Quaker Women

One nineteenth-century commentator noted the 'public' character of Quaker women as signalling a new era in female history. This study examines such claims through the story of middle-class women Friends from among the kinship circle created by the marriage in 1839 of Elizabeth Priestman and the future radical Quaker statesman, John Bright.

The lives discussed here cover a period from the late eighteenth to the early twentieth centuries, and include several women Friends active in radical politics and the women's movement, in the service of which they were able to mobilise extensive national and international networks. They also created and preserved a substantial archive of private papers, comprising letters and diaries full of humour and darkness, the spiritual and the mundane, family confidences and public debate, the daily round and affairs of state – and fond but frank views on John Bright, his home life and his hostility to their participation in the women's movement.

The discovery of such a collection makes it possible to examine the relationship between the personal and public lives of these women Friends, explored through a number of topics including the nature of Quaker domestic and church cultures; the significance of kinship and church membership for the building of extensive Quaker networks; the relationship between Quaker religious values and women's participation in civil society, radical politics and the women's rights movement.

This new study is a must read for all those interested in the history of women, religion and politics.

Sandra Stanley Holton is now a Visiting Fellow at Trinity College, Dublin. Her previous publications include *Suffrage Days* (Routledge, 1996); *Feminism and Democracy* (Cambridge University Press, 1986) and with June Purvis she co-edited *Votes for Women* (Routledge, 2000). Some of her earlier research into the Priestman–Bright circle has been published in *American Historical Review*, *Victorian Studies*, *Journal of Women's History* and *Women's History Review*.

Women's and Gender History
General Editor
June Purvis
Professor of Sociology, University of Portsmouth

Emmeline Pankhurst
A biography
June Purvis

Child sexual abuse in Victorian England
Louise A. Jackson

Crimes of outrage
Sex, violence and Victorian working women
Shani D'Cruze

Feminism, femininity and the politics of working women
The Women's Co-operative Guild, 1880s to the Second World War
Gillian Scott

Gender and crime in modern Europe
Margaret L. Arnot and Cornelie Usborne (eds)

Gender relations in German history
Power, agency and experience from the sixteenth to the twentieth century
Lynn Abrams and Elizabeth Harvey (eds)

Imaging home
Gender, 'race' and national identity, 1945–64
Wendy Webster

Midwives of the revolution
Female Bolsheviks and women workers in 1917
Jane McDermid and Anna Hillyar

No distinction of sex?
Women in British universities 1870–1939
Carol Dyhouse

Policing gender, class and family
Britain, 1850–1945
Linda Mahood

Prostitution
Prevention and reform in England, 1860–1914
Paula Bartley

Sylvia Pankhurst
Sexual politics and political activism
Barbara Winslow

Votes for women
June Purvis and Sandra Holton (eds)

Women's history
Britain 1850–1945
June Purvis (ed.)

The women's suffrage movement
A reference guide, 1866–1928
Elizabeth Crawford

Women and teacher training colleges 1900–1960
A culture of femininity
Elizabeth Edwards

Women, work and sexual politics in eighteenth-century England
Bridget Hill

Women workers and gender identities, 1835–1913
The cotton and metal industries in England
Carol E. Morgan

Women and work in Britain since 1840
Gerry Holloway

Outspoken women: British women writing about sex, 1870–1969
An anthology
Lesley A. Hall

Women's history, Britain 1700–1850
An Introduction
Hannah Barker and Elaine Chalus

The women's suffrage movement in Britain and Ireland
A regional survey
Elizabeth Crawford

Students
A gendered history
Carol Dyhouse

Women in the British army
War and the gentle sex, 1907–1948
Lucy Noakes

Quaker Women

Personal life, memory and
radicalism in the lives of women
Friends, 1780–1930

Sandra Stanley Holton

First published 2007
by Routledge
2 Park Square, Milton Park, Abingdon, Oxon OX14 4RN

Simultaneously published in the USA and Canada
by Routledge
711 Third Avenue, New York, NY 10017

Routledge is an imprint of the Taylor & Francis Group, an informa business

© 2007 Sandra Stanley Holton

Typeset in Garamond 3 by
Florence Production Ltd, Stoodleigh, Devon

All rights reserved. No part of this book may be reprinted or
reproduced or utilised in any form or by any electronic,
mechanical, or other means, now known or hereafter
invented, including photocopying and recording, or in any
information storage or retrieval system, without permission in
writing from the publishers.

British Library Cataloguing in Publication Data
A catalogue record for this book is available
from the British Library

Library of Congress Cataloging in Publication Data
A catalog record for this book has been requested

ISBN 978-0-415-28143-1 (hbk)
ISBN 978-0-415-28144-7 (pbk)

In Memory of Reginald Stanley,
Ida Stanley and John Holton

And for my daughter, Flora,
Keeper of my garden and
Sunshine of my life

Contents

List of illustrations — xi
Acknowledgements — xii

1 Introduction — 1

2 Margaret Wood (1783–1859): Quaker spinster and shopkeeper — 9

3 Kinship, money and worldliness — 29

4 Rachel Priestman (1791–1854): a 'public Friend' — 47

5 Marriages, births and deaths: the formation of the Priestman–Bright circle — 64

6 Religion, family and public life — 80

7 Sisters, marriage and friendship — 96

8 The single life: Anna Maria Priestman (1828–1914) and Margaret Wheeler (1817–1905) — 110

9 Family, friendship and politics: Helen Priestman Bright (1840–1927) — 131

10 Marriage, money and the networked family — 147

11 Helen Clark, family life and politics — 163

12 The changing order: family, friendship and politics in the late nineteenth century — 181

13 Suffragism and democracy 200

14 The Priestman–Bright circle and women's history 222

Abbreviations in notes 231
Notes 233
Select bibliography 264
Index 275

Illustrations

1.1	The kinship networks of Helen Priestman Bright Clark	3
2.1	Margaret Wood (1783–1859), mid-late 1850s	10
2.2	The Wood family of Bolton	14
2.3	The Bright family of Rochdale	16
4.1	Rachel Priestman (1791–1854), *c.* early 1850s	48
4.2	The Priestman family of Newcastle	52
8.1	Anna Maria Priestman (1828–1914) as a young woman	111
8.2	Margaret Tanner (1817–1905), *c.* late 1860s	122
9.1	The wedding party for Helen Bright and William Clark, 1866	145
10.1	The Clark family of Street	149
10.2	Sophia S. Clark (1849–1933) in middle age	153
12.1	Helen P. B. Clark (1840–1927), *c.*1890	186
12.2	The Clark family outside Millfield, *c.*1897	194
12.3	The three Priestman sisters, *c.* 1897	197
14.1	Helen and William Clark on their Golden Wedding anniversary, 1916	224

All photographs are by courtesy of the Trustees of the Clark Archive.

Acknowledgements

My thanks must go first to the trustees of the Clark Archive, C. & J. Clark, Ltd, Street, Somerset for their generosity in allowing me to undertake this research and for giving their time to talk to me about the history of their family, and also to the Archive staff for their patience with what became a far larger task than I had anticipated. I am grateful, too, for help during this project from the staff of the Friends' House Library, London; Women's Library, London Metropolitan University; the Archive Department of the Library of British Political and Economic Science, at the London School of Economics; the Manuscript Department of University College Library, London; the Manuscript Department at the University of Cambridge; Rhodes House Library, University of Oxford; the Bodleian Library, University of Oxford; the National Library of Scotland, Edinburgh; the Local History Department of Bolton Public Library; the Local History Department of Rochdale Public Library; the Archive department of the Save the Children Fund, London; the State Library and Archives of the Republic of South Africa, Pretoria; the Barr Smith Library, University of Adelaide; the Library of Trinity College, Dublin.

My thanks to the Australian Research Council for the funding that made this research possible in the first place, and latterly to the Irish Research Council for the Humanities and Social Sciences for funding for a related project on networks. The University of Adelaide also funded some of the travelling and other costs involved in this research. The Humanities Research Centre at the Australian National University, Canberra hosted a period of study and a conference on aspects of religious history. The Institute of Historical Research, London provided stimulating seminar series and library resources, as well as somewhere to find a cup of tea and lively discussion; Professor Phyllis Mack and the Rockefeller Foundation, Bellagio, the Women's History Network, the Quaker Studies Association, Bath Spa University, and Leeds Metropolitan University issued invitations to contribute lectures and papers that helped me think through much of the material presented here or in related articles. Professor Pat Thane at the Institute of Historical Research, London always had helpful ideas about where to turn when I stumbled across yet another topic or question that was new to me. A seminar at the Institute of International Integration Studies, Trinity College, Dublin given by Professor Supriya Singh, of the Royal Melbourne Institute of Technology University, gave me both valuable conceptual tools and a greater confidence to tackle some of the issues around 'women's money'. Lastly, a joint project with Professor Bob Holton at Trinity College, Dublin helped me more fully appreciate the global context of this research, and confirmed for me the value of microhistory, and a focus on particular persons and the networks they create.

My thanks, too, to George Holton, Anthony Macri, Robin Haines, John Harwood, Ngaire Naffine, Eric Richards and Di and John Collins in Adelaide who provided the warmest hospitality during the last stages of writing this book, and similarly to Polly Holton, Jan and Mike Dougall, and Bronwen and Arun Holden during numerous periods of research in England. My thanks also to the anonymous readers of the original outline and of the first draft of this book whose comments and suggestions made the process of writing and of revision so much easier – and to Victoria Peters, Philippa Grand and Emma Langley at Routledge, and Sue Leaper at Florence Production, for their seemingly infinite patience.

Projects requiring lengthy research and writing always involve considerable sacrifices for those near and dear to the writer for which no amount of thanks seems sufficient – I promise I won't do it again.

1 Introduction

'Thou art most terribly dear, to leave thee is agony, but I know God can make hard things easy.' So Elizabeth Bright wrote to her husband of less than two years, John Bright, as she lay dying from consumption in 1841. She was at their lodgings in Leamington Spa where they had gone to consult an eminent physician. John Bright was making one of his brief returns to their home in Rochdale, to complete the stocktaking in his family firm, and to participate in an election there. The doctor believed there had been some improvement in her condition but she continued, nonetheless, to prepare herself for death: 'perhaps a brighter day may come, sometimes I believe it will but I try and wish to look the other way.' John Bright returned to help nurse his wife as often as business and electioneering allowed, and her sister, Margaret Priestman, provided day-to-day care. Hopes for Elizabeth Bright's recovery proved unfounded and increasingly she looked for some spiritual intimation that her soul was saved. Though she felt that even in a short and seemingly blameless life she had done much wrong, she also believed 'there is mercy and I have prayed for it'.[1] For, the Priestman and Bright families were members of the Religious Society of Friends (often called 'Quakers'), a church in which the influence of evangelical religion, especially its emphasis on personal salvation, had grown in previous decades.

As she lay dying, Elizabeth Bright asked that her bible and watch be kept for her infant daughter, Helen, and that her text book and a brooch containing some of her hair be given to her husband. As death approached she called her sister to her, and asked her to be kind to John Bright: 'He has been a good husband.' She requested all present to kiss her, saying her farewells 'with the calm of one whose most cherished ties to earth had been gently loosened'. Those present watched anxiously for evidence of her salvation, and recorded her last words: 'God has forgiven me' and 'Poor Mamma.' They took comfort also in observing no fear or struggle in her passing: 'her head drooped a little, a sweet smile lighted up the face of death and without a groan . . . her purified Spirit ascended to the God who gave it and to the Saviour who had redeemed it.'[2] Elizabeth Bright had made a good death, and she remained a symbol of feminine goodness and piety in family memory thereafter.[3]

The continued upbringing of her infant daughter by close kin was also among Elizabeth Bright's last requests. During the previous months Helen Priestman Bright had been cared for at the home of her Priestman grandparents, Summerhill, in Newcastle. Subsequently, she returned to Rochdale and the care of her aunt, Priscilla Bright, who managed John Bright's household, One Ash, until his second marriage some years later. Priscilla Bright kept in constant touch with the Priestman family through letters to her close friends among the remaining Priestman sisters, most especially Margaret Priestman. Margaret Wood, aunt and neighbour of Priscilla and John Bright, similarly recorded life at One Ash for an extended cousinage in the United States that she shared with the Bright family. Regular visits between Brights and Priestmans continued, too, and her Priestman aunts eventually took over the education of Helen Priestman Bright for some years. In this way, she became the hub of a Quaker circle that encompassed several generations of the Wood, Crosland, Bright and Priestman families in Britain, one that had extensive links with kin in the United States through the Wood and Bancroft families (Figure 1.1, and subsequent Figures for each family). The significance of what, for brevity, I will call the Priestman–Bright circle extended beyond the emotional life of its members: it also created, preserved and extended a 'networked family' that might variously serve the pursuit of business interests, humanitarian campaigns, the reform of the Society of Friends, and middle-class radical politics that latterly included the campaign for women's rights.[4]

To a degree, the continuing strength and coherence of such connections rested on the creation and preservation of family memory. Letters, diaries and memoirs of the dead provided emotional, psychological and spiritual resources for the women and men of this circle, as they did in many other middle-class families. These papers served both as memorials for the dead, and as their gift to the living: readers might through them refresh their memory of the dead, find comfort for grief, confront their own mortality, celebrate goodness and piety, seek exemplars for spiritual growth and enlightenment, alleviate loneliness and sorrow, and preserve extensive bonds of kinship, despite physical separation and the passage of time.[5] The gathering in of such material was undertaken originally only for an audience comprising near kin. It served to express and reaffirm shared religious, political and social values, not least in terms of the place of churches within civil society, and the space they provided for the enactment of forms of Christian citizenship for women as well as for men.[6] It also served as a chronicle of family life and its connection with larger economic, social and political processes.

The creation and preservation of this family archive was a task largely undertaken by the women of the Quaker families concerned. Male kin might also from time to time keep diaries and write family letters and memoirs of the dead. But it appears to have been the women of this circle who ensured the continuing life of family memory by beginning the systematic creation, collection and passing on of such an archive, largely now contained within the Millfield Papers and the Sarah Bancroft Clark papers, both comprising

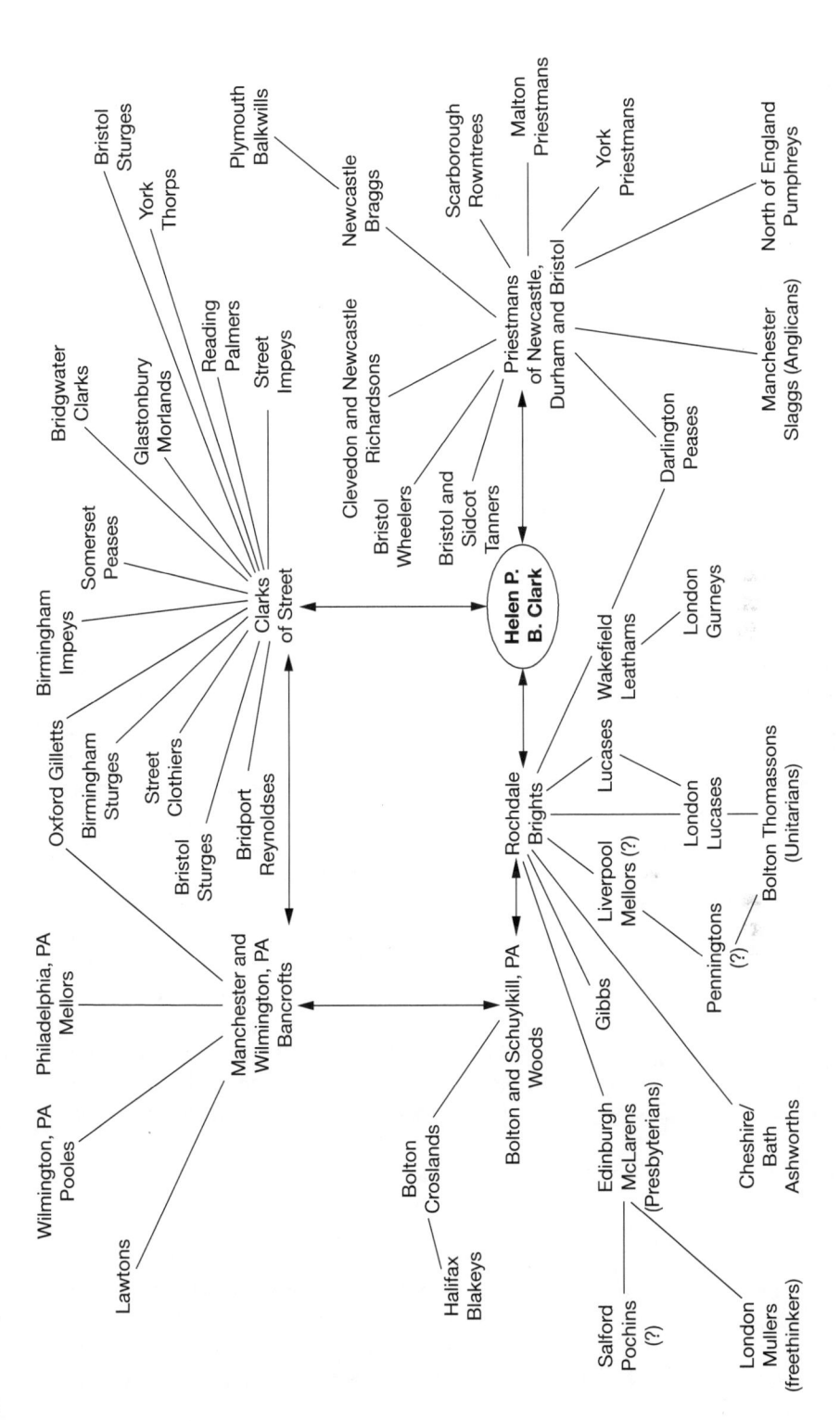

Figure 1.1 The kinship networks of Helen Priestman Bright Clark (with location where known, and religious affiliation where this is known not to be the Society of Friends)

women's private papers for the greater part.[7] These sources provide a perspective on history through the written reflections of a group of related Quaker women from the modest but comfortably placed ranks of nineteenth-century shopkeepers and manufacturers. They include accounts of the spiritual life, domestic relationships, sewing groups, philanthropic societies, and close emotional relationships that formed female worlds among more well-to-do women at this time. But the women of this family circle also lived alongside men, of course, and the interests, activities and values of both sexes clearly overlapped, where they did not merge, at many points. Therefore, such sources provide not only 'insider' views of women's worlds,[8] but also accounts of how women's prescribed roles within the family related to other worlds – of church government, of theological disputation, of voluntary organisation, of business, of politics, of class relations, of cultural pursuits, of various modes of intimacy between the sexes, of what it might mean among these circles to be Quakerly and womanly at this time. Such an archive offers, then, a fresh viewpoint from the more conventional materials of history: government papers, parliamentary debates, newspapers and so on, sources that overwhelmingly reflect how the world looked from the perspective of men, and of men in public life, belonging to various elites among their own sex. It also holds representations of a past world as understood through a particular religious mentality. This encompassed a considerable variety, as we shall see, but reflected, nonetheless, a distinctive meaning with which such women might invest their own lives, not least in a shared understanding of the relation between the past of their families and their own present.

Quaker women as a generality were better known at this time for the nicety of their domestic arrangements, for their good works, for their thorough if practical education and for notions of female modesty that led them in general to shun the public eye. The Anglican anti-slavery campaigner, Thomas Clarkson, promoted such a stereotype in his account of Friends, for example.[9] But women Friends also appeared distinctive among their sex, and Clarkson concluded that such difference arose from their 'public character', noting, for example, how they might hold most of the offices in their church and take part in their own business meetings. Such participation, he believed, encouraged among women Friends the 'thought, and foresight, and judgment' that gave them this 'new cast' of character. He associated such an advance with a fuller realisation of Christian values among Quakers than among other congregations, where 'Women are still weighed in a different scale from men.' On the basis of such observations, he declared: 'This is a new era in female history.'[10] His account contained a degree of overstatement, as we shall see, and more recent accounts of the position of women Friends in this period continue to veer between celebration and a more muted assessment.[11] Nonetheless, the significance of the roles of Quaker women as ministers, elders and overseers of the church, as probably among the first women to begin to limit their fertility in the nineteenth century,[12] and as philanthropists, humanitarians and reformers all suggest a picture that moves beyond the stereotype of the domestic, retiring and modest woman Friend. So it may not seem so surprising that the presence of Quaker women has begun to be charted among the leadership of the radical wing of the women's movement from the mid-1860s.[13]

The presence of Unitarian and Quaker women has long been routinely noted in general histories of the women's movement. Now a more complex understanding is emerging: women Friends were not to the fore in the intellectual and ideological foundations of the women's movement in the 1840s and 1850s, for example,[14] a role largely undertaken by a number of 'radical Unitarian' women whose ideas about women's position have recently received more extensive recognition.[15] The Priestman–Bright circle joined the women's rights movement at a later stage, and they were also unusual among women Friends in such participation, as well as in their involvement in radical politics more broadly, and in their efforts to reform the government of the Society of Friends. Clearly, Quaker women differed among themselves as to how to enact the 'public' character identified in them by Clarkson, and those differences suggest changing understandings of women's nature and their proper place, of the meaning of 'public',[16] and of the proper relationship between church and polity.[17] The preservation of so many of their letters and diaries allows the historian to explore subjective understandings of such issues and of how these women engaged with the discourses of gender, class, race, religion and politics that surrounded them. Family relations were central to the roles women were able to play in civil society and in public life, and sources such as these also allow us to reconstruct particular domestic cultures, to examine them for distinctive characteristics and to explore further the role of gender relations in the creation of the middle class. They make it possible, that is to say, to view public life from the perspective of the domestic arena. In this case, the active creation, collection and preservation of personal papers among this circle of women suggest the importance of family history and memory in their understanding of the relationship of the present to the past. Such material also suggests the possible sources of union between personal and public selves, not least in responses they contain to the contemporaneous debate on 'the woman question'.

The response of members of this circle to evangelical religion will receive particular attention. A number of studies of the middle class in this period have established the importance of evangelicalism as a cultural force in shaping ideologies of gender difference, in the formation of class-consciousness and in the creation of civil society.[18] Similarly, histories of the Society of Friends have emphasised the profound impact of evangelical beliefs on nineteenth- and twentieth-century Friends, especially as a major factor in the revival of Quakerism.[19] The influence of evangelical religion also led to serious tensions and eventual schisms with the Society of Friends, in both Britain and the United States in this period. Its impact was various and complex among the Priestman–Bright circle, shaping the religious outlook of its members in differing ways, not least in their relation to public life. Money, too, shaped the values and opportunities available to these six women. Middle-class women's relationship to property in this period was also complex, especially after marriage. It reflected a mix of legal restrictions and the decline of dower rights, along-side the growing use of marriage settlements and trusts, as well as informal understandings and domestic cultures that might challenge conventional expectations on such matters. Though the evidence is patchy, the sources examined here suggest the significance of what will be termed 'women's money', how it was constituted and controlled, how it informed gender relations within the family and the roles women might play both within middle-class enterprise, and outside the family, in this period.

The nature and content of this family archive allows an examination of what Amanda Vickery has termed the 'unpredictable variety of private experience'.[20] Its method is that of a 'microhistory' that explores the lives of particular persons, their relationship to each other, their mentalities and subculture, and their understanding of larger processes and structures.[21] Its form is that of collective biography and the subjects selected here are examined in terms of their particularity, not for their typicality, or as exemplars.[22] The discussion will focus on the lives of six women, selected from among three successive generations of this kinship circle to allow the narrative to move across time. Marriage among this circle of women seems often to have been less constraining than the conventions of the day might lead us to expect. Equally, the period covered saw new opportunities arising for single women among the middle class. So, of each generation one of those selected was married and one was single, allowing also a further point of comparison as marriage and spinsterhood placed women in a different relation both to their families and to their society. My choice was directed also to some extent by the power of individual voices, some of which emerge more strongly than others from the archive because of the forcefulness of a particular personality, individual powers of expression, a reflective turn of mind, contingencies in the survival of documents or a mixture of such elements. They share, that is to say, a particular ability to communicate between the living and the dead, to represent the self with some force in what was written and still may be read.

The creation and maintenance of family memory among this circle was encouraged through oral storytelling and its written recording, through the passing on of houses, furniture, books and, most of all, of old diaries and letters. Hence, some of the idiosyncratic declarations and expressions of my first subject, Margaret Wood (1783–1859) remain current in family memory even today. Almost two hundred years after her birth, subsequent generations of her kin might sit in her rocking chair, 'very handsome, but high and severe', enjoy the sampler on 'Industry' that she sewed as a pupil at Ackworth School, read her family chronicle, journal and letters, share recorded memories of her from those who had known her in life, and so learn from her cultural legacy.[23]

A very different sensibility from Margaret Wood's emerges from the letters, memoranda and memoir of Rachel Priestman (1791–1854), a Quaker minister and mother of Elizabeth Bright, whose story is considered next. Later chapters move on to discuss the lives of two members of the next generation, Margaret Priestman (1817–1905), subsequently, Wheeler and then Tanner), eldest surviving daughter of Rachel Priestman, together with that of a younger daughter, Anna Maria Priestman (1828–1914) who remained single; and, for the next generation, their niece, Helen Priestman Bright (1840–1927, subsequently, Clark), who was also Rachel Priestman's granddaughter, and Margaret Wood's great-niece. Prior to her marriage, Helen Priestman Bright sometimes joined Margaret Wood, her servant-companion, Eliza Oldham, and a second cousin, Jane Crosland, to form a lively 'hen household' of spinsters. The records relating to unmarried women such as these are much less complete, however, for the last generation studied here, reflecting their lessening embeddedness in family life. That change, in turn, was linked to new opportunities for single, middle-class women, changes evident in the life of Sophia Sturge Clark (1849–1933), sister-in-law, neighbour and friend of Helen P. B. Clark. She was a former kindergarten teacher active in local associational life, and among the earliest women elected to public office, as a member of the school board in her home town, Street, in Somerset, and who until mid-life kept a diary that reflected upon her position as a middle-class 'daughter-at-home'.

The Priestman–Bright circle was built upon kinship, and shared religious, social and political values. Kinship was a two-edged sword, among this circle at least, reflecting not only 'an assumed gender order', as Leonore Davidoff argues,[24] but also the means to confront and challenge that order. Here, the sibling relationship was especially important, for sisterly care might nurture, protect and enable the less fortunate among sisters and nieces, and was fundamental to the construction and maintenance of this circle. The sibling relationship provided, too, a model for civil society and a metaphor for social action, helping create the network of women activists that grew from mutual friendships shared among it members. Thus, Helen Priestman Bright may have remained 'a motherless child' in the eyes of many of her closest kin, but she several times expressed her thankfulness for the richness of her emotional relationships with a number of her aunts. Family relationships also led to the lifelong friendships she made among her cousins, and with many outside her own circle. So, the relationships of sister, aunt, niece and cousin figure as largely as those of mother, daughter and granddaughter in this account. For, these papers provide ample evidence of their importance beyond domestic life.

The lives of these six women covered a period from the 1780s to the 1930s, one of great economic, social and political change. The growth of industrial capitalism, major shifts in religious belief and practice, the emergence of new classes, political contestation and democratisation, shifting constructions of public and of domestic arenas, changing understanding of gender differences, and more especially of women's place in society, all shaped these lives. This study will focus on particular aspects of such change: the domestic culture of the Priestman–Bright circle, especially as it related to gender relations, and to roles outside the family; the role of kinship in the creation of networks in which were united personal, church and public life; the mobilisation of such networks for business, religious and political ends; the varieties of religious experience among this set of women Friends, and the implication of such experience for their participation in larger arenas; the changing place of single women among families of 'the middling sort' such as these; the relation between personal life and public action in their lives. What follows is an account of such change, as recorded principally through the writings in which a group of women kin recorded, rehearsed and reflected upon their lives. Such a project is possible because of the collection and preservation of their personal papers, a collection by which they rendered themselves subjects of history, simultaneously private and public, domestic and political, restricted and expansive, constrained and free – like and unlike ourselves in terms of how such contradictions might be expressed, reflected upon, remembered and represented.

2 Margaret Wood (1783–1859)
Quaker spinster and shopkeeper

Quakerism and oppositionism

In 1821 the throne of the United Kingdom passed at last from George III to the Prince Regent. The coronation became an occasion for civic demonstrations of loyalty throughout the country that summer. Rochdale, an old Lancashire market town then being transformed by the mills of the growing cotton industry, played its part in the national celebrations. Five-year-old Priscilla Bright (1815–1906) was on a visit to an aunt, Margaret Wood (1783–1859), a sometime pastry cook of Bolton who now kept a confectioner's shop in Rochdale. As the child rushed to the window to watch the festivities, her aunt admonished: 'Come away, child! He's na but a pauper, and I have to help keep him.'[1] The story illustrates Margaret Wood's lack of respect for king and coronation, her notable capacity for blunt speech, and an idiosyncratic view of the world that often found expression in bathos and paradox – here, the image of a crowned head of state standing cap-in-hand before a provincial shopkeeper. But its reiteration through family memory serves also as a reminder of the origins of the Religious Society of Friends in the turmoil of the English Civil War and in the egalitarian values of the Levellers of that period, origins evident in a continuing rejection by Quakers of state religion and of a church headed by the monarch.[2]

Quaker theology maintained that a seed of the divine, the 'Light Within' or 'Inner Light', existed in everyone. Such a doctrine had implications for the religious leadership of the Society, and its ministers were voluntary and unpaid. A sense of calling to the ministry was generally encouraged (or discouraged) by the elders of a local meeting, and became formalised when a Friend was recorded as a minister by their local Monthly Meeting (the organisational grouping of a set of neighbouring 'meetings for worship', and the basis of representation within the government of the Society). The notion of the Inner Light also had implications for the position of women within the church: as it was universal, women as well as men might feel 'called' and be recognised as ministers.[3] During Margaret Wood's lifetime women ministers were prominent in the religious leadership of the Society in some regions, and notably so in York.[4] Women also served alongside men as elders and

Figure 2.1 Margaret Wood (1783–1859), mid-late 1850s

overseers, responsible for ensuring compliance with church discipline among members of their meeting. But in other respects Quakerism conformed more closely to the conventional gender hierarchy, and women Friends had no standing within the national government of their church. This resided in the Men's London Yearly Meeting and with the body that was, in effect, its executive committee, the Meeting for Sufferings. Women Friends had successfully campaigned in the late eighteenth century to establish their own London Yearly Meeting together with local counterparts.[5] These sat simultaneously but separately from the comparable men's meetings, and in an advisory and consultative position only. Women's meetings might send concerns and suggestions, in the form of minutes, to the comparable meeting of men Friends, but they had no formal powers to ensure their consideration.

Quaker opposition to the union of state and religion in the Church of England was maintained despite decades of persecution under both Protector Cromwell and the restored monarch, Charles II. But with a new interpretation of the doctrine of the Inner Light by the theologian, Robert Barclay early in the seventeenth century, Friends came largely to eschew political activism. Barclay insisted that the Inner Light was something quite separate from human nature, an element of the divine that might be found only by the suppression of 'the creature' within and a passive waiting upon inner illumination from the Holy Ghost. This turn toward quietist mysticism also informed the increasing seclusion of Friends within their own religious communities, and a withdrawal, as far as possible, from worldly, 'creaturely' concerns. Members of the Society cultivated a sense of themselves as 'a peculiar people', increasingly marked out from their neighbours by the adoption of 'plain' dress and 'plain' speech, as well as a distinctive vocabulary. The discipline of the church allowed a Friend to marry only another member of the Society, on pain of 'disownment' if this rule was broken. Children of Quakers enjoyed membership of the church as a birthright. Others might become Quakers 'by convincement' but the Society of Friends had ceased by the eighteenth century to be the proselytising, evangelistic church of its early years.[6]

So, in many places Friends had become, by the late eighteenth century, a socially exclusive and secluded community. But such seclusion did not mean an end altogether to the fundamental oppositionism of Quaker church culture, an oppositionism that was written into the discipline of the Society. Friends were required to refuse all taxes levied for the maintenance of the Church of England, even though such refusal might mean imprisonment or more usually, by this period, the distraint of goods. The manners of their church enjoined civility to all, but refused deference to any worldly authority. So Friends were similarly required to resist other aspects of the established order, for example, by refusing to take oaths, or to serve in the militia or the magistracy. Though the mode of such protest was that of social seclusion, civil disobedience and passive resistance, it was nonetheless generally more rigorous than the oppositionism among other churches within 'Old Dissent'. It required a direct and continuing confrontation, albeit peaceful, with the state.[7]

For Margaret Wood, then, church history, culture and discipline all informed her lack of respect towards the new king: he represented both a state-maintained religion and government by aristocracy. In some areas such Quaker oppositionism might find expression also through political radicalism: around the turn of the nineteenth century Rochdale Friends received spiritual guidance from a Lancashire minister, Joseph Wood (apparently, no relation), who was also known for his radical political beliefs, beliefs that were shared by many of Margaret Wood's kin.[8] She also identified herself with the industrious classes and against the landed classes, an identification reflecting a shared sense of dispossession and economic vulnerability that led many of her kin to emigrate to the United States. Despite her oppositional values, however, the quietist religious sensibility of Margaret Wood left her out of sympathy with political radicalism, and indeed, with any active involvement in national politics. It also left her out of sympathy both with the 'rational religion' of the Unitarians, and with the evangelicals' emphasis on Bible-study as the principal religious guide. Like most Friends, she valued the scriptures but believed they could only properly be understood with the aid of the Light Within.

Family, community and migration

The Wood family of Bolton (see Fig. 2.2)

Margaret Wood and her closest kin had their origins among tenant farmers in the Lake District who in the latter decades of the eighteenth century emigrated or left the land. Those that stayed in Britain continued to struggle economically, however, in the growing industrial centres of the Manchester region. So Margaret Wood's only surviving brother, John Wood jnr (1781–1849), followed earlier generations of his kin and emigrated to the United States with his first wife and children in the years following the Napoleonic Wars. Their father, John Wood snr (1747–1804), had also once contemplated taking such a step, as he struggled to make a living in Bolton.[9] But, instead, he had stayed and gradually established a modest business as a clog maker and shoeshop keeper there. That business, it seems, was continued by his wife (another Margaret Wood, 1751?–1828, formerly King) for some years after his death. Perhaps it did not suit their only surviving son or perhaps it was incapable of supporting more members of the family, for, as we have seen, Margaret Wood also followed a different trade from her parents. Between 1805 and his emigration, John Wood jnr is recorded, variously, as a mustard manufacturer, a cotton-twist dealer, a cotton spinner and an accountant in Bolton. He briefly moved to Manchester as an accountant and then to a farm where he described himself as an accountant and auctioneer.[10]

Family correspondence suggests that he left for the United States in expectation of finding a more equal and open society. He is reported to have declared of his new country: 'We have a Government it is true, but we never feel it . . . Never mind if people like England and Taxation let them enjoy their taste – it is not mine.'[11] But similar aspirations evidently transferred themselves also to the oldest of the four Wood sisters, Elizabeth (1777–1845). She travelled to the United States as a single woman for reasons that are not known, returning in 1797. That homeward voyage was undertaken while Britain and France were at war, on a ship that was twice boarded by enemy forces.[12] The evident terror of such an experience did not, however, stop Elizabeth Wood from a second, permanent migration across the Atlantic in 1822, along with her husband, John Bancroft (1774–1852) and their thirteen children.

The Bancroft family of Manchester (see Fig. 2.2)

The Bancrofts shared a similar social standing to the Woods, composed of urban craftsmen and shopkeepers who none the less retained a hope of returning to farming. John Bancroft's family had a timber and chair-making business in Manchester, but he and Elizabeth Bancroft decided at some point in their marriage to take up agriculture.[13] Thereafter they struggled to make a living as tenant farmers in Wales. Landowners were demanding rents that appeared extortionate to struggling farmers like themselves, as they contemplated the prices obtaining for their crops in the years following the Napoleonic wars. Their family was large, and in their last years in Wales the Bancrofts found it difficult to meet even the modest fees required to send one of their younger sons to Ackworth, the school founded in 1778 for 'Friends not in affluence'. Elizabeth Bancroft, like all the Wood sisters, had attended this school, but her younger daughters, at least, did not follow her there. Instead, two of them were sent to a small girls' school in Rochdale, where two of their aunts among the Wood sisters, Margaret Wood and Martha Bright (1788–1830), now lived. By 1821, John Bancroft was not only seeking family help with a son's school fees; he was also looking for family support in his decision to sell up and emigrate to the United States, a plan that would require the export of family capital to finance new endeavours there.[14] After settling near Wilmington, on the Brandywine River in Pennsylvania, he reported 'the Burden of Taxes is scarcely felt, Tithes not at all, and Poor Rates almost nothing'. John Bancroft remained a regular reader of the pamphlets and journalism of William Cobbett. Years after migrating he still avidly awaited the arrival of the *Political Register*, sending £6 to a nephew in England with the instructions: 'I shall be obliged if thou will not omit sending me the Registers *every* month.'[15]

Before migrating, his response to the coronation of George IV in 1821 prompted further evidence of his radical political sympathies, in his references in letters to Queen Caroline. The new king's estranged wife had returned to England from voluntary exile on the death of George III. But her husband refused to permit her attendance at the coronation, and she became a rallying point for radicals such as these. Like many who shared his views, John Bancroft

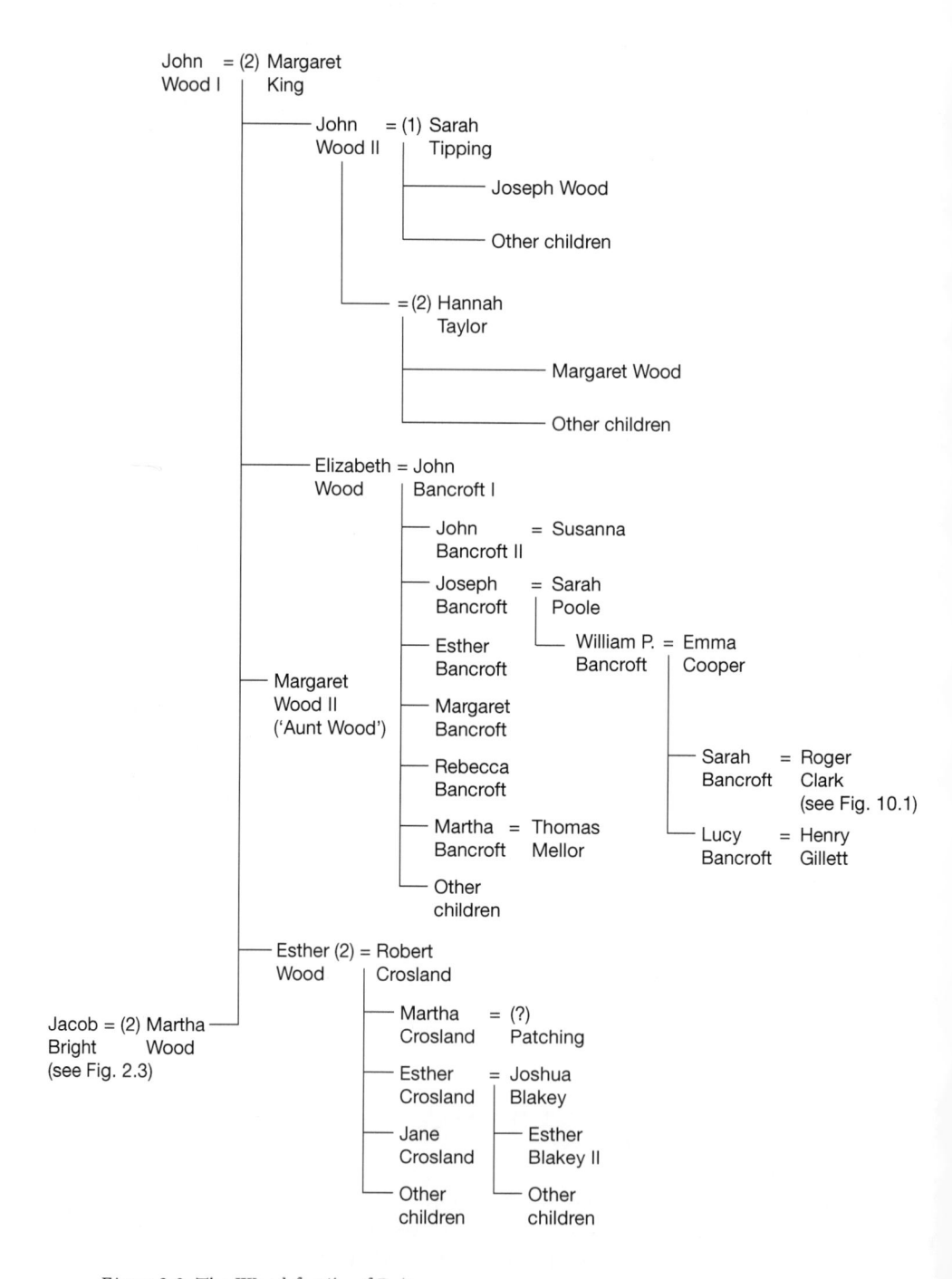

```
John     = (2) Margaret
Wood I        King
         │
         ├─── John      = (1) Sarah
         │    Wood II        Tipping
         │         │
         │         ├─── Joseph Wood
         │         │
         │         └─── Other children
         │         │
         │         └─ = (2) Hannah
         │                  Taylor
         │                  │
         │                  ├─── Margaret Wood
         │                  │
         │                  └─── Other children
         │
         ├─── Elizabeth = John
         │    Wood       Bancroft I
         │
         ├─── Margaret      ├─── John       = Susanna
         │    Wood II       │    Bancroft II
         │    ('Aunt Wood') │
         │                  ├─── Joseph    = Sarah
         │                  │    Bancroft    Poole
         │                  │         │
         │                  ├─── Esther    └─ William P. = Emma
         │                  │    Bancroft      Bancroft    Cooper
         │                  │                        │
         │                  ├─── Margaret            ├─── Sarah     = Roger
         │                  │    Bancroft            │    Bancroft    Clark
         │                  │                        │                (see Fig. 10.1)
         │                  ├─── Rebecca             │
         │                  │    Bancroft            └─── Lucy      = Henry
         │                  │                             Bancroft    Gillett
         │                  ├─── Martha    = Thomas
         │                  │    Bancroft    Mellor
         │                  │
         │                  └─── Other
         │                       children
         │
         └─── Esther (2) = Robert
Jacob = (2) Martha ─     Wood        Crosland
Bright      Wood                    │
(see Fig. 2.3)                      ├─── Martha    = (?)
                                    │    Crosland    Patching
                                    │
                                    ├─── Esther    = Joshua
                                    │    Crosland    Blakey
                                    │
                                    ├─── Jane       ├─── Esther
                                    │    Crosland   │    Blakey II
                                    │               │
                                    └─── Other      └─── Other
                                         children        children
```

Figure 2.2 The Wood family of Bolton

Sources: J.T. Mills, *John Bright and the Quakers*, London: Methuen 1935; W.B. Clark Papers.

sorrowed at the queen's death shortly afterwards and looked forward to the protests that her funeral was expected to occasion. He was similarly saddened at the news of the death of Napoleon – after whom a grandson, born in the United States, was later named.[16] Meanwhile, the Bancrofts sent their eldest son ahead to gather advice and information from their extensive network of kin already living in the United States. On departing England in 1822, they left behind their second son, Joseph Bancroft (1803–74), to finish an apprenticeship with his uncle, Jacob Bright, in Rochdale. For the Bancrofts planned to add spinning to their farming activities in the United States. So Joseph Bancroft remained a member of the Bright family circle at Greenbank, the house that adjoined one of his uncle's mills.[17]

The Bright family of Rochdale (see Fig. 2.3)

The Bright family resembled the Woods and Bancrofts in its social origins, religion, and an interest in radical politics, fostered among the children of Martha (formerly, Wood) and Jacob Bright in their shared reading of the local radical press.[18] Though orphaned and impoverished as a child, Jacob Bright had had a few years schooling at Ackworth and then served an apprenticeship with a Derbyshire farmer as a handloom weaver. At the end of that time he and a fellow apprentice set out together with only a few shillings between them. They walked to the new industrial centres of Lancashire, where textiles were increasingly being produced by machinery within large factories. There, Jacob Bright was fortunate to find employment as a weaver at 5s a week, for his trade was already in decline as mechanised production methods began to displace hand crafts. His religious affiliation, the schooling provided him at Ackworth, as well as his evident abilities, helped in his rise from weaver to bookkeeper, and then salesman on the Manchester cotton exchange for his Quaker employers (the sons of the farmer to whom he had been apprenticed). In 1809, the year in which he married his second wife, Martha Wood, he was lent £6,000 capital by some other local Quakers with which to start his own cotton-spinning business in Rochdale. He received one third of the profits for seven years, by the end of which he had repaid the loan and was becoming a wealthy man in his own right.[19] His political sympathies remained radical nonetheless, and a number of well-known local activists were employed in his mills.

The kinship circle formed by Woods, Bancrofts and Brights was, then, radical in orientation decades before John Bright, eldest surviving son of Martha and Jacob Bright, rose to national prominence as 'the Tribune of the people'. That radicalism grew from a sense of belonging to a class oppressed by a landowning aristocracy; by the protective trade tariffs, notably on corn, that they believed were levied unjustly so as to maintain government by a plutocracy; by an established church that levied rates for its own maintenance on members of other religious persuasions; and by a growing sense of conflict

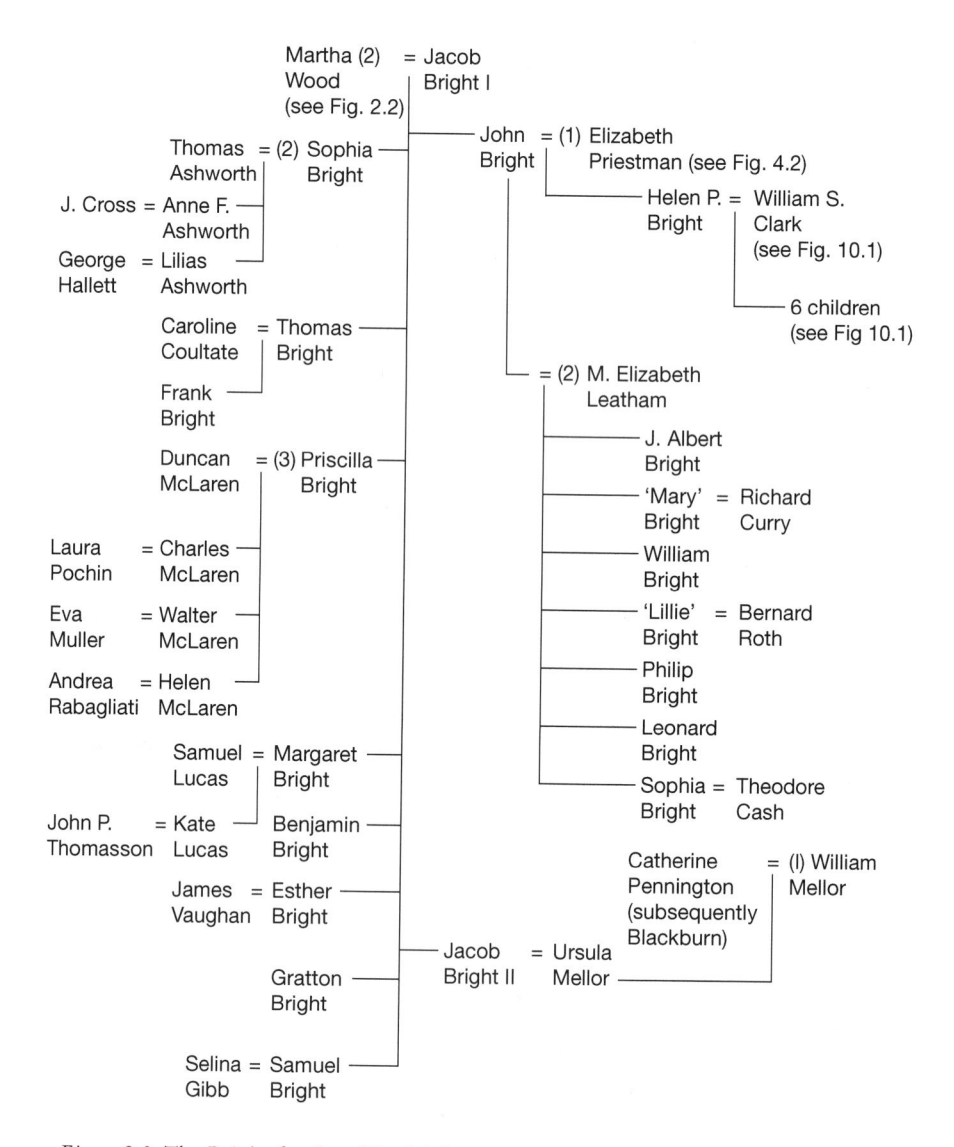

Figure 2.3 The Bright family of Rochdale

Source: J.T. Mills, *John Bright and the Quakers*, London: Methuen, 1935; McLaren family chart, CA.

between those who produced and those who consumed the wealth of the nation. Such a sense of social identity merged the interests of mill-owner and factory worker, of shopkeeper and customer in ways sometimes castigated as entirely illusory and self-serving. So the employment of child labour in the Bright mills has been taken by some as evidence of a cruel hypocrisy among radicals of the middling classes such as these. Yet, many, like Jacob Bright, had themselves laboured as children and recognised the dire economic necessity that it represented among the families of working people. They justified the practice in terms of that need, even as they attempted to relieve it by their care for the wellbeing of their child workers and their families, evident in the provision of educational facilities, savings schemes and neighbourly acts of personal philanthropy. So Martha Bright was long remembered throughout the district for her everyday benevolence and industry on behalf of those in want – the provision of meals, clothing and work for the needy, establishing a night school for the women who worked in the Bright factories, and eventually an infant school for the children of the neighbourhood.[20] She was said always to keep her hands employed in knitting warm garments for the poor, even as she went about her other tasks in the counting house and in managing her household. In this way domestic skills might serve larger ends. Martha Bright's daughters continued to act on a similar sense of the social obligation attaching to their family's prosperity.

Margaret Wood, though with much smaller means, was similarly a frequent source of assistance and advice to her Rochdale neighbours. But her sense of a common identity with the working people around her was also moderated by the evident precariousness of her own early working life. As one of the 'middling sort' who had had to make her own way, she might still, even when living on income from her capital, identify with the 'industrious classes'. But she also retained a sense of her social standing as one quite distinct from that of the poor – into which category she had earlier held very real fears of falling. She recognised a religious duty to relieve want within her community, but she also from time to time feared the poor as a potential threat to the public order and social harmony important to one of her quietist convictions. Indeed, her criticism of that order arose in part from her fear of the political disequilibrium and social turmoil that might arise from the injustice she perceived in the lives of her less fortunate neighbours, as well as in her own.

Spinsterhood, independence and property

In her dismissal of crown and coronation as worthy of attention, Margaret Wood also gave expression to a sense of herself as an independent, self-supporting spinster. In this period, an unmarried or widowed woman enjoyed a legal status, that of 'feme sole', which differed significantly from the standing of a married woman or 'feme covert'. As the latter term implied, the legal personality of a woman became 'covered' on marriage by that of her husband. She could not, for example, hold real property in her own right, or make contracts, or retain possession of any earnings made after marriage.[21] Wealthier families might secure a woman some degree of economic independence after marriage through the creation of trusts. But there were considerable costs attaching to the making and management of such legal instruments, and there is no evidence of their use among Margaret Wood's generation of this kinship circle.[22] It is probable that such women brought a modest marriage portion with them, becoming in return dependent on the goodwill, success, and financial good management of their husbands. Margaret Wood generally welcomed news of coming marriages among her nephews. She was more circumspect with respect to similar news regarding her nieces, for she had few illusions about the position of married women. So she wrote to comfort a niece in the United States, Esther Bancroft, whose marriage prospects had come to nothing: 'well never mind if it be right for thee to marry some other will be found for thee.' Learning of Esther Bancroft's fresh plans to marry some years later, however, she wrote to another niece: 'poor Esther I hope she is likely to have a good husband.' When this courtship also came to nothing, she wrote directly to Esther Bancroft: 'I was pleased to learn thou had miss'd falling into the pit of trouble. I hope some finer prospect will sometime be thy portion.'[23]

In the estimation of Margaret Wood, giving up single life was a dangerous step for any woman. The thing most to be avoided was marriage to an unkindly man, or one lacking the ability to manage his financial affairs successfully. Husbands might prove to be incompetent, devious, or dishonest wastrels. Several such appear in her letters. To this were added the dangers of childbirth and the costs to health of repeated childbearing among families where large numbers of children still remained common, and childbearing generally continued until menopause: Margaret Wood's father had lost his first wife and an infant daughter before marrying her mother; her brother lost his first wife while their children were still young, and among her brothers-in-law, Jacob Bright had lost his first wife and a stillborn child, while Robert Crosland was another widower with a large family when he married Esther Wood. More personally painful for her, her sisters Esther Crosland and Martha Bright died prematurely, and at least three of her nieces died after childbirth, while her nephew John Bright was first widowed after less than two years of marriage, as we have seen.

The best wish of Margaret Wood for any niece or nephew about to marry was that they might enjoy 'a comfortable union', as well as a steady income that allowed a modest housekeeping.[24] The relationship of 'Friend', and the mutuality so central to how membership of the church was understood, extended also to how Quakers thought about marriage. In that sense, it represented the ultimate form of 'Friend'-ship, so that Margaret Wood's principal advice to those about to marry was that they 'cultivate comfortable dispositions towards one another'.[25] Such sentiments informed her father's letters to her mother before their marriage. In one in which he wrote to tell of his safe arrival back in Bolton, he declared: 'my vissits to the has been very agreeable to me When I reflect on the subject it afords me confort ad satisfaction oping it may aford the same to thee it will ever be pleasing to me to add to thy comfort' [*sic*]. He hoped that, should they marry, 'we shall be inabled to be treuly helpful to each other' and that their love would remain 'fresh and blooming'. While believing 'without we have a feeling sure of something more than a Natural fond Passion to join us together it will soon grow cold and dull', he also offered this assurance: 'it would be vain for to set forth my love in the manner some do [but] I have a sufficient degree of sincere and afectionate regare to thee . . . and love thee with a love that will continue from youth to old age.'[26] Because of the rule against exogamy, Quaker marriage necessarily also became a central institution of the church, and was thought of principally in terms of a companionship of two souls. In such ways the domestic culture of Quaker families emphasised an ideal of companionate marriage that put spiritual goals to the fore in that relationship.

Equally, the marriage rules of the Society created particularly dense sets of kinship relations arising from the practice of endogamy, especially as membership of the church continued to decline in the nineteenth century. Hence, many Quakers married among distant kin, and marriage to a second or third cousin was not uncommon: one of Margaret Wood's Rochdale nieces, Margaret Bright, married a second cousin, Samuel Lucas, for example, despite the reservations of her father (and her Aunt Wood) regarding such unions. The social cohesiveness of the church rested to a degree on this complex web of connectedness among its members, one that has led the Religious Society of Friends at this time to be described as 'a national family'.[27] So the consequences of a broken marriage for church unity might be considerable. The lengthy courtships that were general among these Quaker circles were intended to give both parties adequate time to assess the possibility of continuing friendship and spiritual support between partners.

Couples also sought to foster close friendships between the siblings of each, friendships that might strengthen their own family by extending the resources available to it. An unmarried sister-in-law might prove an especially valuable friend to a husband, at a time when life expectancy remained so uncertain, wives might ail, and many men early became widowers. The friendship of Margaret Wood and Jacob Bright proved of practical as well as emotional value to both. The importance of the role of aunt and uncle, but especially of the former, grew out of this ideal of the sibling relationship. Margaret Wood was the only one among four sisters to remain single, but that position did not serve to remove her from the day-to-day obligations of family life. Especially in her role as aunt, it brought with it extensive responsibilities, outlasting those to parents and generally extending far into old age. In Margaret Wood's case these commitments also stretched across an ocean, in her emotional and practical investment in the wellbeing of her nieces and nephews in the United States.

The Wood family's financial position was evidently not one that might support any of its women in a life of leisure. Equally, the financial resources and commercial opportunities that might be available to both women and men of this class remained embedded within the family, and so usually came bearing many obligations of kinship. As the only surviving son after their father's death, John Wood jnr had been 'wont to say he would have to keep his four sisters'. Family memory records how Margaret Wood recalled this with some asperity and 'would refer wryly to her having to keep him', for she was to provide him with an allowance in the straightened circumstances of his old age.[28] That allowance came at least in part from property that she had accumulated for herself. It is unclear how she gained her livelihood between 1804, when her father died, and 1814. Her mother appears to have continued with the family's shoe business in Bolton, for a Margaret Wood (almost certainly her mother, whose namesake she was) is the householder at that address in the 1811 census returns.[29] This household comprised two females and two males who were classified as chiefly employed in trade, so Margaret Wood the younger may have continued to live there. At some time in this period, family memory suggests, she was employed as a pastry cook.

By 1814 Margaret Wood had left Bolton for Rochdale, where her sister, Martha Bright, had lived since her marriage in 1809. Here she made her own way in the world by keeping a confectioner's shop. This business is recorded in a local trade directory for 1814–15, where it appears as a partnership under the names of Wood and Rimington. Thereafter, she is recorded as sole proprietor, though her mother came to live with her some time afterwards (possibly at the time John Wood emigrated to the United States around 1819, or following the marriage of the other single Wood sister, Esther, to Robert Crosland in 1817). In a letter to nieces years afterwards, the younger Margaret Wood acknowledged the help she had received from her mother in establishing and running her business. Mother and daughter shared housekeeping together until the death of the former in 1828. Neither was unusual at this time as a woman who ran her own business. The Rochdale directories for the 1810s to 1820s list scores like them, ranging from shopkeepers to manufacturers, from needlewomen to blacksmiths, from postmistresses to schoolmistresses.[30] But none of their Rochdale grand-daughters/nieces were to follow the two Margaret Woods into business. The success of its mills saw the transition of the Bright family, in the space of a generation, from one composed of respectable, skilled artisans and shopkeepers to one of owners of a substantial industrial concern, and a large employer in their town.

The presence of Margaret Wood within their domestic circle ensured that none of her Bright nieces and nephews forgot their social origins, or the values for which their family stood. They frequently visited Margaret Wood's home, enjoying her conversation, and valuing her role in their family, while she was a regular guest at Martha and Jacob Bright's table. 'Useful' is an adjective that was several times applied to her, and without the pejorative or dismissive overtones it might carry today. Thus, Thomas Bright, second son to Martha and Jacob, reported to his US cousins in 1838: 'Aunt continues and [I] hope always will, a useful and interesting old Maid.' Similarly, family memory summed up the qualities of each of the four Wood sisters thus:

> Elizabeth [Bancroft] the Cleverest
> Margaret [Wood] the Usefullest
> Esther [Crosland] the Gentlest
> Martha [Bright] the Beautifullest.[31]

Such an assessment of Margaret Wood implied her possession of a practical handiness, common sense and a helpful disposition. These qualities she put at the service of her neighbours and local community, as well as her immediate kin. Such usefulness had been fostered by her schooling at Ackworth. In this regard it differed from the education provided there for her youngest sister some years later. For Margaret Wood was taught little of ladylike refinements, but wrote in a plain, if serviceable, hand, while her use of punctuation was erratic, and her spelling sometimes unsure. Moreover, she wrote as she spoke, so that the cadences of her Lancashire dialect, and some of its particular vocabulary, are evident in her letters and journal.

The curriculum for girls at Ackworth had been somewhat extended by the time Martha Wood entered the school in 1797. In particular, closer attention began to be paid to teaching the girls there correct spelling and the art of handwriting, changes that no doubt account in large part for Martha Bright's subsequent ability to use an elaborate copperplate script, make proper use of punctuation and adopt conventional English usage.[32] She had also been allowed a longer time at school, perhaps an example of the greater indulgence that Margaret Wood noted was sometimes shown to the youngest child. All the Wood sisters, however, would have been taught how to prepare business records, including how to issue an invoice, how to keep account books and the basic arithmetic required for such exercises — and they would have been expected to put such knowledge to use. So Martha Bright, according to local historians, took 'an equal part' in her husband's concern, accompanying him on visits to outlying mills, and keeping the business accounts.[33]

Her more privileged schooling may also account for Martha Bright's care for some of the 'refinements' that began to characterise family life among Quakers of comfortable means in this period. She created a debating club and an essay society for her children, where she shared with them her love of poetry, and where she also encouraged them to learn to express themselves clearly both in writing and in addressing an audience.[34] These were skills that her daughters, as well as sons, were to put to the service of radical politics in the years to come. Margaret Wood evidenced no aspirations toward genteel accomplishments such as these, and perhaps this difference from her Bright kin is also bound up in her characterisation as 'useful'. Certainly, the only books she mentions in her letters are religious texts, mostly the memoirs and journals of the founders of Quakerism, like George Fox, or of influential ministers of her own time, like Job Scott.[35] Otherwise her correspondence with kin in the United States concentrated on supplying commercial intelligence and religious counsel, alongside family news.[36]

Most of the business matter in her letters from the late 1820s was not directed at gaining her own living, however, but at helping kin and neighbours to gain theirs. The release she sought in her retirement from shopkeeping was not from the affairs of the world as such, but from day-to-day money making. For her it was the pursuit of monetary gain that was spiritually dangerous, not the everyday world of 'creaturely' activity in itself. She expected those she helped to demonstrate industry, honesty, humility and good management if they were properly to deserve that help. Equally, she continually warned against the dangers of pursuing great wealth, and was increasingly uneasy at the growing prosperity of her Bright kin. In her moral economy, as in that of the Brights, capital held a privileged place, but one that came with considerable burdens of care for kin and community. She lacked, that is to say, any clear individual possessiveness with regard to her own modest wealth.

Long after her retirement, Margaret Wood continued stoutly to assert the attractions of shopkeeping, especially as a means of securing a modest independence for women as well as men. In this she included married women – there were several among her neighbours who continued to keep a shop after marriage, sometimes jointly with sisters and mothers, among them the wife of a local schoolmaster. For her, such an occupation remained an entirely proper application of women's industry.[37] Though none of her Bright nieces and great nieces needed to resort to employment that paid, neither did they lead idle lives, or conform to the more restrictive stereotypes of middle-class womanliness, as we shall see. They, too, strove to become 'useful' members of their family, church and community, albeit in quite different ways. Indeed, Margaret Wood saw several of them embark on a path that challenged both her own Quaker quietism and the newer conventions of middle-class femininity, in their first tentative entries into radical-political campaigning. For, some fresh arenas of public activity were opening as others were closing for women like those of the Bright family. The growth of local associational life, especially organised around church congregations, and most notably those involved in philanthropy, humanitarian and moral reform movements, and radical politics, provided fresh opportunities in public life for the generations of her female kin that followed after Margaret Wood.[38] The patterns of daily life among her Bright nieces came to look very different from her own.[39]

Her advocacy of shopkeeping as an occupation reflected the opportunities that had been open to her as a young woman, and her experience of thereby securing for herself a comfortable if modest independence.[40] It required, however, the right temperament and an appropriate manner. So it irked her when her brother, John Wood, took over a tavern-cum-post office in the United States, for she considered him lacking the necessary disposition for shopkeeping (he had previously agreed with his kin to become an auctioneer in Philadelphia). She reported that her Bright sister and brother-in-law shared her disapproval of this change of plan. The failings that made him, in her eyes, unsuitable as a shopkeeper are only hinted at, but an intolerance towards the views of others and lack of a pleasant manner are suggested.[41] Conversely, she was pleased when two of her unmarried Bancroft nieces set up a store together, a haberdashery business they carried on in conjunction with their oldest brother's tallow chandlery. Margaret Wood was especially gratified when the store prospered sufficiently well for the Bancroft sisters to offer employment also to one of their unmarried Wood cousins in the United States.[42]

The greatest advantage of keeping a shop, to the mind of Margaret Wood, was that it involved much lower levels of risk compared to entering upon 'trade', by which she meant manufacturing enterprises. Setting up a mill needed a far greater capital outlay and kept still more money tied up in stock. Such a concern was therefore necessarily less able quickly to respond to changing economic circumstances and business conditions. She wrote to Joseph Bancroft, the nephew whose mill she helped finance: 'I wish thou could have done something there better than thy spinning business it is so very changable and appears to take so much money to follow it.'[43] She was similarly dismayed when John Wood decided on again 'changing his situation' by starting a spinning concern, something he seems earlier to have tried in England without success. Her fears proved justified, for her brother's mill did not succeed, and he had to abandon yet another enterprise (the mill established by John Bancroft and two of his sons also failed).[44] She sorrowed especially over her brother's failure to provide all of his children with a sufficient education or training in a craft. Some struggled in consequence to find a secure means of earning a living, let alone economic independence. Otherwise, she believed, they might have been better placed to ease the straightened circumstances that attended John Wood's old age: by this time he was an unsuccessful farmer, dependent for some of his wants on an allowance provided by Margaret Wood and Jacob Bright. So she was particularly irritated by her brother's refusal to let any of his children go into service, if that was all that was open to them: 'they are all able to work and ought to keep themselves.' Such nicety was out of place in someone who had himself become a dependent: 'He well knows I've worked for most of what I have, and I dont like it should go while I live to keep idle folks.'[45]

Shopkeeping had allowed Margaret Wood to become a woman of independent means, maintain her position among the industrious 'middling sort', and enact her sense of duty to family and community. But religious values also shaped her economic activity, especially in her fear of the dangers posed to spiritual life by the pursuit of wealth. Despite championing shopkeeping as a worthwhile occupation, especially for women, Margaret Wood valued her release in middle life from the worldly concerns of a commercial venture. For shopkeeping allowed her to accumulate sufficient capital to retire from business in the mid-1820s, when in her early forties.[46] From this time she and her mother lived on rental income from some cottage properties owned by the latter, and from the investments Margaret Wood had been able to make with the profits from her business. By such means she was able to buy herself the freedom that allowed her to pay greater attention to her spiritual wellbeing.[47] Yet the management of her financial affairs continued to occupy her mind, and fill her letters, as we shall see. And there was no retirement from the obligations of kinship, even for an independent single woman. For the relation of sister carried with it considerable expectations of mutual aid and service, expectations that were further extended by the marriage of siblings, and the addition of nieces and nephews to her family circle. Singlehood did not release Margaret Wood from the lifelong responsibilities she felt towards her kin, both those who lived nearby and those far distant.

Margaret Wood's work of kin[48]

Retirement from shopkeeping seems to have brought Margaret Wood a role in which she was never easy — that of family correspondent. It fell to her, perhaps taking over from her mother, to sustain the exchange of news, information and advice between the English branches of her family and those in the United States. This task she found irksome, believing herself to be ill-suited to it. She undertook it, nonetheless, out of a wish that family bonds not be broken, and a deep sense that family memory, involving knowledge of genealogy, individual histories and particular places, was important to leading a meaningful life. In recording and passing on such memory her letters also served to express her own clear sense of self as among the 'peculiar people' of the Society of Friends. In her later years, she derived great satisfaction from journeys she undertook, in England, Scotland and the United States, to places associated with long-dead kin. During such travels she sought also to establish an acquaintance with those of her extensive cousinage whom she had not previously met. In these years, too, she took on the duties of family chronicler, keeping a record (not always accurate) of the births, marriages and deaths occurring among her English kin.[48] Through her letters she sought to foster such knowledge in her nieces and nephews in the United States, encouraging them where possible to come themselves to England to see the places associated with previous generations of their family, and to meet as many as possible of their surviving relations. So singlehood did not prevent her from becoming something of a matriarch, most especially as an authoritative link between her family's past and present. And the correspondence by which she sought to maintain and strengthen the bonds of kinship has also preserved her place in family memory, continuing to connect the living and the dead.

In the early decades of the nineteenth century the Society of Friends in both Britain and the United States experienced internal divisions, between those Quakers influenced by evangelical religion and religious rationalism and those who resisted such influences, led in the United States by the minister Elias Hicks.[49] Evangelical Friends charged their opponents, not always accurately, with denying both the divinity of Christ and the value of the scriptures.[50] Hicksites resisted the evangelicals' emphasis on the doctrine of the atonement and the constant and anguished search for personal salvation to which it could give rise, fearing also the possible creation of a priesthood to direct that search. Between these two bodies of opinion there remained the larger part of Friends who feared that such tensions might lead to schism and separation from their church. Margaret Wood was one such, and for her a far greater danger lay in the spiritual arrogance and dogmatism she perceived on both sides of this debate. Hence, she wrote to a Bancroft niece on behalf of all their English kin: 'we are very sorry to find your minds so much engross'd in the divisions that are in the society about matters if we do not understand them it is best to let them alone.'[51]

Like many Friends she might sympathise with aspects of either (or indeed of both) sides of this contest for the spiritual leadership of the Society. So, she sympathised with the emphasis placed on Bible reading by evangelicals, for example, and was sceptical of biblical criticism. But she also maintained the long-established view among Friends that such reading was best guided by the Inner Light, and not by the establishment of a formal priesthood towards which some evangelicals appeared to lean. So, on this matter when writing to the Bancrofts she counselled tolerance and moderation: 'I wd never persecute for thoughts if peoples actions were good but I always think as the Scriptures are so generally and deservedly believed it is a pity to attempt to lay any part of them waste.'[52] Her sister, Esther Crosland, wrote similarly to John Bancroft at this time, pointing out that many within London Yearly Meeting were as prepared as the Hicksites to stand 'against innovations however trifling'. But equally, Friends in Britain were also being 'continually advised to read the scriptures daily in our families for they are *not* a dead letter' (the Hicksites never, in fact, suggested that they were). Though the tensions ran no less deeply in Britain, she believed the respect accorded both currents of opinion might save the Society from 'an open rupture'. She suggested, too, that the schism among US Friends might result in the very outcome the Hicksites sought to prevent: 'I am afraid that with you, such tumult of altercation in religious opinions, will prove a paving of the way for an oppressive priesthood to take root.' Like Margaret Wood, then, Esther Crosland sympathised with those uneasy at the evangelical influence within the Society, but believed schism was not the way to resolve such tensions.[53]

A similar preference for tolerance and the search for consensus made Margaret Wood doubt the wisdom of allowing the leading evangelical Quaker minister, Joseph John Gurney, to take his ministry to the United States. Her fears appear justified, for tensions continued to grow within Philadelphia Yearly Meeting, leading the Hicksite schism to establish a separate Baltimore Yearly Meeting. John Bancroft and his children were at the forefront of the Hicksite separation, dividing not only their church but their family: Elizabeth Bancroft, Margaret Wood's sister, remained within the Philadelphia Yearly Meeting.[54] Margaret Wood wrote once again to the Bancrofts expressing the anxiety this step caused herself and others of their English kin: 'We were much concern'd and tryed on reading thy account of the state of your family as relates to the Society, one side must be wrong has not hardness of heart and unbelief got in amongst you?' Once again she counselled tolerance and moderation: 'do come down in your minds we must become very little or nothing in our own estimation before we can be in a state of acceptance or have communion with the Father.' But once again her own ambivalence towards evangelical religion was evident in the more conciliatory tone with which she concluded: 'I dont mean to say that you are all wrong I hope not but believe you wish to seek for yourselves and well will it be for us all to do so and when we are all led by the same thing we shall not be divided.'[55] In the years ahead Margaret Wood found herself increasingly in sympathy with the Hicksites, however, and ready to defend her American kin from their critics among Friends in Britain. Her kinship relationships were structured, then, not only by affection, a shared history and linked financial interests, but also by a religious sensibility and the obligation arising from it to provide spiritual guidance and counsel.

As well as spiritual counsel, Margaret Wood also provided practical assistance for her sisters and their families: Jacob Bright, Robert Crosland and John Bancroft became 'brothers' to her and she remained unstinting in her help to them after the deaths of each of her married sisters. Geographical proximity, however, meant that Margaret Wood became especially close to Jacob Bright. That closeness found concrete expression in 1829 when he built a house for her, in which she lived rent-free. It neighboured his factory and household at Greenbank, and was known as 'Mizzy' after an old farm, upon part of which it was built. The circumstances of this act of generosity remain unclear but may have signalled some final settlement of her parents' estate. Margaret Wood, the older, had died the previous year so perhaps it was built in part with capital from the Wood family's estate that now came to Martha Bright. Here is how Margaret Wood described her new home for her American nephew, Joseph Bancroft (previously apprenticed to Jacob Bright):

> He has built two dwellings in one part of which live Wm Bottomly and his Sister and a larger part I live in I have two longe front rooms 6yds square one a parlour and the other a Kitching and behind the Kitching is a Scullery & pantry and behind the Parlour is the Staircase the house is altogether very well finish'd the Parlour Lobby and Stair Case and one Bedroom all molded round the ceiling and a marble fireplace in the Parlour and best Bedroom I have 4 lodging rooms and out of two of them are closets, adjoining and one on the landing also two good cellars, the Lobby is above 4 foot wide and a very nice yard and other conveniences also a pump and a large Cistern which supplys both houses with excellent water the situation is rather high and commands an extensive prospect and most beautiful living it is.[56]

From this time on Margaret Wood lived alone with a servant, and sometimes a niece or great niece, or other occasional houseguests for company.

Martha Bright may already have been seriously ill when her sister moved into Mizzy, for she died in 1830 from an unspecified wasting disease.[57] After her death the daily intercourse between the two households became all the more necessary, both to Jacob Bright, widowed for a second time, and to his children, the youngest of whom, Samuel, was only three years old. By this time Jacob Bright had the assistance of his two oldest surviving sons: John who became the firm's bookkeeper until his election to parliament, and Thomas. Sixteen-year-old Sophia, the oldest of his daughters, took on the role of housekeeper at Greenbank and mother to her youngest siblings, with Aunt Wood near at hand, providing love and companionship, advice and assistance to all. From this time on Margaret Wood also became Jacob Bright's occasional companion on travels for district and regional meetings of the Society, for holidays, or in search of specialist medical advice.

The Croslands of Bolton (see Fig. 2.2)

The relation of sister and aunt structured Margaret Wood's emotional life and at times shaded into that of a mother, especially in providing guidance for her numerous nieces and nephews who were left motherless. For only a year or so after Martha Bright's death, she also watched over the last illness of Esther Crosland, the 'gentlest' of the Wood sisters, and the only other of her siblings still living in England. Esther Crosland is the most shadowy of the Wood sisters in the extant family papers. We know that she was the second wife of Robert Crosland of Bolton, a card maker and importer of Irish linen, and a sometime neighbour of the Wood family. With this marriage Esther Crosland took on the care of her husband's children by his first wife, Mary Crosland (they had had six children, but it is not clear how many survived their mother). Esther Crosland also had five children of her own (though her last baby seems not to have survived), and after her death the youngest, Jane Crosland, became like a daughter to Margaret Wood.[58]

The family was evidently a mobile one, for in 1827 Margaret Wood reported to her Bancroft kin in the United States 'Robert Croslands are about moving again'. Her description suggests that the family's household had by this time become separate from their place of business, a separation also indicated by local registers and directories. The falling value of real estate apparently had made this step affordable for them. Here is Margaret Wood's description of the property, written for one of her nieces in the United States:

> It is a large single house and Stable with a Gigg house and two Cottages at the back and about 1000 square yards of land inclosed in a yard and garden for the rent of £36 ... per year it wd once have given £50.[59]

The birth of her last child in 1830 had marked the onset of a decline from which Esther Crosland never recovered. For some time she was nursed at Mizzy by Margaret Wood, returning to Bolton to die early in May 1831.

Margaret Wood (1783–1859)

The illness and deaths in quick succession of her mother and two of her sisters evidently undermined Margaret Wood's accustomed stoicism, and it was some months before she became reconciled to this last loss. Dispirited and fearful for her own health, she determined on a visit to the United States, to see once more her last remaining sister and brother. There was family business to transact also, almost certainly arising from a final settlement of her parents' estate. Such a commission reflected the standing she had established as a woman of affairs. It provided the opportunity, also, to better inform herself about work and business opportunities there, information of value to neighbours and family in Rochdale. It allowed her, too, to observe for herself the religious divisions among American Friends, and how these were being played out, not least among her own kin. Family ties and obligations continued, then, to inform and shape the emotional, material and spiritual life of this independent, authoritative woman, a life that in its turn speaks of the legacies of religious dissent and civil war, of family separation and solidarity, of migration and urbanisation, of changing religious sensibilities, and of the trials and rewards of an unmarried life for a woman of the middling sort.

3 Kinship, money and worldliness

Margaret Wood and her transatlantic kinship networks

Margaret Wood's visit to the United States demonstrates the extensive kinship networks of which she was an active part. Such a journey was not lightly undertaken, and she justified it in terms of the family commissions she attended to there. When Elizabeth and John Bancroft had followed John Wood to the United States in 1822, for example, their vessel had lost a sail, and the mate was badly injured. They had passed icebergs, whales and an overturned schooner, some of whose crew they had been able to rescue.[1] Margaret Wood's voyage was to prove fully as eventful, and the seriousness of the undertaking was recognised by the male kin who sped her on her way. She travelled to Liverpool via Bolton, taking home two of her Crosland nieces, Martha and Jane, who had evidently been staying with her at Mizzy after their mother's death. There she spent a few days with Robert Crosland, who then accompanied her to Liverpool. Her ship had been selected and her ticket had been organised by John Tipping – an uncle of her Wood nieces and nephews in the United States (see Fig. 2.2) – with whom she dined that evening. Jacob Bright came from Rochdale the next day, taking her to meet the ship's captain, and seeing her onto its tender.

She set sail for New York on 28 July 1831, and for the first few days was able to enjoy the ample meals provided for cabin passengers like herself. Her first breakfast on board was 'quite in the American style roasted or boiled potatoes, massed Ducks, Beefstakes, cold Ham and tongue with tea and coffee and eggs'. She was also still well enough to minister to the passengers in steerage with some of the brandy she had brought with her, for most became sick on their first night at sea. She gave an equally pleasurable account of her breakfast on the second day of her voyage, one of 'Lobscouse [a Liverpool stew], fried egg and bacon, broil'd Salmon and cold tongue and Ham, with tea and coffee and roasted potatoes'.[2] The ship was still not a hundred miles from Liverpool, however. Once they reached the open ocean, seasickness became general and her reports of her meals tail off after recording the killing of a calf, the liver of which was cooked for breakfast. Most of the passengers, she reported, were now 'rather squalmy' and little was eaten. Following the next ten days and more of rolling seas Margaret Wood wrote in her journal: 'I have dreamt a good deal about some of my good friends that I have left behind me.' Reflecting on this, she declared: 'What a favour it will be if we are all permitted to land safe on our destined port. I trust it will be numbered among the numerous blessings of my life.' When the ship subsequently became becalmed for a week, Margaret Wood remarked in her journal that 'Patience is a virtue very needful in a Sea Voyage': she would think very carefully before ever recommending it to anyone else. Then her ship encountered a fearsome storm when 'the atmosphere seemed all of a blaze from 3 to 4 in the morning'. Lightning split the ship's main mast: 'Oh never to be forgotten the awfulness of that stroke.'[3]

When she and another woman ventured to open the cabin door they found the captain and men 'all aroused as dead men . . . Paleness and tears was in every face.' Three of the crew had been injured and one had been struck blind. Neither the captain nor the crew had ever previously experienced anything 'to equal it for dreadfulness', 'the air was one continuous fire all night'. During the day that followed, Margaret Wood found herself almost unable to speak, surely an unusual experience. Eventually, she recorded, 'I got some relief by tears', as one of the company read a prayer thought appropriate to their situation. The next day she and her companions rose 'with pleasant countenances', 'being I trust much impressed with feelings of gratitude for our mighty escape from a watery grave'. The next day brought another storm, and a waterspout was seen some miles off. The ship had now been becalmed for eight days: 'Oh it is very tedious sailing against the current . . . our company is very impatient to land but think it best to endeavour after resignation altho' very hard to get at.' It was another eleven days before they reached New York. In the interim, captain and steward had a falling out and the passengers feared themselves 'in imminent danger of having a sad fray'. Margaret Wood reported herself 'quite unnerved' by the time the pilot came aboard the next day.[4]

On their arrival in the United States some years before, the Bancrofts were met by some 'cousins', and the whole party was given lodgings by two other families, including yet more cousins, the Halliwells (spelt variously in the family papers that remain). Margaret Wood left similar testimony to the density of the social networks of which she was a part, encountering an old acquaintance, one James Merrit, as soon as she disembarked. She was straightaway invited by him to come and lodge with his family. By this time, Margaret Wood had become a significant source of information within her hometown on economic conditions in the United States. Now she used the opportunity to extend and bring up to date such knowledge, and was evidently a skilled interrogator. Meeting briefly a young man with whom she could claim only a most attenuated connection, she extracted the information that he was 'very nicely situated in a Merchant's office', being paid $500 a year, plus perquisites. She took the opportunity to visit still more old friends among the Quaker community, again encountering others quite by chance as she walked around the town. New York she declared 'a very gay looking City' with 'every accommodation that most towns in England have'. She continued to make her accustomed bright-eyed and quirky observations of the world around her, declaring that she now understood why visitors from the United States rarely brought an umbrella with them to England. In their country, she reported, 'It rains so much from the ground.'[5]

After three days in New York, Margaret Wood took a steamboat for Philadelphia where Wood and Bancroft kin were waiting to welcome her. Preparing herself for this occasion, ten years and more since their last meeting, Margaret Wood confessed to her diary: 'I felt myself restrained from thinking much of my relations lest I might be disappointed, so endeavoured to keep as quiet in my mind as I could.' She feared she would not recognise her nephews, who were still boys when she last saw them, and was relieved when three young men came rushing up to her on the quay 'and took me by the hand with such smiling faces saying here she is'. These were Joseph and Henry Wood, and an old acquaintance from Bacup in Rossendale. A few steps on she was greeted by her 'poor Brother', her usual appellation for John Wood. Elizabeth Bancroft was waiting for her at a nearby tavern, with another old acquaintance: 'it was indeed a comfortable meeting to what I had anticipated'.[6] She and her sister set off by stagecoach to visit John Wood's home at Schuylkill. There she found she would not have recognised any others of her English-born Wood nephews and nieces. She was gladdened, though, to find her brother 'so comfortably situated' in his post office-cum-tavern. She was reassured also to find his older children 'all able to get their own living and clever in their professions'. His younger children, too, she believed 'will soon be able to get trades in their hands' (though she was subsequently to revise this optimistic assessment of the younger Wood family's prospects). On a subsequent lengthy visit to her brother over the winter, Margaret Wood noted how his tavern was a favourite meeting place for English migrants: 'it is very natural to all to feel an ankering after their native land, although they have nothing real to complain of in this.'[7]

After this initial brief visit of a day or so, John Wood accompanied his sisters back to Philadelphia, travelling in the sort of light carriage that Margaret Wood noted was kept by most families of their sort there. The Bancrofts' home in Providence was some fifteen miles from Philadelphia, and was reached by boarding another steamer, to Wilmington, where they were met by John (her brother-in-law) and Thomas Bancroft (a married nephew) in their family carriages. Once arrived in Providence, Margaret Wood met four of her Welsh-born nieces for the first time, Margaret and Sarah (born in 1807), and Esther and Martha (born in 1814): 'The meeting was to me truly gratifying.' The travels that Margaret Wood undertook to visit family and friends over the next ten months reveal once more how extensive and far flung was her social network. Again, there were many unanticipated meetings. On one occasion, visiting Philadelphia to deliver some of the letters she had brought from England, she encountered a couple who, she recorded, had 'very dishonourably left England just before I left. I spoke to them and told how wrong they had done, but they vindicated themselves in the act.' Perhaps this was the exchange with former neighbours who had left many bad debts behind, stored in family memory in more explicit terms: Margaret Wood: 'I can't think how thou sleeps abed o'nights, thinking o those to whom thou owes money in Rochdale,' to which she received the reply: 'I can't think how they sleep abed to whom I owes it!'[8]

As she travelled around the homes of her married Bancroft nephews, Margaret Wood noted the ingenuity of many of their business arrangements. Visiting some corn factors, the brother and sisters of Sarah (formerly Poole), wife of Joseph Bancroft, she described the advanced design of their flour mill on the Brandywine river. Here the wheat was not touched from the time it was taken from the boats into the warehouse, until it reached the barrels as flour. She recorded, too, the economics of farming for the Philadelphia and Wilmington meat markets, the considerable fortunes accumulated by some of those who had arrived relatively poor, not always to their best advantage in her view. She was impressed, though, by the property of her nephew Samuel Bancroft, describing the prospect from her chamber window there as 'truly delightful', encompassing a farm and thick woodland for a radius of a quarter of a mile, as well as 186 acres of 'nice arable land', 'a capital stone built house' of three storeys with four large rooms on each floor, 'cellared all under with a good spring house for milk and butter, two good barns, and shippons underneath', as well as two long milling sheds, housing for carts and carriages, a chamber oven, and several outhouses, all in good condition. There was also on the property a waterfall 'suitable to erect a mill upon which they have done to carry on the flannel business with his father'. All this had cost $1,500, some part of which had evidently been borrowed, for Margaret Wood also recorded that her nephew was paying $40 a year in interest.[9]

Elizabeth and John Bancroft's own enterprise was by this time quite large. Sixteen male employees lodged in their household, alongside their own unmarried children, making 'much work for the girls'. The women of the Bancroft family had to wash, sew and cook for all of these. Almost always when Margaret Wood recorded the lives of her unmarried Bancroft nieces, they were busy with some such task, or helping with the work of their oldest brother's store. The washing and sewing seem to have been their particular responsibility (as they were for John Wood's daughters). The various Bancroft households were not without domestic servants, but their maintenance required substantial labour, and such help was evidently hard to recruit. Margaret Wood's own most frequent contribution as a guest was in needlework, mending stockings, helping a niece to finish the shirts needed for John Bancroft's employees, and the wife of a nephew to complete the layette for the baby that was soon expected.[10]

She also cooked the plum puddings for the Christmas festivities in John Wood's home. On another occasion she provided a 'scaled flour pudding' for her Bancroft nieces, 'the first I've made since I left home'. She also copied out some family recipes for another friend made during her travels. These are the only times she seems to have practiced her own former trade, however, though good cooks were especially hard to come by, as she recorded. This scarcity was reflected in quite different employment practices from those known to Margaret Wood in England. So it was, for example, that she was called on to help in the confinement of a nephew's cook, who already had one small child living with her in the household. Such an arrangement would not have been considered in England, but was necessary to retaining such service in the United States. Similarly, young girls might be bound into service as young as five or six, their employers finding their keep and clothing, and usually sending them away for a year's schooling in return for their help in the house. The young woman might then decide whether or not to stay in their service at around the age of eighteen.[11]

Not all those met by Margaret Wood on her travels had fared well, however. An old acquaintance, John Hustler was once again unemployed after some casual work wool sorting when she encountered him in Philadelphia. She recalled that he 'once saw better days' when he lived at Yeadon in Yorkshire. Ralph Taylor, probably an in-law of John Wood, told her how trade was so poor that he had moved his workshop into his dwelling to save on costs. The climate was sometimes inhospitable. Margaret Wood experienced cold so intense that she could not sleep, and recorded temperatures that froze the streams and stopped the waterwheels powering the Bancroft mills. And many of her kin were frequently sick with 'the ague' (malaria), including Elizabeth Bancroft whose health remained uncertain for the whole of her sister's visit, and who endured a succession of fevers for which she was several times bled.[12]

During this visit Margaret Wood arranged the loan that helped her recently married nephew, Joseph Bancroft, establish a new mill. Several of the letters she wrote home during her travels were to Jacob Bright, and at least one was informing him of a draft she had authorised Joseph Bancroft to draw on his account. It is likely that Jacob Bright was, with herself, an executor of her mother's estate, and Margaret Wood may also have been using his counting house as her bank. Jacob Bright also appears to have provided some of this loan, as half the interest was considered his to dispose of in later years, probably as trustee for his daughters. Often, this interest was repaid through complicated movements of money and goods within this extensive kinship network, rather than through banks. So we learn that Thomas Mellor who married a niece, Martha Bancroft, sometimes paid the interest on a similar loan by sending sacks of flour back to England. At one point, Margaret Wood suggested such a form of payment might be more advantageous to Joseph Bancroft (perhaps with the corn factoring business of his wife's siblings in mind).[13]

Economic, financial and commercial intelligence, especially as it concerned her US kin, formed a large part of the material in her travel journal. As she came to prepare, in the early summer of 1832, for her journey home, however, she also began to record the extent of her emotional investment in her relationship with these siblings and their families: 'The thought of separating is very tiring as they are the only near relatives I have left but still my native spot invites me strongly, I wish they had never come to far from home.' She found especially difficult the thought of leaving her nieces who, she recorded, 'above all cleave to my feelings more than all, having had more to do with them than any others'. (This is not otherwise evident in her journal, focused as it is on impressions of places and people that she met outside her family, on family finances, economic conditions and religious and public affairs.) Meanwhile, she continued to make her farewells, many of her new friends travelling miles to see her for one last time: 'I felt it kind in them to show me such respect.' Thoughts of taking leave from her American family she found 'almost more than I can bear'.[14]

These feelings did not lessen with distance, and after her return home she still pined at such separation, especially from sister and nieces. She and Elizabeth Bancroft continued to dream of each other, and Margaret Wood wrote to a niece: 'I wish we were a bit nearer without having that great pool between us.' She continually assured them that they remained always in her thoughts:

> I often, very often visit in spirit you dear girls, for you do feel very near to me and it wd be very pleasant to have you nearer to me, but the distance is almost frightful at times to look at yet I could venture again if I had a commission but that will never be.

Margaret Wood frequently urged her younger kin to come on a visit to England, offering to help with the fares. This wish was several times answered, though inevitably not as fully as she desired. Her niece, Martha Mellor visited England with her husband and her ailing sister, Margaret Bancroft, in 1837. Other nieces and Joseph Wood also followed their aunt's urgings.[15]

For the present, Woods and Bancrofts travelled with her to New York to help her choose a vessel. Finding a ship proved difficult, for in England the Reform Bill was presently before parliament, and its passage remained uncertain. Many in New York expected it would fail, and that revolution would follow. A cholera epidemic was also raging. So the ship on which Margaret Wood had intended returning did not sail: 'the Captain told me he durst not venture on account of the state of the country.' She finally found a berth on a ship whose captain was prepared to sail. When the pilot boarded their vessel at Holyhead he was met with many anxious enquiries, and brought mixed news: the Reform Bill had passed, but the cholera epidemic was especially severe in Liverpool where Margaret Wood was to disembark. She sent word to Jacob Bright to come and help her with her considerable and unusual baggage, which included a green parrot, three grey squirrels and two flying ones, American bird skins, a plant of Indian corn and corn meal, and a peacock tail wrapped in an oilcloth, many of them presents from her US kin to their English relations.[16] En route home she stayed once more in Bolton, catching up no doubt with her young Crosland nieces, one of whom, Jane, came to live with her again for a while. She was collected from Bolton by Thomas and Sophia Bright with their little brother Sam in the family phaeton, and taken back 'to my own habitation which they had been painting and papering and made all very beautiful against my return'. John Bright had been attempting to improve the garden at Mizzy with a stand of trees. Her comments on this much-favoured nephew had begun to take on a wry edge by this time. She reported on his efforts to an American niece: 'I dont think it looks much prettier, that hardly could be it was very nice before, I never saw such a prospect.'[17]

Oppositionism and radical politics

John Bright was evidently beginning to move beyond the tastes, aspirations and station of his aunt. Radical politics were already his absorbing passion, an enthusiasm frowned upon by more conventionally pious Friends at this time. John Bancroft continued to keep a disillusioned eye on events in Britain, and had written to another English nephew after the passage of the Reform Act, fearing he would now no longer consider following him to the United States: 'the Farmers as well as others may be looking for better times'. One mutual friend had given it as his opinion 'that the great change that is to be brought about in England will be now done peaceably'. John Bancroft remained sceptical: 'I am not of that opinion, time will show which is right.' He continued to urge all who could to sell up and join him in his new land: 'but I suppose some will only laugh at me as usual.'[18]

John Bright had begun his working life alongside a number of radical activists employed in his father's mills, and is said to have been fired into still fiercer opposition to the established political elite under such influences. Throughout his life he kept on his desk a jug commemorating 'Peterloo' in 1819. Though he was only a boy at the time of that event, he knew eye-witnesses to the carnage inflicted when a sabre-wielding militia, assisted by cavalry, were ordered to disperse the peaceable crowd attending a demonstration in St Peter's Field in Manchester. During the political turmoil that preceded the passage of the 1832 Reform Bill, John Bright painted 'Hunt forever' on the walls of his father's factory (a reference to the radical orator, Henry Hunt). He had hurried south in hope of watching the final debates on the Bill, hearing of its passage as he reached London. The Reform Act was followed by a successful campaign by the Brights and their Rochdale friends and neighbours to have their town granted representation as a parliamentary borough.[19]

Parliamentary reform altered the ways by which a deeply imbedded oppositionism might be expressed among Friends, placing men like John Bright in a different relationship to the state, as voters, and serving to encourage the greater integration of Quakers of a radical cast into local political life. Such an advance served in turn to throw further into question the long-standing values of quietism advocated by their church. For the preceding century and more, passive resistance and civil disobedience had been the preferred mode of protest by Friends. Jacob Bright had regularly had his property distrained upon for the church rates demanded by the local vicar, which he refused to pay. Now, in the years that followed the Reform Bill, John Bright came to national prominence in a fiercely fought campaign against church rates in Rochdale (the local vicar, in his capacity as a magistrate, had also been among the 'butchers' of Peterloo). Such resistance became widespread in these years, and served to draw Quakers of radical convictions, such as John Bright, into a much more active political role.[20]

Both Jacob Bright and Margaret Wood were uneasy at such developments. While Jacob Bright shared his son's political outlook, he was less in sympathy with the vehemence with which John Bright pursued the matter, the intemperate language he sometimes adopted, and his increasing presence in the public eye. All this represented a shift away from the long-standing quietist values of his family, and the temperate expression of political difference that came with it. Jacob Bright was evidently on good terms with a local landowner and Tory candidate, for example, but when that neighbour called on him to ask for his vote he refused, while softening that refusal with his accustomed civility and good humour.[21] For her part, Margaret Wood shared the hostility of the Brights to the established order, and especially to a state-sponsored church. But she was not at all in sympathy with radical agitation or programmes for change. Writing to one of her Bancroft nieces after her return from the United States she reported: 'most of the public talk is now who they must send up for members of parliament and sad work it makes our Radicals are for Annual Parliaments but I should be very sorry to have them.' Though many of her kin were absorbed in the selection of a candidate and the election that was to follow, for herself she wrote, 'I take very little interest in the choice'. She found some satisfaction, however, in the likely return for Rochdale of the Whig rather than the Radical candidate. Should the latter win, she feared, 'we shd soon be in a state of Anarchy, & that wd be worse than ever we have been'. She took heart, too, in the relatively good economic conditions at this time, so that 'there appears no disposition at present to any thing like riots or disturbance'.[22]

Friends as deeply quietist as Margaret Wood might express the oppositionist heritage of church and family in support for the Whigs; they might be gladdened by the enfranchisement of the 'industrious classes' among male kin, and the establishment of their town as a parliamentary borough. She lived to see her nephew, John Bright, become a radical icon as 'the Tribune of the people'. But few of her generation wished to have any active connection with political life, or readily and openly supported the fully-fledged radicalism of her nephew. His growing career as an agitator was rather a cause for concern. Even so, she too became drawn into a more active engagement with public affairs in the years that followed and also observed her Bright nieces begin to enter the political arena, in the agitation against the Corn Laws in the 1840s. This campaign was to take John Bright to a seat in the House of Commons. Less than a decade after her death, a number of her nieces and great-nieces were also to be found at the forefront of the emerging women's movement. Shortly, they were also to begin to press for a more equal part for women in the government of the Society of Friends. The pattern of their lives was, then, to be very different to Margaret Wood's, and not simply in terms of their greater prosperity.

Margaret Wood and many older Friends were troubled by the increasing openness of their Society to outside, worldly influences, influences that were changing the habits and manners of a younger generation of Quakers. She regretted, for example, how some of her nephews and nieces had abandoned the now-antiquated second-person pronoun, 'thou', when addressing correspondents. (The use of 'you' when addressing a single person she found un-Quakerly for its want of warmth, or its suggestion of deference.) Her younger kin were similarly beginning to abandon some of the plainness of dress that had helped Quakers distinguish themselves as 'a peculiar people'. She was especially uneasy about the Brights' pursuit of ever-greater wealth. A modest financial security was her own goal, and represented for her a means rather than an end, making it possible to concentrate on spiritual concerns and on helping others where she could. Nothing pleased her more than being able to report a legacy that left a female acquaintance in a position to live 'in a nice snug way' on £300 a year.[23]

Family money and women's money

As we have seen, Margaret Wood was glad to retire from shopkeeping in her early forties. The period in which she lived has been identified as one when middle-class women, single as well as married, became increasingly excluded from economic activity, and therefore from the ability to acquire property. Most of the discussion has concentrated on married women, for the dower right of widows became completely eroded in the 1830s, while married women's rights over property remained severely limited until the last decades of the nineteenth century. Yet, a growing body of evidence suggests a much more complicated picture, and a considerable variety among middle-class women in their relationship to property, for example, in the use of trusts to circumvent coverture and thus provide some independence and security for married women. Women might also exert control over family property as executors, guardians and trustees. Similarly, the value of a wife's capital, however small, to family enterprises is also increasingly apparent, for it represented a flexible resource and one not infrequently sequestered from the reach of a husband's debtors by means of trusts.[24]

The modest wealth of a single woman like Margaret Wood shared similar advantages. Hence, property held for her a meaning beyond individual self-interest or personal rights deriving from law. She understood all her property as in some sense 'family money', with the potential for part at least to become 'international family money'. Her sense of ownership was shaped by four aspects of her social position: the first pertained to her personal life as member of an extensive kinship network, reflected not just in her patterns of letter writing and of visiting, but also in her grasp of genealogy and family history, and her detailed knowledge of the particular financial standing, abilities and needs of kin; the second derived from her position within the middle classes, as a petite bourgeoise with business experience and an understanding of finance, however small scale;[25] the third derived from the ethical precepts embodied in the discipline of the Society of Friends, and an ascetic attitude to consumption; the fourth, from an apparent recognition among this family circle of a component of family money that might best be termed 'women's money'. Its gendered character recognised the economic contribution of women, followed female lines of inheritance across at least two generations, and was intended to ensure some financial security for women. But it was also flexible and might be directed by women to help with family enterprises. For Margaret Wood, all her property constituted Wood 'family money', while some of it also became transnational family money, meanings that might cut across, but not entirely extinguish, its character as 'women's money' for a generation or so.[26] There were potential tensions, that is to say, between the different meanings that her property held for Margaret Wood, but these were pragmatically managed by her so as to assist a new generation in establishing their own enterprises, and to relieve the needy among her kin in ways that still acknowledged that that portion of the Wood family money over which she had control had also largely the character of women's money.

With regard to her personal needs, Margaret Wood estimated that an income of about £300 a year might easily provide for a single woman. Leonore Davidoff and Catherine Hall have estimated that £200–£300 per annum was the minimum needed to maintain a middle-class way of life for an average family.[27] Margaret Wood had only one live-in servant, so this estimate would suggest that her style of living was not particularly frugal, especially as she lived rent-free. But she evidently planned, being a single woman, on sometimes needing to provide for others. Certainly, being able to maintain a household of one's own was central to her notion of a snug independence, and she pitied, and helped as she could, those women living alone and able only to afford to board in someone else's household. Her concern for Jane Crosland, an unmarried niece left with an income of only £25 per annum, was resolved, for example, when that niece came to share her home at Mizzy. She also provided small allowances for John Wood and his wife, and for Elizabeth and John Bancroft in the straitened circumstances of their last years, from the interest generated by the loans she had made to Joseph Bancroft in America, not from her income from investments at home. Towards the end of her life, when she lived in greater retirement, she declared herself able to manage comfortably on £100 a year.

In references to her mother's real estate in letters to her US kin, Margaret Wood made a less than clear-cut distinction between her own and her mother's property during the time they lived together.[28] Most likely, this reflected a pooling of their current incomes, the share her mother seems also to have taken in the confectionary business, and the understanding that Margaret

Wood jnr was to inherit this real estate.[29] After her mother's death, she equally saw all her capital, both the inherited part and that part she herself had created, as in her care for subsequent generations of her kin. She was its steward only, and her personal rights over it were strictly limited in her own mind by the needs of other members of her family, especially as her numerous nephews and nieces in the United States grew to adulthood and began to establish their own households.

After her retirement and the death of her mother, Margaret Wood's income derived from dividends on her bank shares as well as some cottage rents, together latterly with the interest paid by her US kin on the loans made to them – some £50 per annum. It seems likely that at least part of this loan came also from the estate of her dead sister, Martha Bright, most probably itself a share in the inheritance left by their mother, or deriving from a marriage settlement. For Margaret Wood's correspondence suggests that it was clearly understood to be Wood family money. Moreover it was money over which the women of that family had prior rights, though Jacob Bright had some say over its use, probably as an executor or trustee for his dead wife, or daughters. The way in which, too, Margaret Wood distributed her surplus resources during her lifetime suggests that she understood John Wood jnr to have already received in full his rights in Wood family property. Most likely he would have needed to realise the capital tied up in the family concerns in Bolton prior to moving to the United States. As we have seen, the main beneficiaries of their mother's estate appear to have been his sisters, and principally Margaret Wood the younger, the only single sister. Possibly, Margaret Wood the older had brought some property with her at her marriage. Almost certainly she had helped create what little wealth the family accumulated, by assisting in her husband's business. And this remained women's money for one further generation.

The younger Margaret Wood gave various accounts of her own wealth to members of her family in the United States. Her letters reveal that in 1843 she estimated her total property to be worth about £1,700. By 1854 she expected to leave to her US kin alone an estate worth some £1,200. References to her intentions with regard to legacies for her Bright and Crosland nieces and nephews in England suggest that the capital she retained at home was of almost equivalent value, so her total estate some five years before her death is likely to have been around £2,200–2,400. She commented: 'I seem to have more to leave than I expected considering how I've been robb'd [it is likely the local vicar was in her mind here], but my *wants* are very few so *that* leaves me plenty while I keep at home.' The limits she placed on her own consumption meant she was also able to allow her US kin the use of a substantial part of her capital while she lived, effectively exporting it across the Atlantic in the form of loans and gifts to them, as we have seen.[30] At certain times she indicated that she was acting as the agent of Jacob Bright and his children, notably in the disposition of half the interest due from the American loan that had been made from Wood family money. Moreover, the generosity of Jacob Bright towards Margaret Wood in the matter of the rent for Mizzy seems to have been part of a reciprocal gesture that acknowledged her own readiness to assist needy kin across the Atlantic: it may even be that it was built with the money that Martha Bright inherited from her mother.

How was it, then, that Joseph Bancroft became the most immediate and extensive beneficiary of his maternal aunt during her lifetime? The rationale for this was never expressly stated, but may be inferred. To begin with, he was the child of her only remaining sister. Quakers as a general rule rejected traditional attitudes regarding primogeniture, and the men among this kinship circle sometimes expressly stated that no such principle had shaped their legacies. None the less, daughters in these family circles generally received a far smaller legacy from their fathers than did their brothers, while the position was generally reversed in terms of the estates of their mothers. Her loan, then, appears to have recognised Joseph Bancroft as a proxy for Elizabeth Bancroft's rights in their mother's estate. But there were thirteen Bancroft children, so why was he singled out? When his family migrated to the United States in 1822, Joseph Bancroft was left behind in England, finishing his apprenticeship with Jacob Bright, as we have seen. He lived altogether for seven years separated from his own immediate family, as neighbour of Margaret Wood, and most likely as a member of the Bright household. He was, then, the nephew best known to her, and a story recording some mischief he entered into with his younger cousin, John Bright, in these years suggest that they enjoyed the freedom of her house.[31] So Joseph Bancroft had a special claim on both her and the Bright family, in his aspirations to set up a mill of his own.

Jacob Bright's involvement with this loan most likely derived from his position as widower of Martha Bright, and as father of her daughters. His approval of it evidently helped ratify the loan in the minds of all parties, Joseph Bancroft standing for his mother's interest, and Jacob Bright for his dead wife's interest in Wood family money; in this way it remained 'women's money' in the understanding of all the parties until the death of the younger Margaret Wood. She herself needed to call on the interest from this loan for a brief period only, when she found herself 'rather kept tight' in 1839, after the failure of the Liverpool and Manchester District Bank: 'If you get the Liverpool and Manchester Newspapers you'll see what mad work has been going on with the Capital, such enormous sums [in loans made] but without any security whatever, or even, advising with all the Directors.' Many of the directors, who included Jacob Bright, were Friends, but they had been provided with only a limited record of the bank's affairs, 'so that for the last seven years none but those who had a hand in lending has had any knowledge of it'. In all, £200,000 was lost. Margaret Wood's personal loss amounted to £200, following shortly after some other unspecified loss of a similar amount – possibly the successful claim of the vicar to a property, the lease on which she had considered her own. She was confident, however, of her capacity to recoup some of these losses: 'in another year I hope in some degree to redeem myself, in money matters'. The likely size of her estate fifteen years later suggests that she did indeed succeed in the intervening years in recouping and increasing her capital.[32]

The allowance she gave to her Bancroft sister and brother-in-law came from this interest and followed the failure of their mill, in which two of their younger sons also had an interest. Margaret Wood made her brother a similar allowance from this source but clearly saw this gift as out of the ordinary, made because of his declining health. She also insisted that Joseph Bancroft pass it on to him in tranches as seemed necessary, rather than in one lump sum a year. John Wood seems to have pressed for an increase in this allowance, but she insisted that it remain at £20 per annum, commenting 'I am short enough myself.' She found it difficult to understand why the ten acres farmed by John Wood failed to produce more profit: 'my brother seems to be carried on very strangely dear man.' She would have gone to see into his affairs herself but no longer felt strong enough for such a journey, declaring in 1847: 'I feel myself an old woman.'[33] Otherwise, she used her means largely to assist the children of her Bancroft sister, who received by far the larger part of the financial assistance offered to kin by Margaret Wood while she lived.

She would clearly have liked to be in a position to help her brother's children more while still living, but did not feel free to do so, either in terms of the disposition of part of her annual income, or of the large part of her capital that she released in the form of loans to her Bancroft nephew. She was particularly concerned, then, when John Tipping, maternal uncle in England of her Wood nieces and nephews in the United States, failed to acknowledge their rights in the estate of their maternal grandfather. Here, again, informal understandings about a component of family money that was women's money is evident, along with female lines of inheritance. But Sarah (Tipping) Wood had died shortly after she and her family emigrated. Physical distance appears to have reduced her brother's sense of obligation to her children. Margaret Wood learned from her nephew, Joseph Wood, how useful a little Tipping money would be to assist them with their own efforts to establish a milling concern. She looked into the matter on their behalf, and learned that John Tipping was 'very slow at parting with his money indeed his Sisters and he are all at variance thro' his dilatory disposition and greediness together'. He made no effort as executor to settle his father's affairs, though two sisters who still lived were 'both very much in want' of their inheritance. Some years later she reported how one of them had recently died while their father's estate remained unsettled. It was all too easy for brothers to prevaricate, especially where such funds were tied up in some ongoing family enterprise. Joseph Wood eventually travelled to England, with some assistance from Margaret Wood, perhaps in hopes of securing aid from his Tipping uncle for a new business he hoped to start. In the event, John Tipping made no contact with him, and reneged on an undertaking wrung from him by Margaret Wood that he would help with his nephew's travelling expenses.[34] She attempted some more equal distribution of her overseas property between Bancroft and Wood nephews and nieces in the final reckoning that was to follow her death, however.

The prior rights of her Bancroft nieces and nephews in her estate was recognised also in Margaret Wood's appointment of Joseph Bancroft as her executor, and the informal will that she sent him regarding the legacies to be distributed from her capital in the United States. He was the most obvious choice as the money concerned was tied up in his business, and would have to be released for the wider distribution that she wished to happen after her death. Clearly, she realised that this would require planning and might only be achieved gradually. Hence, in her original will, she stipulated that if it was not convenient for Joseph Bancroft to release some of this capital immediately, the other beneficiaries must wait 'while he can do it comfortably to himself'. Should any try to coerce him, they were to receive only half the legacy she had stipulated. Such informal wills would appear to have been commonplace among Quakers such as these in this period. They relied on the trust, honesty and fair dealing that Friends sought to cultivate in their business dealings, and on the surveillance of co-religionists and kin. But evidently not all Quakers were fair or trustworthy in these matters.

As we have seen with regard to the related Tipping family, such an arrangement left enormous control in the hands of those asked to execute the wishes of the deceased, and they might not always act according to the expectations held by other intended beneficiaries. Margaret Wood evidently had faith in the honesty and capacity of her nephew, but even so she sent him repeated instructions on the matter: 'thou may think I write a deal about my little property, but as I know, when I make my exit, I shall not return to rectify mistakes.' For his part, he was assiduous in clarifying her intentions in detail, and assured her 'thou need not fear my thinking thou instructs me too much in the matter'. New probate regulations came into force in Britain shortly before her death; regulations she believed would make leaving a formal will far too expensive a proceeding. She considered this an unwarranted tax on her estate, and continued to rely on her wishes being widely known among her family, and respected by those to whom she gave the responsibility for enacting them.[35]

While a 'snug' independence was central to her notion of living a good and useful life, Margaret Wood saw any greater prosperity as a spiritual snare and danger. Her religious beliefs led her to understand the pursuit of wealth for itself as a distraction from the care of the soul, one that might encourage greed, dishonesty, arrogance and worldly pursuits. She was increasingly uneasy, then, with the growing aspirations she detected among her Bright nephews and nieces: 'thou knows they have always been much indulged, so that they naturally look to be gratified in the same proportion as they get older.' She worried about the growth in the Bright family fortunes, and a similar pursuit of wealth among her Bancroft kin in the United States. Such aspirations, she feared, might threaten their spiritual wellbeing: 'Oh it is a good safe state to be low in our minds keep from being too much exalted it is then that we shall be taught of "His Ways" which are indeed pleasantness and all his paths are Peace.' She claimed here to be drawing on her own experience: 'for while I look'd for and expected great things I got nothing, but when all brot down and satisfied with food and raiment the *Great Dispenser* of every good saw meet to entrust me with more.' So she continually urged that her relations not become too absorbed in the search for wealth: 'I do believe if we are desirous of first seeking the Kingdom of heaven we shall be partakers of all things that are necessary and the humbler that our desires are the more we shall be entrusted with.'[36]

Margaret Wood claimed to live frugally, or at least more frugally, according to her own observation, than many among her family in the United States. Certainly, her needs for household assistance were satisfied by one housemaid, at least after she lived alone following her mother's death; and the maid she employed in the last years of her life, Eliza Oldham, was like an adopted daughter as much as a servant. Margaret Wood was free with her advice on how her American kin might adjust their domestic expenses, especially when they came seeking loans: 'tho' provisions may be cheap take care to keep them so, by using them as carefully, as if they were dear, but not to be covetous, nor wasteful.'[37] A story recorded about her illustrates both her frugality and its limits: 'When beggars came to her door, she said why didn't they eat porridge; nothing could be better. Perceiving that she ought to try it herself, she praised it for several meals but finally said: "Take it away, lass, I can eat no more of it."' But her open-handedness to those in need was also remembered, a generosity that extended to giving freely on behalf of others close to her. Once, when John Bright and his family were away from home, she loaned his children's 'fat and sleek donkey' to a travelling tinker, while the overworked donkey was given rest and food in one of the Bright paddocks.[38]

Just as her religious beliefs shaped her attitudes to money and how it should be used, they also determined her view of good business practice. The reputation of Friends for fair and honest dealing in commercial transactions has long been emphasised as a factor in the economic success of many Quakers in this period. Yet it is clear from Margaret Wood's correspondence that her co-religionists were not uniformly honest. Indeed, one of the functions of her letters was to disseminate knowledge of, and to elicit intelligence concerning, the trustworthiness of Friends on either side of the Atlantic. So, she would advise about emigrants who left bad debts behind them, or who had fled the punishment they anticipated for some crime or misdemeanor: 'upon enquiry I find very few that have left here but have done as long as they can without coming under the lash of the law, and so they flee to America.'[39] She warned also of those whose business sense she thought questionable, for example, one who, she claimed, 'lost his money by speculating in land expecting to get rich *too* soon'. She kept an eye also on the manners and business behaviour of family members, and might issue sharp reminders of the financial responsibilities of her kin to their creditors, or deflect any suggestion of loan-seeking that she thought improper or inappropriate.[40]

In such matters she was forthright about the lower standards she believed to hold among US Friends in their financial dealings: 'I think England is preferable to America, there is more confidence to be placed in each other here than with you, in the way of trade.' Similarly, she advised another nephew seeking her aid in finding English backers for his enterprise that there was little faith in the security of loans made to businesses in the United States. She was especially angered by the case of a US minister who married a widow of her acquaintance while travelling in his ministry in England, and persuaded her to let him export her capital back to the United States. Margaret Wood believed he had used his certification as a minister to protect himself from too close enquiries into his financial position prior to the marriage, and that his sole purpose in the marriage had been to obtain his wife's fortune so as to extricate himself from financial difficulties in his home country. In her view, US Friends had fallen down on their obligation to warn their English co-religionists of his uncertain financial standing, indeed had helped him mask this by authorising him to bring his ministry to England: 'It has been a sad thing that friends should have recommended him here as a minister, if I was in Philadelphia the Orthodox friends should know what a creature he is for I know they are deceived in him.'[41]

She also let it be known when she thought acquaintances in the United States might do more for kin left behind in England. Here she evidenced a particular concern for the financial difficulties of the elderly and of women and children who had been left behind in England when sons and husbands emigrated (sometimes without warning).[42] She evidently became an important channel of communication between families and friends separated by migration but without the means themselves to exchange letters. So she passed on to working people on both sides of the Atlantic the latest advice, for example, on the state of the labour market in each country. News of deaths and of possible legacies was another common theme in her letters.[43] In all these ways Margaret Wood practiced the good neighbourliness that was enjoined by her religious beliefs, and upheld the manners and morals that attached to these.

Margaret Wood and the Religious Society of Friends

Margaret Wood made what appears to have been her first visit to London in 1838, to attend the Yearly Meeting of Friends, accompanying some of her Bright nieces. They made the journey there by rail in the remarkable time, then, of fourteen hours, and having stopped to dine on the way. For some forty miles the carriages were drawn by horses, as the railway to London was not yet complete. The unaccustomed speed of their journey left them with a week for sightseeing, 'looking over the wonders of this Great City, which are many'. During the Yearly Meeting, she reported the growing anxiety among some Friends concerning the new modes of living that were becoming evident among church members. It was decided that local committees appointed by Monthly Meetings should visit all Quaker families locally 'in order to stir up to more diligence in the attendance of Weekday Meetings and to bring up their families in a religious life and conversation, and in plainness of speech etc etc'.[44] Margaret Wood shared such concerns as we have seen, concerns that confirmed her in her increasing appreciation of Hicksite Friends that followed her visit to the United States.

At the time of that visit only her sister, Elizabeth Bancroft, continued to attend the meetings of the 'orthodox' Friends in Pennsylvania. John Bancroft and all their children attended the meetings of the Hicksite separation – if they attended meetings at all. For Margaret Wood found that some of her nephews were married to women who remained among the orthodox Quakers. These couples preferred to attend no meeting rather than to attend separate meetings. For her part, at this time Margaret Wood avoided associating with Hicksites outside her own immediate family, feeling she 'dare not so far avow affinity with them altho' I think there are many precious souls amongst them'.[45] When similar tensions grew within London Yearly Meeting, however, it was evangelical Friends who chose to break away, a significant number of 'Beaconites' within the Manchester Monthly Meeting resigning en bloc in 1836.[46] Margaret Wood reported these events in detail to her Bancroft kin, for many of the Beaconites had been their former neighbours and friends. She was by this time more sanguine about such ruptures, noting there were many more within Manchester meeting whose sympathies lay with the Beaconites, but who were not prepared to resign from the main church: 'so that its likely the Society will have some trouble before we get settled again, I hope it will do us good we wanted shaking and rousing and its likely we shall have it with this.'[47]

Like many Friends, she was glad to observe a greater engagement among her co-religionists in open discussion of the issues raised by these theological divisions – even though she continued to believe schism unnecessary, and indicative of spiritual arrogance. For her own part, her essential quietism and her faith in the Inner Light made her increasingly sympathetic to the Hicksites, and more ready to articulate openly her own unease at the influence of evangelical Friends, as this continued to grow within London Yearly Meeting. So, she took comfort from the interventions of Sarah Grubb at the 1838 Yearly Meeting, as this influential woman minister sought to encourage thoughts of reunion in the hearts of the evangelical separatists. She was equally distressed, though, to observe how Sarah Grubb seemed 'almost to stand alone,' and how she was mocked by some of the younger women Friends present. These she watched 'pulling faces at the dear woman . . . who wd have thought such changes wd have been'. She noted also, and regretted, how in the context of these divisions, women ministers appeared less and less ready to speak at Yearly Meeting. One of the fears held by many Friends concerning evangelical influences was the challenge too literal a reading of the scriptures might bring to the ministry of women – if the authority of Pauline hostility to women preachers were ever to be invoked, for example.[48]

Margaret Wood was an authoritative figure in her own right among family and community, though that authority derived from her business acumen, the material resources at her command, the family, business and church networks of which she was a part, her ability to obtain and to share business intelligence, and her readiness to help others in business and family affairs. The money held and created by women such as she was a valuable family resource, especially when new enterprises required fresh funds, or where the ups and downs of family fortunes left some members in need. Her authority allowed her to guide, advise, admonish and, if necessary, help her kinsfolk on money matters. But the manners and interests of a younger generation of Friends were changing, not least in terms of their growing political involvement with which she had no sympathy. Some of her Bright nephews and nieces were also less and less ready to conform to the discipline of the Society of Friends. At least four of her Bright nephews and nieces were disowned or resigned because of a refusal to accept all aspects of that discipline: Thomas, Priscilla, Esther and Jacob Bright jnr all married non-Quakers, the two men also becoming non-believers. John Bright conformed to the discipline of the church in his choice of Quaker wives, at least, but he opposed the marriage rule. He joined with those who have been variously termed 'the liberal party' or 'the moderates' within the Society who sought to soften church discipline in such matters – a group that contained both evangelical Quakers such as his future parliamentary colleague, Joseph Sturge, and Friends like himself who resisted any imposed doctrine.[49]

None the less, religious affiliation still held Quakers together far more closely that theological disputation might separate them. Through his first marriage to Elizabeth Priestman, John Bright's home circle came into intimate connection with her more evangelically inclined family. Rachel Priestman, his future mother-in-law, kept spiritual memoranda, and wrote memorials of the dead as well as copious letters. These reveal a quite different religiosity from Margaret Wood's down-to-earth, if devout, religious certitudes. Rachel Priestman's inner world was altogether more troubled. For her, the salvation of the soul took on a quite awful dimension, one that placed a most terrible burden on her as both a mother and a travelling minister for the Society of Friends.

4 Rachel Priestman (1791–1854)
A 'public Friend'

The Bragg and Priestman families (see Fig. 4.2)

The cholera epidemic reached Newcastle, home of Quaker minister Rachel Priestman, in November 1831.[1] Hers was a fearful religion, quite unlike the calm certainties of faith that shaped Margaret Wood's vision of the world. The advance of a disease that might bring sudden death led Rachel Priestman to write one of the frequent memoranda in which she had for many years recorded her spiritual trials: 'very deep have been the serious conflicts that the poor mind has been introduced [to] lest the solemn message should come at a moment when the soul was unprepared to meet the Judge of the whole earth.' Under this and other trials she confessed: 'I have found it hard work to bend without murmuring to the divine will but at times the Lord's power has subdued self and bowed all within me to resignation ... but Oh! the resistance, the wickedness of the human heart.' In all, 801 died in one of the worst local outbreaks of the epidemic (a large proportion of them from among the poor). All Rachel Priestman's family survived, but her life gave numerous occasions for such anxiety and sad reflection, as we shall see.[2]

She was born in 1791 in Newcastle, above the linen draper's shop kept by her parents, Margaret and Hadwen Bragg (1761–1840 and 1763–1820, respectively),[3] and often recalled memories of a happy childhood there for her own children. Her mother (formerly Margaret Wilson of Kendal) assisted in the family shop until well into middle age. The Braggs's business prospered and they were able to build a house beyond the walls of the old city, Summerhill, where Margaret Bragg combined horticulture, dairying and beekeeping with her other daily tasks.[4] The couple were figures of some standing among Newcastle Friends. Hadwen Bragg was appointed first as an overseer, and then as an elder of that Meeting. He was remembered long afterwards as 'instrumental in promoting the firm, yet tender exercise of the discipline of the church'. A note to Margaret Bragg when recovering from a serious illness suggests a sweetness of character: 'The notes of the Cuckow and the Chaffinch, with the Blackbird, are cheering, the Grass may be almost seen to grow, all around seems revived.'[5]

Figure 4.1 Rachel Priestman (1791–1854), *c.* early 1850s

Margaret Bragg was a figure of still greater authority among Newcastle Friends: as well as being an elder of the meeting she was also a minister, like her mother before her. She had first felt herself called to the ministry a few years after her marriage, and in this role became a person of considerable standing, supposedly ruling 'her household and possibly Newcastle Meeting with a firm hand'. Others thought her a busybody.[6] After her death in 1840 her local Monthly Meeting recorded Margaret Bragg thus: 'endowed with a very superior share of natural ability and possessing an active mind she was induced to take part in the management of a variety of affairs beyond the generality of her sex.' A more prosaic recollection provides us with a different image of her, dispensing the 'hot cloved elderberry syrup' that she provided for Friends after their annual Book Society auction.[7]

Rachel Bragg, the older of two surviving daughters, was sent away to school in the south of England at the age of twelve. Her formal education lasted for three to four years, and was spent mostly at a school run by Elizabeth English in Alton, Hampshire.[8] She passed her holidays in the London area with maternal aunts, when she formed lifelong friendships among her Smith, Messer and Stacey cousins there. The calendar of the Society ensured, however, that she saw her more immediate family from time to time, for example, during their visits to London for Yearly Meeting. Some of her schoolbooks have been preserved, and show that accounting and bookkeeping were part of her school curriculum, as well as French — a mix, then, of the practical and the genteel. A companion from her school years recalled 'an exemplary girl', already of a serious cast of mind: 'There was no levity in her natural disposition and her heart had already been softened by the drawings of the Holy Spirit.'[9]

Rachel Bragg's own recollections of her childhood are less anodyne, regretful of 'the wickedness of my own heart even in childhood'. She retained vivid memories of 'an awful sense of the consequence of wickedness and the state of the wicked' within herself at this time. But even before the age of twelve, she also recalled, she enjoyed 'precious periods of the sense of the presence of God in our meetings of worship'. When attending Yearly Meeting, too, she remembered how 'my mind was so powerfully visited with the outflowings of divine love . . . and I was brought at times into a state in which the language was raised, "draw me and I will follow thee – thou Jesus whom my soul loves".' Looking back on her young womanhood she wondered: 'Oh my God what was I that thou wast mindful of me, but a poor fallen lost creature, for whom in unbounded mercy my Saviour had laid down his life.'[10]

She returned home around the age of sixteen, and evidently retained a broad range of interests, continuing to 'indulge her thirst for knowledge of almost every kind, tho' especially that connected with science and natural history in which she took great delight'. Anxious about having begun the study of Italian and of Euclidean geometry, she reprimanded herself: 'learning tho' commendable, is not requisite, it is not necessary to form a Christian'. Indeed, attention given to such endeavours was, she feared, 'hurtful and will retard our progress to Christian perfection'. Believing it might indicate vanity and pride, her pleasure in learning thus became in her own mind 'a snare'. She told herself 'time is precious and ought only to be employed in what is really useful', and turned instead to 'objects of practical benevolence'. Good works served her spiritually in two respects, then: they displaced other pursuits that might endanger a proper Christian humility; they might aid the individual soul to move nearer to salvation.[11]

Rachel Bragg's recollections of her early womanhood suggest that neither she nor her sister Mary worked in the family business. The latter did not marry and appears in adulthood to have become, in effect, her mother's housekeeper, while Rachel Priestman became Margaret Bragg's occasional companion during travels undertaken in pursuit of her ministry. At other times, the Bragg sisters spent periods away from home staying with kin. It was during such a visit, to Kendal in 1813, when providing company and comfort for a recently widowed aunt, that Rachel Bragg began to be courted by Jonathan Priestman, a Newcastle tanner. He came from a Yorkshire family of farmers and tanners and at this time was employed in a tannery belonging to some of his Richardson cousins.[12] Rachel Bragg at first declined his offer of marriage, but subsequently accepted it. She explained her 'change of sentiment' in these terms: 'I concluded that [with] thou who possessed the most distinguishing and desirable qualities as well as natural and spiritual, [I] could alone taste the most exquisite pleasure of exalted friendship.' In her letters from this time, she rehearses the notion of friendship that was central to Quaker ideals of marriage, expressing the belief that entering such a relationship with 'less romantic ideas' promised 'congenial minds to heighten each others comforts, divide their sorrows' and 'quicken our feeble desire after purity and holiness'. She was at this time reading Hannah More's *Christian Morals*, which she recommended to Jonathan Priestman.[13]

He was still a man of very modest means, as a will made at this time attests. He had served an apprenticeship with his older brothers at his father's tannery in Malton. The illness and death of a cousin, Isaac Richardson, provided him with the opportunity to take over the management of the Richardson tannery in Newcastle, for his kinsman's own sons were as yet too young. Subsequently, he became a partner in that business, and eventually went on to establish his own separate tanning and glue-making businesses.[14] Only a gift of £1,500 from his father placed him in a position to marry, and he made a confidential request that this sum should go to Rachel Bragg should he die before their wedding. The practical requirements of marriage were also assisted by Hadwen and Margaret Bragg, who, 'anxious to keep their daughter near them', enlarged and divided their house at Summerhill (perhaps this is why Jonathan Priestman asked that the £1,500 still go to Rachel Bragg should he die). So after they married Summerhill also became the home of Rachel and Jonathan Priestman and their family.[15] Both households were known among Friends for their hospitality, and it was said of the Priestmans: 'Their door was ever open to welcome anyone of whatever colour or creed whose errand was of mercy to mankind, or for the advance of social opinions, however new and unpopular they might be.'[16]

Rachel Priestman's hopes for her marriage appear to have been fully realised in the many trials that lay ahead of her, at least in terms of the support she found in a husband, 'in whom my very life seems entwined and dependent upon'. Jonathan Priestman remained her 'Beloved friend', and the couple wrote regularly whenever they were separated by business, family concerns or the ministry to which each was called. In one such letter she wrote: 'my heart turns to thee with such deep and tender interest that I am glad to embrace a few moments to tell thee so . . . couldst thou read my heart thou wouldst see all there thou couldst desire of affection for thee, tender love for our dear family.' Even here, though, she saw yet another possible snare for the life of the spirit: 'Oh! the danger is that these should prevent me from uniting with thee my dearest earthly friend in loving above all our heavenly Father – in this duty thou must strengthen the feeble efforts of thy absent RP.'[17] Such sentiments suggest a warmth to their relationship that is at odds with the characterisation of Quaker marriage as 'puritanical'. But it suggests also that the Priestmans' marriage shared in an 'encompassing culture of abstinence' that, it has been argued, explains changing patterns of fertility among Friends over the course of the nineteenth century, with 'unmistakable signs of general and conscious fertility control' among Quaker families from 1850 onwards.[18]

Evidence from this particular family circle would support such interpretations, but it also suggests considerable variety among its members with regard to the fertility of their marriages. The Braggs married relatively late: she was in her thirtieth year and he was two years younger; and they were sometimes separated by her call to deliver her ministry away from their home. Nor was their family of four large by the norms of the time (though at least two other children are known to have died in infancy). Rachel Priestman married in her early twenties, and bore at least nine children, seven of whom survived to adulthood, and the last of whom was born in 1834 when she was in her mid-forties. It was usual for women Friends in these circles to breastfeed their babies rather than to employ wet nurses. The number and spacing of the Priestman children suggests that lactation provided some control on the couple's fertility, with the period between births probably further extended sometimes by sexual abstinence: Elizabeth (b.1815), Margaret (b.1817), Hadwen (b.1820), Rachel (b.1823), David (b.1824), Jonathan (b.1825), Anna Maria (b.1828), Mary (b.1830), Emily (b.1834). Of these, only five were living at the time of Rachel Priestman's own death.[19]

The domestic culture of the Priestman family

The increasing separation of home life from shop, factory and counting house among the middle classes of this period has been associated with the advance of new ideas of domesticity, ideas that in their turn emphasised gender differences, and served to restrict the roles open to middle-class women. Such accounts tend to conflate changes in the sexual division of labour within families with the emergence of notions of 'separate spheres' for women and

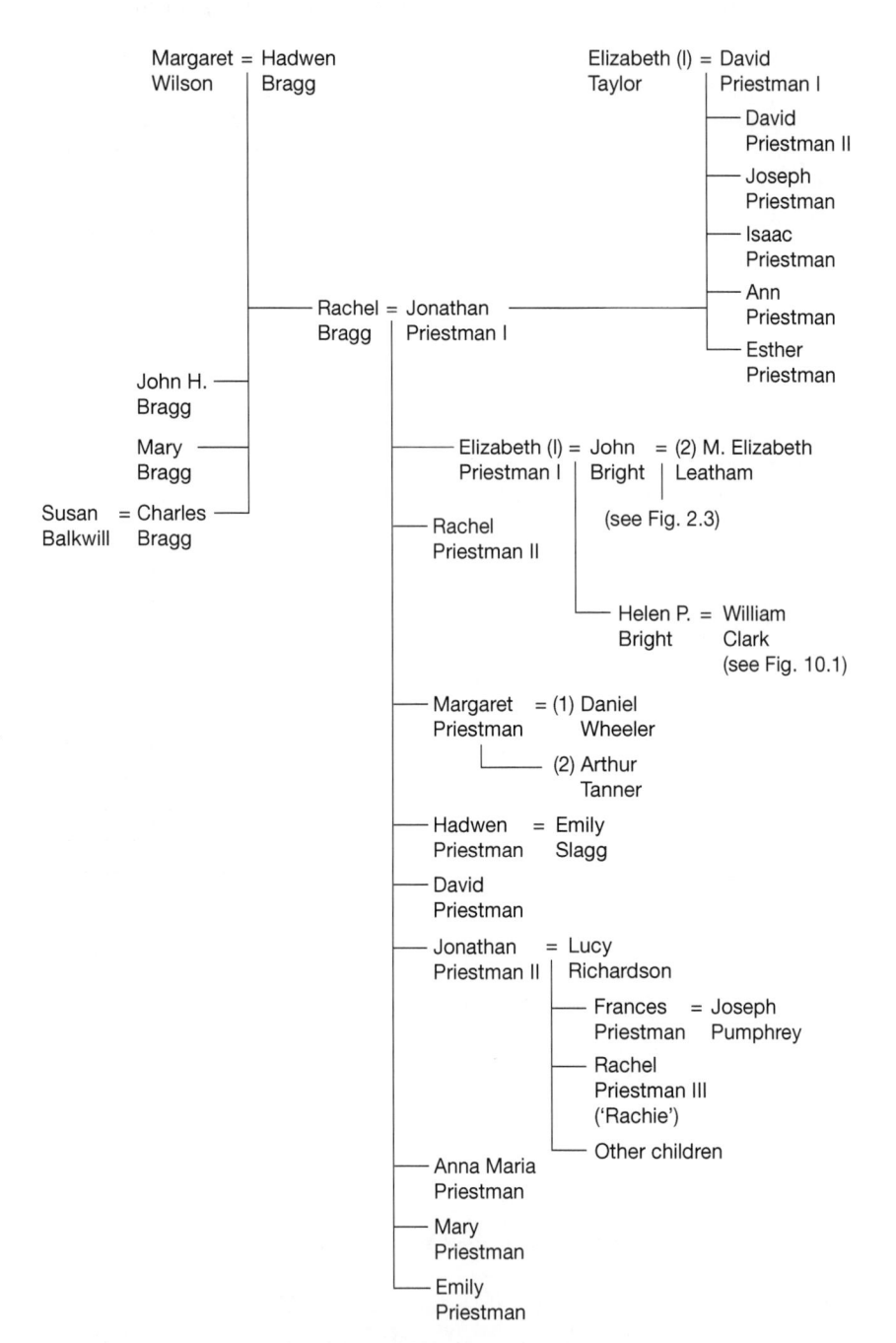

```
                Margaret  =  Hadwen                Elizabeth (I)  =  David
                Wilson       Bragg                 Taylor            Priestman I
                                                                    ├── David
                                                                    │   Priestman II
                                                                    ├── Joseph
                                                                    │   Priestman
                                                                    ├── Isaac
                                                                    │   Priestman
                                                                    ├── Ann
                                                                    │   Priestman
                              Rachel  =  Jonathan ─┤                └── Esther
                              Bragg      Priestman I                    Priestman
            John H. ─┤
            Bragg
            Mary ────┤                  ├── Elizabeth (I)  =  John  =  (2) M. Elizabeth
            Bragg    │                  │   Priestman I       Bright     Leatham
Susan  =  Charles ───┘                  │                    (see Fig. 2.3)
Balkwill  Bragg                         ├── Rachel
                                        │   Priestman II
                                        │                    └── Helen P.  =  William
                                        │                        Bright       Clark
                                        │                                    (see Fig. 10.1)
                                        ├── Margaret  =  (1) Daniel
                                        │   Priestman       Wheeler
                                        │               └── (2) Arthur
                                        │                       Tanner
                                        ├── Hadwen    =  Emily
                                        │   Priestman    Slagg
                                        ├── David
                                        │   Priestman
                                        ├── Jonathan   =  Lucy
                                        │   Priestman II  Richardson
                                        │                 ├── Frances   =  Joseph
                                        │                 │   Priestman    Pumphrey
                                        │                 ├── Rachel
                                        │                 │   Priestman III
                                        │                 │   ('Rachie')
                                        │                 └── Other children
                                        ├── Anna Maria
                                        │   Priestman
                                        ├── Mary
                                        │   Priestman
                                        └── Emily
                                            Priestman
```

Figure 4.2 The Priestman family of Newcastle

Source: R.S. Benson (comp.) *Photographic Pedigree of the Descendants of Isaac and Rachel Wilson*, Middlesbrough: William Appleyard, 1912; A.O. Boyce *Records of a Quaker Family, The Richardsons of Cleveland*, London: Samuel Harris, 1889.

men, even while acknowledging the lived overlap between domestic and public worlds. Yet that division of labour continued to require middle-class women to participate in civil society, most notably in the work of benevolence, and in church life. The evidence regarding the Priestman–Bright circle suggests not only that the worlds of men and women might meet in both the public and private spheres, but also that women made their own spaces within civil society. It is more accurate, then, to speak rather of a gendered division of labour within both the public and the private spheres. As Simon Morgan argues, we should rather think of the public sphere 'as something which itself was constituted around gender division and inequality'.[20] New arenas in public life were also providing women with fresh opportunities beyond kitchen and parlour (or demonstrating the public as well as private functions of such space), in debating clubs and literary societies. Margaret Bragg was to the fore in the formation of both a book club and an essay society among Friends in Newcastle, for example, and those groups often met in her parlour.[21] Equally, a number of recent studies have demonstrated that the exclusion of women from political life was never as complete as the proscriptions of the prevailing domestic ideology might suggest.[22]

Recent analyses of middle-class Quaker domestic life in this period have similarly found that it did not altogether reflect the conventions of the domestic ideology, and have argued on such grounds for its particularity: Sheila Wright, for example, emphasises the relatively egalitarian nature of Quaker marriage; Elizabeth O'Donnell suggests that such 'non-oppressive' marriage relationships may have inhibited any earlier development of a feminist consciousness among women Friends; and Helen Plant argues that the integration of domestic responsibilities and religious authority in the lives of Quaker women created more fluid notions of gender difference among Friends than was general among the middle classes.[23] The evidence regarding the Bragg and Priestman households confirms the increasing withdrawal of women Friends of this class from business activity in the early decades of the nineteenth century, and the companionate ideal of marriage that was pursued by many Quakers. It also suggests that the relationship of men and women to domestic and to public worlds, and the sexual division of labour between them, was more complex that those prescribed in the conventional domestic ideology of this time.

So, while Rachel Priestman specialised in domestic management and Jonathan Priestman in manufacturing, neither was restricted to only one sphere of action, for the education of Quaker girls, and the religious values and church structure of the Society of Friends served to cut across such divisions. Notions of femininity and masculinity might, in consequence, be less divergent. Hence, Jonathan Priestman could be found reorganising his working day so as to spend time with a new baby; or cooking small puddings to soothe the stomach of an ailing infant; or overseeing spring-cleaning when Rachel Priestman was away from home delivering her ministry.[24] Moreover, 'home' among this circle of Friends was not simply a place of retreat and seclusion, the 'haven in a heartless world' celebrated in the conventional domestic ideology of this period. Instead, it was a relatively open space where religious and ethical values might be enacted, where the obligations of citizenship as public service might be performed with the like-minded from the broader community, and where recreation might be shared with co-religionists. Such openness was required by the sociability central to Quaker church culture, by personal commitments to the cause of social and moral reform as well as to good works, and by the hospitality provided for visiting lecturers on temperance or the abolition of slavery, as well as travelling ministers. So the participation of Priestmans and Braggs in civil society and in public life might take place within the walls of Summerhill as well as in town hall or meeting house.

Equally, the letters of Rachel Priestman to her husband and to her mother suggest that from her home she was both able and willing to look after their business interests when he or her parents were away. She was not routinely involved with the family firm, as her mother had been when living above the Braggs's shop. But she might nonetheless report on railway shares, scrips and 'trade letters', alongside the arrangements for a public meeting, the passage of a Bill through parliament, or a due subscription to a charity – as well as pie making, the health of her children and lost household keys. If she was never an active participant in the family business in the way her mother had been, she nonetheless knew enough to check on, and attend to matters of business. Like Margaret Wood, she also imbued business activity with religious and ethical meanings. Hence towards the end of her life, in July 1853, she recorded in a memorandum: 'Stocktaking has been gone through, endeavours blessed, if only Oh! my God, basket and store be but given with thy approving smile, and united with grace to rightly use.'[25]

If the growing prosperity of their families allowed women like Rachel Priestman to live and work largely within the home, her religious values meant that she did not enjoy a leisured existence. The 'right' use of that prosperity required various forms of community service, especially in terms of personal benevolence towards poor and sick neighbours, and the provision of education for working people and their children. Rachel Priestman was active in the British and Foreign School Society, for example, and together with her husband and children took a special interest in a local infant school and orphanage, and in the Sabbath School that 'marked a new departure in local aggressive work among Friends'. Braggs and Priestmans also supported a range of humanitarian and moral reform endeavours of long-standing concern to their church, like the peace movement. They also increasingly worked alongside members of other churches in bodies like the Bible Society. Generally, such work was organised between separate societies of men and the associated 'ladies' auxiliaries. Those auxiliaries might be the more effective of the two, as was the case with the Bible Society, for example, though women were initially excluded from the government of that body.[26] So while Jonathan Priestman became one of the first teetotallers in Newcastle in the mid-1830s, Rachel Priestman and her daughters were to the fore in the Newcastle Ladies

Society for the Suppression of Intemperance. The Priestmans were also remembered as 'indefatigable' in the anti-slavery movement, a concern shared by the Braggs.

The introduction of the Priestman children to such activity was an important part of the upbringing provided at Summerhill, and her observation of its effects was a great comfort to Rachel Priestman. Hence, Margaret Priestman regularly taught alongside her father at the Sabbath School he had established for the children of the poor. As a child she also recorded attending a 'bazaar', a sale of work, where Margaret Bragg supervised a stall alongside Lady Ravenscroft and her daughters (most probably in support of the anti-slavery or temperance movements). In these ways, the Summerhill families conformed to the picture suggested by Elizabeth O'Donnell, of prominent families of Friends becoming part of the local Dissenting 'radical municipal oligarchies' that began to challenge the established elite in Newcastle through their participation in civil society and, latterly, in local government.[27]

But such a characterisation serves to obscure the genuine and active sympathy of the Summerhill families for those less fortunate than themselves. Popular sympathies were also evident in their political values, for in the case of the Priestman family at least, a leaning towards evangelical religion proved compatible with political radicalism (as it did in notable Quaker radicals of the day like Joseph Sturge, another evangelical Friend). Indeed, the immersion in a variety of good works encouraged by evangelical beliefs offered an alternative way of life to the social seclusion and quietism that had previously marked communities of Friends, and might further sustain radical values. Unlike the Wood, Bright and Bancroft families, no surviving evidence suggests any long-standing radical-political associations. However, the home of Rachel and Jonathan Priestman was later recalled as one 'where intellectual activity existed side by side with a strict form of Quakerism; where the utmost refinement of manner was combined with the warmest of popular sympathies, and where the strongest opinions were urged in the gentlest tones'. They were also recorded as 'deeply interested in the passing of the first Reform Bill'.[28] Such evidence suggests that they, too, sustained the oppositional political values evident among Woods, Brights and Bancrofts, though the channels by which these were promoted (or sustained) among Friends in the north east remains unclear. Indeed, the Priestmans appear if anything still more radical in their politics than their future son-in-law, for they supported universal suffrage, a demand he came to believe should be put aside until the Corn Laws were repealed.

So, in such circles evangelical religion had not served to displace the deep-seated oppositionism of Friends, but rather may have formed a link between a commitment to moral reform, philanthropy and humanitarianism and political radicalism. In such ways, the spiritual and the material, the private and the public worlds of Rachel Priestman were interwoven in her everyday life by her religious beliefs. Though her life was deeply 'domestic' in character, she was never confined to a separate sphere. She evidently felt 'at home' enacting business and public as well as domestic roles. But it was her faith, as much as economic relations, and community, church and family patterns of association as much as business, which maintained the bridges she might cross between them. Her ministry became the principal channel through which her inner world took on a larger significance, one that regularly required her absence from family and domestic responsibilities, and sometimes took her on distant travels.

Spiritual life and the memoranda of Rachel Priestman

Clearly, the religious sensibility of Rachel Priestman differed considerably from that of Margaret Wood. Such differences may in part have been temperamental, but they reflected also the varying impact of evangelicalism among early-nineteenth-century Quakers. Evidence of personal salvation for herself and her family remained her most pressing need. She constantly examined the state of her inner being for any questioning of the dispensations of Providence. She repeatedly reminded herself of the mysterious nature of God's love and immersed herself in the language of bloody sacrifice, in images of the suffering Christ on the cross. The keeping of her spiritual memoranda became the means by which she examined in the light of her religious beliefs the many and varied difficulties that marked her life, thereby revealing, also, the meanings she gave to such emotional and spiritual trials. In contrast, Friends of a quietist faith, such as Margaret Wood, found almost barbaric notions of a god who would see his son crucified to atone for the sins of humankind, and predestine any number of souls to perdition. (This was a misapprehension of the belief of evangelical Quakers like Rachel Priestman, who saw the crucifixion as a voluntary act on the part of Jesus, not as an outcome determined by God.) Quietist Friends instead sought to maintain a steady, patient, spiritual passivity as the likeliest route to salvation. Where Margaret Wood seems never to have been troubled by religious doubt, Rachel Priestman's spiritual life was marked by recurring spiritual rebellion.

Such rebellion came to her especially at times of grief for the loss or suffering of someone close to her, and acquiescence in what she understood as God's will was not always readily achieved. She managed such inner turmoil by writing memoranda for herself of these periods of despair, having first begun to keep intermittent accounts of her various travels after leaving school. The memoranda that for her family came to constitute her spiritual journal began in 1820, prompted by the grief she experienced on the death of her father, Hadwen Bragg. Thereafter, they focused principally on her attendances at Quarterly Meetings, and the Yearly Meeting in London, recording also the births, illnesses and spiritual development of her nine children – and also the deaths in infancy of a son and a daughter that occasioned further anguish. The form and language of these memoranda were borrowed from published texts of this kind, as well as also emulating the similar memoranda kept by her mother and father.

This is how she learned to give shape and meaning to her emotional and religious experience, also fostering, perhaps, the hope that such a record might help subsequent generations of her closest kin. For, whether it was intended or not, such material continued to find readers across many subsequent generations of her family, as we have seen with regard to the letters of Margaret Wood. The preservation of similar unpublished memoranda and letters, and the creation from them of memorials to the dead, helped create and sustain the unusually extensive family memory among Quaker kinship circles like those of the Priestman and Bright families. For such material might not only provide a source of religious guidance, but continue to nourish recollection of long-dead family members as well. In this case, Rachel Priestman's memoranda were ordered and put together by her oldest surviving daughter, Margaret Wheeler (shortly to become Tanner) with reminiscences collected from family and friends, to create a memorial to Rachel Priestman. By such means, what had been a comfort to Rachel Priestman in times of deep despair, became also a consoling legacy to her children. Such material provides, too, a rare record of the life of an unassuming woman of little note and how she understood her world. The survival of such material allows us to recover something of the lives of persons of modest standing who otherwise left little trace of their existence, and who are unlikely to find a place in the grander narratives of government and nation.

For Rachel Priestman herself, the writing of memoranda helped her to move forward from the tragedies of everyday life, if not always in the direction she desired for herself. So the resolution of the inner, spiritual turmoil prompted by her father's death in 1820 was shortly followed by a call to the ministry. And, like many women ministers, she represented this call as one for which she thought herself unfitted and which she would have denied if she could.[29] When her third son, David, died in infancy a few years later she turned once more to writing a memorandum in her efforts to become resigned to his loss: 'It has been a solemn stroke, a heart-rending separation, yet mercifully mingled with many alleviations.' She sought to comfort herself and her dead child with this hope: 'dear babe, thou canst not return to us – but we may possibly come to thee, and we crave to be made fit to participate in those joys.'[30] The death of her sister, the declining health of her mother and fresh anxieties arising from serious illness among her children prompted further religious doubts in 1829, doubts renewed a few years later during the cholera epidemic, as we have seen.[31] By the time of her last pregnancy in 1834, Rachel Priestman was in her mid-forties, an age when physical decline, sickness and death was an increasingly frequent event among her family and friends. She feared that neither the baby nor herself would survive the coming birth, and 'from that time death was so present with me'. The child, Emily Esther, was safely delivered, but lived only ten months: 'How shall my pen pourtray present events . . . her beautiful little remains, lovely even in death, are peacefully resting in the North Room.' This death also brought back memories of David, for like him her baby daughter died of 'water in the head'. This loss, like many previous bereavements, became the occasion for Rachel Priestman to question her own worthiness for salvation: 'We mourn but desire to bend resigned to Him who gave and who has taken away, ... but nature is weak, very feeble – and I have humblingly to acknowledge myself vile indeed, ... my rebellious heart has been too busy with earthly things.'[32] Though she attempted 'gratefully to number remaining blessings' in order to rouse herself from grief, she remained troubled by her own failure inwardly to acquiesce in the death of Emily Esther: 'But Oh! the buffetings of my soul! the many omissions towards my dear babe which I now regretted and that sweet presence of my Saviour which has often cheered, was not permitted to comfort my drooping spirits – an almost continued gloom remains with me.' So instead she sought to ease her sorrow by immersing herself in a variety of good works.

The education of the Priestman children

Evangelicalism also shaped the education that the Priestmans provided for their surviving children. Friends with the means generally sought to give their children a 'guarded' education, usually at home during their early years, and at a Friends' school where possible thereafter. Looking back on the upbringing of her children, Rachel Priestman found consolation in believing that they had been guided past many hazards to their spiritual wellbeing: 'Youth is a dangerous part of our path thro' life.'[33] Evangelical influences informed both the Priestmans' choice of a governess, and the subsequent resignation of that governess some years later. Esther Stickney joined their household in the mid-1820s and resigned her position following the departure of the evangelical 'Beaconites' from the Society of Friends. By this time she had shared the Priestmans' home for almost thirteen years, and overseen the education in early childhood of all their children. Letters between Eliza Stickney and her grief-stricken youngest charges give evidence of the deeply evangelical cast of mind that she brought to her work, with which she had also filled the minds of her pupils.[34] This was no doubt why she had been selected by the Priestmans to be their governess. But it would seem that her evangelical beliefs had now become so strong that she felt it necessary to follow the Beaconites in separating from the Society of Friends. Looking back on their long association, Rachel Priestman recorded: 'it was a period of very serious feeling to me, a subject of much solicitude, that we might act according to Christian principle, in our movements towards this dear friend, whose conclusions, in leaving our loved Society have felt very trying to us.'[35]

One of her older daughters, Margaret Priestman, left a record of the orderly, busy routines of the Priestman household and schoolroom, in a brief journal that she kept for a few months towards the end of 1824. This records that she was usually up by around 6.15 a.m. and had dressed and made her bed by breakfast at 8 a.m. The morning was spent 'in school' from 9.15 to 12.30.

Then she spent an hour or so nursing the new baby, David, before dressing for dinner at 2 p.m. This was followed by a brief visit to her Aunt Mary Bragg to help in the making of a bride cake, before returning to the schoolroom for more lessons from 3 to 5.30 p.m. Tea was taken with Mary Bragg on this occasion – perhaps to relieve Rachel Priestman with a new baby in the house. After tea the children played 'at caping verses' with their aunt till 7 p.m., returning home for bedtime at 7.30. Her diary suggests that the children also had school on Sunday afternoon, after attending meeting in the morning. Margaret Priestman's lessons might be abbreviated if Rachel Priestman had need of assistance from her older daughters in the management of her household. 'Culinary and domestic occupations' might sometimes take up a school day, ones Margaret Priestman seemed to enjoy, perhaps because of her admiration for the housewifery skills of her grandmother, Margaret Bragg. This brief diary was almost certainly kept at the suggestion of her mother, perhaps in preparation for the arrival of Esther Stickney, and was a further way of teaching Margaret to keep a careful account of how she used her time: '1 hour spent sillily today' was a not uncommon self-assessment. This daily exercise appears to have come to an end shortly after the death of the new baby in the household: 'Dear Brother David has been very poorly latterly, and . . . expired very quietly with out a strugal age 5 mo and a half. Much regretted, Sweet lamb.'[36]

Arrangements in the Priestman schoolroom suggest that other values were also being acted out there. First, all the Priestman children received an advanced academic education for Quakers of their class and day, one that went beyond basic literacy, numeracy, accountancy and domestic skills to include the learning of French, German and Latin – accomplishments unknown to their Bragg or Priestman grandparents, and ones extended to both the daughters and sons of Rachel and Jonathan Priestman.[37] Latin was something few Quaker governesses would have been able to teach, and so William Doeg was employed to teach this subject and modern languages. His presence in the schoolroom was evidently not appreciated by the Priestman children, for Margaret wrote to a friend in 1826: 'we are very happy, but we have a Latin master who comes three times a week.'[38] The relationship between the Priestman children and William Doeg indicates their possession of high spirits, a keen sense of justice and a fearlessness in voicing dissent. They had more than a little fun and mischief at their schoolmaster's expense, turning the schoolroom into a regular battle of wills.[39]

William Doeg kept a notebook in which he recorded the misbehaviour of each of the Priestman children, one that suggests equally that he had little aptitude for commanding their respect, obedience or attention to the work in hand. Margaret, we learn, 'very incorrectly performed her Latin lessons' – nineteen words to be parsed on a slate – one day, and compounded the offence by arriving late in the schoolroom the next. On another occasion, he wrote: 'Margaret has given way to no small degree of equivocation in regard to her French lessons this evening.' When reprimanded for her 'indifference to want of punctuation', he recorded, she adopted 'a haughty supercilious and contemptuous demeanour – stigmatising W. D.'s proceedings as tyrannical, unjust, etc.'. Her brother, Hadwen, was perhaps the most recalcitrant, frequently arriving late, unwashed and in dirty clothes. William Doeg recorded his 'continued instances of disobedience and *perverseness*; and some impudence in language'. When put to work in a corner for his misdemeanours, Hadwen 'persisted in petulantly exclaiming I cant see – I cant see, do thee hear W. Doeg, I cant see'. Even the youngest under his direction, Rachel junior, became adept at the game, declaring: 'I'll try to displease thee as much as ever I can' while throwing a book on the floor, trampling on it and saying it made 'a very comfortable footstool'. Quite how or why William Doeg and the Priestman family endured each other for over two years remains unclear – perhaps the gentleness, poise and equanimity of their parents help mediate these unhappy relationships, for the children made sure their dislike and sense of injustice were known to all.

The Priestmans sent their oldest child, Elizabeth, away to school in London in 1830. Here again, the Priestman's values were in evidence: Susanna Corder was a Friend so that her school in Stoke Newington provided a 'guarded' education that conformed to the Quaker values pursued in their own home. But the curriculum included classical languages and science subjects, the latter taught by visiting male lecturers.[40] The choice of this school suggests the valuation that the Priestmans placed on intellectual life, and their more substantial ambitions for the education of their daughters than was common among Friends at this time. However 'guarded' the education there may have been, Elizabeth Priestman returned home with tastes and aspirations that were at odds with those prevailing at Summerhill. Whatever their openness to the world in terms of evangelical belief and cross-denominational campaigns for moral reform and public benevolence, Rachel and Jonathan Priestman otherwise remained 'plain Friends'. So after school-life in London, Elizabeth Priestman had 'felt parental restraint on some points difficult to bear'. Rachel Priestman looked back on what she believed 'a very critical period' in her daughter's spiritual development. The family tensions to which it gave rise were eased by Elizabeth Priestman spending most of her time with her grandmother, Margaret Bragg, whose influence gradually restored family harmony and brought her back into closer sympathy with the ways of her parents' household. Rachel Priestman believed that in these ways her daughter's 'guarded position' had proved a particular blessing.[41]

Following the example of her grandmother and her mother, Elizabeth Priestman began to keep memoranda concerning her spiritual life from 1838, memoranda her mother gathered together with letters and family reminiscences as a memorial to her daughter after her early death.[42] The deaths from influenza, and close together, of two of Elizabeth's uncles, Joseph and David Priestman jnr acted as the first prompt to this exercise. She had learned the appropriate vocabularly and composition of such records, perhaps from reading those kept by her mother and grandmother. Now she recorded how she had found the bereaved households in Malton: 'stunned and overwhelmed with the shock – Oh! how little do we know what a day may bring forth ... May we then seek to be ready when our awful summons comes!' Called with all the family to David Priestman's deathbed, she reported: 'He wanted to see us to tell us of the mercy of God, of his peace, to assure us how sweet the prospect of eternity now felt to him.' Elizabeth Priestman absorbed this lesson well and continued to ponder on these and others deaths known to her in the months that followed: 'Blessed Jesus I would commit my soul into thy hands, thou canst do all for me and thou knows how feebly alas! But how truly I love thee and washed in thy blood, may our trust be in thee.'[43] So the education and upbringing provided for their children by the Priestmans was strongly shaped by the concerns and imperatives of evangelical religion. Elizabeth Priestman stayed on in Malton for some months more, as a companion for her bereaved aunts. In this way, and like her mother before her, she fulfilled that expectation of mutual care between nieces and aunts that was part of the domestic culture of these, as of Margaret Wood's, kinship circles.

A 'public Friend': the travelling ministries of Rachel Priestman

Several times in her life Rachel Priestman felt a call to travel and take her ministry to Friends elsewhere, always after some period of extreme personal emotional and spiritual turmoil. These were also prompted, however, by the disruption that evangelical beliefs brought to the Society of Friends. In 1835, shortly before the Beaconite schism, Rachel Priestman had visited her mother's kin in Kendal, and recorded how it had provoked in her 'varied feelings – the present state of our Society leads to deep conflict – may it eventually conduce to the salvation of souls'.[44] For, one of her Braithwaite cousins there had married into the Crewdson family, members of which were to lead the Beaconite schism; another Braithwaite cousin married Anna Lloyd, a Friend by convincement who also became an influential evangelical minister. The latter's travelling ministry among Friends in the United States helped provoke the Hicksite schism among those who rejected central tenets of evangelical religion, such as the unquestionable truth of the scriptures.[45] So, in this instance the intimate relations of family life might prompt Rachel Priestman to public action in the form of a travelling ministry, by which she sought to prevent the loss of family members to religious schism.

The older Priestman children showed a keen interest in these issues, too. Margaret Priestman attended London Yearly Meeting in 1835 and sent an account of proceedings there to Esther Stickney. It suggests the range of theological issues that were now seriously beginning to divide Friends. A woman minister, for example, 'expressed her fear of a form of prayer – she did not appear to approve of set periods of prayer. Was afraid of the wisdom of man etc'. Daily family prayers and bible readings were by now a common part of the routine of Quaker households like the Priestmans, as they were to become at John Bright's home, One Ash, under the influence of Elizabeth Priestman. But many Friends continued to believe that prayer ought to be a silent, individual exercise directed by the promptings of 'the Light within'. According to this view, those chosen as ministers might best be trusted to verbalise spiritual leadings in meetings for worship, and even then prayer ought to occur spontaneously under the direction of divine inspiration. Margaret Priestman also reported how another prominent woman Friend spoke against teaching a child of Christ's suffering on the cross until their minds were first prepared by learning of the love of God. For evangelically inclined Friends like Margaret Priestman, this made no sense: 'but how my dear E. [Esther Stickney] can the love of God be more wonderfully proved to the simplest child ... such a sacrifice must fill the heart with love to god and to Jesus Christ.' Similarly, Margaret Priestman disputed this Friend's advice against too much reading, especially on theological issues: 'there seemed to me such a setting up of our books – such a desire to turn to our first principles in *them* as though they were not in the Scriptures.' She was glad that a cousin (most likely, Anna Braithwaite), had responded 'that if our early friends were now living they would direct us to the Bible', even while acknowledging that 'there must be the influence of the blessed Spirit' if such reading were to provide spiritual aid.[46] This was a position that sought to acknowledge the particularity of the religious view of Friends, and most especially the centrality of a dependence on 'the seed within', while also promoting the evangelical emphasis on Bible study and the authority of the scriptures.

London Yearly Meeting continued, then, to rehearse the issues that had led, in the Philadephia Yearly Meeting a few years before, to the Hicksite separation by those who sought to resist the influence of evangelical theology. In the British case, it brought about the 'Beaconite' separation by evangelicals impatient at resistance to their beliefs. Many Priestman kin, especially on the Bragg side of the family, became part of this separation. We have already seen Rachel Priestman's sorrow at having to part, in consequence, with Esther Stickney. For the Priestmans, like Margaret Wood, could not condone schism. Membership of the Society of Friends remained central to their sense of identity, and hostility to the established church was never very far below the skin. For Margaret Priestman, as for so many Friends of her generation, theology and politics were inextricably entwined. So, on visiting Durham Cathedral, she described it as a place: 'fitted for high perhaps holy thought but I confess I am too much of a reformer to like to see such a building while things remain as they do, or at least to derive unalloyed pleasure from these remnants of priestcraft.'[47]

Rachel Priestman answered a fresh call to minister when attending the 1839 Yearly Meeting with Jonathan Priestman, 'under the deeply exercising, and humbling belief that my heavenly Father called for an act of dedication very hard to my natural disposition, the visiting of the men's meeting'. Her discomfort at the prospect was eased when another woman minister,

H. C. Backhouse, appeared under a similar 'concern' and accompanied her there. Rachel Priestman experienced great solace in the spiritual support she experienced while so publicly giving voice to her call: 'surely I have great cause to adore and bless that gracious God, who ... was strength indeed in the hour of need when I believed the time was come to make a public surrender of my will, by acknowledging the exercise I was under.'[48] A similar call led her to take her ministry also to the Pickering Monthly Meeting, 'an engagement of duty' perhaps occasioned by similar religious strains among its members who included many of her husband's kin. Rachel Priestman at last returned to 'our loved home' at the end of September 1839. She was in good time to prepare for the wedding of her eldest daughter, Elizabeth, to Margaret Wood's nephew, the Rochdale cotton spinner and aspiring radical, John Bright.[49]

5 Marriages, births and deaths
The formation of the Priestman–Bright circle

The marriage of Elizabeth Priestman and John Bright

Among Quaker families at this time, siblings played a considerable role in the promotion and maintenance of marriages, not least in the creation of extensive and long-standing networks. Margaret Bright introduced her brother, John, to his future wife, Elizabeth Priestman, at the General Meeting of Ackworth School in 1837. His sisters also constructed a pretext for him to visit Newcastle some months later to renew the acquaintance.[1] The Durham Quarterly Meeting of the Society of Friends provided a further opportunity for their meeting (not an occasion, Margaret Wood shrewdly noted, that John Bright usually attended, 'but ones apt to guess').[2] The two had met perhaps only four times when, in the autumn of 1838, he sought the permission of Jonathan Priestman to ask Elizabeth Priestman to marry him, explaining: 'From the circumstance of my residing at so great a distance from you, I find myself in a somewhat unfavorable position and in some degree compelled to make this avowal more abruptly than in other circumstances would be desirable.' He assured them that it was only after 'the most mature and serious consideration' that he determined to make his offer now.[3] Her parents were, by this request, 'brought into much solicitude . . . and were earnestly desirous that true judgment might attend our decisions'.[4]

Both they and their daughter took many months to think over the matter, before agreeing to further meetings and the exchange of letters between the two. Some months before Elizabeth Priestman had written in one of her memoranda: 'I am nearly 23, how innumerable are my blessings! But how cold my heart.' She prayed: 'dear Lord! With Thee would I make fresh covenant, that thou mayst be my all.' To this end she planned a regular period of 'evening retirement' for religious contemplation. But she found her thoughts constantly interrupted by more 'creaturely' concerns.[5] For at this time she was still considering a previous offer of marriage: 'How the cares of earth fill our hearts, sadly annoyed with earthly thoughts tonight, preventing the humble prayer for pardon and peace in the blood of Jesus.' Her anxieties on this matter continued for several months more, until finally she declined this prior offer: 'Varied indeed have been my feelings. . . . I cannot describe the relief it was to me, when the affair was in plain terms dropped. I was satisfied it could not be right to let it go on, even in the way it was, without a stronger feeling of interest and I hope and trust I have done right.'[6] Shortly afterwards, her parents' told her of John Bright's wish to propose, and when she considered this second suitor, she confessed regarding the first: 'Had I known what was so soon to succeed that view, I should have wished the first to have been settled earlier.'[7]

Quaker women carried a very considerable burden of responsibility in decisions regarding marriage. Proposals were rarely turned down out of hand, for they were seen as providential (and were generally first addressed to parents who might refuse to allow a courtship to begin). Should a woman accept a proposal, she remained free to withdraw from such an understanding right up to the time appointed for the marriage if any doubts arose in her mind as to the likely harmony of the union. Responsibility for domestic happiness lay with both partners, but a woman was understood to be the better judge of its likelihood. A Quaker woman would come under severe censure if she was thought to have accepted a marriage proposal on romantic grounds alone and without due reflection, or if she appeared to be simply flirting, or playing with the feelings of the man concerned. Quaker courtship among circles such as these tended, in consequence, to be a protracted affair, where the woman, if attracted to a suitor, tested out his companionability and harmony of outlook and temperament as a potential husband, while those closest to her sought outside advice on her behalf regarding the character and ability of the man concerned.

John Bright was invited to Summerhill some weeks after his letter to Jonathan Priestman, when he sought Elizabeth Priestman's permission to write to her. She refused, but he wrote nonetheless. Their subsequent correspondence conformed to the cautious conventions of Quaker courtship. So, he began by expressing gratitude for the kindness he had met with from her family, and acknowledging the sacrifice that Elizabeth Priestman would make in leaving such a home. He suggested only careful consideration and high motives had led him to seek their marriage. Noting that it was fourteen months since their first meeting, he declared he had come to value one in whose mind '... are united the excellencies which will be of priceless value to him who may be found worthy to possess thy confidence and affections'. He made it clear, also, that he had delayed making his proposal until 'my prospects in life were sufficiently fixed to justify further proceedings'.[8] John Bright must have felt confident of the outcome, for he was already building a house, One Ash, for his intended bride.

Elizabeth Priestman, however, also followed the conventions of Quaker courtship in the oblique reply she sent to this first letter. She neither refused nor accepted his proposal, explaining that she found it difficult to express what she felt on 'a subject of such deep importance and on which not only my present, but what is of far more importance my eternal happiness so much depends'. So she looked for evidence that the marriage would be 'in accordance with the will of my Heavenly Father, without whose blessing there can be no true happiness'. She confessed herself ignorant of his religious views, and therefore sought further evidence of their compatibility in this respect: 'I can only look forward for the blessing of God, on a union with one whose views are similar; one to whom I could look for strength and encouragement under every spiritual temptation and trial, and whose chief aim is the glory of God.'[9] Here was a potential hazard for John Bright's hopes of marriage: his religiosity was of a very different cast from that shared by Elizabeth Priestman and her parents, one far more akin to that of his aunt, Margaret Wood. He wrote to his absent sister, Priscilla Bright, of the quandary he was in: on the one hand, he was sympathetic to Elizabeth Priestman's emphasis on the spiritual companionship she sought in marriage: 'I am not surprised at this from her excellent education and from the opinion I have of the purity of her heart and conduct, and I only fear I fall far short of her standard she has fixed herself'; on the other hand, he was puzzled how to reply, 'inasmuch as I cannot boast of great religious experience and if I did, it would prove that I was not religious'. How to negotiate this difference of outlook between his own liberal Quakerism and the concerns of more evangelically inclined Friends? He decided on another visit to Summerhill, in order to 'express myself by word of mouth and to endeavour to dispel any fears that may exist in this ground'.[10] In the meantime, he assured her he truly valued the religious principles of Friends, and 'deplored many departures from them in practice'. This was as close as he allowed himself to come to expressing his and his family's reservations concerning the doctrinal influence of evangelicalism, and the schisms that had come in its wake.[11]

During this second visit Elizabeth Priestman agreed at least to a correspondence. In his next letter he reported himself 'humbled and instructed' by the piety he had encountered within her family circle. He hoped his replies had been satisfactory in the long conversation he had had with Margaret Bragg, about the circumstances necessary for Elizabeth Priestman's happiness: 'I answered with great candour and freedom.' Margaret Bragg evidently took a close interest in her granddaughter's marriage, for Margaret Wood also reported a visit she made to Rochdale 'to see the situation where her Granddaughter was to come to, Jno Brights intended wife'.[12] Jonathan Priestman had earlier made such a visit in order to help his daughter come to a right decision. During this time, decided differences of temperament, manners and outlook on the world emerged between the Priestman and Bright families.[13] John Bright was stung especially by Jonathan Priestman's suggestion that he was a domineering presence within his own family circle. It was a criticism that had some substance, from evidence in John Bright's letters to his sisters. He had been a frail child, quite literally wrapped in cotton wool for the first few months of his life, when Jacob Bright had supposedly kept his son cradled in his arms as he went about his business. Now, though, he denied being 'the object of very particular attentions on the part of our family', and acknowledged that 'forbearance and self-denial' was to be looked for in a husband.[14]

He also sought to establish himself as an essentially domestic man: 'I think I have inclinations, feelings and habits, which entitle me to be called a domestic character . . . and humbly hope to be preserved from arrogance and self-sufficiency.' In similar vein, he declared: 'In the word *Home* there is a magic to which very few are insensible, and those few are much to be pitied.' In this last statement he was responding also to a much more significant reservation about their marriage among members of the Priestman family, and not least in Elizabeth herself. This concerned his political activism. The Priestmans may have been even more radical in their political sympathies than John Bright. But like many Quakers they still held back from active participation in national politics. Jonathan Priestman had been especially disturbed by evidence of John Bright's 'political engagements' when he visited Rochdale, and Elizabeth Priestman by the warmth with which John Bright sometimes expressed his political opinions. He acknowledged her fear that 'violent political partisanship frequently works in destroying domestic comfort' and takes 'men almost constantly from their homes'. But he explained the duty he felt to be involved in local elections, claiming that his intervention, and that of like-minded voters, had ensured less corruption and less drunkenness. Again, he sought to calm her disquiet by appealing to questions of principle and of shared values: 'I believe the honest exercise of the Franchise to be a solemn duty, and that there are occasions on which we may not shrink even from a prominence in these matters, but I also believe it is dangerous to encourage relish for political excitement . . . I think I feel on this subject as thou does.' These were turbulent times, with unrest over the new Poor Law, for example, continuing to stir up popular disturbances in his own region. However, now he downplayed reports of continuing unrest in Lancashire: 'We are as peaceable as ever; I cannot discover the slightest sensation in the public mind, and the whole is a frightful monster existing only in the fertile imaginations of the Newspaper Gentry.'[15] From this point on his letters dwelt much more on their mutual interests in moral reform and benevolence, especially temperance, anti-slavery and the British School society.

In January 1839 he was once again allowed to visit Elizabeth Priestman and to accompany the Priestman family to meeting, signs that an acceptance was now likely. Before returning home, he renewed his offer of marriage and this time it was accepted without equivocation. He wrote to apologise for leaving 'somewhat abruptly' afterwards, so emotionally drained he had found himself denied speech, and unable to express 'how full my heart was'. Once again, he acknowledged 'the hallowing influence of religion and devotion' that he experienced at Summerhill, and the spiritual self-examination to which it led him: 'I have to deplore many serious deviations from the safe path, I have to struggle with a strange apathy and indifference to the most important of duties, and at times, almost fear I shall never be able to shake off the weight which holds the spirit in fetters.' He claimed that since meeting Elizabeth Priestman and being accepted by her, 'I have felt a very sensible change in my mind and thoughts and tendencies . . . I am much less advanced than thou art, but I feel also that I can be animated and encouraged by thee.' In such terms John Bright rendered himself a religious calling for Elizabeth Priestman.[16]

They married in November 1839 when the Newcastle Meeting House was 'crammed, many standing in the aisles' in order to witness the event.[17] Though the Priestmans were 'plain' Friends, the wedding dress worn by Elizabeth Priestman combined Quakerly restraint with fashionable detail and expensive cloth.[18] Equally, the wedding breakfast demonstrated the temperance values of the Priestman family, jellies and blancmanges all prepared without the usual addition of wine and spirits. The Brights' wedding journey was spent in the Lake District, visiting sites connected with the origins of the Society, and also with the history of their respective families.

Life at One Ash, Rochdale

Margaret Wood kept her US kin abreast of these events in terms that made clear her disapproval of the lifestyles being adopted by her Bright nephews. Here is her description of One Ash:

> it stands about 200 yard from mine, a genteel square building with three parlours and a good Kitching with Pantries on one floor, and two good cellars, one for the Laundry, and the other for the Larder, and a place to take the Ashes that fall from the Kitching; a wide Entry and Stair case with five lodging rooms, only two stories high, the ground before and behind the house laid out very nicely with flags to walk all round, it stands high and commands a good prospect, it has cost above £1200 and the furniture of it will cost not far short of a thousand pounds so you see they are beginning high enough . . . I don't like to see them begin in so large away, but I hope they will sometime see the folly of it.

Such folly arose, in her mind, both from the social aspirations of which it spoke, but also from the uncertainty she believed to characterise 'property in trade', that is in manufacturing.[19]

Elizabeth and John Bright were welcomed to One Ash by her sister, Margaret Priestman (1817–1905). As the next oldest, and still unmarried sister, it fell to her to make their new home ready to receive them, just as it had fallen to Sophia and Priscilla Bright to help their brother with the furnishing, equipping and decorating of the house. Unmarried sisters had a particular role at this time within the marriages of Friends of their social standing, helping the bride to settle into her new life as a wife and find her place in a new community. There was also a considerable amount of hospitality required of a newly married woman, for bride-visiting by other Friends within the local meeting was one of the more demanding aspects of this period in a marriage. There was, too, a new set of servants to come to know, servants who, again, had generally been chosen beforehand by the family into which the woman was marrying, though in this case it appears that Margaret Priestman had also brought with her a servant from Newcastle. She stayed on at One Ash for some weeks to help her sister.

Back home in Summerhill, Margaret Priestman remained her mother's chief assistant in the running of that household, and it would seem that she herself became especially skilled in housekeeping as a result. So, it was sometimes she who replied to Elizabeth Bright's requests for recipes and advice on other housekeeping matters. In her new home, Elizabeth Bright pursued the love of gardening that seems to have been shared by many of the Priestman family, making her own additions to the grounds. She also continued with the kinds of voluntary work that she had undertaken in Newcastle, notably in visiting among her poor neighbours. Those who had been her particular care previously now became the responsibility of her younger sisters, while Margaret Priestman took over her former role in the local women's temperance auxiliary. In such ways, the marriage of a woman might also reshape to some extent the lives of her unmarried sisters.[20]

Elizabeth Bright's life in Rochdale was to be brief. Even so, in that short time she was able to leave some mark on her new community, and to establish a particular place in the memory of some of her servants. The Brights' manservant, Benjamin Oldham, kept her memory fresh for many decades after her death, and through his friendship with both John Bright and their daughter, Helen Bright, established a relationship between his family and the Bright family circle that lasted another fifty years at least. As well as philanthropy towards the poor, Elizabeth Bright continued to participate in a range of humanitarian and moral reform movements, especially those of abolition and of temperance. Her particular contribution to Rochdale was the establishment of a voluntary school for the children of the poor – her sisters-in-law had, under their mother's guidance, early become involved in adult education among Bright employees for many years, while the factory employed a teacher for its child employees. So just like the Priestman women in Newcastle, her duties as wife of a local employer extended also to a range of public roles in her community. She appears to have had no association with her husband's firm, however, except in the educational provision for the younger children of the workers there.

The anti-slavery movement was beginning, controversially, to bring women into roles that went beyond their usual part in public life as the largely silent auxiliaries of men. John Bright was among those British Quakers dismayed by the increasing prominence of women in the leadership of the 'ultraist' wing of the anti-slavery movement in the United States, led by William Lloyd Garrison. This current among abolitionists demanded the immediate and uncompensated end of slavery, and allowed women a much more prominent role, for example as public speakers.[21] The presence of Garrisonian women delegates from the United States at the 1840 World Anti-Slavery Convention in London caused dissent within the anti-slavery movement in both countries. John Bright wrote to his wife of his concern at such developments: 'I should hardly be pleased to hear of thy taking so prominent and may I say unfeminine a part.' But during their courtship he had also assured her that he had not thought her 'forward' when she accompanied him to a session of the British Association, for, he remarked, she was behaving exactly as his sisters would.[22] Some of his sisters, together with his father and Margaret Wood, also attended some of the sessions of the Anti-Slavery Convention when in London for Yearly Meeting.[23] So he did not think women's proper place was entirely in domestic retirement; but he did believe their role in public life should be restricted to a supportive, auxiliary, if well-informed and educated, role as the helpmeets of men.

British Friends, in general, proved unwelcoming to the women delegates from the United States, who included a prominent woman minister from the Hicksite schism, Lucretia Mott. She met with a much warmer response from Unitarian women who, like her, were also subsequently to promote public discussion of women's rights.[24] John Bright's relationship with the anti-slavery movement was complex: his opposition to slavery was unquestionable, and he was subsequently a major donor to the fund established to buy the freedom of the fugitive slave, Frederick Douglass, who had been a guest at his father's house. But he questioned the priority over domestic reform given to this cause by some leaders of Quaker opinion, such as Joseph Pease (a member of the Priestmans' extensive cousinage and one of the few Friends to have entered parliament by 1840). Pease's support for abolition was contrasted unfavourably by John Bright with a speech he had made against the call for an enquiry into the Corn Laws. John Bright declared this position as a disgrace both to the individual concerned, and to the Society of Friends:

> half a million of his fellow men declare a certain Law (passed by a borough mongering parliament, surrounded by the military to keep the people from pulling the House of Parliament down during their pretended deliberations, but in reality their perpetuation of a horrible robbery) to be an atrocious violation of every principle of justice and a direct wrong and robbery inflicted on them, and yet a member of the Society of Friends above all men, is found in the ranks of those who insultingly refuse to listen to a statement of the wrong, and who scornfully resist every, even the slightest most moderate attempt to remedy it . . . The MP for South Durham is asking questions about the Coolies and British Guiana, and cannot see the 'world of agonies at his feet' . . . The Slave trade is dark in its features, but our starvation Laws may attempt a rivalry without being charged with excessive impudence.[25]

The priority he demanded for domestic reform, his choice of language and the temper of his remarks, would all have troubled the Priestmans, and Elizabeth Bright voiced her family's concerns regarding the violence of his feelings and his language. He apologised but explained: 'I felt deeply such a declension from good feeling and principles and wish heartily no "friend" were in parliament so to act.' Jonathan Priestman continued to counsel his son-in-law to adopt a more temperate tone, and to avoid the temptations of public life. John Bright listened to such criticism with good grace, but responded in terms that could have brought little comfort to the Priestmans. So he wrote to Elizabeth Bright, who was visiting her family:

> I feel thankful to thy dear Father for his advice, I shall not forget it, and I will try to profit by it. But having naturally and by education a detestation of oppression and cruelty, and having deeply observed and considered the malevolent workings of an irresponsible Oligarchy and a grasping Priesthood, I cannot at least, I do not always control the expression of feelings which partake of a harshness, which though not a whit more than they deserve, yet is greater than my own welfare requires or warrants.[26]

The Priestmans remained anxious about the evident effect of his involvement in political agitation on John Bright's position with the Society, and its potential also to disrupt domestic life and spiritual growth. In the early months of his marriage, his principal concern was with the growing opposition to tithes and church rates, a cause that united nonconformists of all persuasions, and provided an important basis of middle-class radical politics at this time. So, for example, John Bright wrote jubilantly to Priscilla Bright about a court decision on church rates that he believed would 'rather stagger our Tory wardens'.[27] Shortly afterwards, he led a local protest against church rates in Rochdale, haranguing a crowd in the churchyard and leading a resistance that provoked a similarly successful court battle. By the following year, however, his letters were, instead, full of news from the recently formed Anti-Corn Law League, which had its offices in Manchester; of summaries of reports on parliamentary divisions on the corn law; and discussion of the contents of the *Patriot*, possibly the Leeds radical journal of that name, marking a clear shift away from the religious issues that otherwise shaped the politics of Dissent.

John Bright's increasing immersion in politics occurred alongside the slow decline in the health of Elizabeth Bright that first became evident in the spring of 1840. She was also in the early stages of pregnancy and had recently nursed John Bright through smallpox. Hydropathy remained the preferred form of medical treatment in this family circle, and the couple decided to take a seaside holiday with the Priestman family at Tynemouth. Elizabeth Bright's health continued poor, however, and she stayed on at Summerhill after her husband returned to Rochdale. She found this separation hard, and John Bright wrote from One Ash: 'Do not feel sad my darling – I fancied thee having a "cry" after going to bed, and I would fain have had thee rest upon my shoulder, but my dearest will endeavour to be happy and well for my sake as well as for her own.' Meanwhile, he attempted to maintain the household routines she had established, standing in for her, for example, in the daily Bible reading with their servants: 'My darling I thought of thee, I loved thee more than ever for thy wise counsel to me – Oh how I prize thee for this and similar goodness.' On her behalf, also, he visited local cottages to recruit children for the British School in which she took a special interest, and tended the flowers she had added to the garden at One Ash: 'for thy sake I esteem them.' Day by day he looked for news of her improvement, regretting that he lacked the nursing skills she had demonstrated during his own illness.[28]

Birth and death in the Priestman–Bright circle

Elizabeth Bright was kept in Newcastle also by the declining health of the grandmother who had guided her away from adolescent rebellion some years before. Now Margaret Bragg provided one last lesson, in how to make a good death, having recognised her declining powers and delivered her final ministry. Most likely, that ministry had concerned an issue that had been preoccupying her for some time, the growing resort among evangelical Friends to the sacrament of baptism. The founders of the Society had rejected such observances, and after searching the scriptures, Margaret Bragg had come to the conclusion that evangelical Friends were mistaken on the matter. Her studies of the scriptures had confirmed her own belief in 'the Spirituality of the Christian dispensation', and thereby reaffirmed her Quaker belief in the 'Inner Light'. Certainly, her last ministry relieved her mind sufficiently on matters of religious concern for her to begin afterwards to prepare herself for death. As she did so, Margaret Bragg acknowledged 'a degree of supporting faith', though she was not as yet in a state of complete readiness to depart life – as she expressed it, she 'had still some will left'. So, she remained interested in the news from Yearly Meeting then taking place in London. When her physician confirmed that death was near, she called her family round her and explained: 'I had rather go now I am prepared, I know that it will be trying for you at any time but I should be glad to be taken now.' On the evening before her death she declared: 'I seem done with temporal things, I have done what I could for my children and for my Friends.' At the very close, her family believed they heard the words 'trials', 'patience', 'sanctified'.[29]

Writing to her husband afterwards, Elizabeth Bright wrote: 'Oh! How beautiful she looks with that Heavenly calm which death only wears. Her very countenance tells us that every trial is past, and that her soul is admitted into perfect peace.' Rachel Priestman once more eased her grief by making a memorandum of this time, in which she gave thanks for the divine comfort that came 'to dart into my drooping soul secret touches of his reviving love ... gently pointing, sometimes to the Christian's hope, sometimes to the duties'. Like her mother, Elizabeth Bright also managed her grief through the memoranda that she kept of this time, and the letters she wrote to her husband. There she veered between a conventionally pious acceptance and a more troubled grief: 'I try to be thankful that all is so peacefully over, that mercy has indeed been mingled with the bitter cup.' One of Margaret Bragg's last gifts to her had been to remove the fear of death: 'As I bent over her and kissed her cold lips and hands I could almost long for the same happy home – death had lost its sting – there is nothing awful there.'[30]

Margaret Bragg's memoranda were preserved among her papers by subsequent generations of her family. They provided her female descendants with an example of a strong, capable, authoritative woman, who had provided spiritual guidance within her family, and religious leadership within her church. She was also a woman of some wealth by her death, and through two amendments to her will also made clear her wish that her daughter receive an equivalent inheritance to the son who had taken over the family business, Charles Bragg (a second daughter had predeceased her, while a period of insanity in her older son had left him incapable of managing his own affairs, so she had already established a trust for his care). She left an extensive list, also, of the remembrances that she wished servants, friends and poor neighbours to receive, one that suggests both her industry, in references to rugs worked and napkins spun, and her substance, in references to the disposal of her furniture, silver and 'libary'.[31]

Some months after her mother's death Rachel Priestman paid a prolonged visit to One Ash to oversee the confinement of Elizabeth Bright. She was accompanied by another daughter, Rachel junior, who acted as nursemaid to the baby girl who was safely delivered shortly after their arrival. So the bonds between niece and aunt were established early, and Rachel Priestman junior stayed on for some weeks more after her mother returned home. The Brights took some time choosing a name for their firstborn, always a matter of great interest among the families of Friends. Eventually, they settled on 'Helen', an unusual choice for it bore no family or religious significance, but rather reflected, perhaps, the literary interests and social aspirations of her parents.

Elizabeth Bright remained weak, and evidently struggled with motherhood. On the first anniversary of the Bright's marriage, Rachel Priestman wrote to her daughter, 'My precious child, still mine tho' another claims thee', concerned at news of broken nights and a disordered stomach that made it difficult for Elizabeth Bright to eat. Her mother sought to ease any discouragement at the situation: 'Providence has ordained a degree of love to exist in a mother's breast that smooths many a rough scene – and makes things easy that would otherwise be hard to bear – and the sweet smile and unfolding powers endear daily.' She also advised, 'don't sit up late, walk out when suitable but don't fatigue thyself too much and take what nourishment thou canst. After a poor night thou must take a sleep when baby has gone from thee.' She herself was already devoted to her first grandchild: 'dear little bright eyes! I should like to see them'.[32] John Bright tried to calm the growing anxiety among his wife's family, painting a picture of domestic contentment for them, alongside a bashful, manly detachment regarding the baby's charms: 'its Mother is looking over my shoulder and smiling so sweetly upon me whilst I write this, that I cannot write anything severe.'[33]

But Elizabeth Bright's strength continued to decline, to the point where she could cradle her baby for only a few minutes at a time. Margaret Wood and Sophia Bright took turns in coming to stay with her while John Bright was away at business during the day, or out at meetings in the evening. He, too, took over nursing the child when at home, finding a capacity for, and pleasure in, this task that evidently surprised him. He stored up every seeming gain in his wife's condition to cheer the family at Summerhill, but was unable altogether to hide his own fast-growing anxiety. It was decided to try a holiday among her family, and to consult a senior physician in Newcastle, Dr Headlam. It was increasingly evident, however, that Elizabeth Bright was 'consumptive', that is, had fallen victim to tuberculosis, a disease that took many young lives at this time. Further advice was then sought from another noted physician, Dr Jephson, at Leamington Spa, while their baby daughter with her nursemaid stayed on with the Priestmans at Summerhill. Margaret Priestman joined them to help nurse her sister and to keep her company when John Bright was away. An absence in the summer was necessarily prolonged, for it was stocktaking, an important part of the business routine in family firms, and John Bright was the company's accountant. Jacob Bright snr had also, at this time, decided partially to retire from business, and to let some of his mills to his oldest sons. So John Bright was in the midst of setting up John Bright and Brothers, the firm that shortly took over two of his father's mills for a rent of £1,000 a year.

He also felt obliged to participate in a parliamentary election then underway in Rochdale, for he had been among the sponsors of an Anti-Corn Law candidate. He rebuffed the suggestion of Jonathan Priestman that attention to politics was inappropriate in such circumstances. Her parents wished to visit Elizabeth Bright, and he suggested it would be especially appreciated if this could in some part cover his own absence. Meantime, he assured his wife: 'Oh my precious Girl, my heart longs to find . . . thou art still improving a little.' Such news, he wrote, 'would be as sunshine to my soul'. He assured her that he would not be absent 'at the call of pleasure or of selfish enjoyment or unimportant occupation'. But the Rochdale election was one in which every vote was needed for 'the cause of Free Trade and freedom of industry'. He was missing his baby daughter, too: 'how I should enjoy to nurse her awhile.' Meantime, he attempted to cheer Elizabeth Bright with frequent letters full of news of their home and garden, of neighbours in Rochdale, and of the Anti-Corn Law League offices in Manchester.[34]

Members of both Bright and Priestman families visited Leamington during that summer, sharing with Margaret Priestman some of the burdens of nursing. Even so, as autumn approached, she was near complete exhaustion, for Elizabeth Bright was no longer able to wash or dress unaided. Margaret Wood was readying herself to travel to Leamington to relieve Margaret Priestman, when Elizabeth Bright's condition rapidly worsened. She was now too weak to write to her husband, but dictated a letter that Margaret Priestman forwarded to him, to which she added her own urgent hope that he might soon be 'liberated to return'. John Bright hurried back to Leamington, and wrote of his own despair to Priscilla Bright: 'it is no light affliction to see the sweetest, dearest and tenderest wife wasting away, and myself wholly powerless to give strength or relief.'[35] Rachel Priestman snr now looked for a summons, writing to her sick child: 'I have awoke early this morning, and unable to sleep my heart has turned with unutterable love and interest towards thee.' She told of the severe mental conflict their separation caused her. While recognising there was little now she might do for her daughter, she wrote: 'yet I can but now express my love and longing feelings to be again beside thee.' The Priestmans also wondered if Helen should be brought to Leamington, to ease the sorrow that now looked certain to lie ahead for John Bright. His letters to Rachel Priestman snr from this time veered between clinging to any hopeful sign, and expressing his deep despair at his wife's increasing weakness and pain. Dr Jephson, too, alternated between sombre warnings, and an unwillingness to give up on her case. Rachel and Jonathan Priestman received a summons in time, it would appear, to be present at their daughter's deathbed. Elizabeth Bright's body was taken back to Rochdale for burial in the graveyard of the Meeting House there.[36]

Margaret Priestman stayed on after the funeral to oversee the care of her baby niece, and to help Priscilla Bright, who now had charge of both her widowed father's household at Greenbank and her brother's at One Ash. This period of living side by side in a shared grief confirmed their friendship, one that became lifelong despite their subsequent marriages and the considerable geographical separation that followed from them. They were often left together in the house with baby and servants, for John Bright's grief made him restless, dyspeptic and unable to settle back to business and everyday life in Rochdale. Brothers and brothers-in-law tried distracting him in shared recreational pursuits, and eventually took turns to act as his companion in a holiday taken at Blackpool. He wrote home daily, either to Priscilla Bright or to Margaret Priestman, sometimes so deep in his own sorrow that he was forgetful of others: 'forgive the grief which will still rise and choke utterance – thou hast grieved and wilt long, . . . but a husband's loss is far far beyond what a sister can feel, however much she may have loved.'[37]

Sometimes he found 'the soul elevating view of ocean' eased his pain, but at other times 'the rolling sea, and pebbly shore' simply reminded him of the pleasure Elizabeth Bright had taken in such scenes. His letters were frequently fretful and self-absorbed: 'After all Blackpool is a sorry spot, and pleasure would be about the last commodity I would expect to find in it – the sea always excepted.' At other times, he experienced 'a gleam of gladness' that his wife's suffering was at an end, and acknowledged his debt to his sister-in-law: 'thou are very good to be so content in thy solitary governorship – I have no fear for Helen under thy care'. At other times he become over-anxious about the child's health, less sure of the wisdom of women. So he asked Priscilla Bright to ensure Helen's nursemaid was warned against 'too much exposure' to the cold, damp weather: 'I should feel uneasy at being away from home, but I think Margaret has much firmness and will do as well with her present position as most of her sex.'[38] By the time Margaret Priestman was called home to Summerhill, her friendships with Priscilla and with John Bright were firmly established – indeed it was later suggested that she and her brother-in-law might have wed if marriage between a woman and a widowed brother-in-law had not been illegal.

A shared devotion to Helen, and the visiting to which it gave rise, further consolidated the links between the two families, binding still more tightly the Priestman–Bright family circle in ties of love, friendship and mutual obligation for another seventy years and more. Frequent letters between them also helped maintain these links. John Bright, as well as his sisters, kept up a continuous correspondence with the Priestmans, writing regularly also to his schoolgirl sisters-in-law, Anna Maria and Mary, letters expressly aimed at keeping in their minds their relationship to his motherless child. He regularly visited Summerhill with Helen, and while his own relationship with the child became ever fonder, he acknowledged the rights of the Priestman family to a share in her upbringing, and the enjoyment of her company. She was a lively, cheerful child, sometimes wilful, always responsive and loving, and too young to understand the sorrowfulness of her circumstances, or the sadness of those most close to her in these years. She became a firm favourite with her great aunt, Margaret Wood, a fondness she returned in good measure. Her nurse also made friends with her youngest aunts when they first went to Summerhill to stay. Ann Sayles's letters to Anna Maria and Mary Priestman provided regular bulletins of every small advance made by the child, providing another tie between the two families in Rochdale and Newcastle.[39]

The household of Jacob Bright snr saw its own troubles in these years. A younger son, Benjamin, was in poor health, and none of the water cures proved of any assistance. John Bright took him away to try mesmerism, again without success. One by one, too, Jacob Bright's older children were marrying and leaving home. Thomas Bright, one of the partners in John Bright's new firm, married a non-Friend, Caroline Coultate, daughter of a Bolton doctor, and was disowned by the Society of Friends. Sophia, the oldest of the Bright sisters, and previously mother to her younger siblings, as well as her father's housekeeper at Greenbank, married a well-to-do widower and land agent, Thomas Ashworth, in 1840 and moved to her new home in Poynton. John Bright was present at the marriage, and recognised its particular significance for his family, writing to his ailing wife: 'my heart was full and the tears trickled down my face as I walked up home . . . when I see our home forsaken, my old home being broken up, it is rather more than I can bear.'[40]

The poor health of Margaret Bright Lucas, the first of the Bright sisters to have married, became a fresh source of anxiety in 1842. Jacob Bright snr had resisted her marriage in 1839 to a London Friend, Samuel Lucas, for his own mother had been a Lucas, and like many of his co-religionists he opposed the marriage of second cousins. Samuel Lucas was also 'a gay Friend', that is, one who rejected the plain ways of his co-religionists. A further reason was suggested by Margaret Wood in her letters to their kin in the United States: the Lucas family was not as financially as successful as the Brights, and their family business seemed unlikely to be able to support all seven of the Lucas siblings.[41] Samuel Lucas established a series of businesses of his own in the years ahead, but none of them prospered: financial worries were among the many trials that marriage and motherhood brought for Margaret Bright Lucas, until her father subsequently settled a significant sum on her some years later. Both she and Priscilla Bright appear to have been liable to severe postnatal depression, though the condition was not then recognised as such. Priscilla Bright was concerned at her sister's state when she went to care for her at this time. She and her siblings felt the Lucases too grudging in the medical advice sought for their sister. They tried to persuade Jacob Bright to intervene in the matter, but to do so would have been to challenge the authority of Samuel Lucas and his father. So, Priscilla Bright took matters into her own hands, taking her sister away from her home, travelling around various spa towns in search of a water cure that might suit her sister's condition, apparently at their father's expense. John Bright looked on supportively, as well as with some amusement, at this challenge to patriarchal attitudes, for he was deeply fond of all his sisters, and still grieving for his own dead wife: 'My Father *hardly* can agree with thee in the propriety of your proceedings – I cannot censure you and hope your plans may be found beneficial to dear Maggy – I have faith in the water cure and hope you will find encouragement to go through with it.'[42] Patriarchal authority would appear less than robust in families where women were accustomed to exercising their independent judgment in such ways, and, moreover, to require male heads of family to foot the bill.

Grief, memory and life writing

Further troubles similarly befell the Priestman family in the period after the death of Elizabeth Bright. The health of Rachel Priestman jnr was already a cause of concern when she had accompanied her mother to help in Elizabeth Bright's confinement. Following her sister's death, her particular correspondent at Greenbank was the youngest of the Bright sisters, Esther, and she told her of the unhappiness also of the Priestmans at the disownment of her older brother, Hadwen. A lack of 'serious' religious observance appears to have been at the centre of the concern about him, together with a suggestion that his name had been 'coupled with sin and shame'. Hadwen Priestman's disownment also ended his hopes of marriage, presumably to a woman Quaker, because of the damage done to his reputation among Friends. Rachel Priestman jnr observed his suffering and that of her parents, especially her father – 'such mild yet exquisite sorrow' – and commented: 'It seems to me rather hard that friends should be in such haste to deprive of a membership which was never asked, and which might perhaps [given time] have been valued.' Birthright membership was to become another issue taken up by those who sought to reform the Society, and to moderate the sometimes strict surveillance of those too young as yet, perhaps, to value such an inheritance. Margaret Priestman was a little more circumspect in her reaction to this episode, though she questioned why the overseers, having acknowledged decided improvement in her brother, 'saw fit upon the strength of reform to blast his hopes of happiness' (a further reference to the end of hopes regarding marriage).[43] His alienation from the Society was further compounded by his marriage some years later to an Anglican.

The health of Rachel Priestman jnr did not improve, and her symptoms increasingly indicated that she too was a victim of consumption. In these circumstances, she was especially gladdened by the return of Margaret Priestman from One Ash: 'what a comfort an older sister is'.[44] Eventually, her parents heeded the advice of John Bright and sought treatment first at Leamington, then at another spa in Malvern. She was now so weak that travel itself was a considerable trial for her. After the discouraging opinions of the doctors consulted, she began to prepare for death, asking Priscilla and Margaret Bright Lucas, also at this time at the spa, to visit and make their farewells. Jacob Bright snr and Samuel Lucas both opposed this request, but again the Bright sisters disregarded the wishes of father and husband. Rachel and Jonathan Priestman accepted there was now nothing more to be done, and, remembering Elizabeth Bright's death the previous year, answered the wish of their daughter to go home to die before she became too weak to travel. John Bright, with his infant daughter, met their train at a station en route, so as to make his own farewell, and to allow Rachel Priestman jnr a final sight of the child she had cared for at birth. Not yet nineteen, she found great difficulty in coming to terms with the prospect of death, and the physical and mental sufferings of Rachel Priestman jnr in her last few weeks of life were great. Her mother was constantly by her side to provide religious counsel, and to pray with her for the salvation of her soul. Her worn and anxious family were comforted by her increasing acceptance of death in her last days, and treasured any sign that she had found salvation. She died leaning on her father's shoulder with the words 'Happy, happy, happy.'[45]

The period that followed the deaths of two of her daughters within a year of each other, and the deep depression into which Jonathan Priestman now fell, brought for Rachel Priestman snr another period of intense spiritual turmoil. She sought to ease her grief by compiling a memorial for each of her daughters from their own memoranda and letters. Their schoolbooks, diaries and letters were also gathered together and preserved. These became a precious legacy for her surviving daughters, and for her motherless granddaughter, Helen. Elizabeth Bright emerges in her mother's memoir as a young woman who had successfully overcome her earlier rebelliousness to become an exemplar of womanly goodness and Christian piety. Such mementos were ones to which Helen Bright might turn as she forged her own strong identity in the years ahead, and despite recognising in herself a very different spirit. In time, she also inherited custodianship of the papers of the Bragg and Priestman families, bringing them together with further papers from her Priestman aunts, and with the material she herself gathered from Bright and Wood kin.

So far, sources such as memoirs, letters, diaries and memoranda have been mined here to create a picture of Quaker domesticity, and a narrative of family life among the kinship circles of Woods, Bancrofts, Brights, Braggs and Priestmans. But it is also evident from such an account that the domestic sphere impinged upon, and equally was shaped by, the larger worlds of civil society and of public life. The domestic culture of these Quaker circles involved a sexual division of labour, but one that was never absolute. It was also one where daughters might be valued equally with sons in the distribution of family property. The authority of women was recognised not only in spiritual matters, but also in the care to be provided for family members. Most importantly, for this argument, the domestic life of these families encouraged deep and long-standing emotional attachments between members, placing a particular emphasis on the sibling relationship both in arranging and in sustaining the bonds created between families through marriage. John Bright might voice conventional views as to women's proper sphere, but the imperatives that drove his political career not only required the support of female kin, but also served to legitimate their participation in political campaigning, as we shall see.

The Priestman–Bright circle came into being because of events in the private lives of its members. In time, however, it also took on the character of a network, one mobilised to further business, religious and political as well as domestic goals. Equally, the demands of business and of politics might cut across personal relations and the life of the emotions. Public and domestic worlds, peopled as both were by men and women, could never be entirely distinct from each other, and the sexes might pursue shared as well as different roles within each.

6 Religion, family and public life

'Public Friends': grief, vocation and politics

Rachel Priestman experienced a further crisis of faith after the deaths, within a year, of two of her daughters, and yet again this resolved itself in a call to a travelling ministry, one endorsed by London Yearly Meeting in the spring of 1843. Events in her personal life once again prompted her to follow her calling as a 'public Friend'. This time her response required leaving her family, voyaging to the United States, and travelling extensively there to deliver her ministry. It was a year before she felt released to return home. Some Friends were evidently uneasy at her being licensed for such a task, and she had reservations of her own, writing to Priscilla Bright: 'My prospects are undescribably solemn – no doubt many will question their propriety but this I must leave. If I may be permitted to have a conscience void of offence it will be all of mercy and what I do desire.'[1] Her fears proved well-founded, and she recorded a reprimand published against her after she held a public meeting in Washington, from women who declared it 'unscriptural' for one of their sex so to do.[2]

Grief also led John Bright to a new vocation, parliamentary politics. In the days immediately after his wife's death, he was visited by Richard Cobden, a leading figure in the Anti-Corn Law League, to offer his commiserations. Here is how John Bright later recalled this conversation:

> I was in the depths of grief, I might almost say of despair, for the light and sunshine of my house had been extinguished. All that was left on earth of my young wife, except the memory of a sainted life, and a too brief happiness, was lying still and cold in the chamber above us. Mr Cobden called upon me as his friend, and addressed me, as you might suppose, with words of condolence. After a time he looked up and said, 'There are thousands of houses in England at this moment where wives, mothers, and children are dying of hunger. Now', he said, 'when the first paroxysm of your grief is past, I would advise you to come with me, and we will never rest till the Corn Law is repealed.'[3]

John Bright accepted this counsel and by the end of 1841 was undertaking the extensive travels on behalf of the League that were to fill the first few years of his widowerhood. In this return to political agitation, he moved still further away from the quietist piety of earlier generations of Friends. In time he came to represent this path as his own particular calling, making a direct analogy between his work for the League and the religious ministry pursued by Rachel Priestman in the United States, each appealing to religious values to legitimate their departure from a more conventional path.

Rachel Priestman's absence from home left Margaret Priestman (1817–1905) to take over the management of Summerhill, a role she evidently relished. It occurred alongside her own growing involvement in the campaign against the Corn Laws. Both she and Priscilla Bright provided moral and practical support for John Bright as he began to establish his place on the national political stage. Interpretations of women's participation in these campaigns as simply reflecting sentimental notions of 'women's mission' are not altogether adequate in the case of the Priestman–Bright circle. They conflate the radical reforming legacy of Quakerism with the evangelical imperative to good works. They also ignore other meanings implicit in women's special duty to good works, not least the sense of citizenship that might inform such action. As we have seen, the former was central to the sense of self among members of families like the Woods, Bancrofts and Brights. It was a perspective that the younger generation of Priestmans, clearly more shaped by evangelical values in childhood, responded to initially with some equivocation in young adulthood. But such equivocation did not survive their introduction to political activism through the campaigns of the Anti-Corn Law League. In the changed political environment that followed parliamentary reform, radical activism became the mode through which the surviving Priestman sisters increasingly acted out their sense of Christian citizenship, one deriving from a combination of religious values, given gender roles and class interests.

The winter of 1841–2 proved especially harsh for working people. In such circumstances, support for the League might appear no more than an extension of the personal benevolence these women Friends provided for those in need among their neighbours. This was the meaning, for example, that Rachel Priestman jnr gave to her work on behalf of a League bazaar, before she became too ill for such participation: 'the poor people will need a great deal of help this winter I think, so many were without work in the summer'. Acknowledging the 'depression and misery and starvation' she saw around her, she gave a political as well as a religious caste to her duty to relieve such suffering, not only as a Christian but also as a citizen: 'such however is the state of our dear country, it would be wrong to hide it from ourselves or to cease to feel for those who suffer.'[4]

Women were present at some of the early demonstrations in support of the League in Manchester, and subsequently took on an altogether more prominent role, for example, in public tea parties on behalf of the League, for which they organised the speakers and provisioned the tables. Paul Pickering and

Alex Tyrell show how these new departures were accompanied by a significant shift in the rhetoric of the League, in which moral and religious arguments were added to political-economy grounds for demanding abolition of the Corn Laws. The League's lecturer and organiser, Colonel George Thompson, had reinforced this fresh direction in the autumn of 1841 by calling a 'Convocation' of religious ministers in support of repeal. He also asked for 'the public cooperation of women' in the collection of a petition for this reform addressed to the Queen, while declaring: 'Think not I would have you throw off the woman . . . No I would have you put it on.' Women in Manchester collected 100,000 signatures during the winter of 1841–2, prompting many elsewhere to a similar effort resulting in an additional 250,000 signatures. The League's fund-raising that winter also drew on the skills women had learned in their philanthropic and humanitarian work.[5] Here were shared activities that further strengthened the bond between the Priestman and Bright sisters, ones for which Margaret Priestman showed a special enthusiasm and aptitude, and which involved women working alongside men for a political cause.

Tensions between the leaders of working-class and of middle-class radicalism increased in these years as they divided on the best path to secure social reform. As we have seen, manufacturers like John Bright and merchants like Richard Cobden believed economic reform must have priority. For them, repeal of the Corn Laws meant not only cheaper bread, but also an alteration in the conditions of trade that would increase employment and wages. Working-class radicals, and notably the Chartists, in contrast gave priority to political reform, especially in terms of adult suffrage and further parliamentary reform. Efforts to unite the two movements proved ineffectual, and Leaguers increasingly confronted a challenge from Chartists in appeals for working-class support. Serious class conflict appeared possible in the summer of 1842 when 'the Plug Plot' was organised among the textile workers of the Manchester region. Striking mill hands marched through the textile towns, insisting that those working the mills 'turn out', and ensuring the shutting down of production by emptying the boilers that ran the machinery. When the protesters arrived in Rochdale, John Bright himself ordered that his mills be stopped so as to avoid conflict and to indicate his sympathy with the suffering that had prompted such action. He had some discussion with the protesters, lending one of his carts as a platform for an impromptu meeting of, by his estimation, some 600–800 outside One Ash, with several hundred women gathered inside his gates and singing Chartist hymns. He reported to Richard Cobden that the protesters had been entirely peaceable: 'In private they told me they wished for no violence, but the time was come for a stand. . . . The villainy of the landed despots may get a shake, or it may end in deeper suffering for the unfortunate men its victims. I know not what is in store, but the clouds are heavy just now.'[6]

Subsequently, he attended a meeting of magistrates and employers where he stood out against a proposal that one factory at least be restarted so as to provoke the protesters further. For he sensed a desire among some 'to have a shot at the people' (memories of Peterloo no doubt informed such fears, for it was the local militia composed of men like himself that had begun the attack on the demonstrators then). Subsequently, he issued an address to the working people of the town that helped to bring about an end to the demonstrations without any further ill-feeling between masters and their employees. Writing to Rachel Priestman snr, he sought to distance the League from these events while defending the protest as a 'passive resistance revolution. ... Suffering caused by law has made the whole population a mass of combustible matter, and the spark now ignited may not be easily quenched.'[7]

The end of 1842 saw the first Anti-Corn Law League meeting in Rochdale, when John Bright was one of the main speakers, while 'the Greenbank ladies', his older sisters, Sophia Ashworth, Priscilla Bright and Margaret Bright Lucas, occupied a box.[8] The Priestman sisters looked with envy on the opportunity the Bright sisters presently had to help with the forthcoming League bazaar in Manchester, and the encouragement to be gained from seeing 'the attention of the public so turned to this great cause'. It was regrettable to Margaret Priestman's mind that Newcastle had yet to follow this example. Rachel Priestman jnr similarly reported having to content herself for the time being with reading League tracts, 'in order to be able the better to put in a word if opportunity offered' when dining at the house of 'a sad Tory'.[9] This failure on the part of their native city was soon to be remedied by Margaret Priestman, but in the meantime the women of the Priestman household put their sewing skills to the service of the League in Manchester. Even the schoolgirls, Anna Maria and Mary Priestman, were encouraged to participate, receiving a half sovereign from John Bright with which to buy some materials to work.[10] Rachel Priestman snr, too, overcame her discomfort with politics so far as to pay one of her daughters' friends, Jane Rooke, to sew on her behalf.

The Manchester bazaar was preceded by a large public meeting where a section in the centre of the hall was set aside for women. The Bright sisters were also among those women who managed the stalls there. Margaret Wood remained sceptical about such involvement with the League, reporting: 'my Nephews and Nieces here are quite full of anxiety and trouble about it, and are some of the number that are preparing for a Public Bazaar to be kept in Manchester ... so that many will be kept shopkeeping for a considerable time.' If the conservative press dismissed such activity as 'political prostitution', her fear was that 'it will all end in "vanity and vexation of spirit".'[11] Margaret and Rachel Priestman jnr wrote to assure the Bright sisters of their family's encouragement and support, and contributed goods and donations to the effort.[12] The Manchester bazaar raised a net sum of £7,500 pounds for the League.

Margaret Priestman then came to the fore in organising Anti-Corn Law League meetings in Newcastle. She found her own city less easy to rouse, however, reporting a general lack of enthusiasm among those she tackled on the matter: 'At first when I met nothing but cold water [on the ACL subject] I got so disgusted with the apathy of my Towns people that I made them all laugh at home by protesting if I had no social claims I would just leave the place.' Her forcefulness of personality, energy and skills came into their own, as she set out to emulate the success of the League's campaign in Manchester. She wondered at the timidity of those faint hearts, like Richard Cobden's wife, who shunned public affairs. So by the summer of 1843 she was organising a successful local 'tea party' on behalf of the League, to which John Bright and Richard Cobden lent their presence. When her 'ladies committee' (consisting of herself and two other women) became dissatisfied with the lack of energy being put into the preparations by the men's committee she met with the latter's agent, and gave him 'a stirring up'. Her women's committee also met with the men's and 'talked affairs over – and more placards were ordered'. In the event, the hall 'was *perfectly filled* . . . It was a most animated and cheering sight.' The gallery had also been filled, and the standing room at the door, too, had been crowded. They had secured attendance from a cross-section of political opinion, just as they had intended: 'and at last *it took* Tories, Whigs, liberals, chartists'; they had also attracted a range of social classes: 'merchants, tradespeople great and small Lawyers – (Bankers I saw not one) – ministers of religion, doctors of Medicine and several very respectable working men . . . Shop owners too there were, and landed proprietors and agents for land.' Richard Cobden had managed a Chartist interruption to her mind 'capitally', while giving a speech that she thought 'a master piece of talent and skill'. John Bright's contribution she reported as *'forcible and beautiful'*.[13]

Undoubtedly, the dressing of the League in the clothes of moral duty and benevolent intention eased the taking of such a step for a woman like Margaret Priestman. Pickering and Tyrrell argue, from such a line of analysis, that women's participation in the League provides evidence of the continuing strength of the ideology of 'separate spheres' for men and women. An alternative reading, however, might remark how readily, and with what facility, women accepted this invitation to depart the norms prescribed by the domestic ideology. Bread, the staff of life, was at once a public and a private fact of life, and by its very nature denied the separation of spheres. This same period saw a shift in the rhetoric of the League from arguments regarding conditions of trade to an emphasis on the feeding of the people, blending, as Simon Morgan suggests, arguments from domestic with those from political economy. Hence, the campaign was given a particular resonance for women: by long-established precedent, they might lead a bread riot if they were among the hungry classes, or organise, provision and staff a soup kitchen if they were from the well-fed classes. Within their local communities it was the women of families such as the Brights and Priestmans who had to confront and address the immediate consequences of the Corn Laws for the poor and the unemployed; they had frequently to look starvation in the face, as they set about relieving the serious distress experienced among their poorer neighbours during the 'hungry forties' with their sewing groups, blanket societies and soup kitchens. The sexual division of labour that supposedly separated public and private spheres served to break down that very distinction. In such ways the hollowness of the rhetoric of the domestic ideology was revealed, and concerns that appeared 'domestic' and 'feminine' in character were revealed to have political and economic meaning.

Equally, kinship was a major mechanism for integrating women into League activities. And family relations between men and women were actual and part of everyday life, as forcibly shaped by physical and emotional needs as by the language of separate spheres. Where language is pliable, bodies are not: they must be tended, loved and nourished, they sicken and they die – all too readily in the nineteenth century, as we have seen, even for families as comfortably situated as the Priestmans and the Brights. John Bright was effective on the public stage because of a substructure of domestic and emotional labour – women's work of kin – that helped maintain him there (as he himself acknowledged, whatever his occasional posturing and masculinist declarations on women's proper sphere). The two worlds were inextricably mixed in life, and through the gendered work of women as well as of men. This realisation was clear to the women of the Priestman–Bright circle as they became drawn into League activities. Of course, women remained in a subordinate, 'auxiliary' position to men in the work of the League, but their appearance on this political stage at least promised a fresh possibility of challenging such subordination. That possibility increasingly absorbed the attention of the women of the Priestman–Bright circle in the years ahead while requiring no abdication from women's estate. They fitted in their public work among the everyday duties of mother, daughter, sister, aunt, niece and neighbour: attending a funeral, helping prepare a house for a brother's bride, cutting out clothes, making preserves, endlessly stitching, educating a child, looking after a sick servant.

Historians of the women's rights movement that arose later in the century have long noted the importance of the League as a training ground in reform politics for women such as Margaret Priestman. Yet she remained ambivalent at this time when considering the growing debate around 'the woman question'. In the United States women were coming to the fore as public speakers addressing audiences on the abolition of slavery. In Britain, the platforms of the temperance movement provided a similar public arena in which women might speak out in support of reform. None of the Bright or Priestman sisters became public speakers at this time, but they were interested observers of this new phenomenon. Some months before her death, Rachel Priestman jnr had written to Esther Bright after attending a meeting addressed by 'a *female* lecturer on Teetotalism'. She had had some misgivings about being among the mixed audience addressed by Mrs Jackson. While she acknowledged that those whose duty it was to speak in public ought to do so, she also admitted she did not like the prospect, and questioned whether such a break with convention was the most effective way for a woman to support a cause: 'if woman would learn to be more useful in her own sphere, in striving to benefit the minds and hearts of those around her privately might she not find sufficient and noble occupation? She need not sign for a participation in the more public works of usefulness . . . does thou not think dearest E. we had better improve the opportunities we have.'[14]

Margaret Priestman was more ready to accept such a departure from the conventions of middle-class femininity. Reporting the same event to Priscilla Bright, she declared: 'I was *deeply interested* and I hope instructed.' It had been a small but attentive meeting, and Mrs Jackson had adopted the strategy of directing her remarks particularly to the women present. Taking 'not the slightest notice of the presence of men' she urged the duty of women to curb 'the iniquity of drunkenness'. According to Margaret Priestman, Mrs Jackson 'apologized for her own novel position with the modest assurance of a Christian in the discharge of what she knew herself to be right'. She acknowledged that men might try to put limits on the help women could offer such a cause, but insisted 'God put none'.[15] Churches had long provided an arena in which a woman might enact aspects of citizenship, and religious values might, as here, be invoked to defend such a departure from conventional femininity.[16]

Though Margaret Priestman was ready to attend and to help organise public meetings she was less ready, as yet, to identify herself as an advocate of 'women's rights'. The Priestmans held radical views with regard to the franchise, believing in 'complete' suffrage – but Margaret Priestman remained, as yet, cautious about a public campaign for the inclusion of women in any such demand: 'I am quite a suffragist but have much doubt how far it is best for *Women* to use anything but private influence in favour of these political rights.' Her hesitation appears to have been largely pragmatic, arising from the fear that the public association of a woman with a claim of so radical a nature must 'inevitably cost her the good opinion of many whose respect she values'. She declared herself surprised, therefore, to discover during the course of an evening party that she was regarded as 'a complete advocate of *Women's rights* – and bear all the odium that attaches to their *unpopular* assertions'. She suggested that Priscilla Bright might be similarly displeased to acquire such a reputation, adding with an ambiguity that again appears to have arisen out of her diffidence regarding such issues: 'The truth is I have my own opinion on these questions and they coincide unfortunately with those of neither party.'[17]

Even so, the growing discussion concerning the position of women remained one of much interest among members of the Priestman–Bright circle, and their views over time became ever more advanced. Priscilla Bright created something of a 'salon' for her Rochdale friends, where visiting lecturers were always sure of an interested audience and a warm welcome, and where such issues came under discussion. She is said on one such occasion to have urged the justice of women's enfranchisement during a visit of the fugitive slave and abolitionist, Frederick Douglass. On another such occasion she defended the philanthropic efforts of Elizabeth Fry against the dismissive scorn of Thomas Carlyle when, he claimed, he 'shook peaceable Brightdom as with a passing earthquake'. He clearly enjoyed his capacity to shock as he revealed his views on a range of questions to 'Brights and Brightesses', especially the latter: 'poor young ladies ... with their abolition of Capital Punishment – Ach Gott!' If he felt some remorse afterwards he soon decided it served them right.[18] Such encounters suggest how larger reform agendas might obscure the gender politics of middle-class radicalism at this time, or serve to subsume women's greater emancipation within those agendas.

For a paradox lay at the centre of John Bright's involvement in radical politics: on the one hand, his burgeoning career as an agitator rested to a marked degree on the practical and moral support of his women kin, not least as housekeepers and adoptive mothers of his daughter, and hosts to visiting speakers and organisers. And in the work of the League he was entirely accepting of women's active and public contribution to the cause. Yet in the years ahead he never lent unequivocal support to the demand for full equal civil rights for women, and sometimes opposed this in terms that might fairly be described as paternalist, if not patriarchal – derisory of women's capacities for public roles, and derogatory towards those men who were in sympathy with such demands. His own masculine identity was complex – shaped by the values of his church and family, by a Romantic emphasis on sensibility, and by a radical notion of upright, independent Saxon manhood. He was capable equally of great tenderness towards those women whom he loved, and of an imperious egotism regarding the primacy he generally placed on his own needs and activities. He was a man unashamed to weep, and to admit to weeping, and suffered from emotional and nervous exhaustion at several periods in his life. He claimed to love home and hearth.[19] Yet, from young manhood he immersed himself in male associational life, and increasingly in that of an expressly political character that took him away from his family circle. As he grew older he was more likely to spend periods of recreation fishing with male friends, rather than at home with his second wife and children. His opposition to women's suffrage became almost as contemptuous as his critique of the establishment. Though he was ever a fond brother, son, father and husband, John Bright was, and remained, uneasy at any pursuit of greater freedom for women, not least in demands for equal rights.

Love, wifehood and singlehood

Love and friendship as well as shared political and religious values contined to bind together the women of the Priestman–Bright circle in these years. Priscilla Bright was often without her brother's companionship in the early years of League campaigning, and that solitude increased with his entry into parliament in 1843, as MP for Durham. Among the Priestman–Bright circle he was often teased regarding his declarations of love of his domestic hearth in the light of his all-to-evident readiness to leave it. But Margaret Priestman also felt for Priscilla Bright in these changed circumstances: 'it is certainly a great sacrifice on your part and must we not believe on his also.' At first she shared some of her mother's fears about the dangers of a life in politics:

'I like less and less the idea of a Parliamentary life for dear John, and some of us shall not be the gainers! Still if it is *right* we must trust that no harm will come to him.' For Priscilla Bright, however, his election victory meant her brother's even greater reliance upon her continuing presence at One Ash. And this in turn had implications for any hopes she held of marrying and establishing a household of her own.[20]

'Romantic friendships' between young women were also common at this time, and provided their own distinctive forms of companionship.[21] The friendship between Margaret Priestman and Priscilla Bright had many of the characteristics of such an attachment: intimacy when they were together, for example, in sharing a room or a bed; physical expressions of fondness; emotional distress at moments of separation; an open-hearted frankness about matters, such as courtship and marriage that was particular to their relationship. Their family obligations provided the occasion both for the times they were able to spend together, and for the partings that all too soon followed such visits. Separation became painful. So, after one departure from Rochdale, Margaret Priestman wrote to Priscilla Bright: 'What is the use of loving people in this world of separation. Shall we agree to be Stoics?' Subsequently, she recorded thinking 'of one far away in her lonely bed thinking of me in mine'. Similarly, after Priscilla Bright made a visit to Summerhill, she wrote: 'My thoughts have followed thee though the eyes that love to gaze upon thee have sought thy loving looks in vain.' Only the hope of other visits made her able to endure the pain of parting from one whose 'whole presence spreads sunshine'. She also wrote: 'I miss thee very much, particularly *at night*, but I dwell on past enjoyment and endeavour to learn a lesson from dear H. [Helen Bright] not to feel for the absent.'[22] Nothing in their correspondence suggests that either understood their mutual attachment as sexual in nature. Rather, it is likely that this conceit allowed Margaret Priestman to adopt a mock tone of authority when seeking to protect the wellbeing of her friend in some of the trials and tribulations of her position at One Ash. It granted her the right to direct Priscilla Bright, for example, to conserve her strength by going early to bed. It permitted her to expect and accept emotional pre-eminence in the heart of her friend. So when Priscilla Bright went away from her on a visit to her sister, Margaret Bright Lucas, Margaret Priestman might write: 'it was very *true* of my dear little Wife to wish for me.' Writing to Priscilla Bright after the death of her sister Sophia Ashworth, Margaret Priestman assured her: 'I often think of you — almost constantly — I ought to have two hearts one for you and one for home.' Such love took on an added value after the deaths of two of her sisters, albeit they had loved her 'with an instinctive fondness'.[23]

Margaret Priestman also believed that the love between herself and Priscilla Bright was an expression of bonds that were particular to the nature of women. So she asked that her friend not share some parts of her letters with John Bright as 'he might think it *sentiment* (for men, the nicest of them, have not a woman's heart)'. She insisted that such love was 'nevertheless *true*'. Women needed also the love of women, however unlikely this might seem to men, and they might look for different qualities in a female spouse: 'It is well for me sweet wife that the power of mind I grant to Man is not a thing thou art desirous thy Husband should *excel* thee in, or I might well despair of filling the position to thy satisfaction.' Margaret Priestman believed, too, that their shared affection for John Bright and their common commitment to the cause of repeal was an element in their love for each other: 'I *guess* our thoughts have met *tonight* and in fancy we both have gazed together upon Brows that merit a Patriot's wreath of Laurel even now for the Zeal and steady battling that surely must at last bring victory.' The particular intimacy of their romantic friendship was evident also in the confidences they exchanged regarding the various men who offered one or other marriage.

The young women of the Priestman–Bright circle had two principal models on which to form feminine aspirations and a sense of adult womanhood: that of the authoritative wife and helpmeet, and that of the 'useful' spinster.[24] Either way, a woman was defined by her married status and her class combined, and, as we have seen, the role of spinster was by no means one that was divorced from the bonds of family life. The 'snug independence' of a Margaret Wood did not release a single, middle-class woman from the duties of kinship with regard to parents, and to siblings and their children; there were as yet no communities of independent professional women that were to provide a further model of singlehood for young middle-class women in the latter part of the nineteenth century.[25] The status of spinster held some attractions for a young woman of Margaret Priestman's disposition. If at times she chafed at the gender and age hierarchies within the conventional household (and especially at the former), at others she seemed a little anxious about her unmarried state. As a young single woman living under her parents' roof, her time was not her own. It was Margaret Priestman's place to assist her mother in the running of the Summerhill household, and to stand in as housekeeper whenever family or religious commitments called Rachel Priestman away from home. She clearly took some pleasure and pride in her ability to undertake this substantial task, and no doubt enjoyed the command over her own time that it allowed.[26]

A religious calling would have allowed her to appeal to another authority, but Margaret Priestman had no intimations, either as a young woman or subsequently, of such a vocation. Nor had she the means (or the need) to make herself an independent single woman. The Priestmans were by now well-to-do, and of an intellectual bent. They gave their daughters a better education than that provided many young women of a similar social standing. At best, however, this might have equipped them to become governesses or companions. Margaret Priestman and her two surviving sisters were, from time to time, to take on these roles, but only within their own immediate family circles, and never in the open labour market. They knew as caring neighbours many of the employees of the Priestman and Bragg businesses. But they appear to have had no close contact with either the tannery or the glue-making factories, nor with the drapery business now run by their uncle, Charles Bragg, either as places of work or as family enterprises.

Here, then, was a generational change of some consequence for Margaret Priestman. Marriage was the most likely way she might achieve a more permanent degree of authority and greater command over her own time, in a household of her own. This was the largest degree of autonomy and independence to which she might aspire, and it was not negligible. The growing prosperity of the Priestmans, together with changing notions of respectable middle-class femininity, meant that the position of housewife had more narrow limits in terms of economic participation than for earlier generations. Yet the withdrawal of married middle-class from the market was not absolute, for their role as consumers grew with family prosperity and a greater readiness on the part of Quakers to engage with more conventional understandings of gentility and style. In part this reflected the upward social mobility evident in both Priestman and Bright families, as well as shifts in notions of respectable femininity. Their withdrawal from activities directed at personal gain also allowed space for the growing aspirations among Quakers for this-worldly forms of self-cultivation: in the learning of languages, for example, and other non-'useful' fields of knowledge. Rachel Priestman had not had the time, once married, to continue her interest in learning Italian or astronomy. But she and Jonathan Priestman ensured that their children had broader 'accomplishments' than they themselves had acquired through their own schooling.

Middle-class wives in Margaret Priestman's generation did not have to carry the same combined burden of household and business activity as their mothers and grandmothers. Equally, married women in this stratum of society now enjoyed expanded possibilities for participation in other aspects of public life. None of this made Quakers distinctive from other women of similar means and social standing. Margaret Priestman had her mother's example to follow with regard to the little weight she might give convention. And even as they became increasingly the norm, such restrictions continued to be challenged. Margaret Priestman's letters from this time reflect a recurring interest in the issue of women's proper sphere of action, the nature of marriage, and a degree of open-mindedness with regard to both that perhaps also explains what might otherwise seem like vacillation on her part.

She was by her mid-twenties beginning to refer to herself, if with some irony, as an 'old maid'. She noted that her stall at a local temperance bazaar had been the only one presided over by a single woman. So she had dubbed it 'the *old maid's stall*', and looked to the presence of a widowed friend, Mrs Hibbitt, 'to help off the things' because her friend had such a wide acquaintance and such winning ways. Perhaps because of her increasing visibility in public life, Margaret Priestman now found herself the repeated butt of rumours regarding marriage – rumours that extended even to a secret marriage to a local Anglican curate, Mr Carr, the brother of Mrs Hibbitt. On hearing of these, she responded: 'I am not a *foolish hearted girl*.' The suggestion that she might have secretly married was particularly painful: 'I felt as though my general character might have spared me the suspicion of (to say the least) so great an indiscretion.' She explained her acquaintance with the curate, which would have been unusual among Friends a generation before, by her friendship with Mrs Hibbit, for whom she felt a special regard as they had worked together on behalf of the Anti-Corn Law League. She also insisted that her heart remained free and that it had always been her practice 'to discourage any attentions which could end in nothing but disappointment'. She also sought to reassure Priscilla Bright by declaring that she had only ever received two offers of marriage – and that one of these had been 'an act of madness'.[27] Even so, the rumours caused her and her family some discomfort, and when she received an invitation to attend the wedding of an unmarried sister of Mrs Hibbit and Mr Carr, she followed the advice of her father and declined. Shortly after, the clergyman was given a living some way distant and the dust settled.

So, if Margaret Priestman was increasingly ready to look forward to becoming an old maid, it was at least in part in hope of escaping the trials of a still-marriageable woman as the focus of rumour, gossip and speculation. She also recognised aspects of her own temperament that might make her unfit for the role of wife, and expressed a determination only to accept a man with 'a soul too noble' to expect her to give up her will to his. As she explained to Priscilla Bright: 'I know my own high spirit too well to believe that *I* should be happy under such slavery, and therefore should never think of subjecting myself to it . . . I write this to relieve thy mind from any fear that in this respect at least I shall disgrace my order – I wish *thou* may do as well!' Further tribulations followed the emergence of another possible suitor, especially her confusion about whether he might prove a good husband or not. Equally, where she found a young man attractive, she generally also came to conclude that he had not sufficient character for a husband, and was no match for her. The identity of her third suitor at this time remains unclear, but it was probably the man she eventually married, Daniel Wheeler. She confided her interest in a consumptive young man whose manners, however, she described as 'bad, that is *singular* though tho'roly gentlemanly, from both habit and principle'. What attracted her was his 'rich mind' rather than his beauty, and what concerned her was a difference in sensibility that she explained in terms of gender differences.[28]

Daniel Wheeler's manner was reserved, and he was considered un-Friendly by some among her circle because of his haughtiness of manner. His dead father, also Daniel, had been a celebrated minister in the Society of Friends, and erstwhile friend of the Czar of Russia, for whom he had undertaken extensive projects of land reclamation by which he had built a respectable fortune. Daniel Wheeler the younger had for many years lived in Finland where he owned and operated some cotton mills. At this time Margaret Priestman still insisted she was not 'in love' with anyone. But it was also around this time that she sought Priscilla Bright's advice on how to conduct herself with a current suitor: 'ought I to seem quite at ease with him if I know all the time that amiable and kind as he is and much as I may respect him, it is not very likely that I could make up my mind to have him *if* he asked me.' She added that she thought such an offer unlikely: 'because I think he would not consider himself good enough for me – do not suppose I say this vainly . . . but I think myself that his mind *for a man* is not equal to mine for *a woman* – and so perhaps I fancy he may think so too.' Margaret Priestman insisted: 'Money, Family or beauty I might dispense with but I *think* not with the absence of a superior mind to my own; and yet unwearied and delicate kindness has such an effect on a woman's head that it would be foolish to say what I would or would not do.' There were others whom she liked better, but 'if you think a person is fond of you it makes a difference – and you do not like to fling the love away that's borne you'.[29]

She was, in consequence, in a quandary: should she be cold, or should she accept such attentions graciously even while unclear about her own feelings? While writing: 'do not suppose my heart is in any *particular* danger, a *warm* heart like mine needs constant guarding', she also worried: 'if you think anyone really admires you very much you feel that your conduct may affect their happiness – and you are anxious to act correctly.' Rachel Priestman always advised her daughters to think nothing of any such attentions until a man had made a proposal of marriage, 'but Priscilla you cannot help seeing that people like you when they always give you preference over other people and if really their love is not of much value to you, your are more able to see this for what the head wishes'. Priscilla Bright, too, urged caution, however, and Margaret Priestman heeded the warning, confessing that still she felt no 'deep regard' for the man in question. She intended now to give no more thought to the matter, believing she might avoid further meetings and that he would soon find another interest somewhere else: 'In the present instance I shall be glad if the impression I seemed to make does wear away. It would I think be better for both.'[30] She added: 'Dearest P. I am more and more convinced that we should be seeking to overturn the beautiful arrangements of a wise providence to assist an identity of character in the sexes!'[31] Daniel Wheeler returned to Finland, but set about selling up his business there, possibly after advice from Rachel and Jonathan Priestman that they could not countenance a marriage that would remove their oldest surviving daughter so far away.

Margaret Priestman once more contemplated a future as an 'old maid' with entire equanimity. She enjoyed a happy home with her parents, and believed that in desiring marriage, 'persons may be seeking what would not be for their real good'. Like Margaret Wood, she thought it a matter best left to providence, adding: 'I do not overlook thy remarks about an old Maid's trials – and I can truly say one of the most fondly cherished wishes of my heart is to see thee *happily* married – but for myself I have no horror of being an old maid. I do not expect it is the happiest state but if it be the one allotted me I durst not even wish it otherwise.' She added: 'as yet I have not found any thing self denying in an *Old Maid's* life . . . tho' I see plainly enough that to many it is one of self-sacrifice – *quite as much, more so than a Wife's and Mother's* with far less joy to atone for the pain and abundantly less credit. Is that admitting enough?'[32]

Her acquaintance with Daniel Wheeler and his sister, Sarah, was renewed when she stayed in London to take part in the great Covent Garden Bazaar held by the Anti-Corn Law League in the early summer of 1845.[33] A proposal of marriage followed shortly, to her apparent surprise. She carefully weighed the arguments for and against such a marriage for many months. Her heart was, she confessed, still by no means engaged. But she was impressed by her suitor's gravity, and the steadfastness with which he pressed the matter. Some months later, in October 1845, Daniel Wheeler was invited to visit Margaret Priestman and her parents in their Newcastle home – a sign that she was at last ready to consider a proposal of marriage. She reported to Priscilla Bright: 'I found D. a very intelligent and agreeable companion, but my heart felt too cold to admit of my allowing him to suppose it was at all touched and I made both him and myself miserable whenever the subject was named.' He decided against pressing the matter any further at this time, and asked only that she continue to consider the matter. At supper the evening before his departure, however, he gave Rachel Priestman cause for concern when 'he assumed an expression of countenance so fixed and unamiable if I may believe Mama for I durst not look at him that she became seriously concerned about his temper'.[34]

Concern now centred on his temperament – was he likely to prove a cold and dictatorial husband? And when the usual enquiries were sent out to mutual friends by her mother, his aloofness and possible arrogance were matters on which information was especially requested, as was his father's record as a husband. Subsequently, Rachel Priestman received a report that Daniel Wheeler's father had been 'a particularly cheerful, kind good tempered man an excellent Husband!', together with a positive opinion of Daniel Wheeler himself. Now Margaret Priestman began to doubt she possessed the courage needed 'to give away your heart . . . once done I might not repent it but dare not do it I want some one to act for me and yet I would not let them, I believe I am altogether unreasonable'. She found herself in a quandary: 'I have every reason to think well of my friend but the love is wanting.' Yet still she did not reject him outright and by the beginning of 1846 Margaret Priestman was letting her closest friends among the Bright sisters know that she had at last agreed to marry Daniel Wheeler.[35]

Priscilla Bright faced still greater complexities when considering the offers of marriage that she received in these years. There was the weight of her existing family responsibilities to her brother and her niece, while neither of her two suitors met with family approval. The first was a colleague of John Bright's in the Anti-Corn Law League, Duncan McLaren, a twice-widowed Edinburgh merchant. But he was considerably older than her and of a different church, while his manner was distant and lacked the spontaneity and warmth to which Brights and Priestmans were accustomed within their family circles.

In marrying him Priscilla Bright would face the likelihood of disownment by the Society, like her brother, Thomas. Her new home would be in Edinburgh, far from Rochdale, and she would, moreover, become stepmother to an already large family by his previous marriages. So some reasonable, not only selfish concerns, may have informed John Bright's opposition to such a marriage. Priscilla Bright turned down Duncan McLaren's first proposal in 1843, in accordance with the wishes and advice of family and friends. Margaret Priestman wrote: 'I think dear P if thou must marry a *Widower* thou might do better than have Mc — .'[36]

Joseph Smith began to court Priscilla Bright in 1844. He was a Friend, young, handsome and another Leaguer. But most of the advice Priscilla Bright received was against such a marriage (on this occasion, opposition seems to have come mainly from her younger sister and brother, Esther and Jacob Bright jnr). Joseph Smith was somewhat younger than Priscilla Bright, and was judged of insufficient weightiness of character to provide a suitable match. Margaret Priestman sought to help her friend by making some comparisons with Duncan McLaren, suggesting 'better *grey* hairs and *wisdom* than youth and emptiness'. Once again she argued that what was essential in a marriage was 'companionship of talent', and that a husband be 'open and good tempered ... for some men are really *unreasonable*, and I pity their wives'.[37] This proposal had come at an especially difficult time. Priscilla Bright continued to be the mainstay of her brother's household at One Ash, and mother to her niece. She was also grieving for her sister, Sophia Ashworth, who in 1844 died from puerperal fever, leaving two more motherless infants with whose care she was helping. In addition, a younger, unmarried brother, Benjamin, was seriously ill at this time and facing death. The Bright family were also in some disarray over a scandal surrounding her father and his housekeeper, Mary Metcalfe, and there was particular concern that some of the younger Brights still lived at Greenbank in such unconventional circumstances. Jacob Bright responded early in 1845 by moving away to a quieter location to live, taking Mary Metcalfe with him as housekeeper. General disapproval led him first to appoint a niece instead as his housekeeper and shortly afterwards to marry Mary Metcalfe, to the dismay of his immediate family. Reporting on these events to her family in the United States, Margaret Wood made clear her disapproval of his behaviour and of 'this cunning serpentine woman'. But she regretted the breach it had brought between Jacob Bright and his children, one she hoped might gradually be mended over time.[38] Family problems were, then, quite simply overwhelming at this time for Priscilla Bright.

In proffering further advice, Margaret Priestman acknowledged the burden of duty that Priscilla Bright owed as spiritual mentor to her dying younger brother, but lent less weight to her responsibilities to John and Helen Bright, or her infant Ashworth nieces. She sought to strengthen her friend's determination to follow her own heart, insisting that marriage was a proper and desirable goal for her whatever her other commitments. In the meantime, both women continued to work toward the coming Anti-Corn Law League Bazaar at Covent Garden. It became especially painful for the Bright women to fulfil the promises they had made with regard to stalls at the bazaar when their younger brother died a few weeks before its opening. Their distress was one of the causes that brought Margaret Priestman to London to stand in for them in supervising one of the stalls, thereby unexpectedly renewing her acquaintance with the Wheelers. The matter of Priscilla Bright's possible marriage dragged on, and became still more complicated when Duncan McLaren renewed his offer that summer.[39] In the event, Priscilla Bright turned down both offers for she could make up her mind to marry neither man. She seems to have reached the decision to reject Joseph Smith more easily than that refusing Duncan McLaren. She felt unable to turn away from the needs of a sorrowing family, a widowed brother, and her three motherless, infant nieces. Towards the end of 1845, she found herself unwell and once again solitary at One Ash, just as her friend reached her own decision to accept Daniel Wheeler.

The wedding preparations of Margaret Priestman, like those of her dead sister before her, involved negotiating between the 'plainness' preferred by her parents and her own aspirations for a degree of fashionability at least. She decided on the innovation of bridesmaids, for example, including Priscilla Bright and five-year old Helen.[40] That same summer saw the repeal of the Corn Laws and the winding up of the Anti-Corn Law League. John Bright now felt free to look for a second wife, and to consider leaving parliament. Here again, the demands of personal and public life continued to work upon one another, while the coming change in her brother's situation quite unsettled the future of Priscilla Bright.

7 Sisters, marriage and friendship

Ashley Grange

The marriage of Margaret Priestman and Daniel Wheeler illustrates once again the readjustments also involved among these circles for other members of the families involved, and most especially for siblings. Margaret Priestman declared surprise at finding herself about to marry: 'single life has had so many attractions'. Her parents, too, found it difficult to reconcile themselves to her coming departure from Summerhill. The situation of Sarah Wheeler, who had been her brother's housekeeper and companion, remained unresolved at the time of the wedding in the summer of 1846 and for some time more. These readjustments were further complicated when symptoms of tuberculosis again appeared in Daniel Wheeler within months of his marriage, while the couple were holidaying in Switzerland. Anna Maria Priestman (1828–1914) had accompanied them and also became ill, staying on at her sister's home after their return to recuperate herself and then to help nurse Daniel Wheeler.[1]

Initially, Margaret Wheeler's mood remained buoyant: 'The house here begins to look quite homish and servants promise well.' She planned to begin with a far simpler style of housekeeping than at Summerhill: 'I find however plenty to do in an unfinished establishment like ours.' But the first few months of Margaret Wheeler's marriage were a testing time, nonetheless, as she nursed both her husband and her sister while getting to know her servants, entertaining family and neighbouring Friends as they came bride-visiting, and negotiating the place Sarah Wheeler might occupy in relation to her household. She also began housekeeping in temporary accommodation awaiting completion of the house Daniel Wheeler was having built for them. So, she was grateful for the assistance provided by her sister-in-law at this time, and it was eventually settled that Sarah Wheeler should live nearby, but separately, and pass her evenings and holidays with the couple. Hence, the threesome spent the first Christmas of the Wheelers' marriage together, reading the latest novel of Charles Dickens, Hood's poems and a Christmas annual.[2] Margaret and Sarah Wheeler remained on friendly terms, together visiting poor neighbours, and dividing between them patronage of a nearby infant school and a local orphanage. They also canvassed and collected for a relief fund to aid victims of the Irish famine, and held regular sewing meetings to provide clothing.[3]

At times Margaret Wheeler seemed almost to resent her husband's ill health, especially when it led him to decide against living in the house being built for them in the Bristol suburb of Cotham. The decision also meant they had to live for a while with Sarah Wheeler until their chosen alternative house, Ashley Grange, became free. The couple finally moved into their permanent home some fifteen months after their wedding. Ashley Grange, 'the well aired house' beyond the city, promised a more healthful and tranquil setting for Daniel Wheeler, as well as proximity to Sarah Wheeler's home, Ashley Down. By this time Margaret Wheeler, too, appreciated such seclusion: 'No doubt it is enhanced for me by the anxieties that have attended my married life.' Her servants comprised a cook, Edwards, a maid, Emma, a gardener and stockman, Gilham, and his boy assistant, Ben, for whom she made a new shirt. When her pig shortly died, she considered herself lucky as Ben had previously worked for a butcher, while her cook knew how to cure hams, pickle meat, and pot lard. Margaret Priestman set about establishing a kitchen garden, and enjoyed her first crops of asparagus and seakale the next spring, which also saw her spring-cleaning.[4]

Daniel Wheeler's declining health was not helped by growing worries about his financial situation. He and Sarah Wheeler had invested largely in railway and banking shares on their retirement to England, and it now seemed that these would not produce the income on which he had planned; worse, as shareholders in joint-stock companies further calls might eventually be made on their capital. So he worried over expenditure on Ashley Grange and Margaret Wheeler was unable to equip her kitchen as well as might be expected by a good cook. The pleasure she had initially taken in her role of 'domestic Associate', the term she preferred to 'wife', began to diminish with a new appreciation of the dependency that went with it. The need for economy brought another troubling suggestion from her husband: that Sarah Wheeler share Ashley Grange with them. Rachel Priestman intervened at this point, strongly opposing such a plan.[5]

The Irish famine reawakened Margaret Wheeler's interest in national politics, for she fully realised that the philanthropy of women like herself was an insufficient response to the unfolding tragedy, and proclaimed the government's response inadequate: 'wherefore this strange delay in opening the ports, whilst ships loaded with Corn have been actually calling off Falmouth to know if the ports were open and then passing over with their precious cargo to the Continent. Alas for legislation.'[6] There were also repeated crop failures in Britain in these years, and levels of distress that saw the gradual repeal of the Corn Laws, and the consequent winding up, in 1846, of the Anti-Corn Law League. John Bright now selected a possible second wife, Margaret Elizabeth Leatham (always known by her middle name). She was sister of a Yorkshire banker who, together with their mother, had been subscribers to the League and John Bright's occasional hosts during speaking tours. The Leathams were substantially wealthier than the Brights, and used to a more luxurious style of life, so John Bright also began to extend and renovate One Ash. The robust prettiness, stolid temperament and piety, and lack of literary and intellectual interests they noted in Elizabeth Leatham made her appear to the Priestmans a very different kind of future wife from the first Elizabeth Bright, even as they did their utmost to accommodate such a change to their family circle. John Bright's second marriage in 1847 also had considerable implications, of course, for Priscilla Bright, as his housekeeper and substitute mother of Helen Bright.

One Ash

Margaret Wheeler maintained her correspondence with Priscilla Bright after her marriage, promising to forget neither her friend, 'nor all the troubles of thy lot'. Now she wrote sympathising with the heartache that her brother's remarriage must entail, likening it to widowhood: 'this will alter thy prospect materially', while 'to resign that sweet lamb will cost thee a mother's sorrow almost'. As she confronted the loss of home and companionship, Priscilla Bright began to grieve for her lost youth and good looks, and for the opportunities to marry that she had let go. Duncan McLaren came once more to absorb her thoughts, as she busied herself on her brother's behalf with papering and furnishing his increasingly grand house, and with training new servants. Margaret Wheeler wrote of her concern at hearing that her friend had become: '*pale and thin* poor child. I wish I could fatten thee up a bit and plant roses once more on thy worn looks! – Pray let other people's troubles alone at any rate (that is where mine are not concerned!) and try to take care of yourself.' She suggested that once John Bright's wedding was over, Priscilla Bright come and stay with her for a period of recuperation.[7]

Priscilla Bright was also left to tell Helen Bright of her father's coming remarriage. The child proved unresponsive, where not openly hostile, to the young woman who was to replace her aunt at One Ash, resenting this challenge to the reign she had held over her doting father's heart. Her high-spirited wilfulness deteriorated all too easily into surly misbehaviour. The Priestman family observed these changes with growing sorrow and misgiving, even as they tried to ease matters by writing to Elizabeth Leatham and her mother and visiting them at their Yorkshire home. They found John Bright's wife-to-be kind and evidently intent on building a good relationship with her future stepdaughter. Margaret Wheeler wrote: 'How one longs that this marriage may prove all that could be wished for him and our sweet pet! It is a comfort to find E. L. so disposed to love our darling and I trust the dear child will love her in return *in time*.'[8]

The differing outlook and values of Priestmans and Leathams soon became evident, however, in Margaret Wheeler's efforts, at Elizabeth Leatham's request, to find a suitable nursery governess for Helen Bright. She put forward the name of Matilda Ferris, a nineteen-year-old who had already held such a post in another Quaker household. Her family was well-spoken of, and the young woman herself was reported 'lively and very fond of children and does not object to living in the nursery – by this I do not understand that she is expected to take any meals in the *kitchen*'. Her view of the proper duties of a nursery governess were that she should have 'entire charge of Helen and her things teaching her romping with her etc etc'. It was soon evident, however, that Elizabeth Leatham was looking rather for another domestic servant, one who would combine the duties of occasional maid to herself with her care of Helen Bright, who would take her meals in the kitchen or in the nursery, and whose pay would be no more than £15 a year. Margaret Wheeler persisted in arguing the desirability of her more accomplished candidate, the appropriateness of allowing a young woman occupying such a role to dine with her employers, and the need to pay her an annual salary of £20. But her advice was not heeded, the suggestion of Matilda Ferris was rejected, and the Priestmans began to worry at what appeared a niggardliness in the arrangements being made for Helen Bright. Divergences in values and in habits between themselves and the second Elizabeth Bright became increasingly evident in the years ahead, despite the best will on both sides. 'M. E.' or 'M. E. B.', as she became in their correspondence, increasingly failed to meet the model of a wife established by the first Elizabeth Bright; nor is there any evidence that she herself aspired to satisfy such unrealistic, if not unjust, expectations.[9]

None of the women of the Priestman family attended the wedding of John Bright and M. E. B. in the summer of 1847, but the couple visited the Wheelers at Ashley Grange in the course of their wedding tour, and the encounter appears to have pleased all parties. Rachel Priestman, with her daughters, Anna Maria and Mary, visited One Ash some months later and Helen and her step-mother then returned with them to Summerhill. These visits appear to have passed pleasantly, but Margaret Wheeler decided it was wise to burn a letter sent by one of her sisters, in which she found some 'very ambiguous' remarks regarding life at One Ash: 'it might be just as well to have its perfectly natural and harmless details out of the way since they were capable of doing mischief if spread.' Helen stayed on with the Priestmans for a prolonged visit after M. E. B. returned home, and their disquiet at the child's evident unhappiness continued to grow as her relationship with her stepmother failed to improve. Seemingly petty things, like M. E. B.'s refusal to indulge her love of rice pudding, began to take on a disproportionate importance in the child's mind – even in the minds of her grandmother and aunts. Margaret Wheeler reported her husband's blunt advice that someone tell M. E. B. of Helen's fondness for the dish, 'and surely her good sense of which he has an exalted idea would at once see the wisdom of meeting it'.[10] M. E. B. was now expecting her first child. Six more were born at regular intervals in the years ahead, lessening still further the time and energy she could devote to her stepdaughter, and ensuring that Helen's visits to her Priestman kin continued, and indeed grew, in their length and frequency.

The changed situation of Priscilla Bright evidently encouraged Duncan McLaren to propose a third time, and on this occasion he was accepted, despite the continuing resistance of many of her friends and family. Unable to marry according to Quaker rules, she also refused to be married in her husband's church, opting for a registry office wedding, perhaps hoping to avoid disownment by such means. But disownment followed nonetheless, though she evidently chose to ignore it for she continued to attend local and Yearly meetings. Her closest friends in Scotland were also Friends or similarly disowned Friends, including the anti-slavery campaigners, Eliza Wigham and Elizabeth Pease, now Nichol (her marriage to a Glasgow University professor had been followed by her disownment). In the years that followed, John Bright and an increasing number of Friends among the reforming current within the Society of Friends began to speak out forcibly against such aspects of church discipline, and to attempt to liberalise the government of the Society. For her part, Priscilla Bright McLaren appears to have happily acted as a marriage broker, finding Quaker wives for those non-Friends seeking Quakerly qualities and capacities in a wife.[11]

Priscilla Bright McLaren soon established close and fond relationships with her seven stepchildren, but in the first months of marriage found her change of circumstances, and the homesickness associated with it, quite overwhelming. She suffered from a range of debilitating health problems throughout her life, not least several episodes of nervous exhaustion. So, within months of her marriage, she left Edinburgh for a prolonged course of the hydrotherapy by which her family set so much store, at their preferred establishment, Ben Rhydding. This had been founded in 1844 to provide a particular form of water treatment devised in Germany, and became a favourite resort of many among the intelligentsia, including Charles Darwin. Treatment involved various forms of bathing, together with 'the wet sheet envelope' and other forms of compression. It was by this time under the direction of Dr William McLeod, joint editor of the *Water Cure Journal*. Treatment might take many months, as it did in the case of Priscilla Bright McLaren.[12] The subsequent birth of her first child, Charles Bright McLaren, seems also to have helped her settle to her new life and situation more happily. Meanwhile, Duncan McLaren continued to build a political career in Edinburgh as an alderman, then as Lord Provost of that city, and eventually as a Liberal member of parliament.[13]

Widowhood

The health of Daniel Wheeler, though, was clearly now far beyond the help of the water treatment. For Margaret Wheeler, his symptoms and his rapid decline in strength must have brought back memories of the deaths of her two sisters some years before. Whatever her secret fears, she continued to talk positively to her husband: 'It is best for Invalids specially not to anticipate evils.' But the treatment recommended by the conventional doctors to whom the Wheelers now turned was 'heroic'. It involved the blistering of Daniel Wheeler's entire back in the hope of lessening the inflammation in his lungs. The burn was slow to heal, however, and appears to have become infected. The least exertion produced 'such a palpitation of the heart' that visitors were discouraged. Margaret Wheeler now reported how her husband suffered also from 'constant irritation of the Bowels . . . often gasps considerably and coughs and his nervous system is far from right'. He became increasingly bedridden and 'a good deal depressed'. Much of her day was now devoted to nursing him and reading to him, for she wrote of how in such circumstances he 'fairly devours' books. Margaret Wheeler turned away her sister-in-law's offers to help nurse Daniel Wheeler, but was grateful for the company she provided him during the evenings, allowing her to catch up with her housekeeping and accounts.[14]

All three now believed that Daniel Wheeler's case was serious, and for her part, Margaret Wheeler began to doubt the wisdom of their medical advisor. But she was uncertain where to turn and afraid of alienating her husband's doctor, even while complaining of his 'heartless indifference'. Such problems became 'a heavy aggravation of our sufferings', and she concluded 'I have lost confidence in Drs.' The pain from the blistering was now so great that Daniel Wheeler was dependent on opiates to gain any sleep. Shortly, it fell to Margaret Wheeler to tell her husband that the doctors had given up on his case and warned that he had not long to live. He died in the early summer of 1848, and Margaret Wheeler found herself a widow within two years of her marriage. She, who had already attended so many deaths of those close to her, was unprepared for the depth of the grief that now overcame her. One consolation was the still deeper friendship she now formed with Sarah Wheeler. She sought some comfort, too, in drafting and redrafting an account of her husband's last days. But she remained subject to depression, and some years later might still record a 'painful sense of desolation and isolation' stirred by memories of Daniel Wheeler when first introduced to his old friend and business associate, Ferdinand Uhde. She had now to find some new identity from that of the 'domestic Associate' in which she had found so much satisfaction and sense of purpose.[15]

Anna Maria Priestman had also come to Ashley Grange to help her sister in Daniel Wheeler's last weeks. Her childhood had been shadowed by family illness and death and separation, as we have seen. Her early education had also been shaped by the fervent evangelicalism of Esther Stickney, who had continued to ply her former charge with anxiety-inducing advice and tracts regarding salvation after death and its alternative, until at last Anna Maria Priestman asked her to leave such matter aside. The illness and deaths of her two older sisters had been the occasion of her and Mary Priestman, two years her junior, being sent away from home to school in Durham. Her schoolmistresses were gentle and kind, and new friendships were soon made. But Mary Priestman's own subsequent poor health had meant that Anna Maria was also frequently without her sister's companionship in her school years.

Witnessing Daniel Wheeler's death she reported how it had come to him quietly and unknowingly, helping to moderate her own dread of dying: 'death does not seem to me quite as it used to do'. Thinking back also on the passing of her sisters, she found death 'less dangerous and dreary now as one by one of those whom we have known and valued here crossed over it in safety to the bright and better land'.[16] The anguish induced by her earlier evangelical beliefs was increasingly supplanted by the comforts of the more reassuring religious outlook to which she was now tending.

Anna Maria Priestman stayed on to provide companionship for her sister in the early months of her widowhood. Her life at Ashley Grange was made more pleasurable by the Wheelers' library: 'I have been luxuriating in books,' she told her cousin and close friend, Jane Pease, after several weeks there. Shortly, her parents also came on a visit, and then her niece, Helen Bright. For, it had been decided that Margaret Wheeler should become the child's governess for a few weeks, as 'that gives her occupation which she was in want of before'. M. E. B. had recently given birth to her first child, and so no doubt was all the more glad to be relieved of the care of her stepdaughter. Her two aunts found Helen 'very sympathising' for her age, and her 'unfailing gaiety' and 'gentleness and affection' helped soothed Margaret Wheeler's grief and sense of loss. Helen's stay was expected to be for about four weeks, though its length remained uncertain, 'depending so much on other persons arrangements'(the coldness of this reference suggested also the increasing distance between the Priestmans and John and M. E. Bright). In the event, the child was still with her aunts at the end of August, when Anna Maria and Mary Priestman took her on a visit with them to their own aunts at Malton.[17]

Anna Maria Priestman frequently shared the education of Helen with Margaret Wheeler in the coming years. So in the early months of 1850 she was once more at Ashley Grange. While Margaret Wheeler taught Helen in the mornings, Anna Maria Priestman took over in the afternoons. She chose French history for her subject, reading to Helen from a life of Napoleon. Such material she believed preferable to the 'little tales for children', which she thought 'must be as prejudicial as the romances we hear so much condemned for older minds'. There was much to enjoy in this role: 'It is extremely nice to have the small child growing up into a companion in this way.' But she also worried that her own present peripatetic life and the distance of Ashley Grange from Bristol prevented her usual immersion in charitable and humanitarian works: 'it seems rather a selfish life, the one I am leading at present'. That autumn, Helen again came under her charge, though this time at Summerhill where Margaret Wheeler subsequently joined them.[18] And so a pattern was established whereby Helen lived with Margaret Wheeler at Ashley Grange during the first few months of the year, at Summerhill in the autumn and early winter where she was joined by Margaret Wheeler, and with her parents and growing band of brothers and sisters for the summer holidays and for Christmas.

Such an arrangement provided Margaret Wheeler with an acceptable solution to the dilemma she found herself in as a young widow of limited and ever-decreasing means. For Daniel Wheeler had been unable to improve his financial position before his death, having decided not to sell his railway and banking shares, against the advice of both Jonathan Priestman and John Bright. His father-in-law had at that time offered to help by buying some shares from him before they fell still further in value, but he had been unwilling to accept even this loss. The income on which Margaret Wheeler had now to live continued to decline, along with the value of her capital. She appears to have been a trustee of Daniel Wheeler's estate, and readily took over its management, agreeing also to continue the oversight of the English investments of his former business partner, Ferdinand Uhde. She kept a close eye on company reports and the payment – or non-payment – of dividends. But as struggling banks and railway companies began to put out calls on their shareholders, she worried that her own growing financial difficulties might undermine the good name of her dead husband, and warned Ferdinand Uhde of the rapidly declining value of the investments that Daniel Wheeler had made on his behalf. However, he continued to declare himself grateful for the advice that he invest in British companies, especially given the unsettled state of Europe following the revolutions of 1848. So while Ferdinand Uhde accepted her advice that no further investments in railway companies be made, he asked that she continue managing his affairs. As she left Ashley Grange to spend some months at Summerhill, Margaret Wheeler instructed her servants to sell whatever surplus produce from the garden they could to a local shop woman: 'It is time to look after the pence if the pounds are ceasing to come.'[19]

Financial affairs provided her with insufficient occupation, however, while many might lay claim to her companionship and assistance: her parents, her sister-in-law, her aged aunts in Malton, her Bright in-laws, her niece. Yet she could identify no one claim as having priority over any other, and she confided in Sarah Wheeler, 'It is a trying and wearing thing to have no one claim that I see is paramount and thus to have to debate each step between conflicting interests. I am often exhausted with painful effort to know what is best to do.' She considered returning to live at Summerhill with her parents, but found the thought of giving up her own home and its memories too difficult. The plan eventually settled on represented an acceptable compromise to her mind: it allowed her to retain an independent household for some part of the year when she could continue as neighbour and companion to Sarah Wheeler; it involved regularly spending another part of the year with her parents, thereby saving something on her own housekeeping costs; it fulfilled her promise to Elizabeth Bright that she would continue to watch over the wellbeing of Helen; it relieved the One Ash family of finding a suitable and affordable governess solely for Helen, ten years and more older than her brothers and sisters; it gave her a useful and interesting occupation that simultaneously allowed her to build a still closer relationship with the child while enjoying the companionship of sisters and parents. The wisdom of the plan was soon evident, for at the end of 1848 Sarah Wheeler agreed to marry William Tanner, a Quaker minister and paper manufacturer of Cheddar. Though they decided to make Sarah Wheeler's house, Ashley Down, their married home, this coming change only intensified Margaret Wheeler's sense of her own desolation, so that the benefits of her niece's companionship and of regular returns to Summerhill became all the greater.[20]

A conviction of the rightness of these arrangements increased as she came to know M. E. B. better, and to see the continuing hostility felt toward her by Helen Bright. The contrast between the values, mores and sensibilities of her own family and of M. E. B. struck her more forcibly than ever when the Brights visited Ashley Grange with their baby son in 1849, as Margaret Wheeler was working out a new pattern for her own life: 'her good humour is marvellous but her face wears ever an expression of health and buoyancy that seems almost to want a shade of anxiety or deep feeling to render it an object of sympathy ... and yet I daresay she knows what it is to suffer.' She found the continuing hostility of Helen Bright to her stepmother a further cause for concern: 'Poor Nelly looked very coldly on her and it did not require much penetration to discover that their minds were formed in totally different moulds. And I can only think of them as one Bird caring for the young of a totally different species.' She contrasted M. E. B's bluntness of speech and insensitivity to the moods of others with Priestman sensibility, which, she acknowledged, often 'partakes more of feeling than judgment'. Margaret Wheeler tried to persuade her niece of the 'folly and impropriety' of such feelings, but admitted: 'my heart ached for the young spirit forced back upon itself at the period when a child so peculiarly needs the fostering guidance of one dear to it. .... Altogether it was *very* painful to see them together.' For her part, Helen told of a life of constant scolding and of her wish that she might live with the Priestmans. Margaret Wheeler felt 'compelled to laugh away her grievances and fortify her over-sensitive mind for a path of early suffering'.[21]

Helen's life was already beginning to fall into an itinerant pattern that was to last until her late teens, with Anna Maria Priestman and Margaret Wheeler continuing to share her teaching, sometimes at Ashley Grange, sometimes at Summerhill. That summer she also accompanied them on a holiday they took in Scotland with Priscilla Bright McLaren. Around this time, Rachel Priestman decided to confront the Brights with her concerns regarding her granddaughter's unhappiness. She assured them that she wished to give no offence and reaffirmed her love for them and for 'the tender bud' that bound them together. Helen had recently asked if she could live permanently with her Priestman grandparents and aunts, and though John Bright already appears to have rejected this suggestion, Rachel Priestman wrote: 'I confess however that I feel our claim increasingly strong.' For the present, however, she contented herself with putting before them another view of the child's behaviour that she felt they may have overlooked: Helen had been too young to comprehend the sorrow of her mother's death, and since then 'her path has been strewn with many comforts', not least the tender care of Priscilla Bright. While John Bright had greatly added to his happiness by his marriage, such a change could not take place 'without a severe shock to the tender feelings of a child': Helen had not only to form altogether new attachments, but also 'to some extent resign one of her less direct associations', and it was mistaken to expect such adjustments to happen quickly. Rachel Priestman expressed sympathy for M. E. B. in her 'delicate' position, insisting she was 'persuaded of her earnest desire faithfully to fulfil the duties it imposes – I feel much for her under this added care.' The Priestmans would be glad to share it, and felt the 'accuteness of separation'. She suggested, too, that Helen was now of an age where she should be allowed 'some little weekly allowance of money'.[22] This letter met with a conciliatory response and an undertaking that her advice would be heeded.

By the autumn of 1849 Margaret Wheeler's financial position was so precarious that she began to think of returning permanently to her parents' home. Sarah and William Tanner offered to take over Ashley Grange from her, a suggestion that she declared left her 'quite unstrung', and she replied wishing she had been spared 'an idea which is almost torture to my mind – that I may be compelled to part with my right to feel at home in the only place dear D. wished me to feel so'. For she had also begun to hope that John Bright might let Helen come to live with her at Ashley Grange for six months of the year. He finally agreed, on condition that she, with Helen and Anna Maria Priestman first spend Christmas with his family. She evidently enjoyed this visit much more than her sister, for she found M. E. B. a kindly and hospitable host, and thought John Bright unquestionably happier than he had been for many years. The quiet routines of the house also suited her after the cares and anxieties of previous months.[23]

Anna Maria Priestman was altogether less happy with life at One Ash, feeling the keenness of the climate and the coldness of the house intensely, finding the daily routine tedious in the extreme, and complaining of the limited compass of M. E. B.'s conversation. A consolation, as reported by Margaret Wheeler, was that Anna Maria Priestman 'exults in John's splendid library', a testimonial gift from the people of Rochdale after the repeal of the Corn Laws. In later years, Anna Maria Priestman recalled a visit to One Ash as the first time she had had access to the plays of Shakespeare. With enjoyment also of the Wheelers' library, her reading tastes had expanded well beyond the religious literature that was largely all there was to be found at Summerhill. Now she became a regular reader, for example, of Carlyle: 'I delight in his ideas so much that even his strange phraseology feels quite dear to me.' In the years ahead she also began to read with approval novels, including books that had scandalised those of a more conventional religious outlook, such as Charlotte Bronte's *Jane Eyre*: 'On the whole I should say the tone of principle and sentiment, pure and high.' So she felt reading it had done her good, for at the time she had been 'forlorn and jaded and sick at heart' and was both 'soothed and refreshed' by the 'beautiful moral landscapes' she found there 'where true and lofty thoughts were the sunshine'.[24]

The arrangement reached between Margaret Wheeler and John Bright meant a new pattern of life not only for herself and Helen, but also for Anna Maria Priestman, who was now expected to spend the first few months of each year at Ashley Grange to help with her niece's schooling. There appears to have been no payment for providing such service, though it is likely that the Brights contributed towards any additional housekeeping costs and may in this way have helped Margaret Wheeler retain Ashley Grange. She and her sisters were also repaid from time to time with invitations to join the Brights on holiday, or during periods of recuperation at Ben Rhydding. The scheme evidently worked well for everyone. When Helen returned to her parents for the summer, Margaret Wheeler was able to report: 'John says she had been so tractable and good since she returned to them that they cannot be too much obliged to me. Is it not a matter of deep thankfulness?' On the strength of such success, Margaret Wheeler felt free to speak openly to M. E. B. 'as to the treatment that I thought would conciliate H. and she is sincerely anxious that the child should be happy'.[25]

After a summer passed with her family, Helen returned to her aunt's care in the autumn, now studying with her for three hours each morning, while in the afternoon she worked alone for an hour and a half on lessons requiring 'simply an effort of attention and memory for both of which', her aunt believed, 'she ought to depend upon herself'. Helen was now enjoying her studies and showed, her aunt believed, abilities above the average: 'now the hard task of claiming her attention to her work is in great measure accomplished, the Teacher's office is a very interesting one'. During the summer break from her duties as governess, Margaret Wheeler had undertaken some 'needful *calculations*' toward an overview of her financial position. This continued to decline, as had the Tanners', and in December 1850, Sarah and William Tanner put forward a new proposal for sharing Ashley Grange with her sister-in-law. This time Margaret Wheeler's response was more measured.[26]

A broken engagement

In these years Anna Maria Priestman attempted matchmaking between one of her dearest friends, Jane Pease, and the younger of her brothers, failing, however, to make them appreciate each other. Jonathan Priestman jnr subsequently began to court her other particular friend, Anna Deborah Richardson, and by June 1850 the couple's engagement was widely known (provoking bitter feelings in Hadwen Priestman who had also hoped to marry her). Within weeks, however, Jonathan Priestman jnr began to doubt the wisdom of such a union, and turned for counsel to his oldest sister, Margaret Wheeler, recently arrived for her summer visit to Summerhill. With her usual practicality, she took matters into her own hands and told Jane Richardson, mother of Anna, of his unease. The couple then met to discuss the matter, amid much distress on both sides. They decided to allow themselves some more weeks to consider the matter, but Anna Richardson subsequently decided on a clean break and ended the engagement.[27]

Jonathan Priestman explained that his doubts had arisen because of 'the disagreeableness of all the relations but the mother' (Jane Wigham Richardson), something about which Rachel Priestman had earlier warned him. When he and Anna Richardson met to discuss his anxieties he had told her of his fears that he could never give 'a sincere welcome' to her family in any home of their own. To his older sister he went further and explained how he would also have shrunk 'from being at all identified with them and that on several counts', though the grounds for such feelings were not made clear (but perhaps were connected with the earlier business partnership between his father and Anna Richardson's). In a postscript he referred to the marriage of John and M. E. Bright, marred, apparently, by the lack of liking by any of his family for her and her family: 'Is M. E. B. happier for her marriage – or at least would a person of sensibility in her position be so?' Though he thought Anna Richardson a very different character, he saw an analogy in the dislike he and his family felt for her father and brothers.[28]

Anna Maria Priestman felt deeply for her old friend, longing 'for tidings of A. D. to whom the past week must have been sad and stormy'. The Richardsons, however, requested no further communication between them, though Anna Richardson sent her a few pencilled lines before leaving home, lines that Anna Maria recorded 'must have cost me as many tears as they did her'. Jonathan Priestman, too, looked very ill, worn and thin, while her mother was 'quite knocked up' by it all, and seemed unable to rest until she had devised 'some suitable scheme' to remove her younger son for a time from persons and scenes 'which must for long recall to him much that is painful and perplexing'.[29] Jonathan Priestman jnr went to stay with his uncle, Charles Bragg, at his country home in County Durham, and was there introduced to another Richardson family, of Shotley Spa, and to the woman who was eventually to become his wife.

Over the subsequent autumn and winter, the whole Priestman family removed to a nearby seaside resort, Cullercoats, then to Tynemouth. For Anna Maria Priestman 'being absent from Newcastle is in itself a boon for it is unpleasant to feel that the very sight of you is painful to those you meet'. She denied any angry feelings towards the Richardson family over the matter, and continued to grieve for her lost friend: 'My regret for *her* pain, for the severing of a friendship which I dearly prized and my sympathy with my brother's distress have darkened my heart.' She confessed the crisis had 'thrown feelings of gloom and recklessness over my whole being', leaving her 'sadly irritable . . . and vexed and angry about little things'. She and Mary Priestman pressed to remain away, and did not return home to Newcastle until well into the following year. Anna Maria Priestman appears never again to have felt at ease within the close community of Friends in Newcastle: 'it does feel such a desolate changed place now . . . not such a pleasant residence to our family as it used to be.' Her parents now made plans to move to a new residence on the outskirts of Newcastle and her father prepared to retire from business. By autumn 1851, Anna Maria Priestman was immersed in preparations for her family's 'flitting' to Benwell House, a substantial mansion set in an extensive estate, through which a river flowed, and on which the Priestmans planned to keep some stock and poultry, carriages and horses.[30]

Within months of this move, the engagement was announced of Jonathan Priestman jnr to Lucy Richardson of Shotley Spa in Durham, to the anger of Anna Richardson's family. Anna Maria Priestman merely commented: 'I trust it may be for the best.' Subsequently, she acknowledged that her family's feelings on the matter were 'very complicated': while she was thankful for the happiness of her brother, she continued to feel regret that 'the sorrow and annoyance he has unhappily occasioned must continue unabated'. After the wedding she reported in herself 'such a feeling of relieved suspense that I thought I could enter into sympathy with a dormouse – such an irresistible tendency to sleep came upon me, from a sense of long withheld rest to the spirit.' She had observed with great thankfulness how Jonathan Priestman and Lucy Richardson affirmed their commitment to each other with a look of 'quiet, deep satisfaction', though not out of any 'heartlessness or want of constant recollection of my poor old friend'.[31]

The couple's new home was Derwent House, near Lucy Priestman's family home in Shotley, and Anna Maria and Mary Priestman were there to welcome them on their return from their wedding tour. The sisters soon came to share a deep appreciation of and love for Lucy Priestman. In time Anna Maria Priestman acknowledged that she made a much better wife for her brother, whom she now believed Anna Richardson would have driven to madness (though she gave no grounds for this curious reassessment).[32] Her old friend never married and subsequently built a house in the Lake District, having determined on the life of a single 'blue stocking'. There she lived in seclusion with a lifelong woman friend, continuing the academic studies at which she excelled, and encouraging the efforts of another old friend from Newcastle, Emily Davies, to establish a Cambridge college to provide higher education for women. Her brother, John Wigham Richardson, never forgave the Priestman family, writing bitterly of the effect of the broken engagement on his sister's health.[33]

Relations between the Priestman and Wigham Richardsons were further soured by the failure of the Northumberland and Durham District Bank. This had been formed from the amalgamation of a number of local banks in Newcastle, and shortly became the main financial institution in the region. From the beginning it was under the management of Jonathan Richardson, who subsequently became one of its directors, and also father-in-law to Jonathan Priestman jnr. Jonathan Priestman snr was one of the partners in the bank, and his personal business standing was important to public confidence in the venture, a confidence that saw it survive the crisis of 1846–7 when another large local bank failed. Jonathan Richardson, however, used his position to make substantial and unsecured loans to another enterprise in which he had a substantial interest, the Derwent & Consett Iron Company. Jonathan Priestman snr later acknowledged privately that he had become increasingly doubtful of the financial standing of the bank, but was persuaded not to withdraw from it for fear of undermining public confidence and causing widespread distress as a consequence. That failure occurred anyway in 1857, and Jonathan Priestman became part of an effort to relieve the pressure this placed on its partners by forming another bank which, however, also closed within a few months. So, like other partners in the District Bank he became liable for its debts. The accountants' report to the liquidators declared a loss of £1,835,150, and a call of £35 per share was deemed necessary, bringing financial disaster to many of the leading families among Newcastle's business community, including the Priestmans and their former Richardson neighbours.[34]

Both Jonathan Priestmans snr and jnr thereafter retired altogether from the banking world. Jonathan Richardson similarly departed from the management of the Derwent and Consett Iron Works, while insisting that the company would eventually be able to repay its debt to the bank. He and most of his family subsequently resigned from the Society of Friends before he could be disowned on grounds of financial mismanagement, if not dishonesty. Jonathan and Lucy Priestman, however, remained within the Society, the former returning his wife's marriage portion of £5,000 as money his father-in-law had not truly possessed. He also took over the management of what now became the Consett Iron Company, overseeing the successful rescue of the firm. By 1865, the liquidators had been able to pay the bank's debtors 19s 6d in the pound, too late, perhaps, to rescue altogether the Priestmans' reputation and good standing in Newcastle. Their supporters, however, including John Bright, continued to insist that the bank would never have failed if public confidence in it had not been falsely undermined. John Wigham Richardson, by contrast, used his own reminiscences to question the honesty of all those connected with the failure of the District Bank.[35] When 'networked' families such as these fell out, be it over personal or business matters, there were inevitably substantial consequences for other family members, their church and their local communities.

8 The single life
Anna Maria Priestman (1828–1914) and Margaret Wheeler (1817–1905)

Spinsterhood and widowhood

Several among the women of the Priestman–Bright circle chose to remain single. Anna Maria Priestman discussed her attitude to marriage in her letters to her cousin and lifelong friend, Jane Pease. When asked about any tendency to 'amativeness' in her own nature, she replied that she was not sure that she knew the meaning of the term. Certainly, she declared, she had never been much subject to 'falling in love'. Though she admitted that her sympathies and affections 'have often been pretty fully engaged on behalf of young gentlemen', she believed she was still too young, in her early twenties, to give such a step any serious consideration. In addition, she would only want as a husband someone who 'sincerely desired to be a follower of the Lamb', and had yet to meet a young man that she considered truly pious. Some years later, she acknowledged having had some passing feelings for one who remained in her eyes 'an interesting creature'. But now, she declared, 'my heart is growing strong again in its maidenly independence – one charm was broken by telling of my folly! But perhaps the power to do so shewed the spell was weakened, poor fellow!'[1]

She received several offers of marriage both directly, and indirectly through her parents. The latter she treated more carefully, writing to Jane Pease: 'I am sad and troubled – do pray for me that I may be guided to do right.' Such a proposal made her feel *'very much aged!* tho' I am for the present at any rate *free as ever* – those words sound so delicious but I would rather talk than write dear Jane.' Evidently she rejected this proposal and was shortly called from home by the needs of Margaret Wheeler, then attending the deathbed of her husband. Anna Maria Priestman had few reservations about the path of singlehood: 'As I write one old maid after another comes into my mind, bright and useful and *unsoured* but only one poor bachelor, and he I'm sure would have enjoyed his life with tenfold zest under the softening influence of some sunny dispositioned wife.'[2] Jane Pease similarly received proposals in these years but like her friend chose to remain single.

For Margaret Wheeler, her return to single life as a widow was difficult, as we have seen: there were not only her financial problems but also the question

Figure 8.1 Anna Maria Priestman (1828–1914), as a young woman

of where she belonged, what her role now might be. She soon returned to her philanthropic and benevolent activities: visiting and sitting on the committees of the Red Cross School in Bristol and the Orphan Asylum; supporting the work of the Sabbath School Society; helping collect a petition for the Anti-Capital Punishment Society on behalf of a woman who had been sentenced to death; participating in the anti-slavery and temperance movements.[3] But these evidently proved insufficient occupation. The needs of her niece, Helen Bright, provided the solution to Margaret Wheeler's search for a new purpose in life and over the next year or so she established a new, peripatetic pattern of living, as we have seen. This allowed her to maintain a home of her own, while spending some part of every year in Newcastle, in both places providing teaching for Helen.[4] Despite continuing tensions between John Bright and the Priestmans concerning Helen's education, this arrangement also served to preserve the emotional bonds between the two families, involving regular visiting between them. This new pattern also relieved the loneliness of her situation. When Sarah Wheeler married William Tanner the couple made her house, Ashley Down, their home. Sarah Tanner's evident happiness in her marriage only increased Margaret Wheeler's sense of loss.

Her arrangements also had implications for Anna Maria Priestman, who assisted with Helen's schooling both in Bristol and in Newcastle, and deputised for Margaret Wheeler when other family responsibilities required her presence elsewhere.[5] Anna Maria Priestman did not share her sister's aptitude for commanding the full and orderly attention of her boisterous charge and she, like her younger sister, Mary, met with continuous demands on their time and energies from others among their kin. Outside their parents' home, sisters, brothers, aunts and nieces held prime rights to such assistance, while they themselves became interchangeable in terms of meeting these claims, as companions, nurses and teachers. Both she and Mary Priestman saw a great deal of illness and death in these years. They shared the nursing of one of their Malton aunts in her last illness in 1853, and then took turns in providing care and companionship for their only remaining aunt and uncle there, both of whom they were also to help nurse through their last illnesses.[6]

Anna Maria Priestman spent a period as Helen's governess at One Ash in the summer of 1851, which coincided with the last illness of Jacob Bright snr and the return of all the surviving Bright sisters to Rochdale. Their presence seems to have unsettled Helen once again, and deepened her hostility to her stepmother. At one point she had declared to Anna Maria Priestman that she hated M. E. Bright, and later admitted that she had then cried for many hours afterwards at having such feelings. Later she confessed to her aunt that she thought the air at Rochdale made her wicked. Anna Maria Priestman concluded: 'I cannot see any more hope of this soon if ever being a fitting place for her to find a happy home.' Jacob Bright had been reconciled with his children for some years now, and he and Mary Bright had come to live at a cottage in the grounds of One Ash. On his deathbed, Anna Maria Priestman reported, he had had a conversation with John Bright 'of a satisfactory and relieving nature to all of them'. His surviving sons were all now established in the family business, so he explained that he was leaving most of his remaining property, largely in land, to his daughters, an arrangement in which his sons all acquiesced. The day after his death, Anna Maria Priestman recorded how at breakfast the faces of John and Jacob Bright jnr were 'running races in sadness and tearfulness'.[7]

Helen's stay at One Ash, and therefore that of her aunt, was extended in these circumstances – unhappily for Anna Maria Priestman, who in a letter to her sister declared: 'Oh! Mary I don't know what I am writing.' Helen was being 'so provokingly stupid' she had forgotten all the things she had earlier sorted out in her mind to include in her letter. She was also increasingly unhappy in the environment of One Ash, in which she found it difficult to correct Helen's 'faults in tone and manner': if M. E. Bright were present, her habitual 'abrupt manner' appeared always like scolding, so as further to 'embitter Helen's mind towards her'. Anna Maria Priestman contrasted the 'more congenial and loving' atmosphere of her own home with that at One Ash, where she found an almost total lack of 'delicate attention to others feelings' that shocked her in its effect on the child. It would seem, too, that Helen saw little of the rest of the family: 'Poor Nelly, I think she must be sick of me,' she wrote, as she so frequently provided the sole companion for her niece. Priscilla Bright McLaren also made clear her gladness that Helen lived much more among the Priestman family than in her father's home.[8]

Anna Maria Priestman learned to adopt a different stance in relation to John and M. E. Bright during this stay at One Ash. When, some weeks later, Mary Priestman was invited to visit them or accompany them to Matlock for a holiday, she advised her sister to choose the latter. She also advised, 'don't be snubbed by John Bright – whatever he says stand up boldly and rebuke him – and if he abuses thee abuse him in return.' It was better to laugh or scowl at him than to withdraw into a hurt silence, she had found, 'and take thy own way in open defiance'. Both he and his wife, in her observation, showed little regard for the feelings or opinions of others, and they had seemed to like her better when she gave up the deference with which she had so long regarded her brother-in-law.[9] Priestman and Bright sisters together came to believe that the sensibilities developed in John Bright by his first marriage became lost through his second. Shared concern for their niece further cemented the friendships among them.

The friendships between the Bright and Priestman sisters sustained the close ties between the families despite such tensions. Margaret Wheeler remained especially close to Priscilla Bright McLaren, for example, and in her widowhood was freer to attend her friend during her confinements, and to holiday with her in periods of convalescence. She stayed for some months around the birth of Helen McLaren (named for their niece). Duncan McLaren had recently become Lord Provost of Edinburgh, requiring him to keep a far larger and grander establishment, with carriage and horses, butler, manservant and footmen now added to a household that had previously employed only cook, parlour maid and nursemaid. His predecessor had given fifty-two state dinners, something Priscilla Bright McLaren was well-suited to manage when well, but not in the depressed condition that it was feared might again follow childbirth. Fortunately, Margaret Wheeler found that the monthly nurse, Mrs Dymond, proved 'a complete host in herself'. It was arranged that she take over the management of the kitchen till new staff arrived, while Margaret Wheeler stood in for her in her nursing duties. In this way, sisterly relations were maintained between Brights and Priestmans, despite the failure of any of the Priestmans to form a close relationship with M. E. Bright.

Religion and reform

Helen enjoyed the drama of the Priestmans' move from Summerhill to Benwell House in 1851. Anna Maria Priestman wrote a description of their new home for another family member, telling of its library, breakfast room, dining room, drawing room, upstairs sitting room, two kitchens, two bedrooms with dressing rooms, and three others. The kitchens were formed by two wings to the house, the first containing the back and front kitchen, laundry room and washhouse, and the second, the storeroom, servants' hall and pantry. She and Mary Priestman shared a bedroom above this kitchen wing, next to one shared by the servants. Helen delighted in the new house, especially the large gardens, the chickens and ducks, and the pony she had to ride.[10]

One of the reasons for moving had been the desire for a healthier environment.[11] A further cholera epidemic came to Newcastle in 1853, bringing a complete 'panic and stagnation of trade', and 'an unexampled fortnight of sorrow and panic and suspense'. Several victims were from the middling classes, so the danger this time was felt to threaten all, not just, as previously, the poor. Town leaders arranged for the provision of Chobham tents on the moors so that 'those Inhabitants who live in the most disgracefully wretched place may remove and enjoy a chance of life while measures are taken to remedy some of the evils of their lot'. Warm clothing was also in great need, and Mary Priestman attended a meeting with her father 'to consider how best to care for the Clothing of the Invalids and for the poor little children left destitute'. Meanwhile, Rachel Priestman went to her brother's shop for a piece of cloth, after which her family, including servants, set about making eighteen vests for the clothing committee. It was unusual now for the women of the Priestman family all to be together in one place, and Anna Maria Priestman reported: 'Right heartily we all took to needle thimble and thread and Mamma sat in the easy chair in the Drawing room with her knitting looking so happy amongst her group of children it was quite pretty to see her whilst Mary seemed not to know how to enjoy herself enough.' Meanwhile, little business was going on and Jonathan Priestman snr kept busy visiting those who lived around his works in Low Friar Street administering medicines, 'for the disease made havoc in that vicinity', though not, the Priestmans were relieved to find, among their own tenants in the cottages they had built, 'a great satisfaction since one might have been anxious as to drainage etc'. But this time two among their employees died and mortality rates were high: 'It has been a fearful visitation but with so many abuses in our midst, it grieves one to hear it called a visitation of God – almost as truly might a Drunkard's death be called so I fear.'[12] As part of the reform party in Newcastle, the Priestmans remained unconvinced that the disease was spread by contagion, continuing to believe that the cause was more likely to be the insanitary conditions in which the poor had to live.[13]

During this period of her life Anna Maria Priestman went through a re-evaluation of the evangelical religious beliefs that had informed her childhood, and more especially the anxiety that such beliefs induced concerning salvation after death. This shift appears to have been prompted, in the first instance, by the disownment of her elder brother, Hadwen Priestman in 1842, for she thought his treatment overly harsh, putting his soul in jeopardy by such alienation from the Society. She wrote to Jane Pease: 'Oh! may thou *never never* know what it is to doubt a dear one's being accepted for Christ's sake before the throne!' This episode led her to question, however, any necessary link between an individual's pursuit of election and ultimate salvation. 'I cannot believe that the child of so many prayers, as he is will be unreclaimed to Jesus.' It was a doubt even the leading evangelical Friend, Joseph John Gurney, admitted to himself, when contemplating the possible fate of an atheistical brother. Further reflection led her to a belief in universal salvation, one for which she felt she had now found biblical support, 'however contradictory it may appear to earthly minds'. She insisted that such a belief broke no commandment and was 'the most probable and plausible' in her own judgement. She also argued that it did not 'detract from the efficacy of the Saviour's blood but rather increases it.' Nor did it lead her to seek to diminish any sense of 'the deep corruption of our nature', reporting how she continued day after day to shed 'bitter tears' over the sinfulness she perceived in her own heart.[14]

The wisdom of the elders of the Society of Friends was further thrown into question for Anna Maria Priestman by the disownment of Priscilla Bright for marrying outside the Society. She wished her co-religionists would 'trust more to their principles and less to their hedge of ceremonies', while fearing that Jane Pease might on that account think her 'very *heterodox*'. Her growing scepticism toward 'orthodox' Quakerism subsequently became evident also in her openness to more liberal currents within the Society of Friends. She was now certain that it was enough to believe in Christ and to strive after God's will. She acknowledged many might fear that such a faith would lead to a 'false feeling of security', but she also questioned the religious value of 'good works' undertaken only to escape punishment. In such circumstances, she argued: 'our activity becomes as doubtful as repose.' After his marriage to Sarah Wheeler, she came to know William Tanner during her visits to her sister in Bristol, and he showed her a more cheerful kind of Quaker piety. She explained to Jane Pease that her changing religious outlook was reaffirmed 'because I see around me [while visiting at Ashley Grange] so strikingly the beauty and strength of a different practice'. Like Rachel Priestman, William

Tanner actively pursued a travelling ministry and his memoirists emphasise his special interest in the religious guidance of the young, especially in assisting those experiencing religious doubt. His approachability and lack of solemnity no doubt helped. Anna Maria described him thus: 'there is mingled an almost child-like interest in every innocent gaiety of heart – and a zest for the beautiful in art and nature ... which allows no trace of gloom or sternness in his profession of religion.' She noted, too, how 'his ministerial engagements do not seem to be taken up as the arduous services which we often hear them spoken of, but rather as labours of love'. She acknowledged that it was her own 'prone-ness to be disheartened and doubtful' that made her look with pleasure on such a character and such a ministry. Increasingly now she felt her own tendency to dwell on the many sorrows of her early life to be 'unchristian'. His example led her to 'long for a sunny religion for my friends as for a choice blessing.'[15]

She offered the comfort of her own new 'sunny' religious outlook during the spiritual trials of Jane Pease: 'It will not be wandering in the wilderness in a solitary way always dear Jane – if we can cling to our God as our best friend and director.' All dogma from this time on she dismissed as speculation, and speculation which made 'so little, or no alteration in what ought to be our daily aim and acts' that it was not worth 'discussing or dwelling upon in thought'. She held to a simple creed: 'To be good ourselves, and to try to do good to others, should be an increasing endeavour to us all, because we shall please our Father in Heaven, quite irrespective of what may be the consequences to ourselves or others if we do not.' She was as likely now to look for moral and religious enlightenment by reading novels such as *Jane Eyre*, or Harriet Beecher Stowe's *Uncle Tom's Cabin*. Discussing Stowe's work she argued that fiction in itself was not wrong, and that the reader should be ready to engage with such a harrowing an account of slave sufferings 'so long as there is a chance of our being able to help'.[16]

Such shifts in religious sensibility are often perceived as further evidence of the secularisation of society over the course of the nineteenth century. But instances such as that of Anna Maria Priestman suggest an alternative interpretation, in terms of a sacralisation of activities previously regarded by Quakers as 'creaturely'; religious values were finding new forms of expression rather than outright rejection. In time, too, Anna Maria Priestman returned to the reading of religious texts, preferring by now to go back to the founders of the Society of Friends. After reading the *Journal* of George Fox she found herself longing for 'more of the same fervent spirit which activated the writer' among her contempories, both within the Society of Friends, and in other denominations. She was increasingly impatient with the lengthy debate the Society gave to what seemed to her 'trifling issues', such as whether or not to allow gravestones in Quaker burial grounds. In time she came to question whether Yearly Meeting held any spiritual value at all, preferring instead the 'hallow, quiet, unpretending, unobtrusive' nature of her local meeting for worship.[17]

A confident hope in universal salvation together with a rejection of sectarian and dogmatic theological wrangling freed Anna Maria Priestman from the anxieties of evangelical religion. It also led her to displace intellectual speculation on theological issues in favour of subjects 'of practical importance'. Chief among these during her young womanhood was her commitment to radical-political causes, especially repeal of the Corn Laws, and her engagement with the ongoing debate regarding a 'fitting sphere' for women. She knew Jane Pease was unlikely, however, to sympathise with her own belief in 'the rapid progress of that cause of humanity', and in general she avoided discussion of matters that she knew to be uncongenial to her friend. So, for example, she restrained her own evident enthusiasm for such when writing to her: 'I must not speak to thee about the Reform meeting in Manchester . . . thou art so indulgent to my own taste for politics that in common gratitude I must not "bore" thee with it.' Similarly, she recounted for her friend's amusement only the disagreements between members of her family and some visitors from the United States: *'they* for *monarchy*, we for republicanism'. The exchange she reassured Jane Pease was made in no spirit of bitterness, but had given 'zest' to their conversation.[18]

Increasingly, she preferred to read works of social commentary and ethical-aesthetic exploration to which she attached religious significance. The work of Thomas Carlyle became especially dear to her. To this she added also works such as John Ruskin's *Modern Painters* and Henry Mayhew's account of the London poor. But such matter served equally to refer her back to her religious concerns and responsibilities. Hence, she explained how Mayhew's book was 'haunting' her, and had put the Yearly Meeting of Friends in a new light, to her mind: 'It is dreadful to think that we meet year after year in the very heart of distress and crime without bending every energy we can spare to its relief.' In her view such obliviousness to sin and suffering was an abrogation of Christian duty: 'to be feasting in a life boat while vessels on all sides are sinking would be as humane.' Her growing sense of alienation from the governing structures of the Society of Friends was evident also in her determination to refuse an invitation in 1851 to become Assistant Clerk to her local Monthly Meeting. She felt unsuited for such a position by her 'want of voice' and 'nervousness', and also by her sense of lacking the 'decided attachment' to the Society of Friends in her view required for such a post. She persuaded Rachel Priestman of the rightness of her decision only by bringing up the family duties that from time to time would require her living at Bristol with Margaret Wheeler and Helen.[19]

Margaret Wheeler similarly placed herself among those Friends she termed the 'onward party' within the Society, seeking a relaxation of church discipline, especially where it concerned Quaker 'peculiarities', and the attendant proscriptions regarding dress, language usage, the use of headstones, and marrying out.[20] She was also among those who continued to uphold and to celebrate the ministry of her sex, especially when a woman minister felt called upon to address the Men's Yearly Meeting. She was equally sceptical of the authority assumed by certain men ministers, who she might refer to ironically as 'one of the Lords of Creation'.[21] On other matters she found the Men's Yearly Meeting to be decidedly behind the Women's Yearly Meeting, for example, in its commitment to the cause of temperance.

Alongside such deliberations, Anna Maria Priestman and Margaret Wheeler were by this time also thinking about the position of women within the Society. Anna Maria Priestman discussed with Jane Pease the emerging resistance among some leading evangelical Friends to the ministry of women. Like Margaret Wood, Anna Maria Priestman viewed such developments with regret and noted the lack of women ministers in a number of meetings within her own locality. She also acknowledged that a passage in Corinthians, drawn to her attention by Jane Pease, appeared to forbid the ministry of women. The question was especially perplexing and pressing, for her own mother felt it her duty not only to offer ministry, but to pursue that calling through travels far afield. The effect of the ministry of a number of women Friends upon her own spiritual life finally convinced Anna Maria Priestman of its legitimacy: 'in listening to their frequently beautiful addresses, their sweet consoling sermons and their excellent advice I think it must be right for them thus publicly to declare [unreadable] and the judgments of their God or they would not be strengthened and directed so, to take part in the ministry.' Of one such woman minister she wrote, 'She is the pillar of the meeting to me.' Jane Pease shared this assessment, though herself deeply evangelical in her religious beliefs, and despite her 'many varieties of opinion' with her friend on other matters, not least politics. Jane Pease was herself recorded as a minister in 1862.[22]

Anna Maria Priestman was comforted by Jane Pease's agreement with her on this question, but explained that it also raised for her broader issues beyond the Society of Friends: 'still we condemn the American practice of women lecturing in public and I do not see where Friends make the distinction between their *condemned* practice and the *approved* one of our own dear female friends.' In the context of nineteenth-century public life, the boundary between belief and politics was often blurred. Movements for humanitarian and moral reform, such as anti-slavery and temperance raised matters of public policy and administration that expanded religious imperatives beyond the meeting house. Such concerns with the pursuit of Christian duty in turn led her to a topic that she saw as closely related to it: 'looking at what a woman can do'. Observing 'so little in the way of action' from men in public life, she argued 'it seems to make it of ten fold consequence to *her* [i.e. women as a sex] that nothing *she* says should be otherwise than of a high and gentle tendency.'[23] Here she was expressing both a sense of gender difference, and her understanding of its consequence for the pursuit of social action as Christian duty. For the time being, Anna Maria Priestman was content to follow such imperatives through her work for moral reform and humanitarianism, and through her support for radical politics. Similarly, Margaret Wheeler's positioning of herself with the 'onward party' within the Society, was of a part with her radical stance on secular issues, and notably the growing discussion regarding the proper position of women.[24]

Public activities, like the campaigns against slavery and against the Corn Laws, however much clothed in domestic and religious rhetoric, were providing the breach that was in time to lead women Friends such as these to challenge any proscription against women's participation in political life. So, though many of Margaret Wheeler's views on gender difference remained conventional, she clearly respected women with strong views and a readiness to give voice to those views, provided they did so in 'an unpretending and pleasant manner'.[25] Her own active immersion in radical politics as a young woman had not survived her marriage, though the revolutions of 1848 drew her constant attention even as she nursed her husband on his deathbed. In widowhood she once again became an interested observer of the political scene. Her support for women's rights was also evident from the earliest days of an organised campaign in Britain, at least as far as becoming a reader of the *English Woman's Journal*, and circulating it among her sisters.[26]

The business of marriage: the courtship of Margaret Wheeler and Arthur Tanner

The marriage of her sister-in-law, Sarah Tanner, had introduced Margaret Wheeler into a new family circle in Somerset. The Tanner family had a timber business in Bristol, to which William Tanner had added paper-making with his mills in Cheddar, from which in turn had grown a wholesale stationery business.[27] His parents lived in retirement at Sidcot and were of a more modest standing, both socially and financially, than either Sarah or Margaret Wheeler.[28] When William Tanner had married Sarah Wheeler and retired (at least partially) from business, management of the Cheddar mills and stationery business had passed to his youngest brother, Arthur Tanner jnr. After his marriage William Tanner led the life of a gentleman while also pursuing his ministry.

Margaret Wheeler soon established a friendship with Mary Anne Tanner, sister of William, and increasingly took her under her wing, to share her love and knowledge of poetry and of German. She also made occasional references to Arthur Tanner, a reclusive and morose character.[29] It was proving a struggle to keep the Cheddar mill profitable, and he was evidently of an anxious disposition. The solitariness of his life in Cheddar left him much time to brood on his problems, for he seems to have shared neither William Tanner's sunny disposition nor his involvement in a range of benevolent measures aimed at the wellbeing of the local work people and their children. Arthur Tanner's 'worn looks' were causing his brother some anxiety by November 1851, but Margaret Wheeler was impatient with such concern: 'A character acquires neither force nor strength for over coddling and I really see so much inability in young persons to fill responsible situations merely for want of their self reliance being cultivated.' The Tanners accepted her suggestion that his sister should be sent to stay with Arthur Tanner to provide some companionship: 'no doubt a wife would be worth more to him but that you cannot provide whilst this you can.'[30]

Perhaps this was intended as a signal of a deepening interest in Arthur Tanner. He had entertained her family during a visit in 1850, possibly as the beginnings of a courtship – certainly the ever-watchful Helen suspected this – and presumably had received little encouragement at that point.[31] He eventually proposed marriage to Margaret Wheeler early in 1853, and they then corresponded during her usual annual visit to Summerhill that autumn, through which she closely questioned him on his religious views. She also pointed out that her hair was now very grey and almost gone, 'which I thought only honest'. She found much that was unsatisfactory about his letters, regularly forwarding them to Sarah Tanner to prove her case. Arthur Tanner was neither a regular correspondent, nor a very expressive one. Within weeks his courtship had become a matter for gossip among Friends in the north, a great annoyance to Margaret Wheeler who was still unable to come to any decision on the matter. She declared herself glad to hear that Arthur Tanner seemed cheerful under such trials, 'because the long suspense is not what I should have chosen should occur and I was anxious . . . that I might know if it gave much pain – perhaps it does not give enough! Who can tell'.[32]

She continued to feel a 'sense of the unfitness of things in some respects as heretofore'. In her own case she doubted she possessed 'the power of entering upon a second engagement of the heart', and there were unspecified health problems of her own that she felt would need to be resolved before she might consider marriage. She also made increasingly pointed remarks regarding their difference of 'tastes and acquirements', the 'negligence of style and want of finish' in his letters, leading to doubts as to whether he would prove 'a companionable person' for her. There was an element of intellectual and social snobbery, at the very least, in her reservations about this possible remarriage.[33] At the same time, another of her barbed comments suggested that his lack of emotional involvement also concerned her. After they had agreed to leave the matter for a few months, she commented: 'It is a comfort to find how soon men console themselves for the loss of affection even when they have accustomed themselves to the idea of its possession!' He responded to coaching in this matter, however, so that in time Margaret Wheeler remarked her growing satisfaction with Arthur Tanner's 'sensitiveness of feeling' compared to 'his first off hand advances'.[34]

She was mollified, too, by a proposal that Oakridge, a substantial and elegant house in Sidcot, might become their married home. Any decision of Margaret Wheeler's to remarry had implications not only for her own financial situation, but also for Arthur Tanner and his family. Now she sought legal advice on whatever arrangements might protect a shareholder from liability: 'probably no Joint Stock Bank does – I am *liable* to the extent of all my property.' What remained unclear to her was whether any second husband of hers would also become so liable. If so, these shares would need to be sold before her remarriage. Both she and her brother, as the other trustee, wanted them sold in the next year or so in any case. She decided, too, on the wisdom of her retaining Ashley Grange, which she had been sharing with Sarah and William Tanner for the previous two years, explaining that the uncertainty regarding the mill's profitability led her to this decision. Should it have to close, Oakridge would need to be given up, and she would then divide Ashley Grange to make a separate home for herself and Arthur Tanner alongside another for her sister and brother-in-law should they want to remain.[35]

So this marriage had implications for others among the Tanner family, and also for the family business. The conditions of marriage being sought by Margaret Wheeler would also affect the running of the Cheddar mill, most especially the resistance of herself and her family to any possibility of living nearby. William and Sarah Tanner continued to express their concerns about the distance of Oakridge from the mill, but Margaret Wheeler urged the supposed unhealthiness of the environment there. She suggested, too, that the horse ride to work that living in Sidcot would require might prove beneficial to Arthur Tanner, and was certainly 'more refreshing and healthy than the *active* service he has been accustomed to give in the mill'. This, she declared, would now have to be deputed to a millwright, while she hoped that an eight-hour day for her future husband 'may satisfy the mill claims'. Margaret Wheeler was already showing the interventions she was prepared to make in the running of the Tanner business on behalf of herself and her future husband. In these indirect ways, she was also establishing the level of gentility that she required from her marriage: a house removed from the workplace, and capable of accommodating a carriage and horse; the cessation of any manual labour at the mill by Arthur Tanner; and hours more consistent with the role of master, rather than simply supervisor, of this part of the family enterprise. She was seeking, that is, to establish greater parity between the social position of Arthur Tanner and that attained by William Tanner on his marriage to her sister-in-law. These negotiations were conducted through her correspondence with Sarah Tanner, and not directly with either of the other two Tanner brothers.[36]

By such means, Margaret Wheeler effectively signalled before her remarriage the importance of her goodwill in encouraging and supporting Arthur Tanner in the continuance of that business. His immediate kin were evidently reliant upon its success as a factor in the viability of the family firm. Indirectly, then, though she was to have no involvement in the day-to-day management of the mill, she made herself a force within the management of the family business, and strengthened her husband's position vis-à-vis his two brothers. By retaining possession of Ashley Grange she also created a possible married future separated from the fortunes of that business. Matters were at last settled to her satisfaction late in April 1854, when Margaret Wheeler wrote to Priscilla Bright McLaren: 'I have ventured once more to cast in my lot in life with another . . . my feelings have had a trying strife

Figure 8.2 Margaret Tanner (1817–1905), *c.* late 1860s

between past, present and future.'[37] For her life was also still very much bound up with the needs of her niece. Helen Bright was, however, approaching the age when girls in this circle went away to school for a few years. Indeed, the courtship of Arthur Tanner had begun to progress once it was clear that Margaret Wheeler would no longer be needed as her governess.

Educating Helen

Her Priestman aunts were more central to Helen Bright's life during the latter years of her childhood than her father's family. Reflecting on this she wrote to her grandmother, 'How very fortunate I am in Aunts, of all kinds, am I not?' As her family life was divided between three households, and, given the distances between One Ash, Benwell House and Ashley Grange, letter writing was necessary to sustain her complex family relationships. So, she was early introduced to the task of letter writing, and encouraged to develop an epistolary style that was entertaining, fond, poised and above all 'informing'. Letters had to amuse with an easy and light-hearted decorum while conveying recent intelligence about those kin with whom she was in touch, and the neighbours and neighbourhood where she resided. They should also show, where possible, some development of character or advance in education, and convey something of the writer's thoughts on interests and enthusiasms shared with the other correspondent – in terms of her current reading, for example.[38]

Helen attained this standard only gradually, of course; some of the letters written by her as a child worried recipients by their lack of discretion, and a directness, even ferocity, of expression that suggested a temperament more akin to her father's than to that of the gentle Elizabeth Bright of family memory. Encounters with her Leatham relations might provoke such outbursts. More generally, however, her letters demonstrate the informal, open easiness of her family relationships, especially among her Priestman aunts and uncles. Those that survive suggest that the culture of letter writing changed relatively little across the several generations of women represented in the family archive, though modes of expression became more direct and open, and handwriting more uniform and less elaborate.

Her Priestman aunts shaped her habits in many other ways, and during one of her stays at Ashley Grange, she reported: 'Anna Maria has begun a journal and I have taken the example.'[39] This was her first attempt at keeping a diary, a practice that gradually became habitual and which she then maintained until the last few years of her life. Recording how Margaret Wheeler had 'made the resolution to eat only 2 meals a day, she having previously taken it into her head that she eat to much', she decided to emulate her aunt. In a spirit of mischief she wrote in her diary: 'I cannot tell I am sure what Mama indeed will think of it she will be horrified – and I fear (perhaps) think M. has starved me'; for a seeming over-indulgence in food was one way the Leathams differed from the Priestmans.[40] The diaries of Helen Bright remained very different from the spiritual memoranda of her Bragg great-grandmother, her Priestman grandmother, and her own dead mother. They rarely record times of introspection, or of spiritual endeavour, though she was of an intellectual bent and, as a young woman, interested in theological debates. In adulthood, too, she only occasionally stopped to anatomise her own thoughts or feelings when writing her journal. Instead, she wrote of the daily round of family life, so that its main function appears to have been as an aide memoire, a useful record, no doubt, for the considerable correspondence undertaken among the women in this circle. Like her aunts, too, she stored a great number of her letters alongside her diaries. In later years she maintained a watchful interest over the ever-growing collection, eventually taking charge of it after her aunts' deaths. In this way a detailed and extensive family memory was created and became a legacy from previous generations to her children and grandchildren.

Her references in the letters and diaries of her childhood contain notably few references to her father's new family at Rochdale outside the periods she spent there, confirming the importance of the Priestmans to her emotional life and sense of self. In temperament, however, she was more akin to John Bright and Margaret Wood. She found her happiness and pleasure in the moment, in contrast to the anxious soul-searching evident in the childhood letters of Anna Maria Priestman, for example. As a child more used to the company of adults than of other children, Helen Bright became a close observer of the adult world, knowing and ever watchful for signs that might augur some change in her own situation. Her entries indicate, too, a surprising stoicism in a child: she recorded writing an ode on the death of her first pet, a dog named 'Charlie' (in whose 'honner' she had previously held a coronation and arranged a feast), while reflecting, 'time flue *so* quickly when Charlie was living, but it seems very different now'. When her grandfather Bright began to fail in the summer of 1851 she reported with a similar matter-of-factness: 'Grandfather is sinking, I daresay he will not live over today.'[41] In later years her diary was also a place where from time to time Helen Bright expressed, sometimes forcefully, her views on public affairs. So it provided a release, perhaps, for feelings that, as she matured, she felt unsuitable for the more public space of a letter.

Accounts of holidays and later of foreign travel also regularly formed part of her diaries. So some of the earliest memories recorded in the first volume concerned a few days spent with the Tanner family at Sidcot. One day, the party went to visit Barleywood, formerly the home, near Cheddar, of Hannah More, the Evangelical writer, moral reformer and educationalist whose work had so inspired William Tanner; even holidays provided object lessons in 'useful' Christianity. During stays with her aunt at Ashley Grange, Helen Bright might also attend the general meeting of the Quaker school in Sidcot, one modelled on Ackworth and similarly established for the children of Friends 'not in affluence'. On such visits she noted the differences between the modernising manners of her circle and more conventional Quakerly habits, declaring, for example, 'the children looked hideous with their little Quaker bonnets' – she appears never to have worn one though her father insisted that she be dressed 'plain' according to the wish of her dead mother. During the rest of this visit, she observed the pupils being examined on their studies, heard a reading class, and also a 'scripture questioning'.[42] She was already learning her place, then, in the higher reaches of the social hierarchy among Quakers, and preparing for a role in the leadership of her church. Already, she identified herself with 'the liberal party' within the Society that sought to move away from the 'peculiarities' upheld by more conservative Friends, and in adulthood, she became a member of the governing board of Sidcot School, working with her husband to improve the education provided there, especially that for girls.

Marriage often meant the removal of her aunts to other cities and towns, like Esther (Bright) Vaughan and Margaret Bright Lucas, both of whom lived in London at various times. These aunts were able to introduce her to still more distant kin previously unknown to her. Esther Vaughan died of puerperal fever shortly after one such visit, following the birth of a daughter who survived her by only a few months. Helen received her copies of Whittier's poems and of Dickens's *Chimes* to help keep alive the memory of yet another dead aunt.[43] If marriage and childbirth sometimes brought the loss of an aunt, the marriage of uncles brought new ones, some of whom Helen became especially fond, including Selina Bright (née Gibb), and Ursula Bright (née Mellor). The latter married Jacob Bright jnr in 1855 and the couple made their first home in Greenbank, his father's old house. Jacob Bright jnr, like Esther Vaughan, was considered a 'gay' Friend, for both enjoyed music, dancing and theatre (John Bright would still leave an evening party when music or dancing began). Like his dead sister Jacob Bright also chose to 'marry out', and became a declared atheist.

Helen gave this account of Ursula Bright to Anna Maria Priestman: 'She is quite a child in many respects, but has read a good deal and thought a great deal too, and tho' she is very gentle and loving, yet has decidedly a character.' She concluded: 'I am very fond of her, and she pets me, and what is highly satisfactory, she has not made Uncle Jacob a bit less kind to me.' In time she also came to appreciate a quirkiness in Ursula Bright that others in her family circle were to find less congenial, and wished her Priestman aunts might come to know her better: 'I don't think people like her much who meet her casually, but when you know her, you find her so singularly good and loving; quite a model of charity and sympathy, and withal very original, and nearly all that is nice.'[44] Unlike her parents, Helen Bright appreciated such departures from conventional femininity, and was glad to be introduced to new possibilities still frowned upon within her own family circle. So, reporting how Ursula Bright one Christmas went to the pantomime in Manchester, she wrote enviously: 'I have a great opinion of the beneficial effects of hearty laughter. Next year I think I shall make a commotion and try to go too.'[45] Her relationship with Emily Slagg who married her uncle

Hadwen Priestman in 1859 was more equivocal. Like him, Emily Slagg was a chronic invalid, and the couple had met at Ben Rhydding. She and Helen soon took the measure of each other, the latter reporting 'last time I saw her she told me with a candour which I admired and which did not break my heart' that she would prefer they visited at different times in future, 'so I said she must contrive it her own way'. They evidently reached some better accommodation with each other, however, for Helen was bridesmaid at the wedding that followed, and gave it as her view: 'Emily is clever and sees the rights of any thing quickly enough. She is also very amusing and affectionate.'[46]

The letters Helen Bright wrote when at her father's home suggest a slowly improving relationship with her stepmother in these years. She now generally looked forward to her stays at One Ash, and feared any change of plan that might shorten her time there, writing on one such occasion to Margaret Wheeler: 'Please excuse such very shocking writing, but it is owing to the far more shocking and agonising state of mind which I am in.'[47] The fondness she felt for each of seven brothers and sisters was certainly the main factor in this, and she in turn became a great favourite with the younger children in her family. Equally, the homes of her Rochdale grandparents, 'Aunt Wood' and her Bright aunts and uncles provided additional lively family circles to which she could turn when life at One Ash became too fraught. She became especially fond of Margaret Wood, who returned her affection in full; Mizzy was always one of the first houses the child visited on her returns to Rochdale, and the household was still more congenial to her when Jane Crosland, a second cousin, was visiting there. The three enjoyed the same kind of humour, and the simple, quiet orderliness of Margaret Wood's arrangements, and her continuing closeness to the local community, appealed to Helen in a way the relative luxury of life at One Ash did not. In her last years, Eliza Oldham also became an important member of Margaret Wood's household, formally a servant, but one to whom her employer seemed as a mother, and whose friendship and love was valued also by Helen. For Eliza Oldham also represented a link with her dead mother, having worked in the Bright mills as a girl and recalling the kindness then of Elizabeth Bright, especially as the employer of her father, Ben Oldham, at One Ash. The latter continued to work for John Bright or his firm for many years, and also shared his memories of the first Elizabeth Bright with Helen Bright.

Helen looked forward, too, to meeting up with aunts and uncles in London for the few weeks around Yearly Meeting. There were regular family parties where Priestman and Brights again came together. This time was generally also used for extending Helen's education in various directions. One year, she began the exercises devised by Dr Roth, aimed at strengthening her lungs and her body more generally, for the fear remained that she had inherited her mother's consumptive constitution.[48] Another time she took language lessons in French and German from a Polish aristocrat and fugitive. 'Le colonel Jules Przyiemski', who was said to know thirteen languages: 'He teaches well and gently, and does not frighten me.' When she learned she was afterwards to return to One Ash with her Mama, Abby and baby, she wrote, 'Oh *most* delightful occurrence', and made a note to herself: 'Remember to ask Papa to give me some mony.' Her tenth birthday was approaching, and she reflected: 'I am realy getting quite aged.'[49]

Helen's attitude to her Leatham relations, however, remained a continuing source of friction within her own family. She was scarcely able in these years to conceal her irritation with her Grandmama Leatham. The two had a serious falling-out during the summer holidays of 1852 when her grandmother said 'a great many very rude and pointed things' against her uncle, Jonathan Priestman jnr. 'So then I just said as many things as I could, and scolded with all my might and main. And she flew into a passion, and I did too, and I fought as hard as ever I could, and to conclude, I have quarrelled *perfectly* with the rude old thing.' She referred to her Leatham uncles as 'clownish brats', and in a postscript to this letter to Margaret Wheeler she wrote: 'I actually pity and dislike Granny L. as much as I love thee.' Margaret Wheeler evidently responded with an anxious letter, and a consolation gift of pocket money. But Helen replied that her aunt was quite mistaken if she thought her unhappy, adding the postscript: 'I don't feel quite easy at taking the half crown dear. I am *much* obliged for it though too [laugh sign].'[50]

John Bright and Margaret Wheeler continued sometimes to disagree over Helen's education – he arguing there were some things that a child might not be capable of learning, she insisting that any learning was possible if the will were there. Helen at this time expressed the fear that a master ('the nasty tribe, I'm so frightened') might be brought in to expand her 'accomplishments'. When the time came to discuss a possible school for Helen, Margaret Wheeler suggested Frenchay, a Quaker school in Bristol already attended by Helen's Ashworth cousins, and close, of course, to her own home. John Bright finally decided, however, on a school run by Emilie Schnell in Brighton, also attended by the daughters of several other Quaker families at this time.[51] The choice seems to have followed medical advice that Helen should go to a school near the sea because of her health. Its nearness to London also made visits from John Bright more practicable. Helen stayed with both Priscilla Bright McLaren and Margaret Wood before making a farewell visit to Benwell House when she was given Rachel Priestman's memoir of her dead mother to read. She continued to seek out objects and sites associated with Elizabeth Bright for many years to come, pressing her father and others to share their memories of this shadowy presence in her life. Increasingly now she felt her own tendency to dwell on the many sorrows of her early life as 'unchristian'.

Margaret Wheeler reported the unaccustomed wistfulness on her niece's face as she farewelled her Priestman grandparents and aunts, and once back at One Ash Helen began to prepare for her departure. She had been given a small telescope, and used it now to study the landscape that she loved, 'the hills, the chimneys and the smoke and factories'. She continued to mock family concern at a persisting sore throat – the shadow of Elizabeth Bright evident also in this regard – and reported herself 'running about and laughing heartily' at such alarm and its accompanying offers of nursing. She arrived at her Brighton school in September 1853, comforted by a supply of gingerbread from Margaret Wood that she found 'very soothing and good', and adapted to her new environment with her accustomed matter-of-factness and occasional black humour. The next day she wrote to M. E. Bright to report her first impressions. The house she found 'pinched', adding: 'My bed would be a coffin, complete if it had a top. I feel rather like Robinson Crusoe cast upon an island.' Emilie Schnell she reported very kind, and the German governess, too. The food she decided was on the whole good and plentiful, 'I can have as much as I can possible cram in (excuse this very inelegant term)', adding though, 'How I long for some fruit.'[52]

There she was to continue with her studies in French and German, but to give up Latin for the time being 'as I can go on with it without a foreigner'. Nor was she to take drawing. She was, however, allowed to attend lectures on astronomy and botany. There were twelve other girls there and she quickly identified three that she liked, one of whom – Harriet Crosfield of Warrington – became a lifelong friend. Helen found her 'more of a child, more petable' than the other girls, and also more 'sprightly'. Subsequently, she was joined by old friends, her cousin, Annie Ashworth, and two sisters from the Ford family of Friends in Leeds. Her fellow pupils were kind, and she tried to be so in return: 'when I am cross I always beg their pardon after'. She concluded that the greatest benefit of boarding school was that 'it teaches one not to be *soft*'.[53] Her main complaint was that she felt so out of touch with public affairs: 'Oh for pity's sake do tell me *always* what is going on, *please* don't forget about Russia and Turkey, war etc, and what our government is doing, in short, a nice little account of everything, please.' She asked, too, to be sent a newspaper whenever anything particular occurred. It was a plea to be repeated in many subsequent letters. Though occasional visits from John Bright no doubt helped fill this gap for her, those visits were far less frequent than she wished, and so were his letters. On one occasion she pleaded: 'Please tell me what is going on in the world; if the yellow fever is any better in New Orleans, and about the Russian question.'[54]

A persistent cough that failed to improve with the 'white powders' supplied by the school's homeopath so concerned her father that she was summoned home until she recovered, studying for a time under his direction. They began translating Caesar together, and she was set arithmetic exercises, and given D'Aubigne's history of the reformation (in English translation) to read alone. As well as helping her father sort his books and papers, she was now able to be of help, too, to M. E. Bright in teaching her brother, Albert. She also accompanied Anna Maria Priestman on a visit to Priscilla Bright McLaren, looking forward to the opportunity to come to know her Edinburgh cousins much better and to share their schoolroom for a few weeks: 'I am in great spirits about it ... tho' those clever, striking and at first very stiff children appear very formidable indeed.' Her reading in these months reflects the literary interests of the Priestman and McLaren families: Macauley on

1688, and the Irish rebellion, Madame de Stael's *L'Allemagne*, Sully's memoirs, the poems of George Herbert, Coleridge, Dryden and Shelley, a textbook on practical organic chemistry. She also read *Lectures to Ladies on Practical Subjects* by Charles Kingsley, F. D. Maurice and others 'for the purpose of getting up a college or something or other'. Helen at this time thought such a proposal 'entirely visionary', and declared herself to be unclear about 'what its driving at'.[55]

But she was now beginning to develop intellectual interests and a desire for self-cultivation that she found unsatisfied when she returned to school. A further respite came in the form of her father's nervous collapse as a consequence of the strains he had come under when opposing the Crimean War. He had maintained the Quaker witness against war in debates in the House of Commons, notably in one of his most famous orations, the 'angel of death' speech. Such opposition increased his sense of isolation both in parliament and in his constituency, Manchester, and he was now unlikely to be nominated to stand in the Liberal interest again in the next general election. His doctors ordered complete rest, and he went to Ben Rhydding to try once more the water cure there, in the company of Hadwen Priestman and of Helen. Visiting them there, Anna Maria Priestman was shocked by the change she saw in John Bright, and avoided all talk of the Crimean War because of the evident distress it aroused in him. On this topic, she explained, 'He has completely over-thought himself.' This meeting broke down some of the antipathy she had come to hold for him: 'poor man he looked so worn down my heart melted towards him.'[56]

Helen subsequently accompanied her father also on a fishing holiday in Scotland, bowing reluctantly to the request from her vegetarian Priestman aunts that she give up plans to learn to fish. Returning to school, she was shortly summoned away once more, to join her father in the prolonged visit to Europe now recommended by his doctors. She longed for such travel, and reported herself 'nearly wild, in an ecstatic state' at the prospect.[57] Together they toured France and Italy, being granted a private audience with the Russian empress in gratitude for the stance John Bright had taken against the Crimean war; taking part in a carnival; watching a masqued ball; having lessons in Italian. During this time, too, Helen pursued her growing interest in matters of religion, reading Chateaubriand's *Genie de Christianisme* and going to hear sermons by Dr Manning in Rome on the worship of the Virgin Mary.[58] After one more term at school, she finally returned permanently to One Ash to live.

Helen Bright's years at school had sometimes been saddened by deaths within her family, for example, that of her uncle, Gratton Bright, who had given her French lessons when she was at home in Rochdale, and been 'a sort of elder brother' to her.[59] The greatest change to her family circle, however, came with the death, in 1854, of her grandmother, Rachel Priestman. Helen Bright was at One Ash for the holidays and was allowed to attend the funeral in Newcastle, and to stay on at Benwell House to cheer her grieving grandfather and aunts.[60] Rachel Priestman's death occurred in Waterford, Ireland while on a travelling ministry. The first signs of illness had seemed to be no more than the symptoms of the 'sick headaches' with which she had long suffered. Subsequently, however, 'gastric fever' (typhoid) was diagnosed, and the Priestman family was summoned to Waterford. There Anna Maria Priestman nursed her mother over some weeks until she appeared to be recovering. Rachel Priestman then urged her to take a short holiday, but in those few days suffered a relapse and died, so that Anna Maria Priestman could only look back on the decision to leave her 'with utter misery'. The body was taken back to Newcastle for burial, John Bright and Priscilla and Duncan McLaren also attending the funeral, during which Anna Maria Priestman told of being visited by 'a feeling of richness in the stillness'. But in the months ahead she found that 'the yearning for her face and voice grows yet more craving and at every turn as we miss her more and more'.[61] Her mood remained troubled and depressed, so that she wrote 'I often think how blessed an early death must be . . . Life looks to me a burden to be borne — a picture torn and tarnished and the gilding rubbed away.'[62] Anna Maria and Mary Priestman now shared the management of Benwell House while Margaret Wheeler postponed her marriage to Arthur Tanner for another year, staying on to sort the papers of Rachel Priestman, and to prepare a family memorial of her mother.[63]

9 Family, friendship and politics
Helen Priestman Bright (1840–1927)

One Ash and Mizzy

The culture of family life among her kinship circles informed Helen Bright's sense of herself as a born radical, and the imperative she felt to undertake public service. Writing to Margaret Tanner to express her gratitude for all the love and kindness shown her by her aunt, she added: 'It feels like a sin receiving every thing and giving nothing in return.' She concluded from the examples around her: 'The only way to make one's little life spread out is to interest oneself in wider things than those that merely concern ourselves and to live in the future as well as the present.' The great changes that had come about in the previous few years, both at home and overseas, convinced her that she was living in a new age.[1] One Ash, and the other households that provided her with homes-from-home, were often on the itinerary of visiting lecturers, activists and reformers from both Britain and overseas, for example. She continued to read seriously, and to exchange views on works of social commentary and political economy, history and memoir, especially with her Priestman aunts. Family relationships and the Quaker calendar also introduced her to friendship networks, national and international, that might both expand her personal life and shape her participation in politics. So, she met potential husbands through such networks, including the man she eventually agreed to marry. Equally, her growing immersion in radical politics provided an added dimension to the renewed companionship she enjoyed with her father, and her continuing closeness to aunts and cousins. Her kinship networks proved enabling, also, in her efforts to secure improvements to the position of women within the Society of Friends at a later point in her life.

By the time she returned permanently to live at One Ash, it had become the large and substantial household of one of Rochdale's principal employers, and a draw to visitors to the Manchester region wishing to pay their respects to John Bright. So its management was a considerable undertaking, and Helen Bright was expected to play a part in it. She no longer confided in her Priestman aunts about her discontents, perhaps appreciating now how any sign of unhappiness on her part troubled them. But close proximity did not improve her relationship with her stepmother – for while she called

M. E. Bright 'Mama', she evidently did not think of her that way (and the Priestmans, too, always thought of Helen as 'a motherless child').Whenever possible she preferred to use her time out riding and visiting. The provision of hospitality was something in which she took considerable pleasure, however, for she liked meeting new people, and looking after visitors, especially those from overseas.

At One Ash the younger Bright children now had a governess, Lydia Rous, and Helen was evidently expected to continue some study under her which she confessed to disliking greatly: 'I am a good for nothing creature. I prefer following my own devices all day to having any thing fixed to do especially when I don't see any use in what I learn such as Algebra and Euclid.' She found much greater satisfaction sequestered away in her father's library where she continued her self-education by exploring its contents, and literature and history remained her preference. Her choices at this time included rereading Bancroft's history of the colonisation of the United States, 'one of the most interesting and beautiful books I have read', Carlyle on Schiller, the first volume of Motley's *Dutch Republic*, a life of Jefferson, and a life of Dr Arnold. Some had earlier been read to her by one or other of her Priestman aunts, so they also revived pleasant memories.[2]

Her choice of reading also suggests a continuing interest in religious issues. She borrowed, for example, a volume of the lectures and addresses of the late Frederick Robertson, a liberal churchman and Anglican vicar of Brighton who had died shortly before she started school there, but whose influence and reputation continued for many decades afterwards.[3] One extract, which she chose to record in her diary for the beauty she found there, may indicate something of her state of mind at this time. It considered 'infidelity', or absence of belief, which Robertson described as the 'state of one who craves light and cannot find it', someone whom, he believed, was often treated in ways 'most unpardonably cruel'. His sermon offered this advice: 'I know but one way in which a man may come forth from his agony scatheless; it is by holding fast to those things which are certain still – the grand, simple landmarks of morality.' Robertson offered this consolation: 'thrice blessed is he who, when all is dark and cheerless within and without, when his teachers terrify him and his friends shrink from him, has obstinately clung to moral good.' Anna Maria Priestman had voiced a similar conviction some years earlier, in her search for a 'sunny religion', so perhaps her influence is also evident in this choice of reading. With Lydia Rous, Helen Bright also attended a lecture by Thomas Cooper on the historical evidence of Christianity, finding in it an effective response to Strauss's account of the life of Christ.[4]

This interest in religious issues never displaced her primary enthusiasm, however: radical politics remained her abiding concern. So she followed the progress of the government's Reform Bill in 1859 even as she declared it 'a miserable sham', for its provisions were too limited to satisfy her radical aspirations. The following year she was able to attend the House of Commons with Margaret Bright Lucas and watch her father speak on a further Reform

Bill that once again foundered when the government could not secure a sufficient working majority. Accompanying another aunt, Ursula Bright, she also enjoyed a 'capital meeting of liberal electors on Mr Cobden's behalf' during the general election that year. She had sought seats for her party at the shop of a clogger as a vantage point on the proceedings, and those seats had been gladly given, she recorded, in memory of her dead mother. She noted, too, that they were among only five women present at the nomination. Together, they also attended the celebration meeting when Richard Cobden was returned once more. There was good news also from Birmingham, the constituency that had invited John Bright to stand in the Liberal interest two years before, and where he was once again successful at the poll.[5]

Sometimes, now, she accompanied her father to political meetings in the north, and when in London might also visit the offices of the *Morning Star*, the paper edited at this time by her uncle, Samuel Lucas, and one that her father had helped establish to promote the views and causes of Radical politicians. Through her father, too, she enjoyed ready access to the Ladies' Gallery from where she watched parliamentary debates, coming to admire other leading political figures, like the future prime minister, W. E. Gladstone. When they were apart, John Bright would write to recommend particular issues to her attention, and advise on which paper to read for the best coverage. Newspapers, and journals like *The Speaker* and *The Atlantic Monthly* were circulated among her family, providing further shared reference points. Mixing in such metropolitan radical circles, she met up-and-coming young men, such as Henry Fawcett, a great admirer of her father's whom she found 'most clever and interesting'. Her diary summary of the events of 1860 focused especially on political happenings, and revealed both the international scope of her interests, and the strong opinions she sometimes brought to them.[6]

Her ties with her aunts and cousins were maintained by exchanges of visits and by holidaying together.[7] She continued, of course, to have at hand the company of her great-aunt, Margaret Wood, with whom she often passed the time in the years immediately after her return from school, finding her 'as kind and cheery as ever'. Theirs was a particularly fond relationship that also provided Helen with the means to relieve by short stays at Mizzy any building tensions at One Ash. When Margaret Wood's strength began to fail in 1859 Helen Bright secured a bathchair so that she might take the invalid out and about. However frail physically, Margaret Wood retained her forcefulness of manner and her pleasure in company. On hearing a caller at Mizzy enquire if 'Old Margaret' still lived at the house, she sent a message for 'Old George' that she was still very much present in the world. Under her direction, Helen Bright extended her knowledge of cookery: 'I devote myself a good deal to make rice puddings, and pastries, and poaching eggs, and I am getting quite accomplished.' Aunt Wood, she reported, 'takes great pains to make me lick all the spoons and eat all the crumbs. Of course I make my bed, and wash up now and then.' Her great-aunt declared herself especially pleased with Helen on these accounts: 'she says I am not at all dainty and am very easy to suit, and fond of cheap things!'[8]

Margaret Wood's last illness overtook her shortly before Christmas 1859, and her nephews and nieces began to gather for her passing. She had continued to share her house with her niece, Jane Crosland, and her maid, Eliza Oldham, who had promised the Bancrofts that she would never leave while Margaret Wood still lived: 'I have a good home and I hope I do not under value it she has always been like a Mother to me and taught me most that I know.' This undertaking led Eliza Oldham to postpone consideration of, or put aside an offer of marriage: 'as for Marrying I feel pretty content wether I Marry this Man or not if he can do better for himself he is at liberty to do so.' Margaret Wood began her last letter to Joseph and Sarah Bancroft in November 1859, acknowledging receipt of payment of some interest. She explained that she could no longer write a long letter 'for I daily feel my weakness to increase', but that she remained able to enjoy 'a little good company'. She also reiterated her belief in the importance of letter writing among kin separated by distance, fearing that the connections that now existed between Bancrofts and their English relatives might cease once she died. Jane Crosland had to finish this letter for her, and expressed the hope that the correspondence might continue through herself. She told how a constant relay of family members now kept vigil by her aunt's bed, while old friends came to pay their last respects.[9]

Helen Bright was among those present at Margaret Wood's death: 'We were very thankful that it was all so peaceful at last.' Jane Crosland supplied a fuller account for her kin in the United States, telling of her aunt's increasing difficulties in breathing and restless nights disturbed by strange fancies. In the day time, Margaret Wood had received visitors as cheerfully and brightly as ever, though she reduced to tears one old friend who had asked how she was, by replying: 'Nothing to boast of' while adding: 'when thy turn comes, I hope thou may have an easier passage than mine'. When her final decline became evident the summons went out to nieces and nephews. Though she was by now rambling a good deal, she seemed to know each of them and frequently kissed their hands, 'saying with great earnestness "I want you – I want you to love the Lord God – do my love – do begin early. I know I have not done as I should have done – but do you."' The next morning she died 'without sigh or struggle'.[10] Nearing the first anniversary of her great-aunt's death, Helen Bright wrote to Margaret Tanner: 'It does not seem so long. I think there is no one whose memory is *greener* and more beloved than her amongst our own circle, and this season brings back all the circumstances of her illness with great vividness, especially to me, as I was a great deal with her, and it was the first death I had *personally* seen.' She found herself still looking across to Mizzy each morning and night 'as tho' I should find things just the same, just as they had been ever since I was born'. A few weeks later, bemoaning the 'normal state of mouselike seclusion' at One Ash, she recalled Margaret Wood as 'a host in herself, and always the kindest of friends and the best of company'.[11]

Jane Crosland and Eliza Oldham eventually returned to live at Mizzy some years after Margaret Wood's death, so it remained a place of retreat for Helen Bright. But she increasingly now complained of the seclusion of life at One Ash: 'Consequently no time is lost in morning calls, which is a great advantage, and duly estimated by me; but still it is rather too quiet – and so – and so, thou sees I have begun to wish for a pony', which she planned to name 'Abraham Lincoln'. Otherwise, she had to look to her dog for companionship: 'my faithful little Tiff, who keeps me in a state of perpetual internal laughter by his funny appearance, and whom I occasionally divert myself by dropping into ponds etc., after which he is always peculiarly affectionate and tries to dry himself on me.' Such a quiet life was invaluable for reading: 'the only thing that disgusts and puzzles me is why with such advantages I don't grow rapidly wiser.' She thought, perhaps, it was because she had 'too many irons in the fire', studying the work of Adam Smith while also curious to read 'the famous and much abused *Essays and Reviews*'. Her reading served also to reinforce her radical sympathies, so that Jefferson's memoirs and correspondence, for example, produced 'a very American and republican fit on me'.[12]

She also found an escape from her home life in the daily sewing classes she established early in the 1860s. The interruption to the trade in cotton during the American Civil War brought widespread unemployment to Lancashire, and this may have been part of a programme established by the Brights to ease the consequent distress among their employees. Such an obligation provided a legitimate means by which Helen Bright might escape the dominion of her stepmother, and she found that she could so arrange matters that it took up practically her whole day. She also enjoyed the companionship of the working-class young women who were her pupils, and the 'smiles and kind enquiries' she met with among them. Later, she extended her efforts to the provision of a night class for the young men in the factory: 'I wish I could do more for them. I should really enjoy teaching if I were better qualified for it.' Such undertakings only vexed her stepmother further, for M. E. Bright was evidently anxious about the extent of disease among working families and the threat it might pose to her own children. Helen Bright was unsympathetic to such concerns, insisting 'there is no fever prevalent that I know amongst the poor people'. She was similarly angered when her stepmother used a case of scarletina among their middle-class neighbours to cancel a meeting at One Ash of the local book society, even attempting to bring about its end altogether. Helen Bright was at this time its secretary, and reported: 'So we had a little scene, which made me devoutly glad I have a fair excuse for taking up any abode elsewhere than in this harmonious dwelling.'[13] Once again she retreated to Mizzy, using as an excuse the coming Monthly Meeting in Rochdale and the house guests it would bring. Visits to her far-flung kin also provided further escapes from One Ash, and in these years she became a regular visitor at the homes of Margaret Bright Lucas in London and of Priscilla Bright McLaren in Edinburgh.

Aunts and nieces

The election of Duncan McLaren to parliament in 1865 added to the many responsibilities of his wife, who now had also to manage a succession of temporary London households. Margaret Tanner remained unconvinced by Priscilla Bright McLaren's declared wish for a quieter and more settled life: 'she may be very weary sometimes, but if I am not *utterly* mistaken she is essentially in her element'.[14] Nonetheless, these new demands on her aunt provided Helen Bright with further excuses to visit London. She was absent on such a visit when a younger brother, Leonard, died from scarlet fever while holidaying with their parents at Llandudno. The grief of John and M. E. Bright was intensified by the separation they then had to endure from their other children until the fear of cross-infection had passed. They remained at Llandudno and buried their son there. Helen Bright's misery was increased by their failure to send her an account of her brother's death, or regular bulletins on the health of her other sisters and brothers. Though anxious to be with them, she had also to conclude that her duty lay in remaining with an exhausted Priscilla Bright McLaren, then nursing her own youngest child through scarlet fever.[15]

She was also always welcome, of course, among the Priestman family. As an unmarried woman, Helen Bright now began to fulfil the long-established kinship expectations of single nieces as companions and carers to aunts during illness – just as her widowed and unmarried aunts had undertaken her care as a child. Mary Priestman, for her part, increasingly in these years took over the care of an invalid niece, 'Rachie' (another Rachel) Priestman, the child of Lucy and Jonathan Priestman jnr. She was severely epileptic, needed constant nursing and had been declared uneducable. Mary Priestman spent several years travelling with her niece in search of a cure, and trying various water therapies in the hope at least of relieving the symptoms of the disease. She refused to accept medical advice that declared the case hopeless, and in time established a regimen that at least relieved the frequency and severity of the fits endured by Rachie. Though she was never able to walk, Rachie did learn to speak a little, and was able eventually to play and to express her delight in such play, and to cooperate with her aunt and nurses as they dressed and fed her. Margaret Tanner was among those grateful for the care Mary Priestman provided for Rachie, thanking her 'from my inmost heart for thy devotion to the precious little Lamb of our fold'. Helen Bright also occasionally helped her aunts with the care of her cousin, for example, on holidays at Cullercoats, where in earlier days her aunts had taught her the pleasures of the sea. Anna Maria Priestman was similarly called on to care for an aged aunt at Malton in her last years, and then to clear the old Priestman family home. So she and Mary Priestman were often apart, and themselves under strain. Helen Bright regularly came to help and cheer them, thereby also comforting Margaret Tanner: 'I don't doubt her visit has left a shining track.'[16]

Following her second marriage, Margaret Tanner led a life of domestic seclusion, in accord with the retiring temperament of her husband, one given over to gardening, sewing and the company of close family. But she was saddened equally by the family needs that kept them all apart, and the effect of such cares on the health of her sisters. When Mary Priestman travelled to Switzerland in the search of rest and medical treatment, Margaret Tanner supervised Rachie's care and was struck by the progress in the child's development. The financial position of the whole Priestman family, including Margaret and Arthur Tanner, had been seriously affected by the failure of the Newcastle and Durham District Bank, and in 1863 Jonathan Priestman died still regretting he was unable to leave his unmarried daughters legacies that would have ensured them an independence.[17] They had a small allowance each after the bank failure, and Helen Bright had written to Anna Maria Priestman hoping this change of family fortune was not making her feel very low: 'Puss [Mary Priestman] says why need you be so *very* miserable on £25 a year *at least*, independent of any business.'[18] But even pooling their resources left them unable to afford their own home. So for a time the sisters lived with their brother Hadwen Priestman and his wife, Emily, who had taken over Benwell House. Both, being more or less permanent invalids, were glad of such care, and usually spent the winter in warmer locations.

When helping Anna Maria and Mary Priestman to sort their parents' possessions after the death of Jonathan Priestman snr, Helen Bright came across some of the family papers gathered in by Rachel Priestman. These had evidently been collected over a lifetime, and stretched back in date to her Bragg and Priestman forebears in the latter decades of the eighteenth century. Helen Bright recognised that presently she had only a modest claim to such a legacy, at least compared to her aunts. But she had also observed how her great-aunt, Margaret Wood, and her Priestman grandmother and aunts, had set about the preservation of family memory, and how such memory had helped maintain the bonds between kin across time and space. Perhaps, as a motherless child, she was particularly aware of how such memory might strengthen a person's sense of selfhood. Whatever her reasons, she used the occasion to express her conviction as to the importance of preserving the papers collected by her grandmother, and her desire that they not be lost or destroyed.[19] After the deaths of Anna Maria and Mary Priestman they came into her keeping, together with additional material from the Wheeler and Tanner families that suggest the intervening custodianship of Margaret Tanner. Helen Bright in her turn was able to add material collected from the families of her father and her husband, keeping safe the memory of forebears, some of whom had died years before her own birth. The family history stored there served to confirm her sense of herself as a Dissenter, Quaker, Radical, reformer, humanitarian, philanthropist and political activist, as well as a daughter, sister, wife, mother, aunt, niece among the industrious, middling sort.

The Priestman–Bright circle and metropolitan radicalism

During a visit to London in 1865 Helen Bright was befriended by Clementia Taylor, wife of the Radical MP, P. A. Taylor. Their home, Aubry House, Kensington, was a centre of adult education for working-class women and men, as well as a social hub for local and visiting political activists. At the regular 'crushes' there, Helen Bright met many of her father's closest colleagues and controversial visitors to London like Garibaldi, the fighter for Italian independence, or Harriet Beecher Stowe, the author of *Uncle Tom's Cabin* (after whom Priscilla Bright McLaren named her second son, Walter Stowe Bright McLaren). Another friendship made at this time was with a visitor from the United States, the black abolitionist, Sarah Parker Remond, a 'very forceful and pleasant person' and among the first women publicly to speak in Britain on women's rights. Together they attended the lectures of Elizabeth Garrett, the first woman to practice as a doctor in Britain. Sarah Parker Remond was at this time training as a nurse, in preparation for a medical education.[20]

Helen Bright also attended the conference of the National Association for the Promotion of Social Science in Edinburgh. This body had for some years now provided a forum for discussion of areas of social reform, philanthropy and humanitarian goals. From the beginning, contributions from women reformers had been permitted, and increasingly women were ready to address its audiences directly (rather than have men read papers for them).[21] On this occasion, Helen Bright was introduced to Emily Davies, then at the forefront of the campaign for the higher education of women, including medical education. At a subsequent conference she heard Lydia Becker speak on the question of women's franchise. 'Universal suffrage' was the goal of many parliamentary reformers at this time, but it became increasingly clear that this demand was not as comprehensive as the term might suggest. Middle-class Radicals differed among themselves over the property and educational qualifications they thought appropriate to enfranchisement, criteria that largely reflected their own class interests. The inclusion of women in the demand was the concern only of ultra-Radicals like Clementia and P. A. Taylor.

The American civil war became the most absorbing international concern of the Priestman–Bright circle in the early 1860s, provoking complex reactions among abolitionist Friends such as these. For many, like the Priestmans, were both abolitionists and pacifists of long-standing. So even as they hoped for emancipation they remained appalled by the devastation of the war. A fear that Britain would be drawn into the conflict was said to have been particularly troubling to Jonathan Priestman in his last years.[22] Helen Bright was less ambivalent, and seemed at times almost to rejoice at the ferocity of battle and the defeat that confronted the South. While her Priestman aunts busied themselves on behalf of the Freedmen's Aid society, she discussed the rights and wrongs of a capital punishment for a Southern leader: 'Certainly he deserves it – and Lee quite as much – but it does not seem expedient to give them any chance of the glories of martyrdom.'[23] But news of the surrender of General Lee was followed shortly by reports of the assassination of Abraham Lincoln, 'a crime of surpassing horror' to Helen Bright as she recalled: 'How much we have loved and trusted the great hearted President.' She attended a meeting in Lancashire to express sympathy with the Americans, but the only women there, she thought, were herself and Jane Crosland. The recent sudden deaths also of Richard Cobden and Samuel Lucas caused her to write: 'This has been a melancholy month, so many good men lost.'[24]

That summer also brought elections that forwarded the cause of domestic reform, however, and more particularly of parliamentary reform. Among the circles in which Helen Bright moved, the issue of women's rights also began to take on more specific shape, in terms of a growing number of campaigns aimed at securing a range of new opportunities for women. Terms such as 'emancipation' and 'liberation' gained political currency through the anti-slavery movement and the struggles for national independence in Europe. The abolition of slavery in the United States, as well as the visits of nationalist leaders like Mazzini, Garibaldi and Kossuth, all posed the question of what constituted the basic conditions of freedom. These movements provided a language and a rhetoric that might be applied as much to the subordination of a sex as to the rights of enslaved peoples or subject nations. Possession of a vote in Britain remained the privilege of a small proportion of adult men, while women had for the first time been expressly excluded from the franchise in 1832.[25] The reform of the Poor Law in 1834 had also taken from women a long-standing right to take part in local government. The 1830s had, too, seen the complete erosion of the dower rights of widows. An ultraist current among Radical–Liberals asserted labour power as the basis of citizenship. But even this might serve to exclude married women from the franchise in Britain. For the legal doctrine of coverture denied them possession of their own person and thereby of the product of their labour; and all women were hampered by restrictive practices in education, the crafts and the professions.[26] Women in Britain came increasingly to understand that for many, including some Radical men, they did not constitute part of the nation – and that that nation was not always one in which they might take a pride, as the response of British administrations to rebellions in India and Jamaica had demonstrated.[27]

The movement for women's suffrage in Britain built on such concerns, and marked, in organisational terms, the emergence of Quaker women into leadership roles within the larger women's movement. Manchester was the power house of the movement, but women from a number of other provincial centres were increasingly drawn into what became by the end of the 1860s a national movement, and a number of these societies shortly established a coordinating body in London. The extensive kinship and friendship networks of Quaker women, networks that served to link the varying provincial centres to each other and to the metropolis, proved especially valuable at this stage.

Members of the Priestman–Bright circle played a prominent part not only in the formation of a number of the earliest provincial women's suffrage societies, in Manchester, Edinburgh, Bristol and Bath, but also in the London Society for Women's Suffrage. They were able to combine their position of influence in the provinces with the place they had established among the Radical political elite in London to challenge successfully for the direction of movement policy. The initial formulation of the demand was in terms of sexual equality, that is, the same qualifications for the vote for women as for men. This was not as straightforward as it seemed, given the effect of coverture on married women, and their inclusion or exclusion from the demand became one of the most divisive issues among women suffragists. In time, too, women suffragists increasingly demanded the vote in the name of those whose care was primarily the responsibility of middle-class women in the existing sexual division of labour: the sick, the poor and the oppressed.[28] Alongside her Bright and Priestman aunts, Helen Bright was among those women Friends who joined the campaign to have women included in the forthcoming Reform Bill. She did so at the same time as she was preparing for her marriage to William Stephens Clark.

The courtship and marriage of Helen Bright and William Clark

As a young woman, Helen Bright's attitude to marriage was cautious and uncertain, recording evidence that suggested to her it was 'a relationship that can be replaced with great facility'. She turned down an offer of marriage from John Thomasson, for example, someone for whom she felt a fondness all her life. He was a Unitarian, and the son of Thomas Thomasson, an old friend of her father's from League days. Thereafter, she remained sanguine about the possibility of marriage. She first met William Stephens Clark while staying with Margaret Tanner during the annual general meeting of Sidcot School, in the spring of 1864. Two of William Clark's sisters had helped her aunt manage a Cheddar school for the children of the working people there. Sometime after this first meeting they began to correspond, but by the end of the year she made clear to him some aspects of her views on religious matters that he found troubling. He had been raised among evangelically inclined Quakers, an influence that had continued when he attended Bootham school, and was taught by Fielden Thorp – an influential evangelical minister within the Society of Friends who was to marry one of his sisters, and go on to become headmaster of the school. Helen Bright, in contrast, leaned toward the Unitarian heresy that had, a generation before, prompted the evangelical current within the Society of Friends to attempt to impose doctrinal unity on their church. She read an essay William Clark sent her on this topic, but explained: 'It does not however much affect the grounds of my difference with you, as I had not doubted the antiquity and genuineness of the books of the New Testament. I reverence and love them, and not the less because I fail to see in them sufficient ground for believing that their writers claimed infallibility or that the divinely sent Son of Man was one with God except in the sense in which he himself prayed that all the world might be one with him.'[29]

The correspondence then lapsed until he wrote the following year to offer condolences on the death of her brother, Leonard, when he also made reference to the pain their earlier exchange had given him. She responded by explaining that she expected by such forthrightness to show him 'that I was a different person from what you had imagined, and that you would therefore not care for me'. This time, however, he persisted in his courtship, and Helen Bright then raised another issue that she thought needed to be clarified: 'It is right you should know that we are not at all rich – in fact I am quite poor. We live simply, but still in more style than we should but for Mama's property, and that is of course settled on her children.' People were apt to think her father wealthy because of the position he had attained in public life, but the opposite was the case, for politics entailed many expenses, and had prevented him from devoting more time to business. She added that her Priestman grandfather had lost most of his money in the failure of the Newcastle bank in 1857. William Clark assured her that he understood her financial circumstances, and that, like her, he preferred a simple lifestyle.[30]

Now she warned that should they marry, she would not adopt the retired ways of her uncle, Arthur Tanner, whose great aim, she explained, was 'to exclude the outer world – a newspaper possesses no attractions for him till it is two days old and a new book is never heard of'. Nor would she follow Margaret Tanner in her accommodation of a husband's preferences in such matters. She thought 'really disgraceful' the decision by a Clark cousin, Eliza Sturge, to promise obedience to her husband though their wedding had otherwise followed the Quaker form, declaring: 'She evidently was not "fitted for liberty".' Meanwhile, they continued, by letter, to test each other's views across a variety of political, social and religious questions. During these exchanges she succeeded in bringing some of his views into greater accord with her own, for example and perhaps most importantly, on the issue of women's rights. William Clark set about reading John Stuart Mill, becoming convinced thereby of the rightness of the demand for women's enfranchisement. Helen Bright responded that she was glad to hear it: 'The idea of your being in favour of universal suffrage whilst you excluded one half your race amused me.' In her turn, she expressed some sympathy with teetotalism – while retaining a right to drink the pale ale usually served during her holidays in Scotland with her father: 'I mean however to be very moderate – and so please don't send me any advice.'[31]

In September 1865 William Clark sought to move matters on by successfully approaching John Bright for his approval of such a marriage. Helen Bright refused any engagement, nonetheless, 'though I respect you, and prize your affection so much that I could never refuse it without pain'. But she suggested that he might come on a visit to One Ash, on pretence of wishing to see the Cooperative Society in Rochdale, which attracted distinguished visitors.[32] That visit, in early October 1865, at last convinced her to agree to marry, and her father visited Street shortly afterwards. Mary Priestman, perhaps the most determined spinster in this circle, sent a teasing letter, wondering how soon it would be before Helen Bright might be found saying ' "William wont let me do" so and so.' Her niece had apparently a habit of ridiculing other people for using such expressions, and now Helen Bright warned her future husband: 'I expect to carry out in practice what I have advocated in theory.' Even after this announcement, she continued to express doubts as to how they should 'get on', adding 'I don't like the feeling of being bound' while promising 'I will try to love you as you deserve dear William, and I hope it will all be right.' Following this letter, she had to assure him: 'It is not among my fears that you will be tyrannical, at all.' In the meantime, she encouraged further visits from him to One Ash, so that he might meet some of her closest friends.[33]

At times, she confessed repenting her decision, for Somerset sometimes seemed 'nothing less than exile', leading her to argue for a long engagement. At others she declared: 'Every year I feel to enjoy the country more, and to long more for a peaceful country life.' She was glad, too, not to be marrying a lawyer, like her friend, Kate Cobden: 'I am glad you are not in that unpleasant profession. There seems to me nothing so satisfactory as a plain manufacturing business – I mean a manufacture of something really useful. I would rather make the necessaries than the superfluities of society.' Nor, she admitted, would she have liked to marry a shopkeeper: 'I am afraid I am not quite free from the foolish prejudices which make a manufacturing business seem more honourable, or respectable than a shop. Isn't it truly shocking that with all my truly democratic convictions I should still have any of this feeling?'[34] She continued to speak her mind forcefully on political matters also. The Jamaica rebellion, she argued, was a direct legacy of slavery: 'What a pestilent race slaveholders everywhere are. It seems almost impossible to eradicate the wickedness implanted by slavery. For I look on these atrocities of the blacks as the result really of white crime.' She was deeply engaged by the political ferment that followed the execution of leading figures in the rebellion: 'One can hardly write about the latter, it is so dreadful.' She reported her father's view that the colonial administrators concerned should be tried for murder, and current attempts, through the Anti-Slavery Society, to raise a subscription to pay for legal advice on the matter. She herself would feel no compunction about a prosecution of men 'who are doing the fiend's work'. John Bright, she said, wanted to see them all hanged, 'strong opponent of capital punishment as he is'. To her mind also, such punishment would be 'a bagatelle compared with this wholesale butchery committed by officials and if there be a law inflicting the death penalty it ought to be carried out. Every day the whole affair assumes a more appalling aspect.'[35]

She also continued to attend major demonstrations in support of the Reform Bill, sometimes with her father, sometimes with her old schoolfriend, Harriet Crosfield. Contemplating her new life, she argued the necessity for subscribing to both American and British newspapers, and insisted: 'I must take the *Manchester Examiner*, or I should really feel exiled.' She also continued to reject any efforts on his part to reform her religious views: 'I discovered in your last letter the clue to your otherwise inexplicable attraction towards me. It must be your love of a missionary life that led you to think you might do me some good.' She was impatient, too, at a letter from Fielden Thorp, his evangelical brother-in-law and former schoolmaster, giving William Clark a good character, but 'written with nearly as much stiffness as a testimonial and quite as vague ... It will take me some time to compile a suitable reply.'[36] In the meantime, in the months before her wedding she determined to spend as long as possible in London with her father: 'Mama will try to persuade me it is my duty to stay here – but I don't see it so at all.' She continued to enjoy the access to political life afforded her as John Bright's daughter: 'I am always thirsting after a London life when anything interesting is going on and am very much dissatisfied with myself for being discontented.' She also planned a visit to Margaret Tanner so as to be near the home of William Clark, mocking the opinion of her stepmother that it would be undignified: 'You know I am not much accustomed to go by Mama's rules.'[37]

They were to set up home in a former farmhouse beside the factory. William Clark planned some extensions, perhaps a large drawing room, so as to approach a little closer the spaciousness of One Ash. On such matters she declared herself 'very practical', desiring nothing beyond their means. She resisted a subsequent suggestion from her Priestman aunts that John Bright buy the more substantial 'Elmhurst' for the couple, arguing it would be too expensive for them to run. But she emphasised the need for a large and comfortable kitchen: 'I don't like the idea of servants being shut up in a close kitchen.' She worried about the niceties of housekeeping that might be expected of her, especially by Margaret Tanner: 'I am a little afraid she may overwhelm me with questions and suggestions about all sorts of arrangements, as they are her forte, and poor thing, she has not much else to occupy herself with.' Books were to be an important part of the furnishing of her home, and the couple had already begun to plan those they would read together after their marriage. She bought Draper's *History of the Intellectual Development of Europe*, a copy of 'dear old Adam Smith', and told of the gift of a copy of Buckle's history, and John Thomasson's present of eleven volumes of the work of Hugh Miller. Subsequently, she bought Harriet Martineau's *History of the Peace*, as part of the reading she was planning for their honeymoon.[38]

From Somerset she went to London, taking lodgings there with Anna Maria Priestman and spending evenings with Clementia Taylor, when she met Elizabeth Garrett, and Frances Power Cobbe, another figure who was gaining prominence in the growing movement for women's rights. She listened to W. E. Gladstone speak during the debate on the Reform Bill, observed her father and J. S. Mill sitting side by side, and heard her father being vilified by one of his most vociferous enemies. Helen Clark wished 'the liberal portion of the Cabinet ... had had courage to propose a broader measure to contend with and let those leave who would not heartily support it.'[39] She then returned home to attend a great Reform meeting that her father was to address in Rochdale, and secured seats for herself and a woman companion, noting the presence also of a few more women, 'some of whom seemed very enthusiastic'. She estimated the hall had held about 6,000, and reported it the most 'attentive, pleasant, good humoured meeting' she had ever attended. Afterwards she returned to London to observe the progress of the Bill in parliament, and to attend the final lectures of Elizabeth Garrett, whose 'pluck and character' she greatly admired. There she met Helen Taylor, stepdaughter to J. S. Mill. His speech on the Bill she regarded as one of the most noble ever made, combining powerful reasoning with 'a generous kindly heart ... I never feel any enthusiasm about intellect alone, that is if it is not directed and illuminated by the moral part'. Her father told her he did not know when he had been happier during a debate: 'he felt as if someone had given him a fortune.' At her suggestion, Mary Priestman planned to give as a wedding present all Mill's works bound in leather. Some days later Helen Bright had the chance to hear Mill debate, rising to speak, she thought, 'like a ministering Friend under a heavy "concern"'. She recorded how the House listened 'in perfect quiet to the enunciation of a Christian morality to which they are too little accustomed ... And this is the man who is called an infidel by many people! Aunt Tilla [Priscilla Bright McLaren] wishes we might have such infidelity to preach in the pulpits every Sunday.'[40]

By now she was able to write to her future husband: 'I miss you dear William, but the pleasant impression of your visit remains, and I really think of the little house with increasing pleasure and diminishing alarm.' Like him, she was beginning to wish the ordeal of the wedding itself was over, but her parents decided on a date in July. In London she watched Kate Cobden trying on 'her wedding toggery', and was then taken by Priscilla Bright McLaren to buy her own wedding dress. Her aunt persuaded her to buy a light moire silk at considerably greater cost than John Bright had anticipated. Afterwards, she confessed herself 'quite oppressed at the thought of it'. Then she and her aunt went looking at furniture together. In addition to all these preparations she was also engaged in helping organise a petition for women's inclusion in the Reform Bill. John Stuart Mill had agreed to press for such an amendment, provided some hundreds of signatures could be obtained from women in support of the demand. She had given the name of Eleanor Clark, William's mother, in the hope that 'your independent Street lady Friends might take an interest in the subject'. Annie Clark, one of her future sisters-in-law, took up the challenge and collected signatures there, while Helen Bright on her return to Rochdale took the petition round her friends and neighbours. She collected eighteen or nineteen signatures and had 'a good deal of amusement' in the process. She had been more favourably received than she had expected, and met with only one refusal, adding: 'The request of the petition is extremely moderate, which I think is the highest praise in most people's estimation.'[41]

Figure 9.1 The wedding party for Helen Bright and William Clark, One Ash, Rochdale, 1866

The Reform Bill was at this time running into difficulties: 'The Bill and the Govt seem indeed in a terrible mess. The conduct of the Tory Party is so glaringly disgraceful that one would think it would alienate the whole country from them.' John Bright she reported 'very much disgusted and disheartened', while she commented, 'it is really sad to see the struggle so slight a measure needs'. For her part, while collecting signatures for the women's suffrage petition she found 'what Friends call considerable seriousness and openness to conviction. I sowed what little good seed I could and hoped no enemy in the shape of husbands or brothers would come after and sow tares'. In such asides, Helen Bright gave expression to the religious resonance with which she imbued her political efforts, and the impossibility, in her experience, of disentangling public questions from the private politics of family life. The 'Jamaica report' further dismayed Radicals such as these, but they were delighted when John Stuart Mill was made chairman of the new committee seeking justice for the victims of the summary executions that had followed the rebellion: 'He will fight any tiger – or all the tigers in the world.'[42]

Shortly before her wedding, Helen Bright sat up with her father, talking over her future: 'He always tells me I shall "find out" various things – meaning chiefly that I shall have no more of my own way after we are married.' She learned that her stepmother's main reservation concerning her marriage was the youth of William Clark: 'I suppose she thinks you wont be *master* enough!' When she responded that she looked forward to them 'muddling along together', her father 'laughed sarcastically and said no doubt we should have abundant opportunity of doing so'. It irked her that he 'always persists in believing me totally destitute of both sense and experience, which rather nettles me'. Some of her Priestman kin at least thought the marriage one of convenience for the Brights, reflecting M. E. B.'s wish to be relieved of her rebellious step daughter and John Bright's wish for a quiet life. Certainly, Helen Bright came to see her marriage as having provided her with the first loving home of her own that she had known since infancy. As the day of the marriage approached, William Clark was scolded for proposing to come to Rochdale the night before: 'Just imagine if the engine broke down. Besides I shall want you to comfort me and screw up my courage.' She was not miserable, but 'very grave and rather frightened and tired'. She suggested they make it known that they would like a very short meeting on the occasion of their marriage: 'I will threaten to faint otherwise – a thing I never did in my life.' Her future husband's phlegmatic manner was another worry: when they came together in the Meeting House to announce their choice of each other as husband and wife, she instructed, 'pray look as tho' we had met before that morning!'[43]

10 Marriage, money and the networked family

Street village and the firm of C. & J. Clark

Helen and William Clark named their first home 'Greenbank', after the Bright family home in Rochdale. She began housekeeping with two servants, and the help of a gardener once a week to provide produce for the table. Her day began with breakfast at 7.30, after which she and William Clark would 'prowl about our small domain' till the factory bell rang at 8.45.[1] The working day in the factory began at 6.30 in the morning. and finished at 6.30 in the evening. Street was an old stop on coaching routes from Exeter to Bath, Bristol and London and still largely an agricultural village. Farms bordered the main village street, including that of Joseph Clark I, William's grandfather. His family had farmed in the surrounding villages for more than 300 years, and had long belonged to the Society of Friends. By 1866, tanneries and sheepskin and shoe manufacture were an increasingly large part of the growing economy of the 'village', however, as Street became a centre of factory production.[2]

The Clark family had played a large role in this change: Cyrus Clark, the middle of three sons, had been apprenticed to the largest tannery in the village and, after marrying the daughter of a glove maker, set up a tannery of his own beside their house. Subsequently, he took his younger brother, James Clark, as his apprentice. As a means of making some pocket money, the latter began in his spare time to make slippers from remnants cut from the sheepskin rugs produced in the tannery. He found a ready market for these 'Brown Petersburgs' with the help of a cousin, Charles Gilpin (later a member of parliament), who was at this time a draper's apprentice in Bristol.[3] These homely commodities became the foundation for a partnership formed by the two younger Clark brothers in 1826, which soon expanded into shoemaking and in time grew into the international company that has since become a high-street presence. So from its very beginnings, C. & J. Clark demonstrated the value to middle-class enterprise of the 'networked family', and the importance of kinship to its functioning.[4]

In the early days of the firm, most of the manufacture was 'put out' to shoemakers in Street and its environs, and made up in workshops in their homes from leather supplied by C. & J. Clark. Wives and daughters might undertake some of the lighter processes, like the 'closing' or sewing together of the uppers, and such shops might also employ apprentices.[5] The Clark brothers introduced the first factory process to Street, building a cutting room that employed only one man in 1829, to supply outworker shoemakers with the pieces for sewing.[6] James Clark subsequently married Eleanor Stephens of Bridport, a former governess, and daughter of a sometime china painter of Bristol turned draper. She brought a marriage portion of £300, while James Clark settled £1,000 on her. They built a house alongside the factory, Netherleigh, where they raised a family of fourteen children, among whom was William Stephens Clark (see Figure 10.1).[7]

Though this family business continued to grow, it also regularly encountered financial problems in the 1840s, caused in part by an unclear demarcation between C. & J. Clark and other family enterprises. Cyrus Clark was also partner with his older brother, Joseph Clark II, in a corn-factoring business, for example. This bought cargoes of corn from their Sturge cousins, Joseph and Charles, in Birmingham, often selling them on at profit before payment was required by their suppliers. According to the account subsequently written by William Clark, the speculative nature of this enterprise was of great concern to his father, James, who sought to persuade his partner and brother to give it up. For the corn factoring often needed to draw on the shoe and rug business to meet its debts. So when the corn business fell into difficulties, the financial standing of C. & J. Clark was also undermined.[8] These problems came to a head in 1840 to 1842, when the brothers faced bankruptcy, and considered emigration. Bankruptcy was one of the grounds for disownment by the Society of Friends, and close relatives were expected to help wherever possible to avoid business failures. In this instance, relatives of the Clark brothers provided loans, and mediated with the firm's creditors. Further loans from family members were needed by C. & J. Clark in the years that followed. The firm's success at the Great Exhibition of 1851 brought some improvement in its fortunes in the early 1850s, though it remained £6,000 in debt to a Clark relative at this time, while poor book-keeping hid its continuing losses.[9]

The eldest son of James Clark, William, joined the company after leaving Bootham School in 1855.[10] He was especially interested in the mechanisation of production, helping invent new machinery, introducing industrial sewing machines from the United States in 1856 (transatlantic networks were helpful here), and recruiting and training three women shoemakers to operate them. Though initially resistant to moving their workplace to the factory, the three women were persuaded by the much higher wages they could earn in machine production. The way to further mechanisation and the adoption of the factory system of production was paved by the shift to riveting boots, rather than sewing them. In the 1860s C. & J. Clark moved rapidly in this direction under the influence of William Clark. He later argued that the factory system

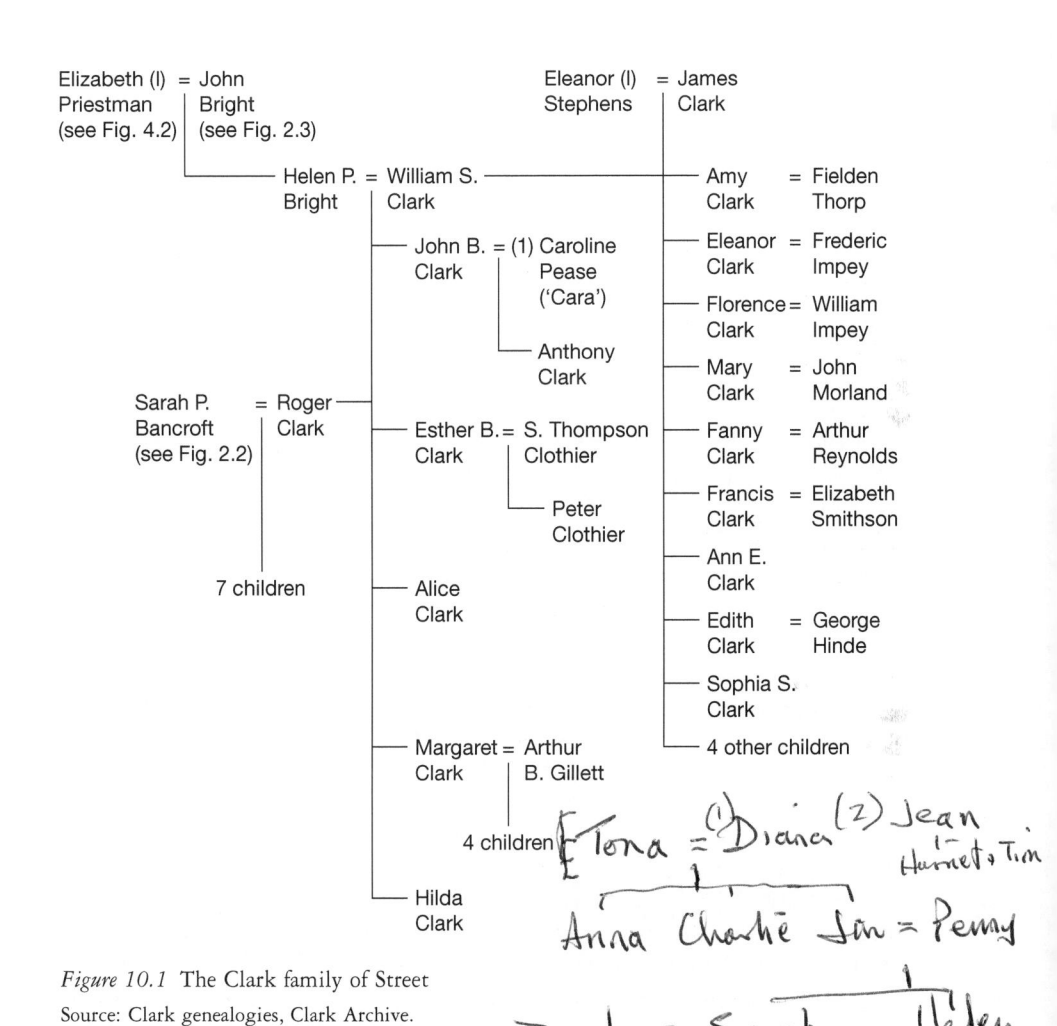

```
Elizabeth (I)  = John                        Eleanor (I)  = James
Priestman      | Bright                      Stephens     | Clark
(see Fig. 4.2) | (see Fig. 2.3)
               |
               └─── Helen P. = William S. ──────────────── Amy      = Fielden
                    Bright     Clark                      Clark      Thorp
                         │
                         ├─── John B.   = (1) Caroline    Eleanor  = Frederic
                         │    Clark      |   Pease         Clark     Impey
                         │               |   ('Cara')
                         │               |               ─ Florence = William
                         │               └── Anthony       Clark     Impey
                         │                   Clark
 Sarah P.     = Roger ───┤                                ─ Mary    = John
 Bancroft     | Clark    │                                  Clark     Morland
 (see Fig. 2.2)          ├─── Esther B. = S. Thompson     ─ Fanny   = Arthur
                         │    Clark      | Clothier        Clark     Reynolds
                         │               |
                         │               └── Peter        ─ Francis = Elizabeth
                         │                   Clothier      Clark     Smithson
         │
         │                                                ─ Ann E.
    7 children                                              Clark
                         ├─── Alice
                         │    Clark                       ─ Edith   = George
                         │                                  Clark     Hinde
                         │
                         │                                ─ Sophia S.
                         │                                  Clark
                         ├─── Margaret = Arthur
                         │    Clark    | B. Gillett       ─ 4 other children
                         │             |
                         │        4 children  ┌ Tona =(1) Diana (2) Jean
                         │                    │                 Harriet, Tim
                         │                    │
                         │                    Anna  Charlie  Ian = Penny
                         └─── Hilda                                │
                              Clark                Paul = Sarah   Helen
                                                         │
Figure 10.1 The Clark family of Street              Rachel  Alex
Source: Clark genealogies, Clark Archive.
```

provided regular hours of work in an orderly setting, and saved apprentices from exploitation by their masters who effectively became middle-men, and who provided erratic patterns of work reflecting their drinking habits.[11] The mechanisation of production at larger centres of shoemaking, like Northampton, was met by widespread strike action. But in Street, it is suggested, C. & J. Clark were isolated from such protest, while the better wages available in their factory offered an attractive alternative for some of the worst-paid agricultural workers in the country.[12]

Despite these innovations, C. & J. Clark faced a fresh financial crisis in 1863. An independent examination of the books suggested that Cyrus Clark now owed the firm nearly £11,000, while James Clark retained a little over £900 in capital in the business. Large loans remained unpaid among the kin who had previously helped keep the company afloat. Subsequently, the net deficiency in the business was shown to be nearer £12,000. When the other assets of Cyrus and James Clark were investigated, Cyrus's account remained in deficit by £4,800, while James Clark was in surplus by £4,450, still leaving a net deficiency. During a private enquiry into the firm's difficulties organised by kin, William Clark prepared a business plan that convinced those concerned that the firm remained viable. Fresh backers were found to bring the firm's loan capital to £19,000. The condition of these loans was that both Cyrus and James Clark relinquish management of the firm, which was now to be placed in the hands of William Clark. In practice, James Clark continued to assist his son with the management of the rugmaking business, but the poor health of Cyrus Clark had already largely removed him from an active role in the firm. Under the conditions of the loan James Clark was allowed to remove no more than £300 a year from the business, while Cyrus Clark was allowed to withdraw only £200 a year. The two brothers entered a new seven-year partnership on this basis in 1864, giving each an interest in the business until the end of that period. The firm's debts were almost cleared over the next decade under the management of William Clark.[13]

So at the time he met Helen Bright he was a young man with a growing reputation for business energy and acumen. He was also a famed athlete locally and was coming to the fore in the associational life of Street and nearby Glastonbury. With his father and Clark uncles he campaigned, too, for improvement in the sanitary conditions of these two towns, through the establishment of a public health board. This was resisted by local landowners for it meant higher rates. They saw the setting up of such a board as a hidden way of subsidising local manufacturers like the Clarks, and argued that these interests should be dealing themselves with nuisances that arose principally from the processes in their tanneries and factories. While he maintained an interest in farming, a figure such as William Clark came to stand for the arrival of a new class within these rural communities, and one inimical to the interests of the established elite there. This new presence saw itself, however, as representing the forces of progress.[14]

The Greenbank family circle and Sophia Sturge Clark (1849–1933)

During the first few months of her marriage Helen Clark began to build closer friendships among her husband's kin. The Clarks shared many of the humanitarian and reform interests common among the Priestman–Bright circle. As a young woman, her mother-in-law, Eleanor Clark, had campaigned on behalf of the radical member for Bridport, Samuel Romilly, for example. Like the Brights and Priestmans, the Clarks had early taken a role in the anti-slavery and temperance movements. And like the Brights and the Priestmans, the Clarks had established an essay society. This regularly produced a manuscript 'Village Album' where contributors practised essay and poetry writing, recounted recent travels, or provided illustrations. So the domestic culture she encountered in Street was one in which Helen Clark immediately felt at home. Her relationship with Eleanor Clark remained cordial, though her mother-in-law in the years before her death became a semi-invalid who kept increasingly to her room, and this prevented them, perhaps, from becoming closer. There were social evenings 'hopping' at the home in Street of some Clark cousins, the Impey family, allowing Helen Clark to joke at her husband's expense: 'We had a pleasant evening, and some dancing, and owing entirely to William's love of dissipation did not get back till nearly 12.'[15] The religious differences between Helen Clark and her husband were never resolved, and while William Clark feared sometimes for her salvation, Helen Clark maintained a mocking disregard for such concerns. In time she learnt to be more careful of his feelings in such matters, while for his part, early worries over the danger to his wife's soul diminished as he observed her essential goodness, most especially in terms of her constant readiness to help and support those in need in their community.

Helen Clark's passion for radical politics and the growing number of campaigns on behalf of women's rights, on the other hand, was shared by her husband and his family. William Clark's sister, Mary Morland and her husband, John, for example, were to join with Helen and William Clark in building up Liberal Party organisation in their predominantly agricultural constituency. Annie Clark was about to set out on a course that led her to an independent life as a professional woman, following the example of Elizabeth Garrett in her pursuit of a medical education.[16] Helen Clark had threatened her husband that she would leave Street if Annie Clark ever married and moved away. Now she wrote to express her sadness at this parting: 'I shall try to comfort myself with thinking of you as one who is really doing something definite for women.' She was equally admiring of the support provided by her parents-in-law, in constrast to the situation of her cousin, Agnes McLaren, who had to overcome her father's opposition to her plans to train as a doctor.[17] Both women were among the pioneer women medical students at Edinburgh who gathered around Sophia Jex Blake.[18]

Another of her sisters-in-law, Sophia Sturge Clark (1849–1933), became a frequent visitor to Greenbank, attracted by the vitality of Helen Clark and the encouragement she received there to overcome her diffidence; as the tenth child she evidently felt overshadowed by her older sisters, and unsure of her place in the world. The account Sophia Clark left in her diaries of her life as a young woman show her days filled largely with cooking, ironing and sewing; supporting male kin in various associations in the town, most notably those advocating temperance; or providing nursery assistance for Mary Morland and Helen Clark. These diaries convey a sense of intense claustrophobia and record her uneasy relationship with the two sisters, Edith and Annie Clark, who, like her, were still single and therefore expected to assist parents, aunts and married sisters. These three seemed to dislike each other's company at this time and constantly squabbled. Helen Clark made clear her liking for Sophia Clark, an unusual experience it would seem from her diaries, and showed her a kindness that soothed her sometimes troubled emotions. So Greenbank became for Sophia Clark a valued retreat. There she also found an unaccustomed opportunity to contribute to conversation and put forward views of her own, and to join in rambles, canoeing and croquet. In sum, her brother's home gave her greater space in which to develop a clearer sense of identity beyond that of daughter-at-home.

Sophia Clark had grown up during the worst of her family's financial difficulties, and her mother was anxious to ensure that her single daughters were able to support themselves. A suggestion came from Fanny Reynolds, one of her older married daughters, who lived with her growing family in Bridport where her husband had a draper's shop. She and some other mothers of young children, unable to afford a governess in their own homes, began to talk of the possibility of together supporting the establishment of a local kindergarten. If Sophia Clark were interested in such an undertaking she might live with the Reynolds family, but she would first have to undertake some further education, and this would need to be paid for. Lydia Rous (former governess to the Brights) was now headmistress of the Mount School in York, and had established a short programme of training for young women who wished to teach. Eleanor Clark discussed these possibilities in letters to her husband, suggesting that they might apply for assistance from their son-in-law, Fielden Thorp, at Bootham. He had already become a good friend to Sophia Clark, sympathising and guiding her during periods of religious doubt, and he duly agreed to help with her fees at the Mount. Sophia Clark looked back on these few months as among the happiest in her life, when she enjoyed a freedom from domestic obligations, together with fresh social circles and the opportunity to make new friends among women of her own age.[19]

On completing her course, she moved to Bridport where she set up a kindergarten and continued her studies at the School of Art there. Her evenings and weekends were spent helping her sister in household chores and the care of her young nieces and nephews. At first, she enjoyed her new environment, but she never settled to her role as a teacher, constantly reprimanding herself for losses of temper with her class, and disappointed at the limited response she was able to draw from them. She was homesick, too, while her relationship

Figure 10.2 Sophia S. Clark (1849–1933) in middle age

with Fanny Reynolds appears slowly to have deteriorated, so that Sophia Clark began to feel her presence in her sister's home was resented. Increasingly she focused on the summer holidays when she might return home to Street. Her parents also wished her return: their financial position was improving as the family firm became more and more successful under the direction of William Clark; Sophia Clark had now a profession to which she might return if the need ever arose; and the health of Eleanor Clark was now so uncertain that she needed more assistance with management of her household.[20]

Sophia Clark began to look for a purchaser for her small school. It took more than a year to sell, but at last she returned home. For reasons that remain unclear, she subsequently took a position at a school in Cornwall, again almost certainly linked to family connections there. But shortly she fell ill with typhoid. Her mother came to nurse her, and it was some months before Sophia Clark had sufficient strength for the journey home to Street. She only ever taught occasionally after this, sometimes as a service to her family – she provided Helen Clark's oldest child with his first lessons – and for a time set up a kindergarten for the children of local working people. But principally she returned for the time being to her role as an unmarried daughter-at-home, and devoted aunt to her numerous nieces and nephews.[21]

Eleanor Clark died in 1879, seemingly simply worn out with bearing fourteen children and caring for the twelve who survived childhood. Sophia Clark's diary entries from this time suggest a sense of loss, but also an odd feeling of detachment, as if her mother had been a mystery to her. She and her unmarried sister, Edith, remained at home to share housekeeping for their father, a position that seems only to have increased the tensions between them. Subsequently, they accompanied him to the United States for a family wedding, and Edith Clark met her future husband on the voyage. Sophia Clark became the only single daughter remaining at home, caring for her father, and at last finding some enjoyment in her position. Shortly, however, she was called to Birmingham to nurse one of her married sisters there, Florence Impey, another consumptive who was losing her battle with tuberculosis. Sophia Clark was fond of this older sister, and drew some comfort from the care she was now able to provide. She was shortly displaced in this role, however, by the arrival of Annie Clark, who had recently completed her medical studies in the United States and hurried straight to Birmingham. Thereafter, Sophia Clark remained at home to care for her father, while Annie Clark subsequently settled in Birmingham and built a successful medical career there.

Motherhood

Helen Clark became seriously ill with a debilitating 'rheumatic' illness during her first return to One Ash in October 1866. She was confined to her bed each day until dinner time, commenting in a letter to her husband: 'It is a stupid plan. Cousin Jane [Crosland] kindly came and entertained me, but Papa never came near me.' Helen Clark told her husband: 'It seems very odd to be without you. I should not wish to become used to it.' Shortly, however, her condition worsened and her Aunt Selina Bright came to nurse her through an illness that left her too weak to travel for several weeks. She wrote to William Clark: 'I cant help in my inmost heart being glad that you miss me and want me back so much [laugh sign] because to be loved is so sweet and I am so dependant on it – I long to be with you very much.' But she also felt it in both their interests that she convalesce before returning home: 'To tell the truth I am rather nervous and ready to do anything rather than become chronically rheumatic.' John Bright had spoken to her 'most solemnly' about the trouble and expense she would become to her husband if she did not preserve her health, adding: 'I could not help laughing so much that he was rather angry.'[22] She was now well enough to read, and whiled away the time with a book by Henry Fawcett on the economic position of the British labourer. As she prepared at last to return to Street, she wrote to William Clark: 'I have a great secret to tell thee – or to speak more correctly, I may have, but I shall reserve it till we meet.'[23] She was pregnant with their first child.

Over the next few months she was busy with visitors and political meetings in support of the Reform Bill, but as the time of her confinement approached she once again became ill, with pleurisy. Several of her aunts once more undertook nursing her, and she wrote to William Clark: 'I think you may be very glad you have married somebody with Aunts [laugh sign].' Describing the arrangements she was making for the nursery, she commented: 'I hope I don't tease you with domestic details and suggestions. Perhaps it is drawing you from your proper sphere [laugh sign].' In a more reflective tone she wrote: 'to tell the truth I feel a vacuum when you go away! The stimulus seems gone.' But she continued to mend 'and I feel that in this as in so much more beside I have the greatest cause for thankfulness, and for a quiet trust in the future'. As she convalesced with Margaret Tanner at Oakridge, she continued to follow elections and parliamentary debates in the newspapers, and to exchange political news and views with old friends.[24]

When the expected date of her confinement approached, in August 1867, Nurse Galbraith arrived and, with the help also of her mother-in-law, Helen Clark delivered a son. She later recorded, 'I fell asleep afterwards and woke well and rested.' She was glad she had decided against having a doctor to superintend the birth: 'W's mother was the very best person I could have had with me. Everything has happened most comfortably. It seems very dreamy to own this baby.' Selina Bright once again came to nurse her and she wrote to her Priestman aunts: 'I have felt perfectly well ever since Baby was born, and am rather tired of being kept lying down.' After ten days she was allowed to leave her bed and wrote: 'I enjoy the feeling of having taken a new lease of life, as it were, and of *William*, who is a thousand times more delightful than the Baby.'[25]

Naming the child apparently gave little trouble, for she and her husband had agreed that he be named John Bright Clark in honour of her father. Helen Clark kept a delighted, watchful interest over the child's development.

In temperament, she reported him 'excessively festive and active and sweet' and 'a delightful little companion, and tho fond of mischief is always very good, always reasonable and never passionate'.[26] By the time the child was about eighteen months old, the Clarks were employing a nursemaid with whom he now slept. The Ashworth sisters also came to inspect the baby, 'examining it much as a geologist would a queer new fossil'. One of the few criticisms she levelled at William Clark was his inability to relate to babies, contrasting this with a picture of John Thomasson cradling his newborn: 'I could not help wishing thou cared as much for a baby.' She had five more children, another son, Roger, and four daughters, Esther, Alice, Margaret and Hilda, this last named for 'the famous Saxon Abbess who ruled men and women from the wild Cliff at Whitby'.[27]

Helen Clark was by now sometimes overwhelmed by the demands of her immediate family, her widely dispersed kin and her political and philanthropic commitments. When she feared herself pregnant again only a few months after the birth of Margaret, she wrote to William Clark: 'I am very low because of my inside, which has shown no signs of coming right – and I feel tempted sometimes to be angry with thee.' In the event, her fears proved unfounded, but she remained away from home for many weeks, searching for a cure among the various water therapies for the severe rheumatism she suffered from time to time.[28] She was irritable and irascible during her last pregnancy, again staying from home for some months and again visiting various water cure establishments to ease her rheumatism. The other children spent three weeks with their Priestman great aunts to allow Helen Clark some rest prior to her confinement, 'the greatest possible relief'. Hilda, her last child, was born in 1881 and she teased her aunts by declaring: 'The Baby is a most uninteresting red thing, and we are all rather at a loss what to do with it as we only wanted a boy, tho' I don't know but that I like a girl in the abstract better.'[29]

The style of parenting of the Clarks was intimate: the smallest child might play around Helen Clark as she brought her household accounts up to date; or sit on William Clark's lap as he had breakfast, begging bites from his plate; or sleep in the Clarks' bedroom, and sometimes in Helen Clark's own bed, for she generally sought such comfort when William Clark was away from home. Both parents shared their love of reading, and especially of poetry, with their children, who were introduced to Milton, for example, from the age of three or four if they showed any pleasure in his work. Both Helen and William Clark also enjoyed outdoor pursuits, taking their children rambling, riding, swimming, skating, sailing and canoeing. There were regular seaside holidays at nearby Burnham, too. Helen Clark had the assistance of a series of nursemaids when her children were young, some of whom remained family friends for many decades after they left her employment, usually to marry.

As soon as a new baby's dependence on her lessened, Helen Clark returned to her work within her local community in which educational provision remained her principal interest at this time. The Clark family had long lent their support to a British School, the principal provider of education for the children of working people in Street, funded largely by voluntary contributions. The Education Act of 1870 allowed for the raising of a local rate to support the establishment of public schools, and Helen Clark reported how the larger part of her Clark kin had now decided to stop supporting the British School so as to 'force a rate and a board'. William Clark's uncle, Joseph Clark II, held by the voluntary principle, however, and was so outraged he declared he would have nothing more to do with educational provision for the town if such a board were established. Helen Clark wrote to the Priestman sisters: 'We only hope he will stick to his laudable resolve [laugh sign].' The school board that was subsequently established became a recurring topic for mirth and mockery in Helen Clark's letters, as she recounted the ensuing battles in which Liberal Clarks defeated Tory Anglicans. But the board provided her and Sophia Clark with their first opportunities for public office, as women were allowed to serve on, as well as vote for such boards.[30]

As her children grew Helen Clark was increasingly able to draw on her aunts to relieve her of their care for longer periods, most especially Anna Maria and Mary Priestman. The years before the marriage of Helen and William Clark had been difficult ones for the two sisters as they struggled to keep themselves on the limited resources that their father had been able to leave them. These appear largely to have been in dividends on shares in the family firm, which they received in quarterly sums. Though they pooled their small incomes, they were able at this time to live together only in the homes of kin: the last of their Malton aunts, or one of their two brothers, or the Tanners' home in Somerset. They continued a peripatetic life for some years after their father's death, with frequent separations, as each nursed or otherwise helped different family members. Mary Priestman also continued to care for Rachie and to pursue a cure for her epilepsy.

By the late 1860s, however, Mary and Anna Maria Priestman had garnered enough money, in part through legacies, to realise their plan to establish an independent household of their own. They settled in Bristol, close to Margaret Tanner and to Helen Clark, and rented a house there in one of the newer suburbs, Durdham Park. Rachie now lived with them permanently, so their staff included a nursery nurse as well as a cook and a maid. The Durdham Park and Oakridge households became extensions of one another, sharing household produce and sometimes servants, nursing or providing holidays for each other's sick servants, and giving hospitality to each others' visitors. Both households received frequent visits from Helen Clark and her children in the years ahead. The hospitality of the Priestman sisters made it possible for their niece to leave various of her children with one or other of them as she shopped, visited or attended meetings in Bristol, Bath and London. She regretted only how much their charges were indulged during such visits, especially by Anna Maria Priestman. She even began to consider whether more sense was to be found at One Ash with regard to managing the mischief of children. But she was grateful that Margaret Tanner retained her skill in bringing unruly children to sweet reasonableness.

Family, money and business

The death of Cyrus Clark, a few months after the marriage of Helen and William Clark, brought fresh financial worries for the firm he had founded with his brother. For though Cyrus Clark had effectively bowed out of the business by the late 1850s, and had withdrawn considerable sums from it before then, one of his sons, Beavan Clark, claimed he should inherit some share in the firm. This claim evidently met with sympathy among others of their kin. The practice of Friends was to resolve such disputes through private arbitration rather than through the courts. A preliminary 'conference' was held early in 1868, when, Helen Clark recorded, 'Wm spoke very plainly, the state of things clearly represented. Beavan, W and myself the only young people present.' She herself believed the claim to be quite unwarranted: 'I think there never was such a case of folly, so injurious every way to himself as Beavan's.' The findings of the arbitrators supported the claim of William and James Clark that the estate of Cyrus Clark had few remaining rights in the partnership, and the matter appeared settled. But Beavan Clark subsequently renewed his claim to a share in C. & J. Clark. Arbitrators were again called in, and another settlement was reached that left the business with James and William Clark on payment of a lump sum to Beavan Clark.[31] He declined an invitation to use that sum to join a new undertaking being planned by his uncle and cousin, and set up in a quite different business of his own. Even so, his family remained bitter over the matter for some time to come, and William Clark wrote a lengthy account of the firm's history as a record of how his and his father's capital and labour had kept the business viable, and able over time to grow substantially.[32] Helen Clark reported that the outcome of the half-yearly stocktaking at C. & J. Clark had proved that the shoe business was making a good profit, 'so that things don't go all wrong together'.[33]

Shortly afterwards, James and William Clark expanded their business interests by going into partnership in a new sheepskin-processing concern with their in-law, John Morland, in nearby Glastonbury. The 'networked family' had not only made it possible for C. & J. Clark to survive a series of financial crises but also became the means by which new family enterprises were established. It had also helped at least one of the Clark sisters, Sophia, establish herself in a profession (probably, her parents were able to support Annie Clark by the time she began her medical education). Equally, the discipline of the church and the arbitration practices fostered by the Society of Friends ensured that such networks came into play, not simply to avoid bankruptcy but also to resolve, without resort to the courts, disputes arising within family enterprises.

Some months after her marriage, Helen Clark finally received details of the money settled on her by John Bright. She explained to her husband that her father had yet to see the draft document himself, and that the meaning of some of the provisions was as yet unclear to her: 'Such things require an interpretation.' A subsequent letter suggests that aspects of the final settlement fell somewhat short of the couple's expectations.[34] The Clarks placed some unspecified financial concerns before John Bright on one of the regular if brief visits he made to their home during the parliamentary session.[35] Helen Clark's marriage settlement was eventually finalised in 1872, and she paid the associated legal costs involved in establishing a trust. This amounted to £5,500 in the form of securities for which the oldest of her brothers, J. Albert Bright, was trustee. The settlement provided that the interest on this sum was for the 'sole and separate use' of Helen Clark, and required that any further inheritance worth over £200 be deposited in this trust. It also allowed her to make a will. Both her Bright and Priestman aunts harboured a sense that Helen Clark had not been treated altogether fairly by her father. But in time, as she came to know more of his financial affairs, Helen Clark was able to put their minds at rest.[36]

John Bright was not always prompt, however, in forwarding the dividends on the investments that were part of this settlement, much of these in shares in railway companies in the United States; on occasion he forgot about the payment for some months. He sent these cheques to Helen Clark who passed them on to her husband. Most likely she was using his business as her bank, like Margaret Tanner with the timber business of the Tanner family. Certainly, she had little time for husbands who took control of their wives financial affairs, retailing family gossip about Emma (formerly Thomasson) and her husband, Stephen Winkworth: 'Emma can do nothing with their money, tho' it all comes from her! and he is wrong on all our questions. Kate [Thomasson, formerly Lucas] and I agreed we should lose all affection for such a husband!' But the apologies that John Bright offered to William Clark when payments were late suggest that some of this income was being used, at least in the early years of their marriage, for domestic, or perhaps even business expenses.[37]

The couple's circumstances were no doubt further eased over the coming years by legacies and gifts received by Helen Clark. Under the condition of her marriage settlement, these had to go into her trust and thus remained her separate property. Mary and Anna Maria Priestman insisted on dividing equally with her the legacy they had received from their Malton aunts, for example. She responded: 'I did not feel as tho' I had any claim to anything your Aunts might leave and feel so still – but I suppose you wont be satisfied without my going shares, so I accept with love and gratitude.' The Priestman sisters were almost certainly seeking to recognise the share that her mother would have enjoyed had she lived, once again suggesting informal female lines of inheritance among families such as these – as well as the lifelong mutual assistance expected of aunts and nieces.[38] Helen Clark seems also to have inherited an interest in Priestman money from her grandfather, and again on like terms to her Priestman aunts, that is, in the form largely of a lifetime interest only.[39] But significantly, Helen Clark firmly refused to accept subsequent gifts her aunts wished to make her from bequests left them by their brothers. Presumably, these came from family money that she did not consider women's money, or perhaps she was recognising the increasing attenuation of women's rights to such money across subsequent generations. Her private property was also significantly increased by a sizeable gift of money from her old family friend, Thomas Thomasson, some years after her marriage, money that again was protected by her trust.[40]

Family networks and public life

Helen Clark was able to keep the close relationships of her single life through a constant round of visiting. Personal life and her keen interest in radical politics might simultaneously be satisfied by such travels in the early years of her marriage. William Clark accompanied her on her first return to One Ash in the autumn of 1866, for this visit was planned to coincide with a major meeting at the Free Trade Hall in Manchester in support of the Reform Bill. Subsequently, they also attended a similar meeting in Leeds with John Bright, who was in the midst of a speaking tour on the question of parliamentary reform.[41] Equally, a major public event in the locality might bring visitors to Street, as when Anna Maria Priestman came to take part in a demonstration in support of the Reform Bill in Glastonbury in April 1867.

Conversely, events in the personal lives of the Priestman–Bright circle might serve as a prompt to local political activity. Thus, the marriage of Kate Lucas and J. P. Thomasson in 1867 brought members of the Bright family to London, from where Priscilla Bright McLaren and John and M. E. Bright moved on to visit Helen Clark in Street. Her father's presence in the town prompted the rapid summoning of a Reform meeting. Helen Clark used this opportunity to raise with him the belief of Mary Priestman that he did not approve of the presence of women at large public meetings, which, she reported, greatly amused him, 'for truly nothing can be further from his real opinion – he said "Ah that only applies to Mama".' M. E. Bright meanwhile went through the Clark factory and 'stocked herself with boots and shoes enough for a centipede's requirements'. This was John and M. E. Bright's first joint visit to Helen Clark's new home, and she confessed to Mary Priestman: 'I had got into rather a nervous state, which however soon departed. Papa was in his sweetest mood and Mama could not have been nicer.' Margaret and Arthur Tanner joined the party, and, ever in awe of her aunt's stately housekeeping, Helen Clark exulted in how she had 'remembered to have coffee after dinner!' Her youngest brother, Willie, was allowed to stay on with her, while John and M. E. Bright agreed to return for a further Reform meeting in Street a few weeks later.[42]

The birth of her first child interrupted Helen Clark's travels away from home for some months and she envied her husband's greater freedom to visit her father in London, or Priscilla Bright McLaren in Edinburgh, and to attend more of the major demonstrations on the Reform Bill addressed by John Bright. But the following spring, she was back in London, visiting or meeting up with Margaret Bright Lucas and Priscilla Bright McLaren, paying calls also on her friends among Radicals there, including Millicent and Henry Fawcett. She took with her a 'speech book', the scrapbook she kept of press reports of the speeches of John Bright, and discussed them with Thorold Rogers, who was then editing a collection of her father's speeches for publication. She now resumed her regular attendance at John Bright's larger public meetings, for the eventual passage of the Reform Act in 1867 was followed by a general election. So, accompanied by Annie Clark, she was present at a major demonstration addressed by John Bright in his Birmingham constituency. Spending time once more with him made her feel 'like a cat in the sunshine', she told her husband. She described the meeting at the Town Hall thus: 'It was very interesting to see the working men at last enfranchised. The unanimity was wonderful. Papa's appeal to them to use their power solely for good, and their response as he went on were very impressive.' But once again her health faltered, and another prolonged absence from her home followed: 'I think I shall not want to roam again for a long time, thou can hardly imagine how affectionately I feel towards thee [laugh sign].' Some weeks later she recorded in her diary how Birmingham had voted-in three Liberal MPs, including her father, while in Bristol his colleague, John Morley, had won by a large majority. But the election also resulted in the defeat of John Stuart Mill, while a Tory headed the poll in Manchester.[43]

The passage of the Reform Act and the coming election, together with the visits of John Bright to Street, encouraged the beleaguered local Liberal supporters to begin to build constituency organisation in Somerset. Thus a visit from John and M. E. Bright coincided with the decision to call a meeting in Glastonbury to form a local party committee. That committee adopted a Liberal candidate and agreed that he was 'to be returned free of expense' (meaning, probably, that the committee had agreed to cover all election costs), an arrangement Helen Clark found 'rather a bold move and very stimulating'. She accompanied her husband on election business and assisted the local Liberal agent, presumably in canvassing. Of one meeting, she reported, 'Good plain speeches were made and the people seemed interested and earnest.' There had been a noisy Tory mob outside who had first rejected invitations to come in and join the meeting. They had entered only as the resolutions were proposed, nearly filling the place, shouting, jeering and hooting for some minutes before beginning to throw eggs. Prominent Liberals, including Helen Clark, escaped from the back of the building, and were followed by the mob until finding refuge in an inn parlour. They had been protected by the presence with them of a local man, C. A. Homfray, 'a great Tory, but a gentleman, though nothing in station particular'.[44]

Some weeks later she received a telegram from her father saying how 'after doing all he could to avoid it', he had accepted office in the ministry being formed by W. E. Gladstone. He had chosen the Board of Trade having declined the India Office, pleading poor health, workload and the 'military business' involved as rendering him unfit for the latter post, together with 'the public mind not being ready to adopt the policy he had advocated and still believes to be the right one'. Some days later M. E. Bright forwarded to her a letter from John Bright. This reported a message from the Queen regarding a lunch that she was to hold for new ministers, and advising him that 'she wished him to do as he liked about kneeling', and to do nothing by way of conventional protocol 'that he felt a difficulty about', an invitation that he had acted upon. Some months later Helen and William Clark travelled to London to hear her father's first speech in parliament as a minister.[45] Priscilla Bright McLaren was once described as the best-represented woman in parliament, because of the number of her close male kin sitting at one time in the House of Commons. Helen Clark was, of course, in a similar situation. By the time John Bright entered government office, Jacob Bright jnr had joined him as an MP, and subsequently joined him also as a Privy Councillor. Duncan McLaren was already in parliament, and remained an MP until his death twenty years later. Two Leatham uncles also sat in the House of Commons at some time, while two of her brothers and two of her McLaren cousins subsequently followed their fathers into parliament. In such ways both Helen Clark and Priscilla Bright McLaren enjoyed extensive links with a radical-political elite in London and in various provincial centres, notably Manchester, Newcastle, Bristol, Birmingham and Edinburgh.

11 Helen Clark, family life and politics

The education of the Clark children

From 1875 the Clarks employed a governess, an Irish Friend, Isabella Pasley. She had been educated at the Mount a few years after Sophia Sturge Clark, and so may well have come with a recommendation from Lydia Rous, now its head, or one of the other Clark connections in York.[1] As well as a common religious affiliation, Isabella Pasley also shared the commitment of the Clark family to radical politics and moral reform. Helen Clark seems always to have had reservations about the character of her governess, however, finding some of her attitudes to children sentimental and 'soft', her discipline insufficiently rigorous. As they grew, the Clark children were expected to be consistently courteous and sociable, responsible and dutiful in both home and community, regardless, or perhaps because of any memory she retained of her own childhood misdemeanours. Various anxieties sometimes made her an inconsistent employer whom it must have been difficult to satisfy. So, she might scold Isabella Pasley for treating some common complaint like a cold with insufficient seriousness, while at other times she suggested the children were allowed too much outdoor exercise and spent too little time in the schoolroom. Nonetheless, Isabella Pasley remained with the Clarks until the younger children were of school age, building numerous friendships among the Priestman–Bright circle, and maintaining the loyal affection of her charges until her death. James Clark, her father-in-law, observed the 'wise and loving training' that Helen Clark provided for her children with considerable satisfaction, believing they were being properly prepared 'to become useful men and women in their day and generation'.[2]

As we have seen, Helen Clark enjoyed the care and company of small children. But she also began to feel overwhelmed as they grew less tractable and more independent, and other demands on her time and energy began to grow. After the birth of her last child, Hilda, she wrote in her diary: 'I have had a quiet month with everything to be thankful for, and have been stronger than last time, perhaps partly because I have nursed baby very little.' She had evidently determined that her family was now complete, but, like her father, always felt a house to be empty without a small child. So, the birth of this last child was bittersweet, and she reflected, on her forty-first birthday: 'If it were not for the pleasure of the children I fear I shd feel old, or at least might dread getting older.'[3] With all of them at home at New Year 1882 she decided the time had come to write 'some little account' of each of them. By this time, John was a concern because he did not look well, and though pleasant 'seems more languid than usual', and had not made many new friends at school. Roger she reported 'very bonny, quite a picture sometimes', both 'affectionate, and full of tears! But very close sometimes and tells little to Wm and me.' His forgetfulness was his greatest failure to her mind. Esther, now nine, sometimes overtook Roger in their lessons but appeared to her mother to be without 'imagination'. She also had some 'very serious' faults, which she tried to improve upon, was 'useful in the house ... and much pleasanter than she used to be.' Alice remained 'nice looking, but has rather lost some of her sweetness. I hope it will come back.' She saw little evidence of ability, 'though her head is good and she seems to be not entirely deficient in imagination'. But she also found Alice 'a nice and very innocent little companion' who 'rather shines when one has her alone'. Margaret she continued to report a 'most quaint and queer and bewitching little creature needing a special pen to describe her.' Hilda is not mentioned in this account: Helen Clark left two pages blank in her diary at this point, presumably with the intention of returning to this task. She had very little time or energy to spare for such reflection over the following years, as the many demands upon her continued to grow.[4]

The schools chosen for their children by Helen and William Clark reflected a mix of concerns: for a sheltered environment that upheld the religious values of Friends, for a healthful environment that promised to maintain their physical wellbeing, for an intellectual rigour to the programme of studies, and for family associations. All the children but Alice attended boarding schools from around the age of twelve, the oldest, John and Roger, attending Bootham, and Esther the Mount, both in York. When Helen Clark accompanied John to school, she had been surprised by the cheerfulness with which he left her, and insisted on fishing him out from among his schoolfellows for a last motherly kiss. Roger went tearfully from home, but his garrulous and sociable nature made school life more pleasurable to him than to his older brother, who became withdrawn and solitary during these years. Esther never let the Spartan conditions at the Mount dampen her usual high spirits. Being in York also enabled her older children more easily to join Helen Clark on her visits to One Ash and to remaining kin in the Newcastle region.[5]

The departure of her three oldest children to school might have lessened the load upon Helen Clark in some ways, but in turn raised fresh fears of illness and disease. Esther Clark, for example, experienced health problems after starting at the Mount, and her mother found fault with the heavy timetable, the pressure of examinations, and the lack of sufficient 'regard for the physical development of the girls'. She outlined these concerns in a letter to John S. Rowntree, the chairman of a board of governors that was entirely male, arguing for more exercise and better food. Rowntree at first disputed her charges, but the matter was shortly investigated, a new regimen established and an invitation issued to Helen Clark to become one of the Visitors that regularly inspected the school. Here again, she had challenged male authority, demonstrating as she did so the continuum that might link personal life and public action.[6] Even so, the health of her children remained a continual worry in these years. For despite the privileged nature of their home and the care provided them, all experienced episodes of serious ill health.

Fears regarding the evidence of a tubercular 'constitution' among both Clark and Bright families now came perpetually to haunt her. The young woman who had been at her marriage energetic, forceful, humorous (if sometimes cruelly so) became increasingly sharp, impatient, ill-tempered and anxious, especially when constrained within her own household. John's tendency to depression, and his increasingly withdrawn and socially retiring manner after his first few terms at school was one source of such concerns. He was liable, too, to severe throat and chest infections, especially after he left school to begin work at the Street factory, when she began to fear that William Clark expected too much from him. Roger was a high-spirited but also sometimes a tearful child, subject to stomach upsets and skin problems from babyhood, problems not helped when he started work in the tannery of Clark, Son and Morland. But the health of Alice proved especially precarious, and she was frequently subject, like John, to severe throat and chest infections. On one occasion, at least, she developed pleurisy, a life-threatening condition in the days before antibiotics, as well as one suggesting a possible susceptibility to pulmonary tuberculosis.[7]

So Helen Clark regularly took one or more of her children to Bristol or Bath in these years, to seek the advice of specialists and homeopaths there. Generally, her medical advisers, Drs Nichol and Baron in Bristol, and Dr Wilde in Bath, confirmed her fears. Usually their advice entailed a period at a place considered more healthful than Street, and generally by the sea – Burnham was close to hand, and for longer periods of convalescence, Bournemouth was favoured. Each of the Clark children was sent to Brighton for a period under the regimen of her brother-in-law, Dr Bernard Roth, to learn the exercises she herself had undertaken with his father as a child when similar fears had been held regarding her health. These exercises appear to have been aimed at straightening the children's spines and expanding their lungs. At other times, a period of rest and convalescence at Oakridge or at Durdham Park with one or more of the Priestman sisters was thought sufficient. Her kinship circle remained central to Helen Clark's ability to manage the care of her invalid brood alongside her public activities and served also to cement family bonds across several generations.

Generally, Helen Clark turned first to Dr Annie Clark for medical advice, and for recommendations regarding consultation with other specialists. She continued, however, to prefer non-invasive and preventative medicine, especially as practised by homeopaths. Her agreement to vaccinate her children against smallpox reflected her high opinion of her sister-in-law, for in the family culture among Brights and Priestmans such procedures were regarded with great suspicion. She was always able, however, to seek Annie Clark's prior advice as to a safe source of the lymph required for smallpox vaccination. She was never convinced, however, by Annie Clark's defence of vivisection, that other great source of radical antipathy to contemporaneous medical science. Three of her children became seriously sick over the winter of 1885–6 just as the ill health of some of her elderly relatives needed her absence from home. So she was all the more grateful that her Priestman aunts were so close at hand, providing nursing and convalescence, and companionship when it was decided to send them all to Bournemouth for the winter with Isabella Pasley.

Alice Clark's case had been especially serious, and once again, she turned to Dr Annie Clark: 'Annie of course is the greatest comfort possible and if she had not been here I think we should have run a great risk of losing the child.'[8] This episode led her to worry about the healthiness of Greenbank as a house, an issue on which she increasingly belaboured William Clark after taking medical advice on the question. She pressed the advisability of building a new house away from the factory and on more elevated ground. William Clark bought land at this time on the edge of Street on which he first built a 'chalet' as a large summerhouse for picnics, and for camping out away from the house by the factory when the weather was suitable. Eventually, it became the site for the new house that Helen Clark wished to see built. In the meantime, William Clark continued with an ambitious programme of civic improvements in Street.[9]

Women and money

Evidence of the informal understandings within these family circles regarding women's money has already been noted. These involved moral, not legal, imperatives, however, and so might readily become the source of family tensions and dispute. The death in 1884 of Hadwen Priestman, brother of the Priestman sisters, demonstrated the complexities that might arise from such informal understandings of 'women's money'. His wife, Emily Priestman was not a Friend and had considerable wealth of her own, but, it seems, insisted on receiving absolutely a larger portion of her husband's estate than was thought right by the Priestman family. According to their family practices and values, a significant part of the wealth that Hadwen Priestman had derived from the family enterprises ought to remain in those businesses, and be enjoyed by his widow in the form of income from shares in them. Income from part of their brother's estate should also benefit in a smaller way the Priestman sisters, especially those who remained unmarried. Hadwen Priestman might also have wished to leave a small legacy for his great-niece, Helen Clark, in remembrance of her mother.

The claims of the Priestman sisters were reinforced by the nursing and other attendance that they had provided their brother and sister-in-law over the years, as both Emily and Hadwen Priestman became increasingly invalid and wintered in the Bristol area. More recently, Anna Maria Priestman had travelled to Cannes to nurse her brother in his last illness. Equally, Hadwen Priestman's poor health had meant that he had taken little part in the family business for many years, a burden that Jonathan Priestman jnr had willingly accepted alongside his other business activities. Jonathan Priestman was his brother's executor, and sought to enact the values regarding family money that he believed were shared by Hadwen Priestman. So an unresolved rift occurred between the Priestman family and Emily Priestman over the matter. For in the face of a threat of legal action, Jonathan Priestman gave over a far larger part of his brother's estate than he or his kin believed to be right. It nonetheless remained far less than Emily Priestman believed to be her due as the widow of Hadwen Priestman, and she refused any further contact with the family. The Priestmans had concerns also over Emily Priestman's increasing interest in Catholicism at this time. Certainly, she eventually bequeathed her wealth to a religious order, in the service of which she passed her last years, and for which they had scant respect.[10]

William Clark also became involved in the complexities that might surround the inheritance expectations of women, in relation to the Ashworth sisters, Lilias and Anne Frances. Their father had died a wealthy man, long retired from his occupation as agent for a large landowner, and living on rents from his own substantial landholdings. So no ongoing business was involved. The Ashworth sisters had grown accustomed to lives of considerable luxury and evidently expected each to be left a substantial independence. Instead, they received absolute possession of only small bequests (and these perhaps derived from Sophia Bright's marriage settlement). Their father left most of his property in trust for them, and one of the trustees he named had a far more meagre sense of their needs than their own. They determined to go on spending as they wished, provoking the resignation of the less amenable trustee. John Bright was the second trustee and their Bright kin were in general sympathetic to their view of the matter, having always held considerable reservations about the outlook and values of their father, and sharing a clear sense of women's rights in family property. The Ashworth sisters pressed John Bright to find a more compliant trustee. Also wishing to be relieved of the office himself, he asked William Clark to take over the management of the Ashworth trust. His son-in-law proved a more accommodating holder of that office, ready to accept direction from the Ashworths on the management of their property, and much more liberal in his interpretation of the conditions of the trust.[11]

The Priestman–Bright network and women's rights

Helen Clark's active involvement in the women's movement served to reinforce her existing bonds with other women among the Priestman–Bright circle, even as they further separated her from her parents in Rochdale. Margaret Tanner, Mary and Anna Maria Priestman, Anne and Lilias Ashworth, Annie and Sophia Sturge Clark, and Helen Clark, together with their overlapping friendship circles, formed a concentration of active supporters of women's rights in the Bristol and Bath region from the late 1860s that enjoyed extensive links with similar circles in other provincial cities and in London.[12] This network of radical activists was united by kinship, friendship and longstanding affection as well as political aspirations and causes. Its members were all fully in support of the demand for women's enfranchisement, the most challenging of the changes to the position of women that was being sought in the mid-1860s. Just as with Helen Clark's Liberal loyalties, private visits and political campaigning often came together, as when she attended the first large-scale public meeting on women's suffrage, which was held in Manchester. Such a development was the source of much displeasure among the more socially conservative members of her family circle, like her uncle, Thomas Bright. By the spring of 1869 Helen Clark was also busy organising a petition for the Married Women's Property Committee, another campaign that had emerged from the growing movement for women's rights. The national headquarters for this committee was in Manchester, and its secretary Elizabeth Wolstenholme, was a friend shared by many among the Priestman–Bright circle, while Ursula and Jacob Bright were on its committee. Jacob Bright also succeeded that year in having women included in a new Municipal Corporations Act, allowing those with the necessary qualifications to vote for some local government bodies.[13]

Shortly, Helen Clark also became involved with a yet more controversial campaign on behalf of women's rights that called for the repeal of the Contagious Diseases Acts. These Acts provided for the medical surveillance of women deemed to be prostitutes by a specialised 'moral' police force established in military and naval centres.[14] The aim was, by removing from the streets those women thought to be diseased, to reduce the incidence of venereal disease among the armed forces. Such women were required to undergo medical inspection and treatment in a 'lock' hospital until they were considered cured (thought the diagnosis, classification and treatment of venereal disease remained subjects of fundamental disagreement among medical practitioners, and there was, in fact, no effective cure for a number of these conditions).[15] The men involved remained free of such surveillance and compulsory treatment. The penalty for women refusing to comply with these provisions was a prison term with hard labour. The first Act had been passed in 1864, and had been followed by extension of such powers in further Acts passed in 1866 and 1868. The nature of the legislation first came to the attention of leading figures in the women's movement at the Social Science Conference held in Bristol in 1869. There, a group of medical men who opposed the legislation called a meeting with the intention of forming a national association to campaign against the Acts. The women of this circle, with their broad-ranging interest in matters of reform, routinely attended such conferences and were beginning themselves to offer contributions to them. But they found women were not invited to join in planning a national association for repeal of the Contagious Diseases Acts. The matter was of so controversial a nature that many men otherwise sympathetic to repeal and women's rights believed it was inappropriate for women to involve themselves with it.

The women of the Priestman–Bright circle thought quite the reverse: such legislation exemplified for them the dangers to women in their exclusion from the parliamentary franchise. But they moved discreetly as they began to organise what became the Ladies National Association (LNA) for Repeal of the Contagious Diseases Acts. Elizabeth Wolstenholme recognised the need for unimpeachable respectability in the leadership of the campaign, for example, and persuaded a widely respected, Anglican philanthropic worker among prostitutes, Josephine Butler, to head it. She in her turn looked to her Quaker women friends as the most likely to be ready to take on such controversial work, and a preliminary conference was organised in the Quaker Meeting House in Leeds. Margaret Tanner and Mary Priestman were to play a substantial role in the work of this organisation, though largely behind the scenes as, respectively, honorary treasurer and secretary, but it had the support of all the women of the Priestman–Bright circle, and of many of their friends among the women radicals in the women's suffrage societies and the Married Women's Property Committee, including two particular friends of the Priestman sisters, Elizabeth Wolstenholme and Mary Estlin. Helen Clark united with Priscilla Bright McLaren, Margaret Bright Lucas and a number of other women kin in this endeavour, but like them recognised the need to tread carefully as they created a national organisation of women repealers.[16]

Individual friends and relations were approached in the first instance, either in person or by letter, to establish their sympathy or otherwise with the cause. Helen Clark found a ready response from her husband and his immediate family, but had to be more circumspect with her father and stepmother. It was decided that someone outside his immediate family should approach John Bright on the topic, and Josephine Butler wrote to him to seek his support for the work of the LNA. Helen Clark heard of her father's response from her aunt, Ursula Bright. He had told Josephine Butler that he was 'of much the same opinion as herself – but the subject did not invite correspondence!' William Clark was at this time on business in the north, and obtained a fuller picture of her father's views on the matter. Helen Clark thanked him for the 'kind and informing' letter in which he had reported them, but added that it had made her miserable for fear that her father 'must be disgusted with me. You know I was averse to writing, for I knew his kind of fastidiousness.' She wished her husband was at hand to advise her, but turned to his mother instead who, she reported, 'quite unites' with the repealers. Other members of her family, including the Braggs, resisted any involvement on the grounds of protecting their children from such knowledge.[17]

Helen Clark continued to receive 'fresh information showing the extent of the evil', and remained of quite another mind. Regarding her father's response, she wrote: 'I do not agree with him. I am far *indeed* from wishing such papers circulated in *families*, but I think *mothers* should know the state of the world, that they may guard their children.' She agreed with the protest that was being planned through a public letter to the press, signalling the beginning of the campaign against the acts by women such as herself and her aunts. Ursula Bright coordinated the signing of the protest among the sympathisers of their family circle. The division among her family over this question was difficult for Helen Clark. Visits to One Ash during these years might create considerable ambivalence in her mind: 'I feel quite festive, and yet the reverse. I can never explain to you the strange medley of most opposite feelings that come over me here.' That ambivalence in turn served to make her value her home and husband all the more: 'But whatever else I feel, I am always most truly thankful for the true and faithful love thou hast given me, ever since I first knew thee. It fills me with a deep content.'[18]

She was several times in these years called on to care for her father during periods of ill health. She found him a nervous invalid, but patient and sweet-tempered. 'He says he cannot remember to have been a day in bed since he had smallpox 30 years ago.' Sometimes, such care interrupted her campaigning activities, so on one such occasion she deputed William Clark to look out a roll of petitions against the Contagious Diseases Acts that she had collated, and then forward them to their local member of parliament. The petition had been gathered from a neighbouring military centre, Wincanton, and contained the signatures of 31 men and 164 women from the town. She also asked him to distribute locally copies of the journal of the LNA, *The Shield*, a task that she usually undertook. Her part in this campaign became, as she feared, a cause for tension between herself and her parents. Jane Crosland – herself a repealer – wrote Helen Clark a 'most disquieting account of what Mama says about the CDA – quite sickening – and most distressing and saddening to me, implicating Papa so much.' Her uncle, Thomas Bright, also declared his regret at having '20 screeching women [a reference to women's rights advocates] nearly related to us'.[19]

Josephine Butler had first come to public prominence in her efforts to care for women brought to imprisonment, sickness and death through sexual labour, and such work gave middle-class women an awareness of some of the debates surrounding the causes of prostitution. But an immersion in the campaign against the Contagious Diseases Acts necessarily brought with it a far greater knowledge of the misery and brutality of some women's lives. It also opened the eyes of women like Helen Clark to the hostility to, and contempt for women evident in underlying attitudes among men of her own class and background. She took heart from the readiness of some men Friends to organise their own society for repeal of the Acts, while continuing to believe, 'our chief hope was in the masses'. After less than a year of campaigning on this issue, she wrote to her Priestman aunts: 'I am low in my mind. The C. D. Acts and things connected leave me no vestige of old fashioned happiness.' Such depression also made her fear a weakness in her own make up: ' I do not think that in a well regulated mind one thing however bad ought to have power to prevent one's enjoyment of the simple pleasure and happiness that are surely God-given.' It was also making her poor company for her husband, 'who does not deserve it, as he is very good and entirely satisfactory, to me as always'.[20] John Bright made clear his disapproval of her involvement in the various campaigns for women's rights in these years. Grudgingly agreeing that one of his younger daughters might visit Helen Clark he wrote: 'I wish that her head may not be filled with the rubbish which seems now so much approved by her Sister and her Aunts.' So he asked her to abstain from any conversation on such matters, believing them false and 'injurious to a young girl'. He also admonished her for beginning to appear on public platforms, following in the footsteps of her Ashworth cousins, and associating his name with agitation of which he disapproved: 'In future our sympathy and the harmony of our thoughts must be considered at an end.'[21]

By this period there was evident a division of labour emerging among members of the Priestman–Bright circle. Margaret Tanner and Mary Priestman increasingly lent their best energies to the Ladies National Association, as we have seen, while the Ashworth sisters and Anna Maria Priestman focused especially on the women's suffrage societies formed in Bristol and Bath at this time. The Ashworth sisters and their Bright aunts were also to the fore in the national leadership of this campaign when a Central Committee of the National Society for Women's Suffrage was established in 1870 at Jacob Bright's suggestion. Annie Clark was, as we have seen, among the group of women now seeking a medical education and entry to the medical profession. Sophia Clark and Helen Clark were active in local government, and the latter also in the campaigns of the suffrage societies, the Married Women's Property Committee and the LNA.

Their part in the women's rights movement (and perhaps the patriarchal attitudes it revealed among some of their male kin) encouraged the women of the Priestman–Bright circle regularly to press for a greater part for women in the government of their church. Helen Clark raised the question through a letter to *The Friend* in 1873, for example. It proved more effective, however, to pursue such change through the local councils of Friends. At the October Quarterly Meeting in Bridgwater in 1884 the women's meeting agreed to establish a committee to consider the question and how it might best be addressed. Several members of the Clark family circle in Street were among its members, including Sophia Clark, Mary Morland, Catherine Impey and Catherine Clothier. Sophia Clark acted as their spokeswoman, canvassing among other members of the committee a series of proposals that would ensure women a greater part, for example, in discussing changes to church discipline. While these found a sympathetic response among some, including Margaret

Tanner and Charlotte Sturge of Bristol, they were judged too precipitate. Instead a much more gradual approach was advocated, one initially focused on educating opinion within the Monthly Meetings of the Society of Friends, and the Women's Yearly Meeting.[22] One reason for this was that many women Friends valued the separate deliberative space provided them by the existing organisation of the church. The merger of the Women's and Men's Yearly Meetings took almost another two decades to achieve. In the meantime, more and more women's and men's local and regional business meetings began to meet jointly.[23]

In the midst of campaigning on a range of women's rights issues in 1869, and while she was visiting her Bright aunts in London, Helen Clark received news of the serious illness of Arthur Tanner, and turned for home. Mary Priestman was already at Oakridge helping her sister with nursing. Arthur Tanner died some days later, by which time Margaret Tanner was also seriously ill. Helen Clark took over the arrangements for the funeral and for the arrival of family members while Mary Priestman now nursed her sister. Helen Clark recorded how, once she could leave her bed, Margaret Tanner visited her husband's body: 'It made my heart ache to see her and feel her desolation. She is dreadfully ill prepared by previous illness to meet this blow.' Margaret Tanner's condition declined further and Mary Priestman refused to leave her sister's side. Other family members hurried to Sidcot in anticipation of a further death. Helen Clark found she was not needed in the sickroom, and as she sat alone in the house that had become a second home to her in her youth, she wrote to her husband: 'I seem to be losing all that is left me of my own mother.' She eased her grief by sitting with her uncle's body in Margaret Tanner's stead, and five days after his death recorded: 'Uncle Arthur looks very nice and natural still. W. and I have put flowers into the coffin. I watched the coffin closed that he might seem cared for to the last.' In the meantime, she delegated to William Clark and to Annie Clark the final preparations for three married-women's-property petitions that needed to be sent off to Jacob Bright, concerned especially for one that had been collected among working women. By the time of the burial, Mary Priestman had also become very ill, but both she and Margaret Tanner eventually recovered. Margaret Tanner remained at Oakridge for the rest of her life, free once again to take up her interest in radical politics and moral reform.[24]

Helen Clark, One Ash and Mizzy

The uneasiness of Helen Clark's relations with her stepmother only intensified with their divergent views on women's rights. She told William Clark: 'the pleasure of being near Papa and the worry of being near Mama are two opposing forces, and it is not easy to calculate exactly what will be the resultant of the two.' Like her Priestman aunts she tended to blame M. E. Bright for any failings they saw in her father. She continued close to her half-brothers and sisters, who often shared her views of the weaknesses they saw in their parents. Her childhood home also retained its attraction for her: 'Every stone in the neighbourhood seems precious to my eyes, and the people are so superior to Somersetshire people – I mean the working people.'[25] She took her three infant daughters with her when visiting in the spring of 1878 while Anna Maria Priestman had care of her two boys.

She stayed for three weeks, during which she also attended a large political meeting in Manchester at which John Bright spoke. His children were encouraging him to 'plain speaking', but in the opinion of his eldest son, Albert, 'Papa now dislikes to make enemies, and has lost his aggressiveness.'[26] The visit seems to have passed without incident, but as Helen Clark and her children were saying their goodbyes, M. E. Bright collapsed. A telegram was sent to John Bright in London but his wife died before he reached home and Albert Bright went to meet him with the news. Helen Clark wrote to her husband: 'I am full of regrets – almost the last thing Mama did was to cut a little lock of Alice's hair – I had no chance to thank her for her kindness to the children . . . You can think that I grieve and wish I had not said many things – and all feel this too. It is just another lesson, and a very searching one.' She wrote again the same day, describing John Bright sitting by the body and recalling the death of his first wife, and of Leonard. Helen Clark felt unable to leave her father for many weeks, especially after the departure of Priscilla Bright McLaren, who 'as you may suppose has left a great blank'.[27]

She was anxious also, before she returned home, to persuade her father to review the financial implications of his wife's death. He had already told her that he thought she and William Clark might as well now liquidate and spend the assets in her trust. She had responded by telling him she had paid £18 in legal costs for the settlement 'and saw no use in tearing up the deed [laugh sign]'. John Bright had suggested they might buy Street House, and she herself was: 'quite of the opinion that we had better get rid now of all American securities. You can think over the Street House idea – if we sold some for building we might make up what we lost in interest perhaps, and then should have a more certain investment than the present, besides having the use and pleasure of the land.' There was also the position of her sisters to consider, especially that of Mary and Lillie who were both about to marry. M. E. Bright left no will (suggesting that the conditions of her trust did not overcome coverture by including the right so to do). The terms of her marriage settlement of £20,000 provided that on her death this money go at once and absolutely to her own children. Helen Clark noted: 'Of course if this is so, Papa's income will be rather affected. He did not seem to mind at all, only saying that it was quite different from what he and Mama had understood.' The money that John Bright had settled on M. E. Bright on their marriage she learned was to go equally to all his children, including herself, 'so that there is no foundation whatever for what Aunt Tilla always said as to my exclusion. Both settlements are perfectly fair and proper.' Helen Clark found it difficult to persuade her father of the need as a consequence for some fresh financial planning: 'Papa is dreadfully procrastinating, poor thing.'[28]

After the death of M. E. Bright, Helen Clark also became responsible for the care and counsel of her younger sisters. All married after their mother's death and needed her help with the arrangements to be made for their weddings, and then the confinements that followed. So Helen Clark grew still closer to Mary Curry and Lillie Roth in these years, and Lillie Roth looked to her especially as her first confinement approached. The situation of Mary Curry, the consumptive sister to whom she was perhaps most attached, gave her different causes for concern in this period, as the school she and her husband had established failed to prosper. Helen Clark remarked bitterly on the disparity between her sister's position and the relative ease enjoyed by her oldest brother, J. Albert Bright, who now held a senior position in John Bright and Bros. Eventually, the school was sold and Richard Curry found a position as a school inspector. The couple then settled in Bath, further extending the family circle in this region.[29]

As well as her sisters, there were also numerous ageing relatives, not least her father, whose care in times of illness she undertook. John Bright was often alone at One Ash once all his daughters married and the two sons still at home were very much absorbed in business and their own social lives. His one outing during a day might be to play billiards at Greenbank with his brother Thomas. One Ash was left in the hands of servants who received very little supervision, and evidence of its neglect became increasingly apparent. Helen Clark suggested a housekeeper be employed, and after John Bright fell violently ill with a stomach upset, this was agreed to. Mary Rowntree, a distant relative and a widow, came to oversee the care of One Ash. She shared John Bright's love of dogs, however, and as his sons married and left home, the presence of three inadequately exercised and supervised animals in the house brought another kind of disorder. With these additional anxieties, Helen Clark's temper did not improve, and her health remained uncertain. In her father's last years, she spent increasing time at One Ash as John Bright complained more and more of loneliness, and as his health declined. Her visits to him appear ones of relative quiet and ease for her in her diaries, and her husband's enquiries about her returning to her own home might sometimes bring a sharp rebuke.[30]

Jane Crosland had returned to live at Mizzy in 1862, but had to leave once more in 1869 when it was needed for a younger member of the Bright family about to marry. Eliza Oldham appears to have moved to Halifax with her. The town was presumably chosen because Esther Blakey, an older sister of Jane Crosland, lived there. Helen Clark was greatly saddened by the removal of her old friends from Mizzy.[31] She was anxious, also, regarding the well-being of Ben Oldham, whose employment was about to end around the same time. Her intervention appears to have secured for him a pension from John Bright's pocket, for it was thought inappropriate to give such support from the family firm – perhaps because of the precedent it might establish. This pension of 5s a week was half what Helen Clark thought a suitable sum, and so she made it up to 10s a week. This she paid in a lump sum every six months to Eliza Oldham, believing she would know better how to use the money than her father. Eliza Oldham was assured that she, too, would always be cared for. After Jane Crosland died suddenly in 1879, Eliza Oldham moved back to Rochdale to care for her father. Helen Clark sought to comfort her grieving friend with a gift of a jacket and the offer of some warm shoes. But the old servant explained that her feet were hard to fit because of bunions, and that any way she felt herself 'well off' with two pairs of thick boots.[32]

Helen Clark was once again able to keep up with news of old friends in Rochdale through her correspondence with Eliza Oldham. The occasional preservation of a series of letters between servant and mistress among the Millfield Papers might variously signal the importance of the content to a mistress, or the depth of friendship that had been established between servant and employer's family. Such a correspondence offers a rare glimpse into the lives of some who might otherwise have disappeared almost entirely from the historical record. In this instance, Helen Clark saw the welfare of the Oldham family as a particular responsibility arising from the history they shared with the Bright family. So she sometimes turned to this old friend for memories of her childhood home, for example, when writing an essay on some of the New Year customs in Lancashire that she missed in Somerset. Her correspondence with Eliza Oldham helped sustain a sense of continuity for Helen Clark between the past of the Bright family and her own present. Eliza Oldham might volunteer memories of when, as a girl, she herself worked at the Greenbank mill, and more particularly memories of the first Elizabeth Bright: 'she used to look in as she went along and all the hands was pleased and the all use to say she is not a bit proud'. She also recalled the kindness shown her father: 'my dear Old Father thought the never was any one like her when it was very wet she told the cook to make Ben a Basin of coffee and bread and Butter and call him in it was not fit for him to be out in the wet, he never forgot it.' (Ben Oldham seems to have been variously employed both at the factory and as an outdoor servant at One Ash, possibly the gardener whose wisdom John Bright sometimes quoted in support of his own patriarchal attitudes. Ben Oldham's last position was as a watchman at the factory.)[33]

After her return to Rochdale, Eliza Oldham wrote to Helen Clark: 'I do feel thankful for my home I *do* that for that I have a comfortable home and my father enjoys it too.' Her grief for Jane Crosland continued to rob her of sleep and to cause headaches, though, and she was in her turn cared for by her niece, Ellen Oldham. This niece also corresponded with Helen Clark and came to help Eliza Oldham nurse her father in his last illness. Various members of the Bright family made farewell calls on him, and Sophia Bright brought jellies and soups. After his death, Helen Clark sent flowers from her garden, which his four granddaughters laid on the coffin that was carried to his grave by four nephews. Before dying, Ben Oldham had expressed his gratitude that he had been 'so well nursed and caired for'. For herself, Eliza Oldham reported that she did not feel lonely 'but thankful that my Father is gone before me, and it wont be long before we meet again'. She herself continued to suffer from serious skin problems and increasingly poor eyesight, problems Eliza Oldham believed to have been caused by the poverty of her family and the hunger they had known before her father had found work with John Bright.[34]

Helen Clark invited Eliza Oldham to come and stay once more for a holiday in Street. But like her employers, Eliza Oldham believed in the efficacy of the water treatment and decided instead to go to Matlock Spa, where she could lodge with another old Bright family servant who now lived there. She also turned down Helen Clark's several offers to pay for consultations with a London doctor suggested by Bernard Roth. She continued to enjoy visits from Croslands, Brights and Clarks whenever they were in Rochdale, as well as from her nieces who were all away in service.[35] She also maintained her friendships among the servants of the Bright family and made several new friends among the servants of the Clark family when she visited Street, sometimes sending messages and good wishes via her letters to Helen Clark.[36] The letters of Eliza Oldham contain a mix of deference, gratitude and affection towards the Bright family. Shared political values also mediated the distance between them in wealth and social standing. For, like them, she celebrated her family's long-standing commitment to radical politics: 'all the Oldhams was called Radicals I know my Father cd not Bear what are called Whigs my Father was at Peterloo and he helped to carry the Drum when they was coming home and they ran over the fields and over hedge and dich out way of the Soldeirs that was gallopin on the road after them.'[37]

So Eliza Oldham continued to follow reports of John Bright's political career in the papers, and kept up with public debates, writing after the assassination of Lord Cavendish: 'I don't know what they wd do in Rochdale if any attempted to hurt Mr Bright we sd no need to go abroad for War we shd have it in our own town.' When it looked as if the Liberal government's 1884 Reform Bill might be thrown out by the Upper House, she declared: 'the Lords will find that they have gone to far and people wont sit down to be treated like this they are more awake to their own interest'. She linked her temperance beliefs also to the welfare of her class, 'where they are kept out of the way of Publick houses and bad company ... there is every chance for the working class to improve themselves.' Her own political allegiances remained with the Liberal Party. Class divisions sometimes emerged through her work for the women's movement, however, and she explained why she had decided against distributing LNA leaflets when attending a meeting of the British Women's Temperance Association: 'our *Ladies* are so particular that I wa afraid to give offence they insist so much on refined speaker and ladylike and they don't *I think* give *due* honour or I should say respect to working women that they find it difficult to get speakers.'[38]

In the past Eliza Oldham had collected signatures on petitions for the repeal of the Contagious Diseases Acts alongside Jane Crosland, and she shared many other reform interests with Helen Clark, who arranged for her to receive the *Woman's Suffrage Journal*, and *The Shield* (the journal of the LNA). Eliza Oldham also requested pamphlets on the repeal question. A widow working in the wool warehouse at the Bright mills offered to distribute them there, 'she is a strong Radical', and hoped by such means to encourage the men she worked with to discuss the issue with their wives. Visiting in Yorkshire the previous year, Eliza Oldham had been surprised at the ignorance she found there concerning the Acts, for she was laughed at and told they applied only to cattle: 'I said . . . but their is one for Women and they ought to know about them.' (The name of these Acts did, indeed, echo others designed to control the spread of disease in livestock.) She herself was qualified to vote in local government elections and canvassed among her women neighbours to do likewise, during 'a sharp contest' in Rochdale. By the end of polling day, she reported, 'I felt quiet Exhausted and my throat was sore', but she had found that an account of the Contagious Diseases Acts was effective in persuading a previously uninterested woman to use her vote: 'she like a many more [*sic*] has never heard anything about them and it is not a easy thing to get Women to *think*. one Woman told me today that she never met a Woman like me it is strange but they are very much more alive to those dreadful Acts in Halifax then they are in Rochdale.'[39]

Her niece, Ellen Oldham, was similarly engaged. Subsequently, she distributed fifty leaflets sent her by Helen Clark. A brother also gave some out to customers at his shop, women who knew him through his involvement in a Sunday School, in this way hoping to reach 'outling districts where they don't see evening papers'. Members of the Oldham family kept up a campaign for repeal in the weeks that followed, continuing to encounter complete ignorance of the Acts and requesting still more tracts to distribute: 'we have to do such a *lot* of explaining they can hardly credit what we say'. The secre-tary of their ward's Liberal Club had been 'allmost the only man' they had encountered who took an interest in the issue. Ellen Oldham reported, too, how her aunt was trying to place a placard in the Co-operative store where it would be seen by a great many, 'she is almost angry with people for not knowing more about them [the Contagious Diseases Acts]'. Together, the Oldhams were also looking forward to participating in the coming School Board elections, and the general election that was increasingly expected. They hoped John Bright would once more be returned for Birmingham and show Randolph Churchill he had made a mistake in choosing to stand there, and in making 'disrespectful remarks'.[40]

The letters of Eliza Oldham also tell of the strategies of women servants anxious about their declining strength for housework. So she reported how another niece, Hannah, had consulted her after a period of illness and they had decided she should enrol at Birkenhead Lying-In Hospital, where they knew the matron: 'she will have to do something for a living Hannah is forty years of Age she will soon be to old for service i thought if she cd get into

Month Nurseing and her sewing together wd be her a living when I was gone.' It seems she provided this niece with the funds to undertake the required training.[41] Helen Clark offered a holiday so that Hannah Oldham might rebuild her strength, as she did during what proved to be the last illness of Ellen Oldham, in which she was nursed by Eliza Oldham. In this case, the Brights provided additional funds so that the washing could be sent out, and good meals and medical advice be afforded.

The Priestman–Bright circle and radical suffragism

The concentration of members of the Priestman–Bright circle in the southwest attracted visiting radicals from overseas, among them in 1882 Elizabeth Cady Stanton, a leading figure in the women's movement in the United States. During this visit she helped celebrate the passage of a further Married Women's Property Act in 1882. Elizabeth Wolstenholme Elmy and Ursula Bright together had largely managed this campaign and the new legislation greatly extended the rights of married women, for example, in giving them ownership of any earnings made after marriage. But it was so amended during its passage through parliament that the doctrine of coverture remained in tact, so there was as yet no end to the divisions in the women's suffrage movement over the inclusion or exclusion of married women from the demand. Elizabeth Cady Stanton sought to strengthen the determination of the radical suffragists of the Priestman–Bright circle, to whom she felt closest, to maintain their support for the inclusion of married women.[42]

Such friendships helped reinforce and expand an international network of women's rights activists that in time created organisations like the International Women's Suffrage Alliance. Equally, such links helped sustain within Helen Clark and her Priestman aunts their own sense of themselves as providing an alternative to the moderate leadership of the suffrage movement in Britain, one that advocated a more radical, because more inclusive, perspective on reforming the position of women.[43] Anna Maria Priestman also established a fresh initiative within the suffrage campaigns in these years in terms of encouraging the formation of local Women's Liberal Associations (WLAs), among the first of which was the Bristol WLA. This new strategy grew out of the frustration she and other Radical-Liberal suffragists felt at limitations put on suffrage campaigners under the national leadership of Lydia Becker, especially in terms of the exclusion of married women from the demand. That limitation was in turn a reflection of current Conservative leadership of women's-suffrage supporters in parliament. Others within the West of England Society for Women's Suffrage (based in Bristol), supported Lydia Becker, however, notably Lilias Ashworth (now Hallett).[44]

Her position as the eldest daughter of John Bright gave Helen Clark a particular value to some of the causes to which she was committed. She did not enjoy placing herself in the public eye, and recognised her own limited talent for public speaking. But she acknowledged as an unavoidable duty the need on occasion to make use of her position as her father's daughter.[45] The prospect of a new Reform Bill in the early 1880s was met with a well-organised and sustained campaign by the women's suffrage societies in which the Priestman–Bright circle played a prominent part. Anna Maria Priestman helped raise a significant fund for the campaign in the south-west of England, for example. Liberal women like these also began to exert more pressure on the National Liberal Federation on the issue of women's suffrage, and to take the issue to major national conferences on parliamentary reform. Helen Clark agreed to attend a major Reform Convention in Leeds in 1883, alongside Jane Cobden, daughter of Richard, and together they addressed the meeting and secured a vote in support of the inclusion of women in the Reform Bill. John Bright presided over the convention, though not over that particular session, and Helen Clark was anxious about his reaction at the soirée that was held afterwards. It seems her father had not yet heard of her intervention, and he greeted her warmly. Subsequently, he wrote her an irate letter that might have distressed her more if her Bright aunts had not supported her action. She was also able to point out his own inconsistency in the matter, for he had voted both for and against women's suffrage in parliament.[46] John Bright was similarly incensed when Helen Clark joined with other figures in the national leadership of the suffrage movement to send a memorandum to the prime minister, W. E. Gladstone, on the issue which they then published. Lydia Becker also opposed such interventions by Radical-Liberal suffragists, for she still sought to distance this campaign from too close an identification with the Liberal Party.

Though women were again excluded from the provisions of the 1884 Reform Act, other campaigns were more successful in these years. 1886 saw the repeal of the Contagious Diseases Acts in Britain. That same year also saw the formation of the Women's Liberal Federation, bringing together the growing number of local WLAs.[47] But the suffrage cause was to be further weakened by divisions within the Liberal Party over Irish Home Rule, as the party split between the Gladstonians and the Liberal Unionists opposed to Home Rule. Duncan McLaren and John Bright moved to the Unionist position. Most of the women of the Priestman–Bright circle of Radical-Liberals remained supporters of Irish Home Rule, and stayed loyal to W. E. Gladstone, despite his refusal to countenance a women's suffrage amendment to the Reform Bill. Lilias Ashworth Hallett was a notable exception and like her old friend, Millicent Garrett Fawcett became a Unionist.[48] These divisions were subsequently played out within the national leadership of the suffrage movement when Radical-Liberal suffragists sought to affiliate local WLAs to the National Society for Women's Suffrage. That body then divided into two national suffrage societies with confusingly similar names, and for that reason they were more generally referred to as the Parliament Street society and the Great College Street society, after the address of their respective headquarters.

The first comprised many Gladstonian suffragists, and the second, led by Lydia Becker until her death in 1890, was supported by Liberal-Unionist as well as Conservative suffragists. Some of the Priestman–Bright circle, including Eva and Walter McLaren, supported both bodies in a spirit of consensus-building, keeping open channels of communication between the two societies.[49]

12 The changing order

Family, friendship and politics in the late nineteenth century

John Bright's last years

Helen Clark divided the last year of her father's life between Rochdale and Street as his health deteriorated. She was concerned also at the continuing shift she observed in his political values toward Liberal Unionism, for which she blamed the influence of her oldest brother, J. Albert Bright: 'I really think practically they are quite out of their minds.' By 1888 her father had become unwilling to talk over politics with her, or with others in her presence, turning her out of the room when one old family friend called: 'I cant imagine why, unless George [Petrie] is seeking light from the Unionist camp!' The state of One Ash was once again worrying. There was much 'food debris' she reported, while 'The dogs are infirm, and I dont advise any one who has not a robust stomach to come here just now.' One was vomiting frequently, 'it is only what Papa calls mucous that he throws up, and then Papa comes with his well known weapon, the steel shovel and tries to get it up. I look another way.' She found, too, that the dogs were never let out properly, 'and the consequences may be imagined'. As a result, she added: 'I never dare step at the bottom of the back stairs, but carefully jump, so that I may clear all the space at the bottom.'[1]

Summoned to One Ash when her father once again fell ill, she reported on how he had, unknown to Mrs Rowntree, cast off his winter underclothing for 'thin things which have never been aired. I dont see how a man's judgment on the Irish question can be much depended on when he does such queer things in private.' She believed such waywardness the reason for the cough that now troubled him: 'As to his outer raiment, he appears to cling to it with as much pertinacity as O'Brien did to his when in prison, for it cannot be got away to be brushed.' Her political differences with her father and brother continued both to exasperate and to amuse her. Her father still avoided discussing Ireland with her but otherwise remained 'most agreeable and sweet'. A further illness some weeks later proved more serious: 'He is very quiet and patient, and quite humble now poor thing. I watched him till 3, and Mrs R [Rowntree] after, Albert being within call ... His voice is good, but he was very feverish yesterday.' She blamed this new episode of ill health on John

Bright's remaining too long in his bath, pointing again to his need now for a full-time personal attendant.[2]

News of her father's decline in the national press brought 'such floods of letters'. One from an old political ally of her father's and a telegram from Mrs Gladstone were especially welcome to her. The doctors now feared that John Bright had also suffered a stroke: 'He is so feeble and his memory seems to fail very much altho' I dont notice that he wanders.' But once again he rallied and shortly she reported, 'he has picked up wonderfully . . . one does not know how far he will ever be the same as before, but he may recover better than one fears.' She hoped, too, that the experience would serve to make her father 'more prudent', and that he would in time become accustomed to his need now for continual 'trained care'. But John Bright's condition went on worsening, and her simultaneous anxiety over the poor health of several of her children left her torn between the two households. She and two of her sisters now took turns to be at One Ash, though they appear not always to have agreed on their father's needs. So on a subsequent visit Helen Clark congratulated herself, 'for I have by a little tact and an accident combined stopped the champagne'.[3]

An election occurred during the summer of 1888, when she and a younger brother, William Bright, stood out as allies in the cause of Gladstonian liberalism and Irish Home Rule. He told her too, how everyone in the House of Commons spoke 'so kindly of Papa, and none more than the Irish Members. Poor thing, how sad it is he cannot put the bitterness out of his head.' One visitor provoked in her father 'such a tirade against the Irish and such a justification (implied) of the whole treatment of Ireland by England that it was very painful, and really I could only, remembering the past, think him quite crazed.' The scandal over Charles Parnell's relationship with a married woman at this time left Helen Clark perplexed. She had never held the leader of the Irish Nationalists in parliament in great respect, but was unwilling to accept, out-of-hand, evidence that would damage the cause of Home Rule. John Bright, she recorded, readily believed 'everything against any Parnellite'. He was at this time diagnosed as diabetic, and at last 'succumbed' to the advice of his family and doctors on the need now for constant personal attention: 'He was astonished, but not frightened. It is much better he should know.'[4]

John Bright's final decline began that winter and was slow and distressing, bringing dizzy spells that 'frightened him dreadfully'. Helen Clark had shortly to accept that 'something had given way in the brain. He is fully alive to the seriousness of it. But what it exactly is nobody knows.' Some black humour was found in the situation, when another younger brother, Philip Bright, claimed 'he has nearly persuaded even Albert that Papa is crazy about Ireland [laugh sign]. He thinks G. O. M. [W. E. Gladstone] and Papa are just alike from age, only at opposite poles [laugh sign].' She prepared for a brief return to Street, but explained that she would have to come back to Rochdale shortly, and asked that William Clark accompany her then. For some dispute had arisen within the family regarding John Bright's property, and she feared 'a tremendous flare up, and the whole thing perhaps put into chancery'. Albert Bright had declared the cause of these anxieties 'the wickedest old man he ever came across' (a reference possibly to one of his uncles who were John Bright's partners in the family business). She returned to One Ash believing that her father's death was imminent, and brought her youngest children with her. Some days later she persuaded her uncle, Thomas Bright, to visit her father: 'He trembled very much and cd not at first summon courage to go up, but I staid in the room and made a little innocent talk and the little interview passed over well.' The next day his doctor told John Bright that he thought death was near. With this advice, Helen Clark recorded: 'He roused up most curiously, sent for Albert and told him things he wished attended to, kissed us all affectionately, slept peacefully, and strange to say is apparently decidedly better today.' She found her father still 'very quiet and cheerful and nice. He says he has not had half an hour's pain all the six months, and he evidently is puzzled at being perhaps so near his end without any pain.'[5]

His family tried to mend John Bright's relationship with W. E. Gladstone at this point, suggesting that he send his old ally a last message: 'Papa seemed taken aback and I thought he was going to be hard, but by and by he said, the tears running down his face "I have never in the least changed my opinion as to the unfortunate course he has taken, but I cannot forget his unvarying kindness to me and the great services he has rendered to the country."' Albert Bright tactfully wrote out a message containing only the latter part of John Bright's remarks, and it was signed and sent off. 'An *exquisite* letter' came from Gladstone by return, which, Helen Clark reported 'nobody could read without crying. It was too touching to read to Papa at the time.' For it now seemed as if her father might live for some weeks more. So she took the opportunity of showing him the plans for the new house being built for her family in Street, realising that he would never now visit it. They were duly admired and later she asked her father about his preference regarding the name of the Clark's new house: he favoured 'Mill Field' over 'Summerhill', despite, or perhaps because of, the memories attaching to the latter.[6]

Though he sometimes wandered, at other times John Bright was lucid enough to have the newspapers read to him, and to share in political talk. He took a ready interest in William Clark's campaign to win a seat on the county council, for example: 'he shd not like you to pay £100 and not get in.' Helen Clark now lived only from day to day: 'Everything is absolutely uncertain.' Increasingly, John Bright became 'restless and wandering and giddy ... and a little irritable now and then poor thing. He is weary and gets almost no sleep and the cough distresses him.' Helen Clark now slept in his room, so as to be at hand when death approached: 'I like to lie on the sofa and hear him when he rambles, his voice is so nice, and his words so well chosen and dignified.' During another lucid period she read him Gladstone's letter 'and he was much touched and pleased and said it was very kind as well as beautifully worded'. Gladstone had also sent one of her sisters-in-law another kindly note about his old friend: 'I fear they think him a great deal more softened than he is. I dont think he is really softened at all.' She also read her father 'a beautiful and most loving address from local Liberals of this ward.' She remained puzzled by his state of mind: 'It is very sad to see such a decline, but of course it is only what all must look for, but perhaps one notices it more in one who has been so powerful, and who still seems in a sense to have lost nothing mentally.'[7]

Now she received news of the sudden illness of Jonathan Priestman: 'I know few lives more valuable, or that if taken wd be more missed, and I am distressed for my aunts.' As he, too, failed to improve, she left One Ash briefly to make her farewell to the uncle who had been to her 'much more like an elder brother than any one else'. On his death she returned to Shotley Bridge for a longer visit to comfort her aunts, before turning at last for her own home. Her concerns for her own children were considerable over the course of this winter, with Alice, Esther and John all being in poor health. Her fears for her older son were confirmed by others who saw him: 'He has the look of one who wd very readily fall into consumption and there is no doubt that Street is a fertile soil for that.' Returning to One Ash, she longed for 'some politically congenial society' and sorrowed for the loss of her father's companionship in this regard: 'It is very sad to think that what pleases us in the papers may trouble and depress Papa. He never says anything.' John Bright died in March 1889, and his family refused a state funeral in accordance with his wishes.[8]

As One Ash was emptied for Albert Bright and his family, Margaret Wood's old servant, Eliza Oldham, was remembered with the gift of a book from John Bright's library. She was also invited to look over the house one last time as it still was, writing to Helen Clark, 'how one dose cling to old things'. John Bright was buried alongside his second wife, and their graves marked with a stone. Helen Clark arranged that her mother's grave now be marked in a similar manner, and Eliza Oldham visited it on her behalf, prompting memories of her own youth as a mill worker: 'I have lived a deal lately in the past such a many things has come to my mind.' Some months later she recalled the day fifty years before when the nurse had brought John Bright's firstborn for her mother to see, sending Helen Clark a birthday present of two cups and saucers that she had inherited from her grandfather. Late in 1891, Eliza Oldham began to suffer with a face ulcer that gradually ate away her jaw, and on her doctor's advice that nothing could be done, she asked Helen Clark to pray for her. In the New Year, Hannah Oldham sought an early release from her engagement as a monthly nurse, and came to attend her aunt through a painful death, writing regularly to Helen Clark with details as to the care being provided. Eliza Oldham's passing that spring ended another living link between Helen Clark and her mother, Margaret Wood and the Rochdale of her youth.[9]

Helen Clark and family memory

In the years immediately following her father's death, Helen Clark regularly sought, through her diary, to assess and comprehend this new phase in her life. The entries reveal an ever more urgent need to mark the passage of time and to note with greater regularity than previously the birthdays of each of her children, and the anniversaries of the deaths of those who remained central to her sense of the past and her own relationship to it. Such acts of remembrance remained important to her until mental confusion clouded her final years. Her moods sometimes reflected a quiet sense of achievement, at other times a deep melancholy. Her children were leading increasingly separate lives at school or at work, so that within her immediate family she encountered greater freedom, but her wider kinship relations brought fresh obligations, especially in the care of aunts and sisters.

At this stage in her life, characterised so much by loss and its expectation, Helen Clark's preference was for books she had read in her early years with those closest to her. Visiting Chippenham, where Sir Samuel Romilly had lived, she returned to his memoirs and reflected on how 'all these scenes and people have passed away – as all are so swiftly passing'. Reading such books served to memorialise for her the long-standing radicalism that had guided the public lives of the Clark and the Bright families. Her diary entries might become a similar act of remembrance: making her regular diary acknowledgement of John Bright's birthday she wrote, 'it is hard to believe it is November, and the dark days at Rochdale seem far off'. Events like the annual meeting of the 'Village Album' also gained a fresh importance to her, for they sometimes served as a communal act of remembrance for those members of this kinship circle who had recently found 'happy release' from the trials of life. Pets had always played an important part in her emotional life, and might now prompt an unaccustomed sentimentality that she would earlier have scorned. So John Bright's Skye terrier, Fly, provided a special comfort to her on the sixth anniversary of his death: 'dear little Fly still here and very affectionate; from the look in her eyes one would think she knew the day'.[10] In these years, a new generation of the descendants of Elizabeth and John Bancroft began visiting Britain, keeping alive the kinship networks that Margaret Wood had been so anxious to preserve, and in this way, too, further strengthening family memory and identity.

In middle age, the preservation of her family's past became increasingly urgent to Helen Clark, and the rereading of old family papers with one or other of her aunts a valued pastime. She spent a quiet day in 1895 with Anna Maria Priestman, for example, 'She reading me many old letters of my mother's etc.' A few months later, on a visit to Newington House, she took the opportunity of reading her father's diaries, at that time in the care of Priscilla Bright McLaren. She returned to them again during a visit in 1897, 'with great and loving interest. So much depends on when and where one reads anything.'[11] So the preservation of diaries and letters continued to provide her with an emotional storehouse, preserving the extensive bonds of kinship that formed her sense of herself and her past, and establishing a repository of family memory as a legacy for the generations after hers. Such acts of remembrance provided precious times of retreat from her round of domestic

Figure 12.1 Helen P. B. Clark (1840–1927), with 'Fly', *c.*1890s

and public duties, but were indulged in only as fitted with her ethic of daily life – hence public life might intervene to displace what she considered a proper period for reflection on John Bright's birthday. Equally, thinking about his life confirmed her own sense of her place in the world, and the duties and obligations attaching to that position.

Visits to places associated with her family also served as 'sites of remembrance', especially in Newcastle and its environs, with all their Priestman associations. Where possible she involved her children in such acts of memorialising. So Roger and Alice Clark joined their parents at the public meeting held to unveil John Bright's statue in Rochdale. She recorded how after an 'exquisite' address from John Morley, the statue was revealed 'amidst an impressive silence' while a band behind played softly 'Should auld acquaintance be forgot'. Thinking back on the day she wrote how she had been especially moved to see the town placarded with immense bills with 'John Bright MP' in large letters: 'One did not see the rest, just that, and to feel it was the last time one would ever see the dear and familiar name so. It seemed like the real and final closing.'[12]

If the memory of her forebears continued to shape Helen Clark's sense of identity, the death of her father distanced her more from national politics, though she retained some access through her uncle, Jacob Bright, for a few years more. She did not lose interest in the fortunes of the Liberal Party, nor did her commitment to women's rights and radical reform decline. But she no longer felt so much in touch with these worlds. The presence of W. E. Gladstone might still draw Helen Clark some distance to a major political meeting, as in the summer of 1889, prompting 'many sad and touching recollections to me'. She continued to admire him as greatly as her father and to support home rule for Ireland despite her continuing doubts as to the wisdom of the Irish Nationalists in parliament. So she wrote to her husband: 'I am fit to explode, what with the conflicting emotions caused by the conduct of the Irish, the Northampton election, the imprisonment of Dillon and O'Brien ... Dillon and O'Brien seem to have no weapons but emotion, now they have resort to imprisonment. If they were all women it wd be said what irrational creatures women are.' Gladstone's death, and Jacob Bright's retirement from parliament because of ill health served further to reinforce her increasing sense of removal from metropolitan politics.[13] She found herself (together with many among her kinship circle) in the last years of the nineteenth century out-of-step with the times. Increasingly, she focused her political goals at the local level, within the women's movement and in the government of the Society of Friends.

The Priestman–Bright circle and the women's rights movement

The influence of the Priestman–Bright circle within the women's movement also began to decline in these years, with the death, for example, of Margaret

Bright Lucas in 1890. In her widowhood, she had become a leading figure in women's organisations, and was at the time of her death a pre-eminent figure in both the British Women's Temperance Association and the World Women's Christian Temperance Union, as well as the United Kingdom Alliance and the Order of Good Templars.[14] A new generation now moved into the leadership of the women's temperance movement, sometimes representing very different values. Lady Henry Somerset became president of the British Women's Temperance Association, for example, and sowed the seeds of further division when she lent her support to the reintroduction of the Contagious Diseases Acts in parts of the British empire. A 'social purity' perspective began to overtake the libertarian values that had informed the early repealers among the Priestman–Bright circle. They now gave their support to the Vigilance Association for the Defence of Personal Rights, while old friends like Millicent Garrett Fawcett moved to the fore in a new body, the Vigilance Society, which instead pursued moral reform through a set of repressive policies.[15] These internal tensions within Liberalism were reflected in growing political differences among members of the Bright circle. Radical Liberals like Helen Clark maintained their opposition to imperialism, aristocratic privilege, protective duties and war and lent their support to free trade, movements for greater democracy at home and the freedom of subject peoples abroad.[16]

The Priestman–Bright network had been further extended by the marriages of Charles and Walter McLaren, sons of Priscilla Bright McLaren, to Laura Pochin and to Eva Muller respectively who both became prominent figures among Liberal women and their organisations. Radical Liberal suffragists in this circle continued to pursue as inter-connected questions the demand for sexual equality with wider social reform politics; hence, their focus on women's organisation within the Liberal Party, and their support for as inclusive a measure of women's suffrage as possible. Their viewpoint reached a wider audience through journals linked to the WLF, the *Women's Penny Paper* and its successor, the *Women's Gazette*, the editor of which for some time was Henrietta Muller, sister of Eva McLaren and close friend of Helen Taylor. The influence of members of the Priestman–Bright circle may be tracked through their columns and those of a similar orientation, for example, *Shafts*, and later the *Women's Signal* once it came under the editorship of Radical suffragist, Florence Fenwick Miller.[17] The editors of both journals looked for and received financial as well as moral support from their friends among the Priestman–Bright circle as each paper struggled to survive.[18] Helen Clark's daughters, in consequence of such connections, began their contribution to the suffrage campaigns principally through the WLF, not the national suffrage societies.

If Radical Liberals such as these sought to realise their suffrage goals through the Liberal Party, other radical suffragists increasingly emphasised their frustration equally with both the national leadership of the suffrage movement and with such a political strategy. They chose instead to form new suffrage bodies, like the Women's Franchise League, established in 1887 by a group that included Elizabeth Wolstenholme Elmy, and Emmeline and Richard Pankhurst.[19] These organisations upheld the Radical-Liberals' inclusive approach to the demand but rejected what they saw as its subordination to Liberal Party interests and a wider reform agenda, including Irish Home Rule. Even here, however, the personal politics of the Liberal Party soon divided the membership of such bodies. Hence, those in the Women's Franchise League who continued to support Charles Dilke after a scandalous divorce case found themselves divided from those for whom he represented all that was worst in male subcultures. So when Ursula and Jacob Bright, firm Dilke-ites, shortly joined the leadership of the Women's Franchise League, Elizabeth Wolstenholme Elmy left to form yet another new suffrage society, the Women's Emancipation Union, in 1892. She found support from other members of the Priestman–Bright circle hostile to Dilke, like Anna Maria Priestman.[20]

The latter also continued, however, to campaign for women's suffrage largely through local Women's Liberal Associations and the WLF. In 1892, when the national leadership of the WLF refused to make women's suffrage a test question for Liberal candidates, Anna Maria Priestman formed the Union of Practical Suffragists to act as a ginger group on this issue among the membership of the WLF. Ursula Bright wrote a number of its leaflets, and Helen Clark and her daughters also lent their support. Increasingly, the Radical-Liberal suffragists of the Bright circle chose to campaign through such splinter groups, ones that adopted a more militant approach to the question, whether it be in seeking to make women's suffrage part of the Liberal Party election programmes, or to bring an end to coverture altogether, or to insist on the inclusion of married women in the demand. And some of the founders of twentieth-century suffrage militancy, including Emmeline Pankhurst and Dora Montefiore campaigned within these radical suffragist bodies at this time, suggesting greater continuities between the nineteenth- and the twentieth-century campaigns for the vote than is sometimes acknowledged.[21]

Priscilla Bright McLaren provides a further illustration of such continuities, for with the help of Alice Clark, at this time working in a shoe shop in Edinburgh, she mobilised support for the *Women's Signal* as it began to fail financially. Subsequently, she also lent enthusiastic support to the suffrage campaign among the women textile workers of Lancashire and Cheshire in the early years of the twentieth century, as did Kate (formerly, Lucas) Thomasson. Though her strength was declining, Priscilla Bright McLaren was still able to visit family and friends in the south, where both her MP sons kept homes in London. She also visited Helen Clark several times in these years and following her departure after one such visit, her niece wrote 'I never felt it more. Yet I am full of gratitude for this sweet and delightful little visit.' Equally, Helen Clark was able to visit Edinburgh more frequently in these years and help her aunt with the organisation of meetings there in support of women's rights.[22] Helen Clark stayed in touch, too, with their mutual friends from the anti-slavery movement and the early days of the women's rights movement, saddened, for example, by the frailty and loneliness of Clementia Taylor, when she visited her in Brighton.

The international networks of the Priestman–Bright circle were also maintained in these years, not just in support of women's rights but also of black rights in the United States and elsewhere. Both Millfield and the home of the Clarks' Impey cousins in Street were regular stops on the itinerary of visiting lecturers on black rights, both from the United States and from Africa. Catherine Impey was also known in the United States as a representative at congresses of the International Order of Good Templars, where she opposed the growing practice of segregation in the temperance societies there. In 1894 she undertook the organisation of a national lecture tour in Britain by Ida B. Wells to expose the horrors of lynching in the South. Frederick Douglass wrote to introduce Ida B. Wells also to Helen Clark and to explain her mission, for he had recently visited Millfield on what proved to be his last tour of Europe.[23] A new body, the Brotherhood Society, grew out of this campaign and Catherine Impey produced and distributed almost single-handedly a journal associated with it that she called *Anti-Caste*.[24] Through its columns, she set out to explain the practice of segregation, and the social and political consequences that followed from it. She also followed the work of some of the first campaigners for black rights in southern Africa. The columns of *Anti-Caste* show that several members of the Priestman–Bright circle, including Helen Clark, were among its small band of subscribers, as well as hosts of Ida B. Wells during her speaking tours in England. Helen Clark also took up the complaint of Ida B. Wells that Frances Willard, President of the World Women's Christian Temperance Union, refused to support the campaign against lynching.[25] Once again, kinship, friendship and family history as well as political values directed and shaped the involvement of women of this circle in movements for black rights.

Helen Clark and her daughters

Knowledge of parliamentary politics formed an important part of the education the Clarks provided for their daughters as well as their sons. At a suitable age Helen Clark took them to London with her to see the House of Commons at work. Here again kinship relations came into play for gaining tickets to the Ladies Gallery through the brothers and cousins who had followed her father and uncles there. The schooling the Clarks selected for their daughters similarly reflected a belief that education should prepare them for a 'useful' life in both public and private affairs. At the age of sixteen Alice Clark was at last considered strong enough to leave home for Brighthelmstone School in Southport, a resort favoured by Victorian consumptives. There were family associations also, for it had been established by Hannah Wallis, who had lived in Rochdale before her marriage and taught two of the Bright sisters. Now headed by her daughter, May Wallis, the school provided a relatively advanced curriculum and was able to prepare its students for the Cambridge matriculation examinations.[26]

Before leaving home for school, Alice Clark travelled to Bournemouth to make what proved to be a final visit to the friend and cousin with whom she had in earlier days shared her lessons. Pollie Morland was dying from tuberculosis, and the shadow of this disease continued to shape the life of the Clark family in the years ahead.[27] When Pollie Morland came home to Glastonbury to die, Helen Clark insisted that her other children also went to make their final farewells. From early adulthood she had accustomed herself to the company of the dying, and was never uneasy in the presence of death. She sought to inculcate a similar ready care and respect for the dying and the dead in her own children from their earliest years, and evidently saw in the knowledge of its rituals the ultimate recognition of a common humanity, and the proper acting out of values of family and community solidarity.[28] Sentimentality about the dead and dying was for Helen Clark not only weak and silly, but lacking in love and due respect.

Isabella Pasley did not share such views, at least where children were concerned, and clearly disapproved of Helen Clark's insistence that her youngest charges visit their dying cousin. In this she may at last have lost entirely the confidence of Helen Clark. The sensibilities of the two women were quite at odds on this matter, one that was fundamental to Helen Clark's outlook on life. She wrote to Isabella Pasley during the Christmas holidays of 1891–2 to let her know that she was no longer required as a governess for the Clark children, and giving a year's salary in lieu of notice. Though the two youngest children were approaching the age when they, too, would be sent away to school, Isabella Pasley had not expected to lose her position quite so soon, or to be informed in such a way. The Clark children were all greatly dismayed at their mother's treatment of their former governness. Isabella Pasley found temporary refuge with friends she had made among the Bright family circle, and then stayed with Dr Annie Clark after enrolling in a series of advanced lectures being held for women in Birmingham.[29] Eventually she returned to settle near Street, establishing a school there. Her former charges remained loyal to her until the end of her life, and joined together to provide an annuity for her old age, by which time she had become a convert to socialism and an active supporter of the Labour Party.

The abruptness of Helen Clark's decision seems largely to have been a response to her growing difficulties with her oldest daughter, Esther, who was rebelling against her position as an unmarried young woman in a middle-class family. She wanted to teach and sought to follow a number of her women kin who had pursued an independent life through a profession in education. Helen Clark decided her oldest daughter might first try taking over the teaching of her two youngest sisters, Margaret and Hilda. The experiment was not altogether successful, but Esther Clark was eventually allowed to undertake formal training as a teacher at the Durham College of Science in Newcastle. She gained a teaching qualification, but became engaged to marry during her studies, and was never to follow her profession in terms of paid employment. Her interest in education continued throughout her life, however, and she served on her local school board for many years as well as the Education Committee of her county council. Helen Clark remained ambivalent about such ambitions among her daughters and Alice Clark turned to her father to support her wish to sit the matriculation examinations for Cambridge University.[30] Other family needs intervened as we shall see, and she never pursued a university education. Margaret Clark, however, was allowed to study at Girton College, while Hilda eventually took up medicine at Birmingham University and qualified as a doctor.

In this regard the daughters of Helen and William Clark were more privileged than their sons. Both John and Roger Clark entered one of the family enterprises on leaving school, though the latter would have liked to have studied medicine. Their business training began on the shopfloor, John Bright Clark learning shoemaking from a master craftsman who supplied the bespoke shoes available from C. & J. Clark, and Roger Clark learning how to clean animal skins for tanning at the factory of Clark, Son and Morland. After school, William Clark had undertaken a short period of further education, studying chemistry at St Thomas's Hospital, to improve his knowledge of dyes and dyeing. Eventually, Roger Clark was also sent to study aspects of industrial chemistry and engineering for two years at the Yorkshire College in Leeds. Possibly his uncle, John Morland, provided an alternative model here, for he had been an outstanding student in the Chemistry Department of the Royal School of Mines, and subsequently applied his knowledge to the sheepskin factory in which he was a partner with James and William Clark. His parents travelled with Roger Clark to Leeds, introduced him to his professors, paid his fees and arranged his lodgings, leaving him 'with much hope that after all our perplexity we had chosen a good course for him'. On completion of his studies he returned to the sheepskin factory for some years, but later moved to C. & J. Clark where in time he became company secretary.[31]

Money, business and family life

After her father's death, Helen Clark continued to visit Rochdale once a year to attend as a shareholder the annual general meeting of John Bright and Bros. She had inherited shares in the firm as part of her legacy from John Bright, one that increased her personal wealth quite substantially. John Bright had originally divided his estate so as to leave by far the largest share to Albert Bright, with a smaller share to each of his younger sons, and a still smaller share to each of his daughters. This form of division was undertaken by Albert Bright as executor, but according to a note with the papers concerning Helen Clark's inheritance, in arranging for these legacies he recognised that his own share was 'excessive'. All four of his sisters received £11,000 in shares, while his brothers received £15,000, substantial advances on the provisions in their father's will. These revisions were negotiated between Albert Bright and William Clark, and the former was also, of course, the trustee of Helen Clark's marriage settlement.[32]

She sought legal advice as to whether this inheritance had to be incorporated into that trust. Her solicitor advised that her trustee would not be justified in retaining this money, but to remove any doubt she might release all her personal wealth from such control 'by power of appointment' in favour of herself. All her wealth would then become directly vested in her as her own 'absolute property'. She seems to have decided against this course of action, as her trust continued in existence for some years more, with her brother as trustee. But it appears that she used £7,000 of her personal wealth to invest in the land for, and the building of, Millfield, the new house away from the village that she felt necessary to better protect her children's health. This was organised in the form of a loan to William Clark from her trust and through her trustee that in turn took the form of a mortgage on that property, on which he was to pay interest at 5 per cent per annum. So in effect he was paying rent to Helen Clark to recompense her expenditure on Millfield. She took full charge of her estate only in 1905, by deed poll, after which this mortgage was also transferred to her. The previous year C. & J. Clark had been reorganised as a private, limited liability company, so she may have kept a separate trust until then to protect her estate from any business difficulties the company might encounter. Her estate received only the interest due on the £7,000 loaned, and the capital was not repaid. Towards the end of 1919, she transferred ownership of the mortgage to William Clark, after serious illnesses in the previous years and a subsequent decline in her mental powers.[33] Presumably, while she lived the mortgage was not an embarrassment to her husband, but it might have become so if she had predeceased him.

After her father's death, Helen Clark's closest identity was with her community in Street, and increasingly the public offices she held were connected with local bodies, rather than the national organisations she had helped establish in her youth. By the 1890s Street was enjoying a continuing process of 'improvement', in large part through the efforts of the Clark family. To ever-expanding employment, railway access, clean water, club, library, public hall, model housing and coffee house were added electricity (produced by the factory), and new educational facilities for secondary and technical education (in buildings offered to the county council by William Clark).[34] Her youngest children graduated in these years from the Band of Hope to the local Templar lodge; began to provide as well as to attend lectures and debates at the village club; helped participants present their exhibits for the annual Chrysanthemum Show and in time produced their own; contributed to the adult schools provided for working men and women; and helped establish the town's fire brigade. The 1894 Municipal Corporations Act, after the intervention of her cousin, Walter McLaren, allowed women to vote and stand for office on the boards of Poor Law Guardians. Though Helen Clark was not successful in the elections that followed, she was shortly co-opted on to the Wells Board

Figure 12.2 The Clark family outside Millfield, *c.*1897, from left to right: Esther, Hilda, Roger, Margaret, Helen, John B., Alice and William Clark

of Guardians, and her work on this body came increasingly to absorb her energies.[35]

C. & J. Clark was by now the largest employer in Street and the surrounding area. In 1889 James Clark retired and the joint capital of father and son in the business was estimated at £79,400, of which James Clark withdrew £23,000. William Clark now entered on a new, fourteen-year partnership with his brother, Frances J. Clark who brought £30,000 in fresh capital. James Clark continued to undertake the daily Bible reading in the factory's reading room at 7.30 each morning, and the relationships within the factory and the values of the Clark family still shaped community life. So, for example, James Clark subsequently bought an old mansion that stood near the factory site, using the house to provide accommodation for a School of Housewifery. This was perhaps the prompt to Alice Clark's interest in housework and cookery around this time. A Technical School was built in these years also. The silver wedding of Helen and William Clark was marked, to their surprise, by a procession of 3,000 villagers to their home, when an address from the employees of the Street factory was delivered. In response, William Clark invited his employees and their families on a day excursion to Bournemouth. The 1890s were also, however, a period of considerable tension between employers and the growing Union of Boot and Shoe Operatives. William Clark continued to resist unionisation, and to hope that no third party would enter his factory while he lived. The company took no part in the 1895 lockout either. His paternalistic style of employer–worker relations, and the relative isolation of Street, meant that the unionisation of C. & J. Clark proceeded only slowly, and wage levels remained substantially below the national rate until the 1920s, resulting in a good deal of migration from the area to the South Wales minefields around the turn of century.[36]

Helen Clark had frequent cause for anxiety concerning the poor health of her children in these years, and the future of John and Alice Clark was substantially reshaped by tuberculosis.[37] The health of her older son had become increasingly precarious from the time he entered the factory. His father was a man, evidently, of quite remarkable energy, and it may be that his expectations of his son, as of himself, were too great for the wellbeing of either. It was decided to send John Bright Clark on a voyage to South Africa. There were business reasons for this visit, but it was intended as much to explore the benefits of the climate there for a possible consumptive. John Bright Clark's accounts of his travels in South Africa suggest that it had proved a gruelling time, involving extensive journeys on bullock carts through the dust of the South African bush. His experience led him to advise against a view of South Africa as 'a comfortable country for people who have anything the matter with them'. So Helen Clark began to urge her husband to lighten their son's workload. He was not strong enough, she was now convinced, for 'full work', and it was not his fault that he appeared to lack his father's strength, either of body or mind. 'He is conscientious and gets worn with worry and pressure.' She now began to argue the need for them to find additional assistance in managing the family business.[38]

Within eighteen months of his return home John Bright Clark's health once again collapsed. Some tests were undertaken by a local specialist and the findings forwarded to Helen Clark by letter: 'He says he fears there are traces of tubercular disease. A great shock and trouble to us.' She went to the factory to ask her son to finish early, and found him feverish. She insisted he stay in bed while a further opinion was sought. In her diary entry on her fifty-first birthday she wrote: 'The saddest day I ever had.' The earlier diagnosis was confirmed and it was advised that the invalid leave for St Moritz as soon as possible. But John Bright Clark was exhausted with a high fever and 'much oppression of mind', and Helen Clark was evidently unsure of the wisdom of such a proceeding. Pollie Morland had, after all, died only the previous year after extensive travels through Switzerland and Italy in search of a cure, one that entailed considerable expense and lengthy family separations. So, instead, the advice of a homeopathic doctor was followed, involving some 'external application' on John Bright Clark's lungs. Roger Clark was at this time also suffering from a recurrence of the eczema that troubled him throughout his life. Helen Clark wished her sister-in-law were nearer at hand 'to help us look after our delicate children!' and Dr Annie Clark came to participate in further family deliberations.[39]

A London specialist, Douglas Powell, was then consulted and figured in Helen Clark's diary as 'the Oracle', for she evidently disliked his manner and doubted the carefulness of his examination of her son. None the less, his advice was accepted and she accompanied John Bright Clark for a stay in Davos. Substantial costs had been and would be involved, of course, in the treatment of John Bright Clark. William Clark had also now to manage the family firm, his household, and his community and political commitments single-handedly.[40] John Bright Clark did not recover his health until the end of 1894, after a stay at Nordrach, a sanatorium established by Dr Otto Walther in the Black Forest. During the Christmas holidays after his return home, Helen Clark was at last able to record: 'tonight we were all happily under one roof, for the first time for 2½ years'. The Clark family became, in consequence, fervent proponents of the Nordrach system of care for consumptives.[41]

In the meantime, his son's illness created a pressing need for fresh assistance in the factory for William Clark. Family memory records that he and Helen Clark had always hoped that one of their four daughters might enter the business. Esther Clark declined the opportunity, and it was offered to their next oldest daughter, Alice Clark, at that time preparing for the Cambridge matriculation examinations prior to leaving school. She accepted, putting an end to her aspirations to study at Cambridge and embarking on an altogether unconventional career as a woman industrialist. She seems never to have regretted her choice. Indeed, her accounts of her work in letters at this time suggest she enjoyed learning both the manual skills in the various processes of shoemaking, as well as the business side of shoe manufacturing.

Figure 12.3 The three Priestman sisters (left to right), Margaret Tanner, Mary Priestman, Anna Maria Priestman, *c.*1897

But that career did not provide a passage into the kind of independent womanhood that a number of sisters, cousins and aunts found through university study and professional life.

Alice and Hilda, the two of the Clark daughters who chose not to marry, each took a somewhat different path, but one that continued to meld private and public lives. They had a variety of models of single womanhood to observe and to learn from. The Priestman sisters remained substantial presences in the Clark family circle, for example, demonstrating how a single life might be lived that combined independence with service to family, community and reform politics. Their homes remained places of rest, convalescence and holidaying for friends and family even as all three continued active in a range of political and reform organisations. The example of Sophie Clark provided yet another model, still living in her father's house after his second marriage in 1892 to Sarah Satterthwaite, a widowed Friend and a notable women preacher and minister. Her diaries cease at the point of this marriage, and as they were carefully preserved up to this time, it seems likely that she stopped writing them. Possibly, they had served the function of tracking and assessing her journey towards a clearer sense of self, a more definite individuality. Her life continued to be shaped by kinship, for example, as aunt to a growing band of nieces and nephews in whose care she continued to assist from time to time. Equally, her father's remarriage may have released her from some of the cares of household management, and left her freer to pursue her own particular interests. For she had by this time established a position of her own within her local community, both in local government office and in various positions within the voluntary associations of the town.

Her kinship relations as aunt and sister also continued to shape, though to a much lesser degree, the life of Dr Annie Clark. She remained in Birmingham where she developed a large private practice and held honorary positions at both the Women's and the Children's hospital there. She also became the highly respected assistant of Dr Lawson Tait, one of the most successful, but also most controversial, specialists in gynaecology of his day. But she also frequently returned to Street for family gatherings, and sometimes joined the Clarks and others of her kin on holiday. As we have seen, she also remained an important source of medical advice and support for the Clark family in their many anxieties regarding the poor health of their children, and readily when called upon returned home or accompanied them to specialists.

Marriage, politics and women's rights

The year 1897 brought the first wedding among the children of Helen and William Clark when Esther Clark married an old family friend and neighbour, S. Thompson Clothier. He was considerably older than she, and her parents had some reservations about the marriage on this account. The couple was also to live in his family home, a substantial but dilapidated house on the edge of Street that reflected his more modest circumstances. It was at least close at hand and Thompson Clothier was from another Quaker family of long-standing in the area. Friends and relatives gathered for the wedding, including Priscilla Bright McLaren and all three Priestman sisters, a reunion that was recorded in a special photograph. Helen Clark prepared for the wedding celebrations under the shadow of a further possible family tragedy, however. For Alice Clark had been unwell for some weeks with symptoms that aroused fears of tuberculosis. This diagnosis was confirmed, though Alice Clark was not told of it until the wedding was over. Annie Clark and Bernard Roth stayed on afterwards to assist at an operation on her throat that was undertaken at Millfield. Alice Clark then followed her brother to Nordrach, returning seemingly cured to take up once again her position in the factory. Her fragile health remained a cause for concern in the years ahead, however. For tuberculosis was an unpredictable disease and might return. That possibility made marriage undesirable, for pregnancy was thought sometimes to strengthen the disease, leaving perhaps more motherless children. Alice Clark appears to have determined on a single life from this time.[42]

Public events that same year gave members of the Priestman–Bright circle grounds for growing optimism, however. The passage of the Municipal Corporations Act in 1894 effectively put an end to one of the main sources of division among suffragists, for it provided for the enfranchisement of married women in an important area of local government, the administration of Poor Law relief. That statutory defeat for the principle of coverture was matched by decisions in the law courts that eroded it still further. So the inclusion of married women in the demand for the parliamentary vote was no longer a cause for division, and the major suffrage societies came together for a conference that led, in 1897, to a reunification under the umbrella of the National Union of Women's Suffrage Societies, headed by Millicent Garrett Fawcett. Helen Clark served as an officer of this body in its early years, and a branch society was eventually established in Street in 1910. A private member's Women's Suffrage Bill was also introduced to the House of Commons in 1897, and was the first such Bill to pass a second reading. It could go no further without government backing, but this success was evidence of a revival in the fortunes of the campaign for women's enfranchisement. A national 'Appeal' on behalf of the demand got underway to produce a new petition to put before parliament. Esther Roper, Secretary of the Manchester Society of Women's Suffrage, was successfully leading a campaign among women textile workers as part of this renewed effort. The demand for votes for women was becoming a live issue once again.[43]

13 Suffragism and democracy

The Priestman–Bright circle and liberal politics

The mood of Helen Clark remained troubled in the last years of the nineteenth century, even as she acknowledged the many good things in her life. Looking back on 1897, she wrote: 'much is to be said, or at least thought, as to this last year, so full of interest and anxieties, with so much blessings added.'[1] Among those blessings she counted the lengthy visit of Priscilla Bright McLaren for the marriage of Esther Clark, and the improved health of Roger and Alice Clark. But matters of state also shaped her emotional life: 'In public matters trouble has rather thickened than lessened at least the sense of trouble has rather increased.' The death of Gladstone in 1898 seemed an especially dark day for both herself and Priscilla Bright McLaren: 'the link that connected her with her past life is broken.'[2] In these years Jacob Bright's declining health forced him to retire from parliament. Ursula Bright was for a time attracted by the growing labour movement, and considered joining the Independent Labour Party (ILP). But her friendship with Annie Besant subsequently led her increasingly to look to religion instead and more particularly to the Theosophical Society, and to turn away from radical politics. The visit Helen Clark made to the couple when in the south of France proved tedious in this respect: 'Theosophy inside, and pouring rain outside.'[3] Jacob Bright's death in 1899 represented the loss of yet another link with her family's radical past. Helen Clark was far less of a monarchist than her constitutionalist father had been. Though she never succumbed to the glamour of royalty as did some in her family circle, the death of Queen Victoria at the beginning of 1901 further compounded her sense of living now in a very different social and political landscape. Recording the event in her diary she commented: 'Very much overwhelmed with the sense of change, all the associations of one's life time altered.'[4]

The reform politics in which she had engaged since her youth was changing in character, a shift evident in the divided response of the Liberal opposition to the wars waged by a Conservative government against the Boer people in South Africa from 1899 to 1902. The pacifist, anti-imperial values of Priestmans and Clarks necessarily led them to campaign against the war, and to sympathise increasingly with the Boer people.[5] Mary Priestman helped organise a peace march, while Margaret Tanner presided over a peace meeting at Millfield, 'with much grace – in a pair of very elegant lavender gloves and a rich silk dress'. Priestmans and Clarks also became involved in a South Africa Conciliation Committee (SACC) that pressed for peace talks, also attending metropolitan as well as local demonstrations against the war. Helen Clark described the annual meeting of her local branch of the SACC in these terms: 'Homely and instructive, not many great, not many noble, not many "Friends", Alas ! Alas!'[6]

Her family also helped organise a series of public meetings for Emily Hobhouse, campaigning against the concentration camps established by the British military authorities in South Africa, and supported her plans secretly to sail for the Cape. Street remained a regular stop on the itinerary of black leaders from both the United States and Africa, and Helen Clark recorded the views of one visiting black bishop thus: 'he fancies England is going to improve matters in S. Africa! Alas!'[7] *Anti-Caste*, the journal of the Brotherhood Society edited by Catharine Impey, increasingly provided material from South Africa, including excerpts from a paper established by John Davidson Tengo Jabavu, who in time became another established friend among these circles, establishing a relationship that was to survive across generations of the Jabavu and Clark families.

The Clarks' children were now at an age to join in such campaigns: Hilda Clark made her first public speech against the war; Alice Clark, too, spoke at a series of meetings in Somerset; John Bright Clark adopted long-established Quaker methods of passive resistance, refusing to pay taxes as a protest against the war; sympathy for the sufferings of Boer women and children eventually took Margaret Clark to South Africa after the war's end, to join Emily Hobhouse in relief work there. Meanwhile the village blacksmith was persuaded to put up a Stop-the-War poster at his forge, though most of the inhabitants of Street supported the war. Threats to the personal safety of the Clark family became commonplace as they spoke out about their belief that the war was driven simply by materialist interests and the pursuit of imperial aggrandisement. Alice Clark recorded how they were hooted home after taking part in a local peace meeting, for example, and they became used to having to pass through threatening crowds.[8]

On her voyage home from South Africa in 1907, Margaret Clark met one of the Boer leaders, General Jan Smuts, and introduced him to her parents when they met her ship. Some days later he travelled to Street for a visit. Helen Clark reported him 'quite young, very simple and friendly', someone 'whom we all at once adopt warmly'. This friendship, too, was to cross the generations (and was to be further consolidated when Helen Clark's oldest grandson, William Bancroft Clark, married one of the daughters of Jan Smuts). So, by the early twentieth century, the separate legacies of abolitionism and of mid-century liberalism continued to find expression among the Clark family in their opposition to racism and to imperialism, and the friendships they formed with both Boer and black African leaders. It is difficult to see how such a balancing act might have been maintained without the warmth of personal friendships, or the values and practices of Quakerism.

The Street branch of the Women's Liberal Federation was suspended for two years during the South African wars – a sign of the divisiveness of the issue. Helen, Margaret and Alice Clark together with their three Priestman aunts attended a conference of Women's Liberal Associations at the end of 1901, where Alice Clark had proposed a resolution against the British concentration camps in South Africa. Now she 'toiled hard' by her mother's account to revive their local branch. Attending its first meeting after this break Helen Clark declared it 'Satisfactory on the whole'.[9] At the national level, there was now a leader of the Federation, in the person of Lady Aberdeen, who shared the Clarks' pro-Boer sympathies. In 1903, too, the WLF at last made women's suffrage part of its programme. The need for a ginger group in the form of the Union of Practical Suffragists now seemed redundant, and the Priestman sisters joyfully wound up that organisation. But, shortly, Anna Maria Priestman found herself under attack from within the Bristol Women's Liberal Association, one of the founding societies of the Women's Liberal Federation in the formation of which she had played so large a part. The Liberal candidate in this seat was not prepared to make women's suffrage part of his election manifesto, and his wife, Mrs Lennard, gathered support among members of the Bristol Women's Liberal Association to resist such a demand. Helen Clark reported how at a special meeting: 'All went off quietly, the women managing well to conceal their annoyance, and Aunt Anna behaved splendidly. A strange affair, however, the Lennards ousting her in fact.'[10]

Women's suffrage remained a contentious issue also within the British Women's Temperance Association (BWTA) in this period, and Helen Clark was among those who spoke strongly in support of the question at an executive meeting in 1898. Lady Henry Somerset, its President, resigned subsequently after being worsted by pro-suffragists among its leadership. Helen Clark also challenged a deputation from the United Kingdom Alliance, seeking BWTA assistance with a great temperance bazaar later in the year, by asking: 'whether these gentlemen were prepared to help us to obtain the weapon the Franchise, at which they seemed to me to look rather foolish, and said nothing. All the women cheered very heartily and many thanked me after, but they were far too willing to work at the Bazaar, and did not, beyond applause, back me up.'[11]

After the reunification of the suffrage movement in the formation of the National Union of Women's Suffrage Societies in 1897, Helen Clark was briefly drawn back into the leadership of the movement, working alongside old friends from her youth, including the Liberal Unionist, Millicent Garrett Fawcett, and a founder member of the Independent Labour Party, Isabella O. Ford.[12] Her daughters, too, found their commitment to women's suffrage leading them away from the WLF and into one or more of the suffrage bodies that now began the final campaign that was eventually to secure the enfranchisement of women. The faith of this circle in reform politics was also briefly restored as those opposed to imperialism regained some ground in the leadership of the Liberal Party. After attending a lunch for Campbell Bannerman, the future Liberal Prime Minister, in Bath in 1901, Helen Clark reported approvingly that there had been only one 'Imperialist speaker' and he had been 'very coolly listened to . . . It was a great pleasure to be once more at a hearty meeting on the right side.' A few days after, there was a large public meeting in Street on 'Internationalism versus Imperialism' to which the audience listened quietly, to her surprise. With the ending of the war Liberals of all persuasions were once again able to work in unity for the next general election. She even found herself back among the platform party at a major London Liberal rally that she attended with Alice Clark, with Campbell Bannerman in the chair. The general election in 1906 brought a Liberal 'landslide'. 'Great news' arrived from family and friends in the northwest, one nephew telegraphing, 'No Conservatives left in Manchester.' Nearer to home, a Liberal candidate was also elected at Wells with 'a fair majority', if less than had been hoped.[13]

The women's suffrage movement and 'militancy'

Two new suffrage organisations were established in Manchester in 1903: the Lancashire and Cheshire Textile and Other Workers Representation Committee (LCTOWRC), formed by Esther Roper, a former secretary of the Manchester Women's Suffrage Society, which aimed at organising working class women to demand the vote for *all* women, not only those with property; and the Women's Social and Political Union (WSPU), formed by Emmeline Pankhurst, alongside whom Ursula Bright had campaigned in both the Women's Franchise League and the Women's Liberal Federation in Manchester.[14] These new societies found supporters among survivors of the Priestman–Bright circle and such veterans of the movement rejoiced in the re-emergence of a well-organised radical current, one based in the northern heartland of provincial suffragism to which they remained linked by long-established family and friendship ties.

So, members of the Priestman–Bright circle were to be found across the growing range of women's suffrage bodies. Old friendships and long-established networks served to link them with the constitutionalists of the National Union, the militants of the WSPU and the working-class suffragists of the LCTOWRC. In its early years, the WSPU was glad to advertise the support offered by Ursula Bright, Lilias Ashworth Hallett, Priscilla Bright McLaren and Laura McLaren. Mary and Anna Maria Priestman became its most loyal supporters among this circle in the years ahead, and Helen Clark and her daughters were also in time drawn towards this and other militant organisations.[15] Their stories illustrate the distortion involved in treating the suffrage movement as if it were composed of two quite distinct and opposing wings, the constitutionalists (or 'non-militants', as the WSPU leadership generally characterised them) and the militants. So 'militancy' continues to be discussed as if it had a quite new, separate and stable character entirely distinct from 'constitutional' suffragism, even where its reference back to the long history of constitutionalism within British radicalism is acknowledged. Cross membership was not uncommon, at least until 1912, mutual sympathy often continued after then, and many suffragists saw both approaches as helpful to each other.[16]

The WSPU was in many ways a fresh expression of the radical suffragism of the last decades of the nineteenth century. Another figure in the early years of the WSPU, Dora Montefiore, had initially chosen to work alongside the Priestman sisters in the Union of Practical Suffragists, for example, and may also have adopted the tactic of tax-resistance in emulation of a protest they had made against the Contagious Diseases Acts many years before. In 1906 she refused to pay her taxes. The 'siege' of her Hammersmith home by bailiffs attempting to distrain on her property, was one of the first 'militant' protests to catch the eye of the national press. Members of the Priestman–Bright circle were able, by virtue of their standing as among the founders of the movement, to keep above the sectarian hostilities that increasingly separated the leaderships of the militant and of the constitutionalist suffrage societies.[17]

Militancy at this time developed further the political strategy that had been pioneered by the Union of Practical Suffragists, one aimed at pressuring the Liberal Party into making women's suffrage part of its programme. Now the Liberal Party was back in power, such a policy was in effect a demand for a government measure of women's suffrage, abandoning the long-established strategy of pursuing this reform through the introduction of private-member Bills. The WSPU's mode of campaigning centred on the staging of large public protests and demonstrations of support, and on what has been called the 'politics of disruption' – interrupting Liberal speakers at public meetings by persistent heckling, and campaigning against them in the by-elections then required if they were appointed to an office in the government. The WSPU quickly adopted a term coined by the tabloid press, 'suffragette', to distinguish themselves from the constitutional suffragists of the National Union.

Marriages and deaths among the Priestman–Bright circle

In 1899 Roger Clark returned from a voyage around the world and announced his engagement to Sarah Bancroft, of Wilmington, Pennsylvania. Helen Clark recorded the effect of this news on her and her family: 'Breathless excitement and astonishment on our part – and sorrowful feelings for poor Cousin William' (Sarah Bancroft's father). For her future daughter-in-law was a descendant of Joseph Bancroft, whose mills Margaret Wood had helped to finance seventy years before. Sarah Bancroft had visited Millfield, like many of her family before her, during a period of postgraduate study at Newnham.

Her sister, too, was subsequently to choose an English husband so the next three decades saw the Bancrofts regularly crossing the Atlantic, as new grandchildren were added to their family. Such a continuation of the transatlantic relationship first created by Woods, Bancrofts and Brights would surely have gladdened the heart of Margaret Wood. Helen, William and Alice Clark attended the wedding in Wilmington, and took the opportunity to make return visits to the many abolitionists and women's suffragists who had become family friends over three generations, including Frank and William Lloyd Garrison jnr, Susan B. Anthony and Elizabeth Cady Stanton. They also toured US shoe factories to observe the new technologies and methods of work that were transforming the industry.

In the next few years, Helen Clark became more settled in her own mind, more content with how she found the world, especially following the marriage of her older son, John Bright Clark, to Caroline (Cara) Pease in 1904. This daughter-in-law was a colourful figure of strong character and unconventional ways, and Helen Clark was delighted with this further addition to the Street family circle. Insofar as she was capable, she was somewhat in awe of Cara Clark, so much like herself in her scant regard for the conventions of femininity. After the marriage she wrote, 'this summer seems to have brought me out onto a broader plain, with more clearness of view, and recognition of many blessings thro' blessing to another.' Some months later she was reading G. M. Trevelyan's history of the American Revolution, which, she recorded, 'made me almost feel young again, the names of men and places bringing back the days when I used to read Irving's Life of Washington etc, sometimes perhaps in One Ash garden, with dear old Tiff [her dog], names so familiar.'[18]

In the presence of Cara Clark a family party might now take on an avant-garde air, as Roger Clark observed when a visitor arrived to find Cara Pease smoking while another family friend, Roland Thurnam, was engaged on his latest knitting project. Her first pregnancy, however, brought Cara Clark close to death. She had become ill shortly before the expected date of her delivery. Helen Clark wrote afterwards of 'a time I cannot describe. The Baby was dead. I told poor John. Then came the question was that to be all,' for Cara Clark's life also remained in danger. She survived after many days of uncertainty, and Helen Clark was the first to see her, apart from her husband, after she regained consciousness: 'It was an effort for her . . . It was touching to me, but we managed quite well.'[19]

Those aunts who had been mothers to her were now moving towards the close of their lives. She and her daughters were frequently at Oakridge to nurse Margaret Tanner, who died in the spring of 1905, having told them 'what a blessing our love had always been to her'. Among the testimonies at her funeral, Walter McLaren recalled a life of public work, despite Margaret Tanner's determined domesticity, while several women spoke of the inspiration she had been to them in their entry into public life. Helen Clark recorded, 'It was altogether very unusual and interesting and came at last to be soothing.'

Some weeks later she and her daughters helped her surviving Priestman aunts prepare the house for sale, taking special care to ensure the preservation of the many family letters they sorted at this time. The following year James Clark died, Helen Clark recording his life as one with 'Nothing to regret and every thing to be most thankful for.'[20]

The Liberal election victory of 1906 brightened the last days of Priscilla Bright McLaren. Helen Clark received news of her aunt's last illness from 'Bennett', longtime lady's maid to Priscilla Bright McLaren. She arrived in Edinburgh to learn that 'the darling creature has passed away peacefully at 2.30, not having opened her eyes that day, or known Charles and Walter'. Helen Clark visited the body and recorded: 'Aunt Tilla looked very peaceful and dignified . . . the house did not seem yet forlorn', but she was, unusually, unable to complete her diary entry for the day of the funeral. A month or so later she returned to Edinburgh with several members of the McLaren family, when they began 'to struggle with the letters'. Some of these she was able to secure for her own family collection, almost certainly the correspondence between her aunt and herself, her father, and each of the three Priestman sisters. She had one further last duty to undertake on her aunt's behalf – securing the future of her servants, and most especially of Bennett, for whom a place was made, albeit not a happy one, at Bodnant, the country home of Laura and Charles McLaren.[21]

These deaths were necessarily a watershed in the life of Helen Clark. Each aunt at different times had stood in for the mother of whom she had no memory of her own, and each had attempted to ensure that Elizabeth Bright remained in some sense a living presence in her daughter's inner life. Their passing, then, was like the death of a parent, and seemed to mark Helen Clark's own entry into old age. Her interest in politics did not wane, but her connection with public worlds became increasingly confined to the triangle formed by her own locality, comprising Street, Glastonbury and Wells, and the larger centres of Bristol and Bath. She continued to visit London occasionally on business connected with the Society of Friends, and maintained her membership, alongside her daughters, of the Lyceum Club. She also returned each year to her old home at One Ash in Rochdale, around the time of the annual general meeting of shareholders in Bright Brothers.[22] Her public worlds, that is to say, now became almost entirely congruent with her private worlds, family, community and church now providing her principal means of engaging with the society and the polity that she still sought to change. Though she continued to maintain her formal membership of a range of moral reform and political associations, she also increasingly made way for a new generation in their leadership, not least in the persons of her six children.

She still found puzzling the new options available to her unmarried daughters for they suggested both comforting continuities and unsettling change. Some of the mystery of the new world for women created by college life was dispersed when Hilda Clark was taken ill with quinsy while visiting Margaret Clark at Newnham. She needed her mother's nursing for several weeks, and Helen Clark was glad of this opportunity to come to know something of college life from the inside. Inevitably, though, this new world allowed Margaret Clark to begin to build a different mental and emotional world of her own, so that her mother found her, when home for the holidays two years on, 'rather preoccupied, much more so this holiday than on previous ones, and causing us a shade of anxiety as to the influence of the new life'.[23]

At the heart of such concerns was almost certainly Helen Clark's resistance to the individualism of scholarly life, its removal from the world of public affairs, and the alternative it might provide to the religious community of Friends, that is to the very values and activities that formed her own sense of right living. Alice Clark, too, expressed a similar sense of unease when visiting Hilda Clark at university: 'She seemed entirely immersed in her affairs.'[24] Both her younger sisters followed paths that eventually led them away from the family and community life of Street in which she herself remained immersed, and Alice Clark must have wondered how different her own life might have been if she had pursued her academic ambitions. Hilda Clark did well in her studies passing her first set of examinations in the first class, an achievement that was evidently unexpected by her family. Helen Clark noted other changes with equal approval – her daughter now departed home cheerfully, 'delighted to go, and looking nice and very much more tidy that usually', while also recording how she left behind a room that gave the impression of 'the flitting of a whole family'. This child, the prospect of whose birth had so taxed her mother, and whose whirligig energies had sometimes disrupted the calm and order of her home, grew in the years ahead into a person to whom Helen Clark felt able to turn for support at times of fresh trials, one who at last seemed content, and more ready to enjoy an occasional period of quiet and tranquillity when home at Millfield. Dr Annie Clark evidently kept a watchful eye on her niece, and in her usual severe manner from time to time offered advice as to matters of professional deportment and development.[25]

In time Alice Clark became the only unmarried daughter at home, and Helen Clark took a special pleasure in her company.[26] But she also almost entirely ignored Alice Clark's work and growing responsibilities in the family firm. It was as if she could comprehend this part of her daughter's life only as an extension of family life. For her part, Alice Clark successfully combined her various roles in both domestic and public life, her mother writing on Christmas day 1906, for example: 'Alice spent all day on Domestic Matters with good results.'[27] Alongside her work in the factory and home, she became in these years her mother's willing and valued companion in shared visits to temperance lodge meetings and in organising public meetings as well as nursing her parents through episodes of illness.[28] She also accompanied them during various travels abroad, for example, on a holiday in Egypt, sharing her father's enthusiasm for archaeology, and more especially for Egyptology. In her mother's accounts, she figures as a generous but somewhat self-contained companion, given to what Helen Clark saw as a doubtful capacity for forming sudden, adventurous friendships among the Egyptian villagers they encountered. The physical fearlessness that Alice Clark had demonstrated as a child in ice-skating and horseriding she now brought to camel-riding – while her parents kept to the more sedate alternative of donkeys. At Tewfik, Helen Clark recorded how her daughter, whose beauty at this time became the stuff of family legend, was 'nearly torn to pieces by rival camel keepers, quite a scene in the midst of which she preserved a calm and smiling appearance'.[29] From her late twenties, Alice Clark began to take her first fully independent holidays, and became, in the years that followed, an intrepid cyclist, sailor and camping enthusiast. By such means she found, while remaining a devoted single daughter-at-home, some space and time of her own, among fellow-enthusiasts for 'the simple life' movement.

In 1908, the Clark family suffered an especially heavy blow. Cara Clark was again pregnant, and appeared in good health and high spirits. A son was safely born in August, but the following day Cara Clark suffered convulsions and lost consciousness. Dr Elizabeth Dunbar was summoned from Bristol, and Hilda Clark, only newly qualified, assisted her. This time, however, Cara Clark did not recover, and John Bright Clark, like his grandfather and great-grandfathers before him, found himself a widower with a motherless child after only a few years of marriage. Cara Clark had in this time won the heart of her mother-in-law and her sisters-in-law. Her death was devastating for Hilda Clark, just then setting out on a medical career. After the funeral, the sisters scattered to the homes of kin to grieve; Margaret to their Priestman aunts, Alice and Hilda to the home of Franklin Thomasson, a second cousin. The beauty of the summer also provided glimpses beyond grief, and Helen Clark recorded a day when the countryside was 'marvellously irradiated as life itself might seem to be after some spiritual visitation in which a divine clearness revealed everything.' She wrote to Alice Clark: 'I seem to be hunting, searching for some clue that is missing both for John and myself. There comes occasionally a faint gleam. Then all relapses and sometimes one could fancy that the last month had been all a dream.' For herself, the baby increasingly provided comfort: 'It is a darling creature, and beyond words strange and pathetic to have in our house. Sometimes I think it looks sorrowful and nurse thinks so too. I love to have it here.'[30]

She turned to Mary Curry, and her sister-in-law, Sophia Sturge Clark, for advice on how best to arrange the child's care. Both strongly urged that John Bright Clark continue to maintain a household of his own, and that the baby remain with him, with help for the time being from his as-yet single sister, Margaret Clark. The nurse also believed the child should remain with his father: 'and *much* as I love having it here I should be most ready for it to go to be at its own natural home for at any rate some time. I write all this because I think we should all agree, and beyond this quiet communication should leave things.' Grief continued to strike her suddenly and unexpectedly, reporting a day that summer 'so beautiful that it seems almost to bring sorrow more freshly before me. I don't know why. The Baby is a delight to me, tho' sometimes makes me very sad when I watch it'. The family strategy seems to have worked: three months later Helen Clark was able delightedly to report how John Bright Clark had for the first time taken his son for a long walk in his perambulator, 'And seemed I thought rather pleased, tho' it must have been a little searching to meet Sunday folks for the first time.' Alice and Margaret Clark each lived at their brother's house from time to time to provide company. Esther Clothier supervised the baby's nurse. Helen Clark's own identification with, and fondness for, the child remained over the following years. Recording his departure for a visit to his Pease grandmother the following year, she wrote: 'I shall imagine its welcome like that I used to receive when I was little at Summerhill.'[31]

As so often in times of trouble, Helen Clark turned to old letters for consolation. After helping with arranging the papers of Priscilla Bright McLaren in late 1906, she had begun at home to sort what she called 'modern' letters – perhaps her own correspondence. In the weeks after the death of her daughter-in-law, however, she looked further back, spending an evening with John Bright Clark, 'reading wonderful old letters of Aunt Tilla (Priscilla Bright McLaren) and Aunt Peggie (Margaret Tanner)'. The year chosen was 1842, that is, the period following her mother's death. She recorded how this correspondence, 'picturing an old world with all the love and all the anxieties which belonged to those who are now all gone', was able to rouse him occasionally out of the withdrawal of his own grief. She confided in Alice Clark: 'I must conceal these letters carefully as they don't legally belong to me, tho' more interesting to me than to any one else living.' Her remaining Priestman aunts seemed also to be going through their papers, in readiness for passing them on to her. When Alice Clark was on a visit to Anna Maria and Mary Priestman in 1909, her mother suggested she might 'get some old letters read and brought back'.[32]

Alice Clark became a frequent visitor at 14 Chenies Street Chambers, the flat where Hilda Clark lived when completing her medical training in London. Here she encountered a community of working women living an independent life of their own, and pursuing careers that were quite distinct from family life – a very different world from her own where business, politics, work and religion melded with family and friendship, and a discrete life of her own was impossible. Hilda Clark at this time formed the friendship with Edith Pye, a senior nurse who was to become her lifetime companion, and to share in many of the humanitarian endeavours in which she became engaged in later years. For her part, Helen Clark still worried that her daughter had chosen a demanding position that would make too many demands upon her – she was again working in a maternity hospital, and the memory of Cara Clark may have shadowed Helen Clark's assessment of such work: 'I don't suppose the men have any idea of the anxiety a woman has about those women and babies.'[33] Helen Clark was also concerned by this time at the extent of Alice Clark's commitments. Not only was her daughter working full-time at the factory, she was also increasingly involved in suffrage and Liberal Party campaigning, alongside her continuing commitments in terms of community associations and public service.

Her fears proved justified, for in 1909 Alice Clark's health began to fail once again in the re-emergence of the tuberculosis that had necessitated an operation a decade or so earlier.[34] This fresh worry coincided with the wedding of Margaret Clark so that Alice Clark was about to become the only daughter remaining at home. A Bristol specialist advised that she take a long holiday away from both work and home, and remain silent to rest her throat. Her mother accepted that such isolation might be necessary, and wrote: 'Well, one must needs apply oneself with devotion to necessities, and at any rate it is well thou art one to enjoy reading and seeing, and not one of the sort who have little inward enjoyment.' When Alice Clark's condition continued to worsen despite this measure, she accepted the need for a period of care in a sanatorium. An old family friend, Dr Rowland Thurnam, had recently opened one based on similar lines to Nordrach in nearby Blagdon. So in January 1910, Helen Clark accompanied her daughter to Nordrach-sur-Mendip, writing afterwards: 'My dear child, it seems very bereaving to have our last dear Prop taken away.' But letters now proved unsatisfactory to both herself and her daughter: 'Every detail is carefully scanned. We wish we could communicate better.'[35]

The regimen at Nordrach required the isolation of the patient from family and friends, while the Clark family now became immersed in campaigning for a coming general election. The prospects for Liberal candidates in Somerset seemed poor and the Clarks' car was needed to transport speakers and canvassers around the constituency, and to the poll on election days.[36] So Helen Clark sought to cheer her daughter with detailed accounts of the family's adventures in electioneering. Many of the working people of their town shared the Clarks Liberal politics, and she told of 'a dreadful rowdy meeting' in Street early on in the campaign when the younger factory women became 'terribly wild and silly – I don't believe the Tories minded at all. It all plays into their hands.' She enjoyed having her brother, Albert Bright, with her at this time, as 'we can narrate many things in which we unite – political especially'. But as the campaign proceeded she had to acknowledge that Liberal supporters were feeling increasingly low about the election: 'Everything seems behindhand.' As polling day approached, she wrote: 'Every thing thickens – cars fly hither and thither.' She herself began to canvass in any spare moment she could find but Liberal Party support in the East Somerset constituency, which the Clarks and the Morlands had done so much to build, was both divided and dwindling.[37]

She was unable to sympathise with the active opposition from the Women's Social and Political Union against all Liberal Party ministers, telling of a visit to Bath where 'A pleasing S and P [WSPU supporter] accosted me at the top of Milson St. She has a craze that she *must* oppose Liberals.' Helen Clark suggested the suffragists could hope for nothing better from the Tories, but her militant colleague remained unconvinced: 'She was pleasing but I fear accounted me a reprobate. I think all these people are simply deluded, like men tariff-reformers.' On a brighter note, she reported, 'Our Liberal women are much reunited I think.' But defeat seemed inevitable locally: 'We are rather in a state . . . How glad I shall be when it is all over.' When the polls closed she accompanied William and his brother to the count, reporting 'almost literally nothing to be seen but blue favours . . . But everyone was very agreeable, probably because they were happy.' The size of the Conservative majority was a particular blow to the local Liberal supporters: 'We were a very sympathetic band sorrowing together. It seems generally thought that the [agricultural] labourers have deserted, under stress of long and persistent [Conservative party] work. The canvas shows 700 promises not kept! All a very serious and novel situation.'[38]

In Street itself, the crowds were angry at the result, and attacked a manager at the Clark factory after he expressed his satisfaction at the Conservative victory 'with more vigour than discretion'. A policeman had had to escort him into the factory, and had advised that he leave by a back way. There had also been some unfortunate stone-throwing in Glastonbury, and the mood in the town was 'unattractive' at present. Some days later it emerged that disappointed Liberal supporters were organising a boycott of the Conservative butchers in Street: 'It sounds amusing but is rather a sad fray.' The Liberals expected also to lose the Wells constituency (the Conservative candidate won with a majority of nearly 1,300), and to retain only two Somerset seats. Visiting her Priestman aunts afterwards Helen reported 'Great political talks are always going on here.'[39] Election work continued for her husband in seats that had yet to poll, while Liberal women in her immediate family circle continued collecting at the polling booths a voters' petition organised by the National Union supporting women's suffrage. A Street branch of the National Union had been formed the better to be able to perform this task, with Sarah Bancroft Clark as secretary. In the end, the Liberal Party held on to government, but only through an informal coalition with the growing force of the Labour Party.

Now she confronted and sympathised with Alice Clark's growing rebellion against the subordination required by her medical advisors 'I grieve over thy spending all thy sweetness away from us.' Her daughter's letters became more and more insistent that she wished to leave the sanatorium. Letters were late and went astray, causing further misunderstandings, so that when Helen Clark was finally able to visit, she found her daughter had barred the door of her room, and refused to discuss matters with her. She wrote afterwards, 'It was sad for me to come away feeling I had only done thee harm . . . I never had such an experience before. I will do all I can for thee.' She began to prepare for Alice Clark's return home: 'Do not dear Alice think ill of me. We have so sought to do for the best, and do not even now feel sure we were misled . . . but thou wilt have to pluck up a little, poor thing.'[40] Two years of a controversial treatment with tuberculin followed, under the supervision of Hilda Clark, and left Alice Clark too weakened to return to her work at the factory. Now she embarked on a search for greater autonomy and independence, and a more self-directed life, one that took her away from her family home and the family firm for a decade or so.[41]

Women's suffrage and a democratic franchise

The greater vulnerability of the Liberal government following the general election opened up greater opportunities for the suffrage campaign, and its parliamentary supporters. The two main parties were now more evenly represented within the House of Commons. While women's suffrage had more widespread support from the rank-and-file of the Liberal Party than from its leadership, the position was reversed in the case of the Conservative Party. Here, many in the leadership favoured the enfranchisement of women of property as a bulwark against the possibility of an increasingly democratic franchise. A number of the leaders of the Labour Party were also sympathetic to women's suffrage. The radical journalist, Henry Brailsford joined with Lord Lytton, brother of a the well-known militant, Lady Constance Lytton, to form an all-party 'Conciliation Committee' of MPs to draft a private women's suffrage bill that suffragist MPs of all parties agreed to support. It provided for the enfranchisement of all women householders, and the wives of householders. In so doing it satisfied the Conservative preference for a property qualification, while making the property required of such small value that it would have enfranchised many working-class women – or so leading figures in the Labour party, such as Keir Hardie, argued.[42]

The advance of the Labour Party, however, proved a more complex benefit. Many of its leading members had recently established a People's Suffrage Federation the aim of which was universal suffrage, the vote for all adult men *and* women. It was a formulation that attracted the support of national organisations of working-class women like the Women's Cooperative Guild. It was one, also, with which a significant current within the suffrage movement was in sympathy. I have elsewhere identified this current as composed of 'democratic suffragists', following a formulation first coined at this time by Margaret Llewellyn Davies, president of the Women's Cooperative Guild. For the time being, however, the main organisations of the suffrage movement held to a formulation of their demand in terms of equal suffrage, and all gave their support to the Conciliation Bill. Their leaderships continued to fear that universal suffrage might easily be diluted to manhood suffrage through the more ambiguous formulation of 'adult' suffrage – a formulation that might mean either all adults, or only all adults among the sex currently permitted to vote. So the Conciliation Bill seemed to provide a real breakthrough. The WSPU announced a truce from militancy during its passage through the House of Commons, and major demonstrations in its support were organised that summer by all the suffrage societies.[43]

Helen Clark had evidently walked in an earlier suffrage procession with Alice Clark, possibly in one of the marches of the Women's Parliament that had become a regular part of WSPU activities from 1907. At this time she could only send her ailing daughter second-hand accounts of the first of these events, and recommendations as to best newspaper reports. The stories she heard when visiting her Priestman aunts made her wish she and her daughter could again have taken part together: 'Thou are such a very nice creature to walk with.' Helen Clark and her daughters lent their support to both militants and constitutionalists at various times, and continued also to take an interest in the suffrage movement internationally. In 1907, for example, Alice Clark had become a tax-resister and was feted by the leadership of both the National Union and the WSPU. Thereafter, she had lent support to a new militant body, the Women's Freedom League, formed after a split among the national leadership of the WSPU. In 1908 she had travelled to Amsterdam, to take part in the conference there of the International Women's Suffrage Alliance. Anna Maria and Mary Priestman meanwhile continued to host visiting organisers and speakers for the WSPU, as well as those militant suffragists escaping from the 'Cat and Mouse Act'. Helen Clark was intrigued to meet one such 'escaped Suffragette' at lunch with them.[44]

In general, though, she and her daughters still campaigned largely through the Women's Liberal Associations and the National Union, while also readily taking part in militant meetings and demonstrations. If she thought the tactics of the WSPU mistaken, Helen Clark continued to be attracted to the daring and courage of many of its supporters, and like her daughters became increasingly disillusioned with the Liberal government. Margaret Clark Gillett was now a mainstay of the Women's Liberal Association in Oxford, counting among her closest friends and political colleagues there, Lady Mary Murray, daughter of the President of the Women's Liberal Federation, Lady Carlisle, Alys Russell, wife of Bertrand (who had stood as a women's suffrage candidate in the 1906 general election), a supporter of the National Union, and Ray Strachey, niece of Alys Russell, at this time also actively campaigning on behalf of the National Union. But Margaret Clark Gillett was also increasingly sympathetic to the use of stone-throwing at the windows of government buildings, a tactic that had been introduced by individual WSPU rank-and-file members in 1908, both in protest and as a means of ensuring a quick arrest.

The Conciliation Bill came before the House of Commons in 1910 and 1911, and passed its second readings. To progress further, however, it needed to gain the support of the government, and this was promised after its successful reintroduction in 1911. If the Conciliation Committee could secure a further successful second reading, the government agreed to allow time for the Bill to become law during the following year. This apparent success and the coronation in the summer of 1911 provided the occasion for more peaceful suffrage demonstrations all over the country. Helen Clark was in London with some American suffragists at the time, members of the Garrison family. Agnes Garrison offered to march with her, her daughters perhaps doubting the wisdom of a seventy-year-old joining in such a demonstration, but she was able to reassure them: 'I have in ambush a 2/- ticket for a seat in a brake if it seems needful.'[45] On the day, she walked the whole route of the procession with a contingent of United States suffragists, though Street also sent a contingent of its own. Agnes Garrison and her mother fell out to observe proceedings from the Albemarle Club. Afterwards, they all met up at a WSPU demonstration in the Albert Hall, and Helen Clark recorded: 'It was curious to hear and see the money coming in by hundreds and fifties and twentys [sic].' She was more impressed with the speaking of Emmeline Pankhurst than of her daughter, Christabel, and regretted only that hunger and fatigue forced her to leave before being able to hear Annie Besant, whose speech was, by all accounts, the most impressive. She was also cheered by the new spirit of optimism and conciliation: 'The women seem to accept fully what Asquith [the formerly anti-suffragist Liberal prime minister] has said, and to feel that they now see an end. It is a great comfort.' She wrote to Alice Clark: 'I wish thou could have gone with me today. My impression is that the crowds, the whole length, were more sympathetic than last time. Certainly I never heard a word approaching a jeer.'[46]

By 1912 Alice Clark determined on a new life for herself in London. She remained on the board of the family firm and enjoyed a small private income from the shares she held in it. With this she lived the life of a private researcher in London, where she was also able once more to take up a more active role in the suffrage movement. She had long shared her parents' interest in history, and with them had kept abreast of new work like that of the Hammonds on the working life of ordinary people. The main prompt to this new direction, however, was Olive Shreiner's, *Woman and Labour*, read while a bedridden invalid between 1909 and 1911. She began working in the library of Friends' House in London, assisting the librarian there, Norman Penney, with his publication of the household accounts of Margaret Fell, wife of George Fox, and with him among the founders of the Society of Friends. Subsequently, she was appointed to the Shaw fellowship at the London School of Economics, to work on a history of women's work in the seventeenth century.[47]

In the meantime, she took up an honorary position at the headquarters of the National Union, as assistant to its parliamentary secretary, Catherine Marshall. It was a position that put her at the centre of National Union campaigning over the next few years. The Liberal Chancellor of the Exchequer, David Lloyd George, had effectively 'torpedoed' the prospects of the third Conciliation Bill when he had announced at the end of 1911 a government measure of manhood suffrage. The consensus so carefully built between suffragists of different parties within the House of Commons was thereby shattered. The WSPU had not been party to the discussions between the government and suffragists, and was thrown into some confusion initially. Christabel Pankhurst played briefly with the possibility of attempting to achieve votes for women through support for full adult suffrage. This was the strategy now adopted by the other major militant body, the Women's Freedom League. Shortly, however, the WSPU leadership decided on a return to militancy but on a much greater scale. The first mass raids on London's west end, and the shattering of shop windows in its famous shopping streets, took place within weeks of Lloyd George's announcement of a new Reform Bill. Militant protest now moved beyond civil disobedience directed at pressuring the government, to direct action aimed at threatening its legitimacy as the guardian of public order. This was a step too far for many of the WSPU's long-standing supporters, and divisions began to emerge among its leadership that led eventually to the expulsion of the Pethick Lawrences, and of Sylvia Pankhurst and her East London Federation of Suffragettes.[48]

The National Union took a number of months to work out its response to the announcement of a government Reform Bill providing for manhood suffrage. Alice Clark returned to suffrage campaigning at just the time its new strategies were being put into practice. Catherine Marshall, in her office as Parliamentary Secretary to that body, was central to this new departure. She and other democratic suffragists had become convinced that the success of their cause now rested with gaining support from the Labour Party and were sympathetic to the goal of full adult suffrage. They now believed it might be possible to secure a measure that ensured both a more fully democratic electorate and sexual equality within the franchise laws. Many of these democratic suffragists were already finding themselves drawn to labour politics, while others subsequently moved in this direction through the suffrage campaigning of the next few years. By the summer of 1914, there were signs that the Liberal government was preparing for an approaching general election, and that franchise reform would be part of its manifesto. There were signs, too, that it was looking to reach a compromise with both the National Union and the East London Federation of Suffragettes, one that promised the hope of a successful women's suffrage measure should the Liberal government be returned once more. But the possibility of a European war also grew that summer.

By the beginning of August 1914 anxiety over the prospect of war had become intense. The speed of events began to overtake the capacity of those opposed to war to organise and protest against it. Alice Clark had only recently arrived in Germany to visit friends, and when war was declared, her mother wrote: 'It is shocking that our fleet had sailed – quite on the loose – like Lufra [her dog] barks to go out when she hears another dog elsewhere. It is, and has been always, a terrible risk to have C. [Churchill] at the Admiralty.' Though normal life continued, she found 'everything clouded with anxiety and with grief at the unnecessary danger we may be in'. The *Manchester Guardian* also seemed to fail her now: 'I miss from it any of the good letters one would formerly have had from faithful friends. People seem dumb (and many gone hence).' For her the recent assassination of the French statesman, Jaures, made him 'a martyr in the greatest of causes'. She also sent a message to Alice Clark's German hosts that 'what ever happens I shall never feel a German to be an enemy'. Her diary records the 'great shock and distress' she felt when finally war was declared. It remained unclear for some days whether her daughter had been able to turn for home in time. In the event, Alice Clark found her way to Holland and telegraphed news of her escape on 9

August, finally reaching Harwich some days later. Many Germans were similarly stranded in Britain. Some were able to seek help from the networks that had created the international women's suffrage movement, and Millfield provided refuge for at least one young woman from Berlin in the weeks that followed.[49]

Helen Clark went as soon as possible to her aunts in Bristol, for whom she feared the advent of war would prove unbearable. She took with her the 'stout letter' that Alice Clark had sent on reaching London, the contents of which 'nearly took our breath away'. She found Anna Maria and Mary Priestman 'wonderful, considering what is happening', and quite able to listen, 'where no slaughter is involved', to newspapers reports. The readiness of the two to take in sick children had not abated and within days they had care of a 'little unlooked for whooping-cougher'. Within a few weeks, however, Helen Clark was summoned to Bristol on the sudden illness of Mary Priestman. She found the house in confusion, as beds were needed for four nurses, and the house was already full to overflowing with recipients of her aunts' accustomed kindness: a young German woman stranded in Britain, an invalid great-niece with troublesome companion, and the convalescent child. She found Mary Priestman half-sleeping but 'always talking, and about the Summerhill family'. Her aunt was able to recognise her still, but became increasingly confused so that Helen Clark feared she 'will never know us again'. When her aunt rallied briefly, she began to doubt the medical diagnosis of a stroke, believing that Mary Priestman might be suffering rather from 'the shock of the war'.[50]

So she stayed to share the night watches with a nurse and her cousin, Fanny Pumphrey. Anna Maria Priestman now also became ill, though Helen Clark was able to record 'really some quite lively talk' with her. Alice Clark arrived next to relieve her mother in the care of those who had so often nursed them both. Anna Maria Priestman died on 9 October, and Mary Priestman on 15 October 1914. Unwell herself, and advised to remain at home by her doctor, Helen Clark was present at neither death. She was able to visit the body of Mary Priestman, however, and to feel some satisfaction in what 'a kind Providence has ordained. Every newspaper makes me more thankful', for her aunts were spared the larger horrors that were still to come from the war. The remains of the two sisters were taken to their parents' vault in Jesmond, enabling kin in the north to hold their own memorial service for them. Family and friends thought of them as among the earliest civilian victims of the war, unable to come to terms with an event that seemed in a stroke to have overturned their lifelong faith in the possibility of social progress and human perfectibility.[51]

Thereafter, Helen Clark tried to pick up the threads of her old life: enjoying the annual meeting of the 'Village Album' where the piano she had inherited from her aunts made its first appearance in her own home; returning to her regular visiting at the Wells workhouse; taking over supervision of the Street tuberculin dispensary established by Hilda Clark; continuing her part in the management of Winsley sanatorium. Her opposition to the war presumably explained her readiness to connive with members of the workhouse staff who 'regularly though rather secretly' received large supplies of excellent meat from a local army camp: 'Somebody there evidently does not like waste!' She asked Alice Clark to attend on her behalf the last meeting of the Ladies National Association, in London, for it was to amalgamate with the London office of the European Federation, opposed to state regulation of prostitution. It seemed especially appropriate that this meeting fell on the first anniversary of Mary Priestman's death.[52] The war years saw many other deaths among Helen Clark's family circle, including her aunt, Ursula Bright, her brother-in-law, Bernard Roth, and her step-sister, Mary Curry.

Paradoxically, the Clarks' family firm prospered because of the war, with government contracts to supply footwear for the armed services. 'In faith and hope' company managers decided to continue with two recent innovations, the Factory school and the firm's 'Welfare Lady'. Helen Clark reported how among a new generation of family members to join the company, Hugh B. Clark was 'rather wild to go off on some of these relief services'. But it was 'firmly pressed on him that the very best thing *he* can do is to try to keep the business going, for the sakes of all the village, as well as ours and his.'[53] Helen Clark recorded how 'every body is busy getting put on Relief Committees' and how 'There is a terrible jam-making going on too.' She wondered 'how soon Government will find out it has meddled with more than it can control.' However, the full order books meant there was no immediate distress in Street itself, and Helen and Alice Clark agreed to help set up a 'colony' in the town for Belgian refugees, and to raise the funds needed for their upkeep. Shortly, she recorded the death there of a young Belgian girl from typhoid, 'one of the fruits of war!' Helen Clark also persuaded one of her male colleagues to make way for a woman relative of hers on the Board of Guardians.[54] Dr Annie Clark, now living with Sophia Clark in Street, also came out of retirement, for there was a great amount of illness in the village, and a shortage of general practitioners. Sophia Clark subsequently cared for her in her last years, and continued on with her long-established contribution to local government until her death in 1933.

War and women's suffrage

The war necessarily disrupted the work of the suffrage societies, though the National Union of Women's Suffrage Societies NUWSS decided to maintain its organisation by engaging in relief work among victims of the economic and industrial dislocation that was one consequence of the war. Serious disagreements arose among its leadership, however, on a number of topics, including the Election Fighting Fund and the support it had promised Labour candidates in specific constituencies.[55] A still more divisive issue emerged regarding where the National Union should stand in relation to the peace movement that was growing among women, both in Europe and the United States. Helen Clark attended the Annual Meeting of the National Union on 4 February 1915, along with Esther Clothier, Alice Clark and Sarah Bancroft Clark, where, she recorded, peace was 'the chief question'. Many in the National Union leadership were internationalists and pacifists, but others, like its President, Millicent Garrett Fawcett, remained staunch 'patriots'. Helen Clark also attended the Caxton Hall meeting where the proposal from Dutch women of a women's 'Congress for Peace' gained unanimous approval, and she and her daughters took an active part in its organisation.[56] She went also, with Esther Clothier, to a further conference focused on the terms on which peace should be secured, and became an active supporter of the Union for Democratic Control, which had extensive links with the women's peace movement.

The association of so many leading members of the National Union with the peace movement was increasingly troubling to its President. An executive committee meeting in January 1915 lasted more than five hours, while Millicent Garrett Fawcett revised a series of resolutions on war and peace that had been drawn up by Alice Clark, Kathleen Courtney (former Secretary of the National Union) and Catherine Marshall. Alice Clark's own position was complex, for, like John Bright she believed war might, if very rarely, be justified to address terrible wrongs, and, for her own part, she believed the resolutions had been improved by these changes: 'Much trouble spent in such matters certainly pays.' Her preference for conciliation and consensus over disputation was evidently valued by the committee, for she was charged with the redrafting of an especially contentious resolution and her efforts met with unanimous approval. She took heart from this: 'I think there are on the Executive people with as widely divergent views as any in the Union, so I hope the consent of the Executive will foretell the unity of the [National Union] Council.' She thought that the resolutions as they now stood offered 'a foundation on which a sound public opinion may be built up', for they committed the National Union to an education programme on the causes and prevention of war. But her hopes proved ill-founded, and the divisions within the National Union grew into an irreparable breach between the peace party and the 'patriots'.[57]

The final split in the National Union occurred over the issue of participation in the Hague conference of women. The peace party believed such participation to be fully in accord with National Union policy. Millicent Garrett Fawcett and her supporters steadfastly refused any official connection, however. A meeting of the National Union's Council was organised for June when many of the leaders of the peace party were unable to attend, and Millicent Garrett Fawcett and her supporters carried the day. Most of the Executive Committee then resigned, including, reluctantly, Alice Clark, for this now left the National Union firmly under the control of supporters of the war. Like many others, the Street branch of the National Union disaffiliated from the central body, and planned to sponsor a delegate to attend the Hague conference. Helen Clark was able to meet some of the overseas figures at the forefront of the international women's peace movement as they passed through London, including Jane Addams. She and her daughters subsequently supported the Women's International League for Peace and Freedom, one of the outcomes of the conference. Helen Clark also pursued the campaign for peace through her local branch of the Women's Liberal Federation.[58] The war was to separate Friend from Friend, and the issue of conscription, which was introduced in 1916, proved among the most divisive for the Society. Among the men of the Clark family, some volunteered for military service, while another of Helen Clark's nephews refused to be conscripted and went to prison. A few left the Society altogether at this time. Helen and William Clark were fully in sympathy with the No Conscription Fellowship, and conscientious objectors were frequent guests at Millfield in these years. Helen Clark also attended the first hearings of the local Tribunal that decided whether or not an individual might justifiably refuse military service on grounds of conscience. It was presided over by her brother-in-law, Francis Clark, and she commented: 'It seemed to me somewhat like a slave market, and others felt it a very sad affair.' Esther Clothier became one of the most effective opponents of conscription and of the war within the Society of Friends. When these questions were discussed at their local monthly meeting, Helen Clark thought the final statements all 'more or less to the point', but there was no overall agreement among its members on the issue of the war.[59]

The course of Hilda Clark's life was entirely altered by the war. She had previously set up in practice in a working-class area of London, so as to offer the tuberculin treatment there. Within weeks of the war's outbreak, however, she began to press for a Quaker relief effort on behalf of refugees from the war zones of Europe. Helen Clark had some reservations about her daughter's 'doings' with regard to this. When she heard a rumour that Hilda Clark had persuaded the Society to send a relief expedition, she wrote, 'We hope there is not truth in this, but are blown about by many winds.' Her concerns appeared to relate to the necessarily hurried nature of the preparations, and her inability, while her aunts lay dying, to give any effectual help. Helen Clark had to be satisfied with buying chocolate for her daughter to take with her: 'I gather it is a really useful thing.' Nor was she sure of the wisdom of Edith Pye joining Hilda Clark in this project, believing her not strong enough and arguing that she 'must be of the greatest possible value to Hilda where she is – an alter ego, such as no one else could be'. Nor did she believe her daughter sufficiently diplomatic about the difficulties she was experiencing with the London headquarters of the relief expedition, and advised other family members to share the typed copies made of her letters only with their inner circle. By the end of the year, Hilda Clark's health deteriorated, and Helen Clark's fears regarding her daughter's 'rash' ways led her to comment 'wisdom lies not in that direction'.[60]

During the first months of the war Alice Clark remained mostly in London. She secured a temporary suspension of her fellowship at the London School of Economics in order to help with relief work among working-class women and children in Southwark, affected by unemployment and the enlistment of husbands and fathers. As such immediate distress eased, she decided to join her sister in her work with refugees, most especially the hospitals for women and children she had established at Samoers and at Chalons. To this end she began to train as a midwife. Helen Clark was as uncertain about this as about Hilda Clark's involvement: 'I hope thou may find some useful end in it. But we both hope thou wilt not undertake any thing too hard.' The decision also meant an end to her fellowship, and Alice Clark did not return to her historical research until the end of the war. She tried to alleviate her parents' fears, reporting that midwifery training was 'a healthy life' and probably easier than hospital nursing. Within weeks, however, her health was giving fresh cause for concern, and Dr McCall, alongside whom she worked, insisted that she go for a period of rest in a fresh-air colony for consumptives in Norfolk: 'I have been planted out in a revolving shelter in a little orchard place near the house. The night was cold. I had some difficulty in washing this morning as water, sponge etc were all frozen hard.'[61]

Now Helen Clark began to argue more forcibly: 'It is impossible for thee to do such continued work, with safety. . . . We hope thou wilt come home from thy present curious abode. Thou would be very acceptable.' Alice Clark's London specialist was pleased with the condition both of her throat and lungs, however, and she shortly returned to her training. By late April she was among the senior students, and told of witnessing the birth of 'a monster', something, she noted that may have led to charges of witchcraft in an earlier era. The last surviving letter from her Battersea address suggests that she came close to completing her training, and a photograph exists with her holding the first baby that she delivered. But no other evidence has so far come to light to suggest that she then went on to practice as a midwife.[62]

During the last months of her training Alice Clark also took on the secretaryship of one of the subcommittees of the Friends' War Victims' Relief Committee (FWVRC), which was overseeing the refugee work in France. Helen Clark wrote: 'We both feel very strongly against thy taking that Secretaryship now. It would have been different if thou had not taken up this last nursing. We said nothing about that . . . but having done that, it does not seem a very wise thing.' Instead, she suggested, Alice Clark should take a real rest for a month: 'Thou looks extremely thin – and thy cough sounds much worse – and I suppose thy taking another course means some sense of doubt. Thou art always some anxiety to us – at times a very great one, and we have suffered so much at times in the past, that we would be thankful to be spared more during what remains of our lives.' It may be that this work in the London office overtook her plans for midwifery in the field, or that she bowed to her parents' wishes. Nor does she appear in the records of the committee as its Secretary. But she was in Rotterdam and Gouda in November 1915, overseeing other aspects of the committee's work for refugees there.[63] Hilda Clark continued to complain about the inefficiency of London headquarters, and its failure properly to support the relief workers in the field.

Antipathy between herself and the overall Secretary of the FWVRC, Ruth Fry, continued to grow. Hilda Clark now carried an enormous workload, one that involved supervision of several relief centres and continual travel between them and the Paris offices of the FWVRC. She was grateful for a visit from a member of the London committee to investigate matters but worried that her letters appeared to remain unread, or if read, not acted upon. Helen Clark was troubled by such reports, but uncertain of her daughter's judgement in the matter: 'I fear she is herself rather worn out. She says the guns and the sight of the villages are so depressing.' But she also began to observe for herself weaknesses in Ruth Fry, noting how on one occasion she had written to *The Nation* but forgotten to give an address to which donations might be sent: 'The difficulty for us is to know how far Hilda herself may be unfit to get on with people through her long work and absence of rest.' So the presence of Alice Clark in its London offices must have come as a considerable relief to her sister, while for Helen Clark it provided an informed source of opinion on these matters. A letter copybook from this period suggests that Alice Clark shared her sister's assessment of Ruth Fry's obstructionism and poor management, while other evidence also began to reach Helen Clark: 'I wish some one could get Hilda sent home. I think she will be ill otherwise. The others all seem to get home.'[64]

Alice Clark learned to drive and spent the last months in France, apparently acting as chauffeur for Hilda Clark, and undertaking routine, light work in the maternity and children's hospital taking temperatures, and so on. But there was evidently another reason for her to join Hilda Clark: signs of tuberculosis had appeared again, and while in France she was evidently undergoing another course of tuberculin treatment under her sister's supervision. Her family were evidently still concerned about her health in the summer of 1917, and waited anxiously for the outcome of a further consultation with her London specialist. Meanwhile, Helen Clark's dismay at the problems experienced with the London office of the FWVRC continued to grow: 'It seems to me very wrong that Ruth Fry should be left where she is, apparently spoiling work. If she were a person without connections she would perhaps have been moved.'[65] She also suggested that Hilda Clark needed a 'second', when Alice Clark returned to her work in the London office. The health of Hilda Clark eventually broke down completely, and she gave up her work for the FWVRC. After a period of convalescence she returned temporarily to her earlier work as a tuberculosis officer in Portsmouth. Her mother wrote: 'Hilda seems to have very curious plans. Poor thing, she never tries anything for long. I am so very sorry for her.'[66] After the war, however, Hilda Clark responded to the growing famine in eastern Europe by persuading the Society of Friends to a fresh relief effort. She directed those operations based in Vienna, and once again turned her direction to the care of child victims of tuberculosis. Alice and Roger Clark also became involved in this work, the former liaising also with the newly established 'Save the Children Fund'.

14 The Priestman–Bright circle and women's history

War, memory and a family archive

Helen Clark, together with Alice Clark and Esther Clothier had spent a few weeks after the death of the Priestman sisters sorting out their effects and gathering together their papers. After her final visit to her aunts' old house she wrote: 'It seemed very strange and sad to come home and have no aunts to write to.'[1] Subsequently, she received her final Priestman inheritance of women's money, far more than she had expected: 'It seems very curious and pathetic, and like the ending of all but the memories of so much, so very much. Very affecting and Wm says the same. The end of all dealing with Newcastle affairs. I am anxious to do rightly in this. It seems as tho' I had to consider the wishes of all those four generous people [her three Priestman aunts and grandfather].' She began immediately to dispense some of this legacy to various charities, in the first instance with gifts, in memory of Anna Maria and Mary Priestman, to funds for women medical students and for women teachers.[2]

Observing the mental decline of Anna Maria Priestman evident in 1913, Helen Clark had written, 'My chief fear now is that I may outlive my faculties.' In 1915 she noted in her diary that she was now seventy-five, 'very strange to say', and increasingly concerned by lapses in her memory over the previous few months. The following March she became so unwell with dizzy spells that she was kept in bed for a month. Hilda Clark returned home briefly to oversee her care alongside Dr Annie Clark. Diabetes and a weak heart were diagnosed, and the former at this time could only be managed by a strict diet. The latter meant she was now allowed only very limited exercise. The Easter Rising in Ireland occurred as she looked forward to leaving her bed, and she returned to a world in which 'public matters seem beyond belief!' The fiftieth anniversary of her marriage took place that summer, which she had understood was to be celebrated quietly with close family. After supper, however, 'the world streamed into the field and gathered in front of the house' where speeches and a formal presentation were made. She was presented with a little golden dish, while William Clark received 'a most beautiful book' containing the signatures of each person currently employed in his enterprises.[3]

Both Helen and William Clark now increasingly resorted to a wheelchair. She also recognised her own growing mental confusion in her diary: 'The last few entries are rather doubtful'. For the meantime, however, she maintained her interest in the world around her, and the various undertakings of her children, but her life of active public service was all but over. She comforted herself by reading and sorting some 'very old letters', but worried about her failure now to remember and mark the anniversaries that were so important to her, especially the deaths of her father and her aunts. She became forgetful, too, about posting letters. When news came of the illness of her last surviving aunt, Selina Bright, her diary entry read: 'I think I wrote to her.' The next day she heard of her aunt's death: 'It my 77th birthday, strange altogether. Much thought of all the recent changes.'[4]

Helen Clark was able, however, to celebrate the 'the wonderful and tranquil change' of women's enfranchisement in the Representation of the People Act 1918, enjoying an article in the *Manchester Guardian* that recognised the role of both Lydia Becker and Jacob Bright. Though the measure did not provide the same voting rights for women and men (this had to wait until 1928), it represented a compromise that had been worked out between members of the government and representatives of the women's suffrage movement. For a time Helen Clark seems to have recovered some of her former vitality, and her fieriness flared again after reading a report in a New York paper of a lynching of a black American accused of shooting two white men:

> Had any such item as this come out of Belgium or Armenia . . . a wave of horror would sweep over the country and there would be an extra rush to the enlistment offices. But when Americans thus debase themselves nobody speaks about it at least no body who is white and we complacently turn to the congenial task of setting up democracy in Germany.[5]

Her interest in public affairs did not abate, and she found much to hearten her in other news, for example, the proposal made at a trades union congress that only governments should be allowed to manufacture armaments and ammunition. She believed that were such a policy adopted by Britain it would deal 'a deadly blow at the whole abominable business of stirring up strife', for she believed England and Germany to be among the greatest offenders in this regard. She welcomed, too, the statement of 'the Trotsky Lenin regime' in Russia that the Anglo-Russian agreement of 1907 'was directed against the liberty and independence of the Persian people and is null and void for all time'. She was grateful for the exposure of 'the shameful treatment' of Persia by a US journalist: 'with one stroke of his pen he has undone one of the least excusable acts of cold blooded imperialism and restored freedom to an innocent nation, as innocent as was Belgium.' Her brief period of optimism was brought to an end, however, by the fear that both her sons were now liable for conscription, which had been extended to men over fifty-one. Events in Ireland, too, led her to record 'We are also feeling with great

Figure 14.1 Helen and William Clark on their Golden Wedding anniversary, 1916

consternation the utter break down between Ireland and England – beyond words to describe.'[6]

Her memory loss continued, however, 'a real trial', leading her to forget to attend local events at which she was expected, and unable to remember if she had written, or what she had written to her daughters. Still, though, she could turn to old letters, letters that took her back 'to another world'. Some saddened but others helped her 'recall what is delightful to bring back'. There were now many weeks when she made no diary entries, including one notable gap of seven weeks around the end of the war. Her last active involvement in politics had occurred shortly before, when she attended a women's meeting to interview her brother-in-law, John Morland, who had become a local Liberal parliamentary candidate: 'Good and useful, though rather dull in some ways but we considered it rather satisfactory. It had cost a good deal of work.' She continued sometimes to attend the meetings of the Wells Board of Guardians, and to visit the workhouse, usually attended by a family member. Her contributions at Board meetings began to reflect the waning of her mental capacities, however, and she was persuaded, very regretfully, to resign. Another fall in April 1919 marked a further stage in her decline, 'I forget to write anything.' When she did remember, her sentences were sometimes left incomplete, or confused, muddling up names from her past with those of the present. She made a further visit to her old home in Rochdale, but though unable to visit all her old haunts, was content at having seen the surrounding hills once more 'so nice and clear'. Her diary entries became more and more intermittent, as did her letters, and their content limited increasingly to the comings and goings of her immediate family circle. Her last surviving postcard to Alice Clark was dated 17 August 1920, and her last entry in her diary on 8 August 1921. Alice Clark's last surviving letter to her is dated 3 October 1921.[7]

There was the consolation, though, that Alice Clark now returned home and oversaw the care of her parents in their last years. She also returned to the factory, to take up a project that her father wished to see further extended while he still lived: 'What I should like if at all practicable would be that thou should set aside the London office work for a time and take this Welfare Work in thy own hands, for a while at any rate, and find more exactly what there is in it before deciding on fresh plans for the future.' He asked her to think over his proposal and ended the letter, 'Goodbye darling child we shall be very glad to see thee back.'[8] Alice Clark agreed and so in their last years her parents had once more a daughter at home to cheer them. William Clark's physical frailty increased as the decline in Helen Clark's mental capacities continued. But at his death in 1925, she was still able with some force to declare the kind of funeral she wished to see, one led by the town's bands, like the funeral of her old adversary on the school board, Captain Butt, and yet another departure from the ways of Friends. Factory and shops closed as the funeral procession wound its way through the village. This year was also the centenary of the company found by Cyrus and James Clark, and the pension scheme it introduced in 1925 to mark this anniversary seemed to Alice Clark a fitting memorial to her father and the business ethic by which he had lived.[9] Helen Clark survived her husband by little more than a year. Subsequently, her children, grandchildren and great-grandchildren conserved and added to the collection of family papers that had been so important to her sense of who she was and what she stood for.

The Priestman–Bright circle and women's history

The use of 'public' and 'private' as dichotomous categories is basic both to ideologies seeking to restrict women and to social theory seeking to explain gender differences. In the first case, historians have long acknowledged the difficulty of using prescriptive material as evidence of actual practice. In the second case, the usage is a valuable heuristic device for finding generalised, abstract patterns in past and present societies. But it is necessarily a crude tool for interpreting the lives of particular persons. Material of the kind collected in the Clark Archive allows the possibility of exploring the play of public and private in the lives of individuals. Looking at such lives in this more rounded way suggests the potential bluntness of such categories of analysis, especially when public and private are treated as quite distinct and separate categories. In the histories of individuals they become, rather, two mutually defining worlds, both cohabited by men and women and both shaped, if in different and ever-changing ways, by gender hierarchies and the sexual division of labour. In recovering the history of women and of gender difference, then, we need to recognise and explore the presence of women in both worlds, and, moreover, not as two different kinds of women – 'typical' or 'average' women (who remain in the domestic sphere) and 'public women' (who somehow escape it).[10]

The material analysed here suggests also the need to modify many existing understandings of the position of middle-class women, providing, for example, a picture of the positive possibilities of spinsterhood in the decades when the problem of 'the surplus woman' was a matter of public debate. Decades before new opportunities in higher education and the professions arose in the latter part of the nineteenth century, middle-class spinsters might, albeit often with a struggle, lead independent and satisfying lives despite their limited economic opportunities. They might expand the shared wealth of their families, as Margaret Wood sought to do in the distribution of her capital and her estate. They might also play a major role in assisting and sustaining the households of married siblings, especially those where wives and mothers died young, as both Margaret Wood and Pricilla Bright did. Single sisters, aunts and nieces continued to play an important part in nuclear households until the early twentieth century at least, especially in terms of the care of those in need of some kind, whether for nurturance or for financial assistance.

In particular, the women in these circles undertook a great deal of the nursing needed among their kin, and single women especially – though men might nurse in particular circumstances, as John Bright nursed Helen when away from their family in Rome, and Jonathan Priestman cared for John Hadwen Bragg in his first period of madness. Wealth and privilege did not protect these families from devastating disease, of course, and the impact of puerperal fever and tuberculosis, especially, on the family life of these circles is notable. But these families had considerable internal resources to cope with what were, at this time, everyday tragedies. Their ability to care for their sick once again rested upon the extensive kinship networks they enjoyed, which by the latter part of the nineteenth century included doctors as well as those practiced in nursing. So the Clarks were several times able to identify quickly new therapies in the treatment of tuberculosis, drawing once again on their social capital, in this case access to new medical knowledge. Such a capacity was as important as the financial means thereafter to act upon such knowledge.

Women's private papers also reveal a more complicated situation regarding their relationship to property than that provided by settlements and wills alone, at least in the domestic culture of these family circles. The principle of primogeniture was generally rejected among these families: family money was to be shared among all the children, or in the case of the childless, nieces and nephews, though daughters rarely received as large an inheritance as sons (Margaret Bragg may have been unusual in expressly desiring to leave her daughter an inheritance equal to her son's). There were also informal understandings regarding 'family money' that fathers, brothers and sons were expected to recognise, whatever the provisions of a will: some chose to ignore these, of course, but others, like Albert Bright, acted out such values when he enlarged the bequests to his brothers and sisters by diminishing his own. Family money also generally contained an element of 'women's money', that is money that recognised the contribution of women, both single and married, to the creation and stewardship of a family's wealth. Attached to women's money were expectations that it would pass to other women, especially to single daughters, to sisters and to the children of sisters for at least one more generation.

As Morris has suggested, money held by women through the legal instrument of the trust allowed an additional degree of flexibility within middle-class family strategies for wealth creation; it also ensured that some part of a family's fortune was sequestered from any failures in family enterprises. Above all, it allowed women, both married and single, a possibility of autonomy and of authority through economic independence from husbands, brothers and fathers, and the right to determine the uses to which their money might be put. It might subvert coverture also by giving a married woman the right to make a will. A growing sexual division of labour accompanied the increasing separation of household and family enterprise, yet the women of these families were not without commercial knowledge or an interest in business matters even if absent from the day-to-day work of the family firm. Wives might still play a significant part in determining business organisation from their parlour, as was the case with Margaret Tanner with regard to the firm of Tanner Brothers. Equally, Helen Clark, protected by a trust, might seek better health for her children by lending her husband her own money to buy land and to build a house away from the factory.

Letters and diaries, especially in a collection as comprehensive as that created by the women of the Priestman–Bright circle, reveal, too, other aspects of the domestic culture of these prospering Quaker families that created substantial social capital, as well as wealth, for its members. At the beginning of the period considered here, that culture was shaped by the discipline and calendar of the Society of Friends. This simultaneously emphasised social seclusion, mutuality and sociability, rendering Quaker homes relatively open spaces where men as well as women were expected to take on a domestic character, and yet, equally, where public ends might be pursued, for example, in church and associational life. The Quaker families discussed here also invested significantly in the education of girls to a high standard, and encouraged continuing intellectual endeavour in womanhood.

The complex patterns of intermarriage among Quaker families also fostered especially dense networks of kinship, and of business and financial obligations arising from such relationships. These were further widened by the friendships encouraged between the siblings of a couple, which in turn assisted the active creation of extensive webs of mutual friendships beyond the family circle. Very often such friendships arose through shared participation in reform movements, for example, the Bristol Unitarian, Mary Estlin, whose friendships among this circle began in the anti-slavery movement and continued through the campaigns of the women's movement. Once established, such friendships were often pursued across subsequent generations of the families concerned, for example, those between members of the Garrison family in the US and the Bright and Clark families in Britain; or, again, between the Jabavu family in South Africa and the Clark family. Once again, personal life and public life became linked through particular persons, and provided further social capital as well as wealth in the creation of networks. By such means both business and political ends might more effectively be pursued, for example, in the repeated salvaging of the family firm of C. & J. Clark prior to its management being handed to William Clark; or in the mounting of a campaign in Britain to protest lynchings in the United States.

The sense of belonging to 'a peculiar people' encouraged, also, an interest in genealogy and family history that in this particular family circle appears to have been reinforced by several factors: the existence of a line of women ministers whose spiritual memoranda and letters were preserved as a valuable legacy; a pattern of family separation through emigration to the United States that went back to the mid-eighteenth century, making letter writing an important part of women's 'work of kin', and fostering a cosmopolitanism that encouraged transnational as well as national networks; the deaths of several young mothers, and the need to preserve some relics of them for their children;

the fostering of especially fond bonds between family members through intimacy across generations and among extended kin.

Moreover, religious imperatives had always drawn some women in to the ministry, as 'public Friends'. Increasingly in this period such imperatives also drew them into humanitarian and philanthropic projects and thereby into the larger civil society that served to link family and public life. There was a clear gender hierarchy within these arenas, and again a division of labour between men and women that often left power and governance with men, but women's presence was nonetheless considerable and provided for the emergence of groups of women possessing the skills, knowledge and sense of duty to participate in public life. So here again the Priestman–Bright circle and its networks reflected the substantial social capital, as well as relative wealth, of these women Friends.

The family culture of Brights and Priestmans was also shaped by long-standing sympathy with radical causes that drew, at least in part, on a particular view of church history that looked back to the radical sects of the English Civil War. The changing political order in the early nineteenth century allowed such largely localised 'oppositionism' to find fresh expression through the national politics of reform, though this transition was not an easy one for the older generation. John Bright was able to present his political ambitions as analogous to the religious calling of Rachel Priestman by invoking a vision of national and church history in which class contestation carried a religious imperative. Equally, the shift from 'corn' to 'bread' in the rhetoric of the Anti-Corn Law League, marked the domestication of a public question and a new space in which middle-class women might participate in radical politics. The central object of the campaign became at once a domestic and a political fact of life while invoking women's long-standing religious obligation to relieve hunger. Here again, a sexual division of labour also helped legitimate such participation: women applauding in the box or gallery, men speaking from the platform; women preparing tea parties and soirées, men taking to the road; women working for and serving at bazaars, men providing some of the custom.

This family inheritance of extensive social capital together with experience of political campaigning was evident in the substantial presence established by the women of the Priestman–Bright circle in radical politics and in the organisations of the women's movement from the late 1860s. These women Friends brought valuable assets with them: strong feminine identities; education and intellectual capacities; experience and skills in organisation and finance; extensive networks both at home and abroad, and especially among communities of reformers; a cosmopolitan outlook arising from church and family history; extensive links to radical male elites in a number of major provincial centres and, later, in the metropolis; and a comparative freedom over their own time arising from their relative prosperity (though constrained nonetheless by conventional kinship obligations). Personal life and political life served each other, family and religious values being acted out in public arenas, and church and public life reinforcing and sometimes expanding personal relationships. The women of the Priestman–Bright circle preserved and passed on this particular domestic culture and the social capital to which it gave rise by the preservation of private papers. These became a legacy for future generations of their families in the archive created by Helen Clark, her forebears and her children. It serves, surely, as an altogether fitting memorial to her and her kinswomen. For its contents challenge many of the conventions of mainstream history, not least in illustrating the role of particular persons and their intimate relations in the arenas of civil society and of politics.

Abbreviations in notes

BAN	Sarah Bancroft Clark Papers, Somerset Record Office and Clark Archive
BC	William Bancroft Clark Papers, Clark Archive
CA	Clark Archive, C. & J. Clark Ltd, Street, Somerset
FWVRC	Friends' War Victims' Relief Committee
HCD	Diaries of Helen Priestman Bright, subsequently Clark
HSHC	Papers of H. S. H. Clark, Clark Archive
MIL	Millfield Papers, Clark Archive
NUWSS	National Union of Women's Suffrage Societies
QDB	Quaker Dictionary of Biography, Friends' House Library, London
RDFC	R. D. F. Clark Papers, Clark Archive
SRO	Somerset Record Office
SSCD	Sophia Sturge Clark diaries
UPS	Union of Practical Suffragists
USJ	United States Journal of M. Wood
E. Bancroft	Elizabeth Bancroft, formerly Wood
Er Bancroft	Esther Bancroft
D. Bancroft	David Bancroft jnr
M. Bancroft	Margaret Bancroft
J. Bancroft	Joseph Bancroft
J. and S. Bancroft	Joseph and Sarah, formerly Poole, Bancroft
Jn Bancroft I	John Bancroft, senior
Jn, II and Sa Bancroft	John Bancroft, junior and Susanna Bancroft
R. Bancroft	Rebecca Bancroft
W. P. Bancroft	William Poole Bancroft
E. J. Bennett	Emma Bennett
H. Bragg	Hadwen Bragg
J. H. Bragg	John Hadwen Bragg
M. Bragg	Margaret Bragg, formerly, Wilson
R. Bragg	Rachel Bragg, subsequently Priestman
E. Bright	Elizabeth Bright, formerly Priestman
Er Bright	Esther Bright, subsequently Vaughan
H. Bright	Helen Priestman Bright, subsequently Clark
J. Bright	John Bright
M. Bright	Martha Bright, formerly Wood
M. E. Bright (M. E. B.)	Margaret Elizabeth Bright, formerly Leatham
P. Bright	Priscilla Bright, subsequently McLaren

Abbreviations in notes

S. Bright	Sophia Bright, subsequently Ashworth
A. Clark	Alice Clark
A. E. Clark	Dr Annie Elizabeth Clark
E. Clark	Eleanor Clark, formerly Stephens
E. B. Clark	Esther Bright Clark, subsequently Clothier
H. Clark	Helen Clark, formerly Helen Priestman Bright
Ha Clark	Hilda Clark
J. Clark	James Clark
R. Clark	Roger Clark
S. B. Clark	Sarah Bancroft Clark
S. S. Clark	Sophia Sturge Clark
W. B. Clark	William Bancroft Clark
E. Crosland	Esther Crosland, formerly Wood
J. Crosland	Jane Crosland
W. Doeg	William Doeg
M. King	Margaret King, subsequently Margaret Wood, snr
M. E. Leatham	(Margaret) Elizabeth Leatham, subsequently Bright, (always known by her middle name)
P. B. McLaren	Priscilla Bright McLaren
E. Malone	Emily Malone
E. Oldham	Eliza Oldham
H. Oldham	Hannah Oldham
J. Pease	Jane Pease
S. Pease	Susan A. Pease
A. M. Priestman	Anna Maria Priestman
D. Priestman	David Priestman, snr
E. Priestman	Elizabeth Priestman, subsequently Elizabeth Bright
H. Priestman	Hadwen Priestman
J. Priestman I	Jonathan Priestman, snr
J. Priestman II	Jonathan Priestman, jnr
M. Priestman	Margaret Priestman, subsequently Wheeler, then Tanner
My Priestman	Mary Priestman
R. Priestman	Rachel Priestman, snr, formerly Bragg
R. Priestman II	Rachel Priestman, jnr
W. Satterthwaite	William Satterthwaite
A. Sayles	Ann Sayles
E. Shackleton	Elizabeth Shackleton
E. C. Stanton	Elizabeth Cady Stanton
E. Stickney	Esther Stickney
M. Stickney	Mary Stickney
C. Sturge	Charlotte Sturge
A. Tanner	Arthur Tanner, jnr
M. Tanner	Margaret Tanner, previously Priestman, subsequently Wheeler
S. Tanner	Sarah Tanner, previously Wheeler
W. Tanner	William Tanner
F. Uhde	Ferdinand Uhde
M. Wheeler	Margaret Wheeler, formerly Priestman, subsequently Tanner
S. Wheeler	Sarah Wheeler, subsequently Tanner
J. Wood I	John Wood, snr
J. Wood II	John Wood, jnr
M. Wood	Margaret Wood, jnr

Notes

1 Introduction

1. E. Priestman to J. Bright, n.d. [July 1841], quoted in 'Memorial Volume', MIL 16/04, Millfield Papers (henceforth, MIL), Clark Archive (henceforth CA), compiled from extracts of her letters and memoranda by her mother, Rachel Priestman, as an act of family commemoration. 'Consumption' was the term applied at this time to a form of tuberculosis.
2. Ibid., for Rachel Priestman's account of her last days in September 1842.
3. On 'the good death', see P. Jalland, *Death in the Victorian Family*, Oxford: Oxford University Press, 1995, pp. 17–38.
4. The importance of kinship and other networks is routinely acknowledged in many histories of the middle class in this period, but is becoming a subject of more detailed interest, notably in R. J. Morris's account of the 'networked family', in *Men, Women and Property in England, 1780–1870. A social and economic history of family strategies among the Leeds middle classes*, Cambridge: Cambridge University Press, 2005. The importance of family networks to Quaker business is examined in L. Davidoff and C. Hall, *Family Fortunes: men and women of the English middle class c.1780–1850*, London: Routledge, 1992 reprint (London: Hutchinson, 1987), pp. 216–25. On women's political networks, see for example, S. Richardson, '"Well-Neighboured Houses": the political networks of elite women', in K. Gleadle and S. Richardson (eds), *Women in British Politics, 1760–1860. The power of the petticoat*, Basingstoke: Macmillan Press, 2000. On the role of kinship relationships and networks in the creation of a women's rights movement see O. Banks, *Becoming a Feminist: the social origins of first-wave feminism*, Brighton: Wheatsheaf Books, 1981; P. Levine, *Feminist Lives in Victorian England*, Oxford, Basil Blackwell, 1990; S. S. Holton, 'Kinship and Friendship: Quaker women's networks and the women's movement, *Women's History Review*, 2005, vol. 14, pp. 365–84; A. Dingsdale, 'Generous and Lofty Sympathies': the Kensington Society, the 1866 women's suffrage petition and the development of mid-Victorian Feminism, unpublished PhD thesis, University of Greenwich, 1995.
5. J. Winter, *Sites of Memory, Sites of Mourning. The Great War in European cultural history*, Cambridge: Cambridge University Press, 1986 has informed my thinking in researching this family archive, though it discusses a very different context. P. Summerfield, *Reconstructing Wartime Lives. Discourses and subjectivity in the oral history of the Second World War*, Manchester: Manchester University Press, 1988, provides a helpful discussion of the complex relationship between discourse, gender and the production of 'memory stores', esp. pp. iv, viii–xi, 1–15, 20. On the creation of family memory among this circle, see, S. S. Holton, 'Family Memory, Religion and Radicalism: the Priestman, Bright and Clark kinship circle of women Friends and Quaker history, *Quaker Studies*, 2005, vol. 9, pp. 156–75. For a wide-ranging discussion on the nature

234 Notes

of archives and of archival research see C. Steedman, *Dust*, Manchester: Manchester University Press, 2001.

6 Churches had long provided a space in which women might enact a sense of themselves as citizens, see, for example, P. Crawford, 'Public Duty, Conscience and Women in Early Modern England', in G. E. Aylmer (ed.), *Public Duty and Private Conscience in Seventeenth Century England*, Oxford: Clarendon Press, 1993.

7 Both holdings of CA. Where possible I refer to the larger part of the Sarah Bancroft Clark Papers (henceforth BAN) held on microfilm at the Somerset Record Office, Taunton. Where I refer to originals held only in the Clark Archive, I will indicate it thus, BAN, CA.

8 For an influential study of a different social stratum that also examines the creation of new public arenas open to women, see A. Vickery, *Gentleman's Daughter: women's lives in Georgian England*, New Haven: Yale University Press, 1998. For ongoing reassessments of women's relation to politics in the late eighteenth century and beyond, see, for example, E. Chalus, 'Women, Electoral Privilege and Practice in the Eighteenth Century', and S. Morgan, 'Domestic Economy and Political Agitation: women and the Anti-Corn Law League', both in Gleadle and Richardson, op. cit.

9 T. Clarkson, *A Portraiture of Quakerism . . .* , London: Longman, Hurst, Rees & Orme, 1806 (3 vols).

10 Ibid., vol. 3, pp. 289–95.

11 Compare, for example, the varying analyses in E. Isichei, *Victorian Quakers*: London, Oxford University Press, 1970, esp. pp. 107–11; S. Wright, *Friends in York. The dynamics of Quaker revival, 1780–1860*, Keele: Keele University Press, 1995, esp. pp. 31–49; E. A. O'Donnell, '"On Behalf of all Young Women Trying to be Better Than They Are:" feminism and Quakerism in the nineteenth century: the case of Anna Deborah Richardson', *Quaker Studies*, 2001, vol. 6, pp. 37–58; E. A. O'Donnell, 'Woman's Rights and Woman's Duties. Quaker women in the nineteenth century, with specific reference to the North East Monthly Meeting of women Friends', unpublished PhD thesis, University of Sunderland, 2000, esp. pp. 227–47; H. Plant, 'Gender and the Aristocracy of Dissent: a comparative study of the beliefs, status and roles of Quaker and Unitarian communities, 1770–1830', unpublished D. Phil. Thesis, University of York, 2000, esp. pp. 19, 32, 57, 74, 124, 152, 238.

12 On Quaker women and demographic change in the nineteenth century, see R. Vann and D. Eversley, *Friends in Life and Death: the British and Irish Quakers in the demographic transition, 1650–1900*, Cambridge: Cambridge University Press, 1992, esp. 133, 177, 243–5, 247, 254.

13 S. S. Holton, '"Educating Women into Rebellion." Elizabeth Cady Stanton and the creation of a transatlantic network of Radical suffragists', *American Historical Review*, 1994, vol. 99, pp. 1112–36; 'From Anti-Slavery to Suffrage Militancy. The Bright circle, Elizabeth Cady Stanton, and the British women's movement', in C. Daley and M. Nolan (eds), *Suffrage and Beyond. International feminist perspectives*, Auckland: Auckland University Press, 1994; *Suffrage Days. Stories from the women's suffrage movement*, London: Routledge, 1996, esp. pp. 24–5, 30–3.

14 For two notable Quaker exceptions, see G. Malmgreen, 'Anne Knight and the Radical Subculture', *Quaker History*, 1982, vol. 71, pp. 100–12; C. Midgley, *Women Against Slavery. The British campaigns, 1780–1870*, London: Routledge, 1992, pp. 1, 44, 56, 77–9, 80, 83, 124, 132, 151, 157, 161–2, 162–3, 164, 166, 171, 173, 175–6, 205, which also discusses another Quaker radical, Elizabeth Pease, later Nichol, pp. 77–9, 162–3, 171, 173, 175–6. See also P. H. Michaelson, 'Religious Bases of Eighteenth-Century Feminism: Mary Wollstonecraft and the Quakers', *Women's Studies*, 1993, vol. 22, pp. 281–95.

15 Notably, K. Gleadle, *Early Feminists: radical Unitarians and the emergence of the women's rights movement 1831–51*, Basingstoke: Macmillan, 1995; R. Watts, *Gender, Power and the Unitarians in England, 1760–1860*, London: Longman, 1998.

16 L. Kerber, 'Separate Spheres, Female Worlds, Woman's Place: the rhetoric of women's history', *Journal of American History*, 1988, vol. 75, pp. 9–39 is a seminal article on this topic. A. Vickery, 'Historiographical Review. Golden age to separate spheres? A review of categories and chronology of English women's history, *Historical Journal*, 1993, vol. 36, pp. 383–414, has been especially influential in Britain. See also A. Vickery, Introduction, in A. Vickery (ed.), *Women, Politics and Power: British politics, 1750 to the present*, Stanford: Stanford University Press, 2001; J. Rendall, 'Women and the Public Sphere', in L. Davidoff, K. McClelland and E. Varikas (eds), *Gender and History: retrospect and prospect*, Oxford: Blackwell, 2000.

17 S. S. Holton, A. Mackinnon and M. Allen, 'Between Rationality and Revelation: women, faith and public roles in the nineteenth and twentieth centuries', *Women's History Review*, 1998, vol. 7, pp. 195–8, and on this point see also Levine, op. cit., pp. 43–4, 37–8, as well as notes 9, 13 for recent interest in this question.

18 Davidoff and Hall, op. cit., has been especially influential here, as has C. Hall, 'The Early Formation of the Victorian Domestic Ideology', reprinted in her *White, Male and Middle Class. Explorations in feminism and history*, Cambridge: Polity Press, 1992, and R. J. Morris, 'Voluntary Societies and British Elites, 1780–1870: an analysis', *Historical Journal*, 1982, vol. 26, pp. 95–118. On associational life and the construction of civil society in this period, see also M. J. D. Roberts, *Making English Morals. Voluntary association and moral reform in England, 1787–1886*, Cambridge: Cambridge University Press, 2004. For an overview of recent debates on the definition and characteristics of the Victorian middle class, see S. Gunn, *Public Culture of the Victorian Middle Class. Ritual and authority in the English industrial city*, Manchester: Manchester University Press, 2000, pp. 12–27.

19 Notably, T. C. Kennedy, *British Quakerism, 1860–1920. The transformation of a religious community*, Oxford: Oxford University Press, 2001, pp. 18, 22, 36, 421; Wright, op. cit., pp. 21–30; Isichei, op. cit., pp. 3–16.

20 So, for example, Morris, *Men, Women and Property*, p. 305 finds a 'mixture of dependency and agency in' the letters of a Leeds widow. See also Davidoff and Hall, op. cit., pp. 209–11, 279–89. Compare M. Berg, 'Women's Property and the Industrial Revolution', *Journal of Interdisciplinary History*, 1993, vol. 24, pp. 233–50. Vickery, 'Historiographical Review', p. 390. This study had also been very much influenced by her notion of 'women's work of kin', see p. 24.

21 'Microhistory' is a research approach that examines the experience, mentalities and subcultures of subordinate and/or atypical groups or individuals. On the epistemology and methodologies of microhistory, see E. Muir, and G. Ruggiero, *Microhistory and the lost peoples of Europe*, Baltimore, MD: Johns Hopkins Press, 1991, esp. E. Muir, 'Introduction'; A. Castren, M. Lonkila and M. Peltonen, *Between Sociology and History. Essays on microhistory, collective action and nation-building*, Helsinki: SKS/Finnish Literature Society, 2004; R. J. and S. Holton, 'From the Particular to the Global: some empirical, epistemological and methodological aspects of microhistory with regard to a women's rights network', in R. Lenton and K. Fricker (eds), *Performing Global Networks*, Cambridge Scholars' Publishing, forthcoming, 2007.

22 For further collective biographies of women, though for differing research agendas, see B. Caine, *Destined to be Wives. The sisters of Beatrice Webb*, Oxford: Oxford University Press, 1986; P. Jalland, *Women, Marriage and Politics, 1860–1914*, Oxford: Clarendon Press, 1986; M. J. Peterson, *Family, Love and Work in the Lives of Victorian Gentlewomen*, Bloomington: Indiana University Press, 1989; J. Hannam and K. Hunt, *Socialist Women. Britain, 1880s-1920s*, London: Routledge, 2002.

23 S. B. Clark, '"Aunt Wood" (Margaret Wood, 1783–1851 [should read 1859])', typescript, 16 August 1968, BC 249/1, W. B. Clark Papers, CA.

24 L. Davidoff, '"Where the Stranger Begins": the question of siblings in historical analysis' in her *Worlds Between. Historical perspectives on gender and class*, Cambridge: Polity Press, 1995, esp. pp. 207, 220.

2 Margaret Wood (1783–1859)

1. Recalled by Priscilla Bright McLaren in old age, and recorded in S. B. Clark, '"Aunt Wood" (Margaret Wood, 1783–1851)' [should read 1859], typescript, 16 August 1968, BC 249/1, W. B. Clark Papers, CA. This suggests Margaret Wood had a pastry cook's shop in Bolton, though I have been unable to confirm this in relevant trade directories. Margaret Wood's correspondence is scattered across separate collections in the Clark Archive, but is mainly held among the Sarah Bancroft Clark Papers. I understand there are more letters in family collections in the United States.
2. On the origins of this church see, R. T. Vann, *Social Development of English Quakerism, 1655–1755*, Cambridge, MA.: Harvard University Press, 1969. For overviews of its history, see J. R. Rowntree, *Quakerism Past and Present*, London: Smith, Elder and Son, 1859; J. Punshon, *Portrait in Grey. A short history of the Quakers*, London: Quaker Home Service, 1984; J. Walvin, *The Quakers: money and morals*, London: John Murray, 1997.
3. P. Mack, *Visionary Women: ecstatic prophecy in seventeenth-century England*, Berkley: University of California Press, 1992; C. Trevett, *Women and Quakerism in the Seventeenth Century*, York: Sessions Book Trust, 1991.
4. S. Wright, *Friends in York. The dynamics of Quaker revival, 1780–1860*, Keele: Keele University Press, 1995, pp. 43–9.
5. On the establishment of separate women's meetings within the government of the Society of Friends, see M. H. Bacon, 'The Establishment of London Women's Yearly Meeting: a transatlantic concern', *Journal of the Friends' Historical Society*, 1992, vol. 57, pp. 151–65.
6. On this quietist church culture, see Punshon, op. cit., pp. 127–51.
7. The link between middle-class oppositional politics and nonconformity is frequently noted, e.g., L. Davidoff and C. Hall, *Family Fortunes: men and women of the English middle class c.1780–1850*, London: Routledge, 1992, esp. p. 22. My usage of oppositionism here is more specific and refers to the particular legacy of its civil-war beginnings to the discipline of the Society of Friends, and within the world view, for example, of John Bright. On this see J. Vincent, *The Formation of the British Liberal Party, 1857–1868*, Harmondsworth: Penguin, 1972 (London: Constable, 1966), pp. 196–7 who emphasises how 'greatly he was soaked in the seventeenth century' and 'dyed in the vat of a certain interpretation of history' that shaped, for example, his 'striking animus' against church clerics. I discuss this point further in my 'John Bright, Radical Politics and the Ethos of Quakerism', *Albion*, 2002, vol. 34, pp. 584–606.
8. J. T. Mills, *John Bright and the Quakers*, London: Methuen, 1935, 2 vols, vol. 1, pp. 129, 163.
9. J. Wood I to W. Satterthwaite (his uncle in the United States), 22 May 1774, BAN 2/3, CA. Marriage to his second wife, Margaret King, and the outbreak of the War of Independence perhaps led him to reconsider.
10. Mills, op. cit., vol. 1, pp. 171–4. See also the entries for John Wood senior and younger in the Quaker Dictionary of Biography, Friends' House Library (henceforth, QDB).
11. J. Wood II, as reported in Jn Bancroft I to his nephew, D. Bancroft, 16 July 1821, BAN 2/11, CA.
12. Reported in an extract, BAN 2/3, CA, from M. Routh, *Memoir of the Life, Travels and Religious Experience of Martha Routh*, York: W. Alexander, 1822, p. 279.
13. As reported in W. P. Bancroft to E. Malone, 7 July 1883; W. B. Clark's family genealogy, dated 15 November 1976, both BAN 2/6, CA, and a Clark–Bancroft family tree, dated June 1960, which accompanies S. B. Clark, op. cit.
14. Jn Bancroft I to D. Bancroft, 17 March 1819; 16, 18 July, 9 September 1821, BAN 2/11, CA. References in later correspondence indicate that this was Heap and Peel's ladies' seminary in Yorkshire Street.

Notes 237

15 Jn Bancroft I to D. Bancroft, 14 October 1825, 23 June, 17 September 1832, BAN 2/11, CA. On the long-established Quaker communities on the Brandywine, see J. Jensen, *Loosening the Bonds. Mid-Atlantic farm women, 1750–1850*, New Haven, CT: Yale University Press, 1986.
16 Jn Bancroft I to D. Bancroft, 18 July, 9 September 1821, BAN 2/11, CA. On the Queen Caroline affair and popular radicalism, see A. Clark, *The Struggle for the Breeches: gender and the making of the British working class*, London: Rivers Oram, 1995, pp. 164–73.
17 W. P. Bancroft to E. Malone, 7 July 1883; W. B. Clark's family genealogy, dated 15 November 1976, both BAN 2/6, CA.
18 Mills, op cit., vol.1, pp. 100–16, 168–85.
19 Ibid., p. 175, citing an autobiographical fragment by John Bright.
20 W. Robertson, *Life and Times of the Right Honourable John Bright*, London: Cassell, 1883, 2 vols, vol. 1, pp. 16–17.
21 On the legal doctrine of coverture and its implications for married women, see L. Holcombe, *Women and Property: reform of the married women's property law in nineteenth-century England*, Toronto: Toronto University Press, 1983; M. L. Shanley, *Feminism, Marriage and the Law in Victorian England, 1850–95*, London: I. B. Tauris, 1989; S. Staves, *Married Women's Separate Property in England, 1660–1833*, Cambridge, MA.: Harvard University Press, 1990; C. Shammas, 'Re-assessing the Married Women's Property Acts', *Journal of Women's History*, 1994, vol., 6, pp. 9–30; R. J. Morris, 'Men, Women and Property: the reform of the Married Women's Property Act', in F. M. L. Thompson (ed.), *Landowners, Capitalists and Entrepreneurs. Essays for Sir John Habakkuk*, Oxford: Clarendon Press, 1994; M. C. Finn, *Character of Credit. Personal debt in English culture, 1740–1914*, Cambridge: Cambridge University Press, 2003; R. J. Morris, *Men, Women and Property in England, 1780–1870. A social and economic history of family strategies among the Leeds middle classes*, Cambridge: Cambridge University Press, 2005.
22 On trusts and the financial strategies of middle-class families, see Morris, *Men, Women and Property*, pp. 254–64; C. Stebbings, *The Private Trustee in Victorian England*, Cambridge: Cambridge University Press, 2002.
23 M. Wood to Er Bancroft, 10 March 1833, 20 July 1838; M. Wood to R. and M. Bancroft, 5 April 1838, all BAN 1/13.
24 E.g., M. Wood to J. Bancroft, 14 April 1829, BAN 1/81.
25 E. Milligan, *Quaker Marriage*, Kendal: Quaker Tapestry Books, 1994.
26 J. Wood I to M. King, 9 July, 25 August 1755, BAN 2/3, CA, copied by W. P. Bancroft, 6 Aug 1884 who believed his aunt, Esther Bancroft, had received these letters from Margaret Wood.
27 B. Lehane, *C. & J. Clark Ltd, 1825–1975*, Street: C. & J. Clark, n.d., p. 4.
28 S. B. Clark, op. cit.
29 Index and Returns for Bolton, 1811 Census, Local History Department, Bolton Public Library.
30 She is listed in a local trade directory as a partner in a confectionary business, Wood and Rimington; *Commercial Directory for Rochdale, 1814–15*, Manchester: Wardle and Bentham, 1814, and solely under her name in the same directory for 1816–17. She was still listed as a confectioner in Rochdale in *Pigot and Dean's New Directory of Manchester, Salford, Etc, 1821–22*, Manchester: R. and W. Dean, [1821], p. 320. On women and shopkeeping see, Davidoff and Hall, op. cit., pp. 301–4. Women in 'polite society' might also, in the days of Margaret Wood's youth, have sold their medicines, or the produce of their farms and households, see A. Vickery, *Gentleman's Daughter: women's lives in Georgian England*, New Haven: Yale University Press, 1998, pp. 154; or pursued an interest in the engineering and the economics of coal mining, and intervened in elections, see J. Liddington, *Female Fortune. Land, Gender and*

238 *Notes*

Authority: the Anne Lister diaries and other writing, 1833–36, London: Rivers Oram, 1998, pp. 22, 48–52, 50, 53–5, 59f, 68–9, 73, 116–17, 117–18, 121–2, 149, 154–5.
31 S. B. Clark, op. cit.
32 See M. Bright's handwriting in M. Wood, Register of Family and Other Events, 1808–58, MIL 17/02.
33 Mills, op. cit., vol. 1, pp. 183, 185; Robertson, op. cit., vol. 1, p. 17. Elizabeth Wood (Bancroft)'s school exercise book from the 1780s, for example, contains exercises in preparing invoices and accounts, BAN 2/6, CA.
34 Mills, op. cit., vol. 1, pp. 262–4.
35 From time to time Margaret Wood recommended, or sent as a gift, works she especially valued, including the memoirs of a Quaker minister, Job Scott.
36 M. Wood to M. Bancroft, 17 March 1827, M. Wood to R. Bancroft, 2 November 1832, both BAN 1/13; M. Wood to J. Bancroft, 30 July 1832; M. Wood to J. and S. Bancroft, 17 September 1838, 5 August 1839, 9 December 1839, all BAN 1/81.
37 M. Wood to J. Bancroft, 27 November 1840, BAN 1/85; M. Wood to Er Bancroft, 16 October 1842; M. Wood to M. and Er Bancroft, 25 March 1843, both BAN 1/13.
38 See the essays in K. Gleadle and S. Richardson (eds), *Women in British Politics, 1760–1860. The power of the petticoat*, Basingstoke: Macmillan Press, 2000. Compare with the discussion in Vickery, op. cit., 256–80, 292–4; F. K. Prochaska, *Women and Philanthropy in Nineteenth Century England*, Oxford: Clarendon Press, 1980, esp. pp. 10–11, 227–8.
39 S. S. Holton, 'Religion and the Meanings of Work: four cases from among the Bright circle of women Quakers', in K. Cowman and L. Jackson (eds), *Women and Work Culture in Britain circa 1850–1950*, Aldershot: Ashgate Press, 2005, compares women across four generations of this kinship circle.
40 E.g., M. Wood to R. Bancroft, 7 December 1839, BAN 1/13, reports her friends, the Sharp sisters in Halifax, doing well in their dressmaking business.
41 M. Wood to M. Bancroft 6 May 1827, BAN 1/13.
42 M. Wood to R. Bancroft, 2 November 1832; M. Wood to R. and M. Bancroft, 5 April 1838, both BAN 1/13.
43 M. Wood to J. and S. Bancroft, 5 August 1839, BAN 1/81.
44 On the various Bancroft mills, see 'Biographical Note', in the records of Samuel Bancroft and Joseph Bancroft and Sons, University of Delaware Library, at www.lib.udel.edu/us/spec/bancroft.htm, accessed 6 January 2006; 'Biographical and Historical Note', Joseph Bancroft Papers, Swarthmore College Library, at www.swarthmore.edu/library/friends/ead/5007banc.htm, accessed 6 January 2006. Further Bancroft business and private papers are held at the Hagley Museum, see www.hagley.lib.de.us, accessed 6 January 2006.
45 M. Wood to Jn II and Sa Bancroft, 9 June 1843, BAN 2/3; M. Wood to Nephew and Niece, 28 June1847, located with M. Wood, Register of Family and Other Events, 1808–58, MIL 17/02.
46 M. Wood to J. Bancroft, 26 July 1826, BAN 1/81, CA.
47 M. Wood to Jn II and Sa Bancroft, 9 June 1843, BAN 2/3, CA.
48 A. Vickery, *The Gentleman's Daughter: women's lives in Georgian England*, New Haven, CT: Yale University Press, 1998.
49 M. Wood, Register of Family and Other Events, MIL 17/02.
50 On these divisions within London Yearly Meeting, see E. Isichei, *Victorian Quakers*, London: Oxford University Press, 1970, esp. pp. 44–53; T. C. Kennedy, *British Quakerism, 1860–1920. The transformation of a religious community*, Oxford: Oxford University Press, 2001, esp. pp. 12–46.
51 Compare with the accounts in T. D. Hamm, '"A Protest against Protestantism"; Hicksite Friends and the Bible in the Nineteenth Century', *Quaker Studies*, 2002, vol. 6, pp. 175–94; C. E. Kerman, 'Elias Hicks and Thomas Shillitoe: two paths diverge?',

Quaker Studies, 2000, vol. 5, pp. 19–47, each suggesting how little divided these opposing groups were theologically. So, the contest is often seen rather in terms of social divisions within the Philadelphia Yearly Meeting, with the spiritual leadership of wealthy urban evangelicals being challenged by less-educated, 'conservative' Friends of modest means from agricultural communities.

52 M. Wood to M. Bancroft, 6 May 1827, BAN 1/13.
53 Ibid.
54 E. Crosland to 'Dear Brother' (Jn Bancroft I), 14 August 1828, BAN 2/3, CA. See also E. Bancroft, 1825 memorandum, in an old Ackworth School exercise book, BAN 2/6, recalling 'a fresh renewal of covenant which I did hope would never have been broken' while in Wales.
55 On the Hicksite schism, see H. L. Ingle, *Quakers in Conflict. The Hicksite reformation*, Wallingford, PA: Pendle Hill Publications, 2nd edn, 1998 (1986). On the Orthodox Friends in Philadelphia Yearly Meeting, see T. D. Hamm, *The Transformation of American Quakerism. Orthodox Friends, 1800–1907*, Bloomington, IN: Indiana University Press, 1992.
56 M. Wood to J. Bancroft, 14 April 1829, BAN 1/81.
57 Ibid.
58 Mills, op. cit., vol. 1, p. 263.
59 Ibid., vol. 2, p. 344 for the Croslands' family tree. Further records relating to Robert Crosland (sometimes spelt 'Crossland') and his household and business include Bolton Poor Law Rate Assessment Book, 1805; Index and Returns for Bolton, 1811, 1821, 1831 Censuses; *Bolton Directory, 1818*, 1821–22, Manchester: T. Rogerson, 1818; E. Baines, *History, Directory and Gazeteer of the County Palatine of Lancaster*, vol. 1; *Slater's Directory of Bolton, 1814*, all Local History Department, Bolton Public Library; entries for Mary and Robert Crosland in QDB.
60 M. Wood to M. Bancroft, 6 May 1827, BAN 1/13.

3 Kinship, money and worldliness

1 Transcription of R. Bancroft, 'Journal of the Voyage from Liverpool to Philadelphia,' 1822, by E. G. Curtis, a great-niece, BAN 2/15, CA.
2 M. Wood, United States Journal (henceforth, USJ), 29 July, 30 July 1831, MIL 17/08.
3 Ibid., 31 July, 4 August, 24 August, 30 August 1831.
4 Ibid., 30 August, 31 August, 1 September, 9 September 1831.
5 Ibid., 11 September 1831; S. B. Clark, '"Aunt Wood" (Margaret Wood, 1783–1851)' [should read 1859], typescript, 16 August 1968, BC 249/1, W. B. Clark Papers, CA.
6 M. Wood, USJ, 14 September 1831.
7 Ibid., 15 September 1831.
8 Ibid., 17 September, 14 November 1831; Clark, 'Aunt Wood', p. 2.
9 M. Wood, USJ, 29 September, 17 October 1831.
10 Ibid, 11 October, 14 November 1831, 18 May 1832.
11 Ibid., 23 December 1831, 4 February, 7 February 1832.
12 Ibid., 29 September 1831, 29 April 1832.
13 Ibid., 18 November 1831, 22 February 1832; M. Wood to J. Bancroft, 30 July 1832, 9 December 1839; M. Wood to J. and S. Bancroft, 6 April 1838, 17 September 1838, 5 August 1839, all BAN 1/81.
14 M. Wood, USJ, 18 May, 15 June 1832.
15 M. Wood to M. Bancroft 7 [?] December 1837; M. Wood to Er Bancroft, 20 July 1838; M. Wood to R. Bancroft, 7 December 1839, all BAN 1/13.
16 M. Wood, USJ, 19 April, 28 May, 10 June, 14 June, 19 June 1832; S. Bright to Er Bancroft, 29 August 1832, BAN 1/93.

17 M. Wood, USJ, 19 June, 11 July, 16–19 July 1832; M. Wood to R. Bancroft, 2 November 1832, BAN 1/13.
18 Jn Bancroft I to D. Bancroft, 17 September 1832, BAN 2/11, CA.
19 J. T. Mills, *John Bright and the Quakers*, London: Methuen, 1935 (2 vols), vol. 1, pp. 259–60.
20 K. Robbins, *John Bright*, London: Routledge and Kegan Paul, 1979, pp. 25–7.
21 Ibid., p. 11.
22 M. Wood to R. Bancroft, 2 November 1832, BAN 1/13.
23 Ibid., 7 December 1839.
24 Compare, for example, L. Davidoff and C. Hall, *Family Fortunes: men and women of the English middle class c.1780–1850*, London: Routledge, 1992, pp. 18, 187–8, 210, 275–9; M. Berg, 'Women's Property and the Industrial Revolution', *Journal of Interdisciplinary History*, 1993, vol. 24, pp. 233–50; P. Lane, 'Women, Property and Inheritance: wealth creation and income generation in small English towns, 1750–1835, and D. R. Green, 'Independent Women, Wealth and Wills in Nineteenth Century London', both in J. Stobart and A. Owens (eds), *Urban Fortunes. Property and inheritance in the town, 1700–1900*, Aldershot: Ashgate, 2000; M. B. Combs, 'Wives and Household Wealth: the impact of the 1870 British Married Women's Property Act on wealth-holding and share of household resources', *Continuity and Change*, 2004, vol. 19, pp. 141–63; R. J. Morris, *Men, Women and Property in England, 1780–1870. A social and economic history of family strategies among the Leeds middle classes*, Cambridge: Cambridge University Press, 2005, pp. 26, 61, 234, 335, 403.
25 For further discussion of this point, see G. Crossick, 'Meanings of Property and the World of the Petite Bourgeoisie', in Stobart and Owens, op. cit.
26 My thinking here has been informed by the work of Supriya Singh, see especially her *Marriage Money. The Social Shaping of Money in Marriage and Banking*, St Leonards, NSW: Allen & Unwin, 1997, which deals with modern marriage, but which conceptualises 'marriage money' and 'market money', and also identifies 'transnational family money', of particular relevance for the discussion that follows. See also V. A. Zelizer, *The Social Meaning of Money*, New York: Basic Books, 1994, which asks how money is adapted to the intimate relations of kinship.
27 M. Wood to R. Bancroft, 7 December 1839, BAN 1/13. Davidoff and Hall, op. cit., pp. 16–17.
28 Margaret Wood's shop was in Market Place, subsequently Yorkshire Street, and a Margaret Wood is rated at 18/- for a property there in the 1825–6 Poor Law Collecting Book for Wardleworth Township (where the Bright family also lived), Local Studies Department, Rochdale Public Library.
29 M. Wood to M. Bancroft, 6 May 1827; M. Wood to R. Bancroft, 2 November 1832, both BAN 1/13.
30 M. Wood to Jn II and Sa Bancroft, 9 June 1843; typescript copy of M. Wood's will, 21 February 1851, shows her leaving a larger share of her estate to the Bancrofts; M. Wood to J. Bancroft, 10 July 1852; J. Bancroft memorandum, 13 October 1852, on further instructions sought from his aunt; M. Wood informal will, 16 June 1854, 'Account of money, amongst my nephews and nieces in America', all BAN 2/3, CA; M. Wood to her Nephew and Niece [J. and S. Bancroft], n.d. [1847] located with M. Wood, Register of Family and Other Events, 1808–58, MIL 17/02.
31 W. Robertson, *Life and Times of the Right Honourable John Bright*, London: Cassell, 1883, 2 vols, vol. 1, p. 39.
32 M. Wood to J. Bancroft, 9 December 1839, 14 April 1829, both BAN 1/81.
33 M. Wood to Jn II and Sa Bancroft, 9 June 1843, BAN 2/3, CA; M. Wood to Nephew and Niece, n.d. [1847] with MIL 17/02.
34 M. Wood to M. and Er Bancroft, 23 October 1848, 12 June 1849, both BAN 1/13.

35 M. Wood to J. Bancroft, 10 July 1852 and his memorandum of his response, 10 October 1852, both BAN 2/3, CA.
36 M. Wood to J. Bancroft, 9 December 1839 (her emphasis), 14 April 1829, both BAN 1/81.
37 M. Wood to Jn II and Sa Bancroft, 9 June 1843, BAN 2/3, CA.
38 S. B. Clark, op. cit.
39 M. Wood to J. Bancroft, 30 July 1832, BAN 1/81; M. Wood to R. Bancroft, 2 November 1832, BAN 1/13. On deviations from Quaker business ethics see also J. Walvin, *The Quakers: money and morals*, London: John Murray, 1997.
40 M. Wood to J. Bancroft, 14 April 1829, BAN 1/81.
41 M. Wood to M. Bancroft, 7 December 1836, BAN 1/13; M. Wood to Jn II and Sa Bancroft, 9 June 1843, BAN 2/3, CA.
42 See, for example, her several interventions on behalf of the parents of Evan Davies, who appears to have been a senior employee of the Bancrofts, including M. Wood to J. and S. Bancroft, 6 April, 17 September 1838; M. Wood to J. Bancroft, 9 December 1839, all BAN 1/81.
43 E.g. M. Wood to J. Bancroft, 30 July 1832, BAN 1/81.
44 M. Wood to Er Bancroft, 20 July 1838, BAN 1/13.
45 M. Wood, USJ, 13 October 1831, 12 February, 31 May1832.
46 E. Isichei, *Victorian Quakers*, London: Oxford University Books, 1970, pp. 44–53; T. C. Kennedy, *British Quakerism, 1860–1920. The transformation of a religious community*, Oxford: Oxford University Press, 2001, pp. 26–31, 69–70, 87–8.
47 M. Wood to M. Bancroft, 7 December 1838, BAN 1/13.
48 M. Wood to J. and S. Bancroft, 17 September 1838, BAN 1/81; M. Wood to Er Bancroft, 20 July 1838, BAN 1/13. The reference here is to Sarah Lynes Grubb (1773–1842), who became a minister at seventeen and was former governess to another Sarah Grubb of Tipperary, see G. W. Grubb, *Grubbs of Tipperary. Studies in heredity and character*, Cork: Mercier Press 1972, p. 94, which also hints, p. 26, at evangelical criticism that Sarah Lynes Grubb 'did not allow family cares to restrict her ministering activities', p. 100. Other research suggests considerable variation between meetings, see H. Plant, 'Gender and the Aristocracy of Dissent: a comparative study of the beliefs, status and roles of women in Quaker and Unitarian Communities, 1770–1830, with particular reference to Yorkshire', unpublished D Phil thesis: University of York, 2000, pp. 32, 74–81 on the challenge to women's spiritual authority from some evangelicals, and compare S. Wright, *Friends in York. The dynamics of Quaker revival, 1780–1860*, Keele: Keele University Press, 1995, pp. 39–49, showing how the spiritual leadership of evangelical women ministers continued to shape that meeting.
49 A. Tyrrell, *Joseph Sturge and the Moral Reform Radical Party in Early Victorian Britain*, London: Croom Helm, 1987, p. 193; E. Bronner, 'Moderates in London Yearly Meeting, 1857–1873', *Church History*, 1990, vol. 59, pp. 356–71; S. S. Holton, 'John Bright, Radical Politics and the Ethos of Quakerism', *Albion*, 2002, vol. 34, pp. 584–605.

4 Rachel Priestman (1791–1854), a 'public Friend'

1 R. J. Morris, *Cholera 1832. The social response to an epidemic*, London: Croom Helm, 1976, esp. pp. 30, 44, 59–61, 63, 71 on the epidemics in Newcastle.
2 R. Priestman, 'Journal, 1820–54', compiled from her memoranda and others' reminiscences of her in her youth, by her daughter, M. Wheeler (subsequently Tanner), MIL 16/01. I use dates where provided here; Morris, op. cit., pp. 61, 91.
3 Hadwen Bragg, son of a Whitehaven shoemaker, served his apprenticeship as a draper there. He married in 1790, two years after establishing his own business in Newcastle, J. W. Steel, *A Historical Sketch of the Society of Friends 'In Scorn Called Quakers' in*

Newcastle and Gateshead, 1653–1898, London: Headley Bros, 1899, p. 125. On Margaret Bragg's family of origin, see J. Somervell, *Isaac and Rachel Wilson, Quakers of Kendal, 1714–85*, London: Swarthmore Press, 1924. For a detailed genealogy of descendants of the Wilsons, see R. S. Benson (comp.), *Photographic Pedigree of the Descendants of Isaac and Rachel Wilson*, Middlesbrough: William Appleyard, 1912.

4 M. Bragg, Account Book for 1820, MIL 15/05, shows her selling butter, keeping orchards, producing honey, employing gardeners and labourers to till fields for vegetables. She also had an interest in another business as a woollen draper and hatter, in partnership with another woman Friend, Sarah Rooke, see, W. Parson and W. White, *History, Directory and Gazetteer . . . of Durham & Northumberland . . .*, Newcastle: White & Co., 1827, 2 vols, vol. 1, pp. 11, 70.

5 H. Bragg, addendum to J. Priestman to M. Bragg, 15 May 1817, MIL 6/09.

6 See the correspondence between M. Bragg and R. Bragg, 29 August, 6 October, 6 November 1809, MIL 12/04.

7 Somervell, op. cit., esp. p. 155; Steel, op. cit., pp. 125, 127, 129.

8 M. Bragg to R. Bragg, 21 July 1803, 29 September 03, 9 February 05, MIL 12/04; E. English, addendum to R. Bragg to M. Bragg, 11 April 1805, MIL 6/03; R. Bragg, school books: Accounting, Bookkeeping and French, MIL 15/06.

9 R. Priestman, 'Journal', n.d., MIL 16/01; E. English to R. Bragg, May 1806, MIL 3/03.

10 R. Priestman, 'Journal', n.d., MIL 16/01.

11 Ibid., February 1810

12 On the Priestman family, see S. H. Priestman, *The Priestmans of Thornton-le-Dale and Some of their Descendents*, Sutton-on-Hull: privately published, 1955; R. Clark, 'Notes, Extracts etc, Roger Clark', an album of fragments collected by a great-grandson of R. and J. Priestman, RDFC (3) I 19, R. D. F. Clark Papers, CA.

13 R. Bragg to J. Priestman, 2 December, 12 December, 21 December 1813, MIL 4.

14 On Jonathan Priestman's apprenticeship, see MIL 3/04; on the position offered him at the Richardson tannery, see D. Priestman to J. Priestman, 31 July 1809, MIL 1/05. For an account of Jonathan Priestman and of the Richardson family, see A. O. Boyce, *Records of a Quaker Family: the Richardsons of Cleveland*, London: Samuel Harris, 1889, esp. pp. 52, 85, 97–104, Appendix F, p. 265 and Table VI. See also, E. A. O'Donnell, 'Woman's Rights and Woman's Duties. Quaker women in the nineteenth century', unpublished PhD, University of Sunderland 2000, esp. pp. 42, 44, 155, 190, 204, 207, 212, 254, 264, 266, 269, 283.

15 D. Priestman to J. Priestman, 28 July, 7 September 1813, MIL 1/05.

16 Steel, op. cit, p. 129; see also, R. Sansbury, *Beyond the Blew Stone. 300 Years of Quakers in Newcastle*, Newcastle: Newcastle Upon Tyne Preparative Meeting, 1999, pp. 162–3.

17 R. Priestman to J. Priestman, n.d., MIL 4.

18 S. Szreter, *Fertility, Class and Gender in Britain, 1860–1940*, Cambridge: Cambridge University Press, 1996, esp. pp. 364, 418–19, 423–4; R. T. Vann and D. Eversley, *Friends in Life and Death. The British and Irish Quakers in the demographic transition, 1650–1900*, Cambridge: Cambridge University Press, 1992, esp. pp. 177, 243–5, 247.

19 Benson, op. cit., pp. 551–61.

20 S. Morgan, '"A Sort of Land Debateable": female influence, civic virtue and middle class identity, c. 1830–c. 1860', *Women's History Review*, 2004, vol. 13, pp. 183–209, esp. pp. 184, 185.

21 Sansbury, op. cit., pp. 155, 164–65.

22 See, for example, L. Davidoff and C. Hall, *Family Fortunes: men and women of the English middle class c.1780–1850*, London: Routledge, pp. 447–9; A. Vickery, *The Gentleman's Daughter: women's lives in Georgian England*, New Haven: Yale University Press, 1998, esp. pp. 254–84 ; J. Liddington, *Female Fortune. Land, gender and authority: The Anne*

Lister diaries and other writing 1833–36, London: Rivers Oram, 1998, pp. 45–50; E. Chalus, 'Women, Electoral Privilege and Practice in the Eighteenth Century'; S. Morgan, 'Domestic Economy and Political Agitation: women and the Anti-Corn Law League'; M. Cragoe, '"Jenny Rules the Roost": women and electoral politics, 1832–68', all in K. Gleadle and S. Richardson (eds), *Women in British Politics, 1760–1860. The power of the petticoat*, Basingstoke: Macmillan Press, 2000.

23 S. Wright, *Friends in York. The dynamics of Quaker revival, 1780–1860*, Keele: Keele University Press, 1995, esp. pp. 51–67; O'Donnell, op. cit., p. 139; H. Plant, 'Gender and the Aristocracy of Dissent: a comparative study of the beliefs, status and roles of women in Quaker and Unitarian Communities, 1770–1830, with particular reference to Yorkshire, unpublished DPhil thesis, York University, 2000, p. 45, 61, 119–24.

24 J. Priestman to R. Priestman, 8 June, 13 June, 23 June, 25 June 1816, 22 April, 6 May 1818, MIL 3/05.

25 R. Priestman to J. Priestman, n.d. MIL 4; R. Priestman, 'Journal', 23 July 1853, MIL 16/01.

26 L. Howsam, *Cheap Bibles: Nineteenth-century publishing and the British and Foreign Bible Society*, Cambridge: Cambridge University Press, 1991, p. 53.

27 O'Donnell, op. cit., p. 62; also, M. Callcott, 'The Governance of the Victorian City' and O. Lendrum, 'An Integrated Elite. Newcastle's economic development, 1840–1914', both in R. Colls and B. Lancaster, *Newcastle-upon-Tyne: a modern history*, Chichester: Phillimore and Co., 2000.

28 Steel, op. cit., pp. 129. See also, Boyce, op. cit., p. 221; Entry for A. M Priestman, QDB.

29 On this point, see Plant, op. cit., esp. pp. 45–55.

30 R. Priestman, 'Journal', January 1834. On responses to child deaths in this period, see P. Jalland, *Death in the Victorian Family*, Oxford: Oxford University, 1996, pp. 119–42.

31 R. Priestman, 'Journal', 21 February 1829; 5 April 1833; 28 April 1833.

32 Ibid.

33 Ibid.

34 M. Stickney to R. Priestman, 26 December 1825; E. Stickney to R. Priestman, n.d.; E. Stickney to M. Priestman, 5 June 1840; E. Stickney to R. Priestman II, 10 February 1842; E. Stickney to A. M. Priestman, n.d., all MIL 26/01.

35 R. Priestman, 'Journal', 31 July 1838, n.d., MIL 16/01.

36 M. Priestman, Exercise Book, esp. entries dated 27, 28 November 1824, and 9 January 1825, also a similar account kept by E. Priestman, both MIL 16/03.

37 See the 'Inventory of Knowledge' made by the younger Priestman children in 1836 and 1839, MIL 9/01.

38 M. Priestman to E. Shackleton, 2 September 1826, MIL 32/04 (1).

39 W. Doeg, 'Book of Misdeeds by Priestman Children, 1831–3', MIL 16/03.

40 O'Donnell, op. cit., pp. 146, 149.

41 R. Priestman, 'Journal', Spring 1830, MIL 16/01, and her introduction to E. Bright, 'Memorial', the account of her daughter's life she compiled from memoranda and letters, MIL 16/04.

42 E. Bright, 'Memorial', MIL 16/04.

43 Ibid., recalling 9 March 1838 and the weeks thereafter; also, 28 May 1838.

44 R. Priestman, 'Journal', March 1837.

45 On Anna Braithwaite and her ministry, see J. B. Braithwaite, *Memoir of Anna Braithwaite*, London: Headley Brothers, 1905; H. L. Ingle, *Quakers in Conflict. The Hicksite reformation*, Wallingford, PA: Pendle Hill Publications, 2nd edn, 1998 (University of Kentucky, 1986), esp. pp. 33–4, 63, 127–9.

46 M. Priestman to E. Stickney, 29 May 1835, MIL 32/04 (1).

244 *Notes*

47 M. Priestman to E. Priestman, 3 April 1837, MIL 31/01(2).
48 R. Priestman, 'Journal', 11 June 1839.
49 Ibid., 27 September 1839.

5 Marriages, births and deaths

1 J. T. Mills, *John Bright and the Quakers*, London: Methuen, 1935 (2 vols), vol. 1, pp. 385–6. L. Stewart, *Memoirs of a Quaker Childhood*, E. Roberts (ed.), London: Friends' Home Service Committee, 1970, p. 31, suggests Priscilla Bright attended Corder's school in 1830, around the same time as Elizabeth Priestman.
2 M. Wood to R. and M. Bancroft, 5 April 1838, BAN 1/13.
3 J. Bright to J. Priestman, 20 September 1838, MIL 34/02.
4 R. Priestman, 'Journal', n.d. (looking back on the events of 1838), MIL 16/01.
5 E. Bright, 'Memorial', selected and copied from her memoranda and letters by Rachel Priestman, 28 May, 3 June, 22 June, 8 July [1838], MIL 16/04.
6 Ibid., 11 August; '11/-' [probably 11 October 1838, the date of her first letter to John Bright, see n. 9].
7 Ibid.
8 J. Bright to E. Priestman, 5 October 1838, MIL 35/01(a).
9 E. Priestman to J. Bright, 11 October 1838, MIL 35/01(c).
10 J. Bright to P. Bright, 12 October 1838, MIL 35/04.
11 J. Bright to E. Priestman, 15 October 1838, MIL 35/01(a).
12 M. Wood to J. and S. Bancroft, 5 August 1839, BAN 1/81.
13 J. Bright to E. Priestman, 8 November 1838, MIL 35/01(a).
14 J. Bright to E. Priestman, 22 November, 8 December, 27 December 1838; E. Priestman to J. Bright, 15 November 1838, MIL 35/01(a) and (c) respectively.
15 J. Bright to E. Priestman, 22 November, 15 December, 27 December 1838, 6 January 1839, MIL 35/01(a).
16 Ibid., 17 January, 30 January 1839.
17 Recollections of W. H. Holmes, quoted in R. Sansbury, *Beyond the Blew Stone. 300 years of Quakers in Newcastle*, Newcastle: Newcastle-upon-Tyne Preparative Meeting, 1999, pp. 158–9.
18 See the photograph and description in J. Tozer and S. Levitt, *Fabric of Society. A century of people and their clothes, 1770–1870*, Carns: Laura Ashley, 1993, p. 91. This dress is part of the collection at Platt Hall Gallery of English Costume, Manchester.
19 M. Wood to R. Bancroft, 7 December 1839, BAN 1/13; M. Wood to J. Bancroft, 9 December 1839, BAN 1/81.
20 E.g. M. Priestman to E. Bright, 13 July 1840, MIL 31/01 (2).
21 N. A. Hewitt, *Women's Activism and Social Change. Rochester, New York, 1822–1872*, Ithaca: Cornell University Press, 1984, esp. pp. 36, 42, 163–6, 169, 254, on the role of Hicksite women among the 'ultraist' abolitionists and women's rights advocates.
22 K. Robbins, *John Bright*, London: Routledge & Kegan Paul, 1979, p. 22; J. Bright to E. Priestman, MIL 31/01(a)
23 E.g. M. Wood to J. Bancroft, 10 August 1840, BAN 1/85.
24 F. Tolles (ed.), *Slavery and 'The Woman Question'. Lucretia Mott's diary of . . . the World's Anti-Slavery Convention of 1840*, Haverford, PA: Friends' Historical Society, 1952, Supplement no. 23, *Journal of the Friends' Historical Society*; K. Gleadle, *The Early Feminists: radical Unitarians and the emergence of the women's rights movement 1831–51*, Basingstoke: Macmillan, 1995, p. 3; C. Midgley, *Women Against Slavery. The British campaigns, 1780–1870*, London: Routledge, 1992, pp. 131–2, 158–9.
25 J. Bright to E. Bright, 30 May 1840, MIL 35/01(b).
26 Ibid., 12 June 1840.
27 Ibid., 27 and 28 May 1840; J. Bright to P. Bright, 9 May 1840, MIL 35/04.

28 J. Bright to E. Bright, 24 May, 25 May, 30 May and 1 June 1840, MIL 35/01(b).
29 Anon., account of the death of Margaret Bragg, MIL 11/04.
30 E. Bright, 'Memorial', June 1840, MIL 16/04.
31 M. Bragg, codicil to her will, 16 February 1829, and memoranda re bequests, 3 April 1837, 5 January 1839, MIL 11/04.
32 R. Priestman to E. Bright, 7 November, 27 November, 28 December 1840, MIL 5/01(2).
33 J. Bright to M. Priestman, 12 November 1840, MIL 35/02, and to A. M. and My Priestman, 5 October 1841, MIL 35/03.
34 J. Bright to E. Bright 25 June, 26 June, 21 July, 18 August, 20 August, 23 August 1841, 35/01(b).
35 J. Bright to P. Bright, 3 September 1841, MIL 35/04.
36 R. Priestman to E. Bright, n.d. [probably August–September 1841], MIL 5/012.
37 J. Bright to M. Priestman, 1 October 1841, MIL 35/02.
38 Ibid., and 3 October 1841; J. Bright to P. Bright, 25 September, 29 September 1841, MIL 35/04.
39 A. Sayles to A. M. Priestman, 27 October 1841, 14 January 1842, 2 February 1842, 2 February 1842, MIL 27/01(T) [signature wrongly ascribed to A. Taylor].
40 J. Bright to E. Bright 25 June, 26 June, 21 July, 18 August, 20 August, 23 August 1841, MIL 35/01(b).
41 M. Wood to R. Bancroft, 7 December 1839, BAN 1/13; M. Wood to J. Bancroft, 9 December 1839, BAN 1/81; M. Wood to J. and S. Bancroft, 5 August 1839, BAN 1/84.
42 J. Bright to P. Bright, 25 September 1842, 28 September 1842, MIL 35/04.
43 R. Priestman II to Er Bright, n.d. [c. November 1841; c. April 1842], MIL 10/03; M. Priestman to P. Bright, 21 April 1842, MIL 31/01(4).
44 R. Priestman II to Er Bright, n.d.[c. November 1841], MIL 10/03.
45 H. Priestman to J. Bright, 14 October 1842, MIL 31/01(2).

6 Religion, family and public life

1 R. Priestman I to P. Bright, n.d., enclosed with M. Priestman to Priscilla Bright, 15 March 1843, MIL 31/01(4).
2 R. Priestman I, USJ, 1 November 1843, MIL 16/02; a printed reprimand among her 'American Miscellany', 2 June 1844, MIL 7/04.
3 J. Bright's speech, unveiling Cobden's statue, 25 July 1877, quoted in G. M. Trevelyan, *The Life of John Bright*, London: Constable and Company, 1913, p. 43.
4 R. Priestman II to Er Bright, n.d., MIL 10/3.
5 P. Pickering and A. Tyrrell, *People's Bread. A history of the Anti-Corn Law League*, Leicester: Leicester University Press, 2000, pp. 120–25.
6 J. Bright to R. Cobden and to R. Priestman I, August 1842, quoted in Trevelyan, op. cit., pp. 80–1.
7 Ibid.
8 J. T. Mills, *John Bright and the Quakers*, London: Methuen, 1935 (2vols), vol. 1, p. 265; Pickering and Tyrell, op. cit., esp. pp. 122–6.
9 R. Priestman II to Er Bright, n.d., MIL 10/03; M. Priestman to P. Bright, 8 February 1842, and see also 26 January, 9 February 1842, MIL 31/01 (4).
10 J. Bright to A. M. and My Priestman, 1 January 1842, MIL 35/03. F. K. Prochaska, *Women and Philanthropy in Nineteenth Century England*, Oxford: Clarendon Press, 1980, pp. 47–72 examines bazaars as a fund-raising method particular to women. On women's benevolence and women's public roles, see also, L. Ginzberg, *Work of Benevolence. Politics, morality and class in the nineteenth century United States*, New Haven, CT: Yale University Press, 1990.

246 *Notes*

11 M. Wood to Er Bancroft, 3 January 1842, BAN 1/13.
12 R. Priestman II to Er Bright, n.d., MIL 10/03.
13 M. Priestman to P. Bright, 6, 27, 31 January 1843, n.d., pm 20 July 1843, MIL 31/01(4).
14 R. Priestman II to Er Bright n.d., MIL 10/03.
15 M. Priestman to P. Bright, n.d. [1842], MIL 31/01 (4).
16 On long-standing notions of women's citizenship, especially as deriving from religious values, see P. Crawford, 'Public Duty, Conscience and Women in Early Modern England', in G. E. Aylmer (ed.), *Public Duty and Private Conscience in Seventeenth Century England*, Oxford: Clarendon Press, 1993 and compare L. Davidoff and C. Hall, *Family Fortunes: men and women of the English middle class c.1780–1850*, London: Routledge, 1992, pp. 419, 447–9 which defines the public sphere as a male-only space in which 'public opinion can be created,' and also argues that men's 'network of association redefined civil society'. Such an account leaves aside the role of dissenting religion in the creation of public opinion, the growth also of women's associational life, and women's creation of their own public spaces. On the latter point, see also A. Vickery, *Gentleman's Daughter: women's lives in Georgian England*, New Haven, CT: Yale University Press, 1998, pp. 225–84, 290–91.
17 M. Priestman to P. Bright, two letters, n.d., pm 16 September 1843; pm 23 July 1844, MIL 31/01(4).
18 Mills, op. cit., vol. 1, p. 269 quoting T. Carlyle to J. Carlyle, 13 September 1847.
19 P. Joyce, *Democratic Subjects. The self and the social in nineteenth century England*, Cambridge: Cambridge University Press, 1994, esp. pp.116–24.
20 M. Priestman to P. Bright, n.d., 2, 16, 28 April 1843, MIL 31/01(4).
21 For an introduction to the literature on romantic friendship, see L. Stanley, 'Romantic Friendship? Some issues in researching lesbian history and biography', *Women's History Review*, 1992, vol. 1, pp. 193–216.
22 M. Priestman to P. Bright, n.d., 12 November 1841, 28 April 1843, MIL 31/01(4).
23 M. Priestman to P. Bright, n.d., pm 27 April 1843; 12 November 1841; 20 May 1842; 1 July 1844, MIL 31/01(4).
24 Davidoff and Hall, op. cit., pp. 18–28.
25 See M. Vicinus, *Independent Women. Work and community for single women, 1850–1920*, London: Virago, 1985.
26 M. Priestman to P. Bright, pm 23 July 1844, MIL 31/01(4).
27 Ibid., 16 February 1844; two letters, n.d., one marked 'Private'.
28 Ibid., 10 June 1844, 26 July 1844.
29 Ibid., pm 15 October 1844.
30 Ibid., 11 March 1843; one n .d., pm July 1844; 18 October 1844.
31 Ibid., pm July 1844.
32 Ibid., 6 January, 15 March 1843, 22 May 1844, n.d., 23 July 1844, 7 October 1844.
33 Ibid., 29 June 1845.
34 Ibid., n.d., pm 20 October 1845.
35 Ibid., 5 November 1845.
36 Ibid., pm 25 October1843, and see also ibid., 2 April 1843, which combined 'love gossip' alongside references to election politics.
37 Ibid., pm 27 February 1845.
38 M. Wood to M. and Er Bancroft, 3 November 1845, BAN 1/13. See also M. Wood to J. Bancroft, 11 January 1845, BAN 1/85; M. Wood to M. Bancroft, 27 June 1845 and 3 July 1845, both BAN 1/13; M. Priestman to P. Bright, 7, 10 March 1845, MIL 31/01(4).
39 M. Priestman to P. Bright, 27 February, 20 October, 5 November 1845, MIL 31/01(4).
40 Ibid., pm 20 October 1845.

7 Sisters, marriage and friendship

1. M. Wheeler to P. Bright, pm 12 August 1846, MIL 31/01(4); M. Wheeler to My Priestman, 9 September 1846, MIL 31/01(2); M. Priestman to S. Wheeler, 9 January 1846, MIL 30/05.
2. M. Wheeler to My Priestman, 9 September 1846, pm 26 December 1846, MIL 31/01(2); M. Wheeler to P. Bright, 26 December 1846, MIL 31/01(4); S. Wheeler, tenancy agreement for Ashley Down, 26 September 1846, MIL 29/02.
3. M. Wheeler [to My Priestman?] fragment, n.d. [August 1847?]; M. Wheeler to My Priestman, 27 February 1847, and n.d. [November 1847?], all MIL 31/01(2); M. Wheeler to P. Bright, 21 January 1847, MIL 31/01(4).
4. M. Wheeler to My Priestman, 3 February 1847, 27 January, 12 April 1848, MIL 31/01(2).
5. Ibid., fragment, n.d., 9 September 1846; M. Wheeler to S. Wheeler, 15 September 1847 and n.d., with D. Wheeler addendum, both MIL 29/14; D. Wheeler to J. Priestman I, 7 January 1847, 11 November [1847], 16 February [1848?], all MIL 29/15; D. Wheeler to R. Priestman, 12 January [1848?], 5 February 1848, both MIL 29/15.
6. M. Wheeler to P. Bright, 21 January 1847, MIL 31/01(4).
7. Ibid., pm 11 July 1846, pm 12 August 1846, 26 December 1846, 5 January 1847.
8. Ibid., 5 January 1847, 21 January 1847; R. Priestman to M. E. Bright, 18 October 1847, MIL 5/01/4.
9. M. Wheeler to P. Bright 16, 17, 19 February 1847, pm 23 February 1847, 1 March, 19 March 1847, MIL 31/01(4). To avoid confusion the second Elizabeth Bright will hereafter be referred to as M. E. Bright or M. E. B.
10. M. Wheeler to My Priestman, 19 November 1847, n.d. [November 1847?], MIL 31/01(2).
11. M. Wheeler to P. Bright, 27 February 1847, MIL 31/01(4); P. McLaren to M. Holdsworth, 5 December 1854, quoted in J. T. Mills, *John Bright and the Quakers*, London: Methuen, 1935 (2 vols), vol. 1, p. 305.
12. For a fuller account of Ben Rhydding and the therapy offered there, see T. Binding, *On Ilkley Moor. The story of an English town*, London: Picador, 2001, pp. 65–90.
13. P. McLaren to M. Holdsworth, 17 March 1849, quoted in Mills, op. cit., p. 301. On the career of Duncan McLaren, see J. B. Mackie, *The Life and Work of Duncan McLaren*, London: Thomas Nelson & Sons, 1888 (2 vols).
14. M. Wheeler to R. Priestman, 12 January n. y., 3 February 1848, 5 February 1848, MIL 29/15; and see also D. Wheeler to M. Wheeler, 3 February 1848, MIL 29/19.
15. M. Wheeler to My Priestman, n.d., 12, 15 April 1848, MIL 31/01(2); M. Wheeler's account of husband's last days, MIL 31/01(5).
16. A. M. Priestman to J. Pease, 29 June, 30 August 1848, MIL 22/01(a).
17. Ibid., 28 July, 29 July, 28 September 1848.
18. Ibid., 11 February, 13 March, 4 April, 15 September 1850.
19. D. Wheeler to J. Priestman, 7 January 1847, MIL 29/15; M. Wheeler to R. and J. Priestman, 22 July, 1 October 1848, M. Wheeler to R. Priestman, 2 September 1848, all MIL 30/01(1); M. Wheeler to S. Wheeler/Tanner (the latter married in the summer of 1849), n.d. [February 1849?], 24 February, 29 February, 25 October 1849, MIL 30/05, and 10 September, 29 October 1849, 32/01; F. Uhde to S. Wheeler, 2 May 1849, MIL 30/03; F. Uhde to S. Wheeler/Tanner, 14 September 1848, 30 January 1849, 20 April 1850, all MIL 29/03.
20. M. Wheeler to S. Wheeler, 11 February, 2 March 1849, n.d., all MIL 30/05; M. Wheeler to S. Tanner, 24 June, 29 October, 9 November, 29 November, 13 December 1849, 3 January 1852, all MIL 32/01.
21. M. Wheeler to S. Tanner, n.d., MIL 32/01.

248 Notes

22 R. Priestman to J. and M. E. Bright, MIL 5/01/4.
23 M. Wheeler to S. Tanner, 26 November, 20 December, 27 December 1849, MIL 32/01.
24 Ibid., 1 December, 13 December, 20 December, 27 December 1849; A. M. Priestman to J. Pease, 12 September 1850, 1 April 1851, MIL 22/01(a).
25 M. Wheeler to S. Tanner, three letters, all n.d.; M. Wheeler to 'dear Sister', 16 June 1850, located among her letters to S. Tanner though the contents suggest it was addressed to M. E. Bright, all MIL 32/01; M. Wheeler to J. and M. E. Bright, 19 September 1850, MIL 31/01(2).
26 M. Wheeler to S. Tanner, n.d., 7 December, 30 December 1850, MIL 32/01.
27 A. M. Priestman to J. Pease, 29 June, 11 August 1850, MIL 22/01(a); J. Priestman II to M. Wheeler, 22 June, 18 July, 7 August, 1850, MIL 10/05.
28 J. Priestman II to M. Wheeler, 22 June 1850, MIL 10/05.
29 A. D. Richardson to A. M. Priestman, two letters, n.d., MIL 26/01(2); A. M. Priestman to J. Pease, 12 September 1850, MIL 22/01(a).
30 A. M. Priestman to J. Pease, 22 October, 29 October, 22 November, 19 December 1850, 10 January, 1 May, 20 October 1851, MIL 22/01(a).
31 Ibid., 9 March, 23 April, 19 July, 25 August 1852.
32 Ibid., 19 September 1852.
33 A. D. Richardson, *Memoir of Anna Deborah Richardson, with Extracts from her Letters*, J. W. Richardson (ed.), Newcastle: privately published, 1877, p. 14. See also E. A. O'Donnell, '"On Behalf of all Young Women Trying to be Better than They are": feminism and Quakerism in the nineteenth-century: the case of Anna Deborah Richardson', *Quaker Studies*, 2001, vol. 6, pp. 37–58.
34 M. Phillips, *A History of Banks, Bankers and Banking in Northumberland, Durham and North Yorkshire*, London: E. Wilson & Co.,1894, provides an account based on public documents. J. Priestman I to M. Tanner, fragment, n.d., 2 February, 23 February, 20 March 1858, MIL 6/09(1) expressed grief and self-blame at the consequences for his children and surviving brother and wife.
35 On the outcome for the Richardsons of Shotley and their local meeting of Friends, see E. A. O'Donnell, 'Deviations from the Path of Safety: the rise and fall of a nineteenth century Quaker meeting', *Quaker Studies*, 2003, vol. 8, pp. 68–88; see also J. W. Richardson, *Memoirs, 1837–1908*, Glasgow: privately published, *c.* 1903.

8 The single life

1 A. M. Priestman to J. Pease, 7 July 1842, 11 October 1845, n.d. [*c.* August 1847], MIL 22/01(a).
2 Ibid., 15 June, 17 June 1848, 15 October 1849, 29 June 1850.
3 M. Wheeler to S. Tanner, 5 July, 8 July, 21 September, 13 December 1849, 2 January 1851, 5 May 1852, 3 August 1853, MIL 32/01.
4 Ibid., 17 October, 8 November, 18 November, 25 November, 19 December 1851, 3 January, 24 February 1852.
5 A. M. Priestman to J. Pease, 29 July 48; 11 February, 12 September 1850; 3 February, May Day 1851, MIL 22/01(a); H. Bright to M. Wheeler, 7 February, 24 March 1851, MIL 33/01(1).
6 A. M. Priestman to Esther [probably Stickney, but located among her letters to Er Bright], 25 October 1852, MIL 22/01 (g); A. M. Priestman to J. Pease, 19 September 1852, 6 February, 4 March, 29 March 1853; 5 November 1854, MIL 22/01(a).
7 A. M. Priestman to her sisters, 24 June 1851, MIL 22/01(b).
8 Ibid., 19 June, 24 June, 8 July 1851; A. M. Priestman to My Priestman, 24 July, 8 August 1851, 21 March 1856, all MIL 22/01(b).
9 A. M. Priestman to My Priestman, 22 September 1851, 22/01(b).

10 Ibid., 26 November 1851.
11 A. M. Priestman to J. H. Bragg, 7 October, 26 November 1851, MIL 22/01(c).
12 M. Wheeler to S. Tanner, 12 September, 24 September, 26 September, 28 September, 30 September, 3 October, 28 October 1853, MIL 32/01.
13 A. M. Priestman to Esther [probably Stickney], 25 September 1853, MIL 22/01(g). Government policy swung back and forth under pressure from both 'contagionists' favouring the isolation of victims, and 'miasmatists' like the Priestmans urging sanitary reform and better housing.
14 A. M. Priestman to J. Pease, 6 March 1844; 2 March 1855, MIL 22/01(a).
15 Ibid., 2 March 1855. See also, J. Ford, *Memoir of William Tanner*, York: William Sessions, 1868, and his QDB entry.
16 A. M. Priestman to J. Pease, 17 October, 9 December 1848, 25 August, 10 September 1852, 21 May, 27 October 1857, 21 October 1858, MIL 22/01(a).
17 Ibid., 29 June 1850, 27 May 1852.
18 Ibid., 8 May, 11 June 1842, 9 December 1848, 15 March 1850, 9 December 1851, 6 February 1854.
19 A. M. Priestman to 'Beloveds', 15 August 1851, MIL 22/01(b).
20 M. Wheeler to S. Tanner, 19 September 1850, MIL 32/01.
21 Ibid., n.d.
22 A. M. Priestman to J. Pease, 13 May, 7 July 1842; 4 April 1850, MIL 22/01(a). See also QDB entry for Jane Gurney Pease (1827–94).
23 A. M. Priestman to J. Pease, 13 May 1842, 7 July 1842, MIL 22/01(a).
24 Ibid., 9 December 1848; M. Wheeler to S. Tanner, 29 May 1850, MIL 32/01.
25 M. Wheeler to S. Tanner, n.d. 1852, MIL 32/01.
26 M. Wheeler to her sisters, 11 December 1852, MIL 31/01(2).
27 On changes in the paper-making industry at this time, see C. Steedman, *Dust*, Manchester: Manchester University Press, 2001, pp. 19–20, 23, 130–1, 157, 165.
28 See QDB for the entries on Mary and Arthur Tanner snr.
29 M. Wheeler to S. Tanner, 13 December 1849; 16 June 1850, MIL 32/01, with A. Tanner to S. and W. Tanner, 20 November 1850, same location.
30 Ibid., 18 November, 25 November 1851, 10 February 1852.
31 H. Bright, Diary (henceforth, HCD), 29 April 1850, MIL 69.
32 M. Wheeler to S. Tanner, 7 January, 13 August, 12 September, 18 October, 28 October 1853, MIL 32/01.
33 Ibid., 10 October, 28 October, 6 December, 17 December 1853.
34 Ibid., 6 December 1853. She offered to send S. Tanner 'a budget' of his letters to illustrate her point, instructing they not be shown to W. Tanner. See also M. Wheeler to P. B. McLaren, 28 December 1853, MIL 31/01(4).
35 M. Wheeler to S. Tanner, 5 December 1853, 28 October, 4 November 1854, MIL 32/01.
36 Ibid., 4 November, n.d., 23 December, 30 December 1854.
37 Ibid., December 1853; A. M. Priestman to P. B. McLaren, 26 March 1854, located among M. Wheeler's letters to P. B. McLaren; M. Wheeler to P. B. McLaren, 29 April 1854, both MIL 31/01(4).
38 H. Bright to R. Priestman; 2 March, 7 May 1853, MIL 57/01. A. Vickery, Historiographical Review p. 409 argues that letter writing was a key component of gentlewomen's household work. For an introduction to the literature on letters and letter writing in nineteenth-century Britain, see B. Onslow, 'Britain: Nineteenth-Century Letters' in M. Jolly (ed.), *Encyclopedia of Life Writing*, London: Fitzroy Dearborn, 2000, 2 vols. See also L. Stanley, 'The Epistolarium: on theorising letters and correspondence', *Auto/biography*, 2005, vol. 13, pp. 216–50.
39 For occasional diaries of the three surviving Priestman sisters, see MIL 16/03, 16/04, 16/05. For an introduction to the literature on women's diaries, see K. Cook, 'Nineteenth Century Diaries', in Jolly, op. cit.

250 *Notes*

40 H. Bright to J. Bright, 7 February 1850, MIL 57/02; HCD, 17 January 1850, MIL 69.
41 HCD, 1 January 1851f, MIL 69; H. Bright to M. Wheeler, 6 July 1853, MIL 58/01.
42 H. Bright to J. and M. E. Bright, 7 February 1850, MIL 57/04; HCD, 17 January 1850, 29 April 1850, MIL 69.
43 H. Bright to R. Priestman, n.d., 15 January, 2 March 1849, MIL 57/01.
44 H. Bright to M. Tanner, 14 September 1855, and also 8 August 1855, 19 February 1856, 5 July 1857, MIL 57/05; HCD, 8 September, 13 September, 16 September, 28 December 1855, 8 March 1856, MIL 69.
45 H. Bright to M. Tanner, 6 March 1861, MIL 57/05.
46 Ibid., 23 October 1859; 16 September 1861; H. Bright to A. M. Priestman, 13 July 1859, MIL 57/06; HCD, 14 Feb 60ff and 15 Feb 60 in overlapping diary, MIL 69.
47 H. Clark to M. Wheeler, 4 July n.y., MIL 33/01(1).
48 See S. Fletcher, *Women First: the female tradition in English physical education, 1880–1980,* London: Athlone Press, 1984.
49 H. Bright to M. Wheeler, 30 June 1852, 1 October 1853, 27 July 1854, MIL 33/01(1); HCD, n.d. [autumn 1851], MIL 69;
50 H. Bright to M. Wheeler, n.d., 7 June, 14 June 1852, 4 July n.y., MIL 57/05. In letters among the Priestman–Bright circle, one or more upright squiggles were used to indicate laughter.
51 The school was located at 27 Montpelier Crescent, Brighton at this time. On the education of girls in this period, see C. Dyhouse, *Girls Growing Up in Late Victorian and Edwardian England,* London: Routledge & Kegan Paul, 1981.
52 H. Bright to M. Wheeler, 28 August 1853, 30 August 1853, 28 September 1853, MIL 57/05; H. Bright to M. E. Bright, 17 September 1853, MIL 57/03.
53 H. Bright to M. Wheeler, 10 October 1853; 27 July 1854, MIL 57/05; H. Bright to M. E. Bright, 17 September, 28 September 1853, MIL 57/03; H. Bright to J. Bright, 4 January 1853 [should read 1854], MIL 57/02; H. Bright to J. Priestman I, 8 September 1854, MIL 57/01.
54 H. Bright to M. E. Bright, 28 September 1853, MIL 57/03; H. Clark to J. Bright, 4 January 1854, MIL 57/02.
55 H. Bright to J. Priestman I, 8 March 1855, MIL 57/01; H. Bright to M. Wheeler/Tanner, 9 April 1855, 17 January 1856, MIL 33/01(1) and 57/05 respectively; H. Bright to her Priestman aunts, 28 December 1855, MIL 58/01; H. Bright to M. E. Bright, 6 February 1856, MIL 57/03; H. Bright to J. Bright, 4 February 1856, MIL 57/02; HCD, 6 January – 16 March 1856, MIL 69.
56 A. M. Priestman to M. Tanner, 21 March 1856, 21/01(a); A. M. Priestman to her sisters, 6 March 1856, MIL 21/01(b).
57 H. Bright to M. E. Bright, 11 November 1856, MIL 57/03; H. Bright to M. Tanner, 29 November n.y., 13 December 1856, MIL 58/01; HCD, 12–16 December 1856, MIL 69.
58 HCD 30 December 1856–25 June 1857, MIL 69; H. Bright to her aunts, 11 February 1857, MIL 58/01; H. Bright to A. M. Priestman, 15 October 1857, MIL 57/06; H. Bright to M. Tanner, 15 October 1857, MIL 58/01.
59 H. Bright to her Priestman aunts, 2 November 1853, MIL 58/01.
60 H. Bright to M. E. Bright, 18 July 1854, MIL 57/03; H. Bright to M. Wheeler, 27 July 1854, MIL 33/01(1).
61 A. M. Priestman to J. Pease, August 1854, MIL 22/01(a); A. M. Priestman to J. H. Bragg, 28 July 1854, MIL 22/01(c). The Priestman sisters also learned of the terminal illness of their former governess, Esther Stickney, at this time, A. M. Priestman to Esther [with her letters Er Bright], 30 June 1854, 3 August 1854, 1 September 1854, MIL 22/01(g); M. Wheeler to S. Tanner, 22 June, 24 June, 16 July 1854, MIL 32/01.
62 A. M. Priestman to Esther [Stickney], 9 March 1852, 3 August, 1 September 1854 MIL 22/01(g).

63 M. Wheeler to S. Tanner 4 August, 5 September, 25 September, 14 November 1854, 6 January 1855, MIL 32/01.

9 Family, friendship and politics

1. H. Bright to M. Tanner, 6 January 1863, MIL 33/01(1).
2. HCD, 21 January, 19, 21, 25 March, 28 October 1859, 3 January 1860, MIL 69.
3. See S. A. Brooke (ed.), *Life and Letters of Frederick W. Robertson*, London: Smith, Elder & Co, 1865, 2 vols. Robertson settled in Brighton near Emilie Schnell's school. Some of his sermons were still being reprinted more than fifty years on, see F. W. Robertson, *Sermons on Religious Life*, London: J. M. Dent, n.d. [1906].
4. HCD, 21 March, 28 October 1859, 3 January 1860, MIL 69; Brooke, op. cit. p. 65.
5. Ibid., 28 February 1859, 19, 29 April 1859, 7 June 1860.
6. Ibid., 10 October 1860.
7. Ibid., 27 May, 24 June, 26 July, 6 October, 8 October, 10 October 1859, 23 June, 5 August, 31 August, 27 October, 5 November 1860; H. Bright to M. Tanner, 23 October 1859, MIL 33/01(1).
8. H. Bright to M. Tanner, 7 April 1858, MIL 58/01; HCD, 2 July 1859, MIL 59.
9. HCD 14, 25, 30 December 1859, 3 January 1860; E. Oldham to M. Bancroft, 17 June 1855, Southport, BAN 1/13; M. Wood and J. Crosland to J. and S. Bancroft, 14, 19 November 1859 and copy of letter from J. Crosland to J. and S. Bancroft, 13 January 1860, both BAN 1/89.
10. HCD, 30 December 1859, 3 January 1860; J. Crosland to J. and S. Bancroft, 13 January 1860, BAN 1/89.
11. H. Bright to M. Tanner, Christmas Day 1860, 6 March 1861 MIL 33/01(1).
12. Ibid., 6 March 1861.
13. Ibid., 20 September 1862, MIL 57/05; H. Bright to J. Crosland, 17 November 1862, 29 October 1865, MIL 58/02.
14. M. Tanner to My Priestman, n.d., and to her sisters, 18 November 1864, MIL 31/01 (2).
15. H. Bright to J. Crosland, 9, 12 November 1864, MIL 58/02; H. Bright to M. Tanner, 10 November 1864, MIL 33/01(1).
16. M. Tanner to her sisters, 20 June 1863, 3 September 1863, 22 November 1866; M. Tanner to My Priestman, 18 November 1864, 11 March 1865, 2 May 1865, 7 June 1865, all MIL 31/01(2); HCD, 1 August 1861, 5 April 1862, MIL 69.
17. J. Priestman I to M. Tanner, 28 December 1862, 12 March 1866, MIL 10/04.
18. H. Bright to A. M. Priestman, 7 April 1858, MIL 57/06.
19. H. Bright to her aunts, 18 March 1863, MIL 58/01.
20. On Sarah Parker Remond, see C. Midgley, *Women Against Slavery. The British Campaigns 1780–1870*, London: Routledge, 1992, pp. 18, 19, 63–4, 143–51, 170–2, 175, 193, 199, 205. See also S. S. Holton, 'Segregation, Racism and White Women Reformers: a transnational perspective', *Women's History Review*, 2001, vol. 10, pp. 5–25. On these social networks, also see P. Levine, *Feminist Lives in Victorian England. Private roles and public commitment*, Oxford: Basil Blackwell, 1990, which also argues the creation of a distinct feminist culture in this period. On some leading figures that emerged from these circles, see B. Caine, *Victorian Feminists*, Oxford: Oxford University Press, 1992.
21. E. J. Yeo, *Contest for Social Science: relations and representations of gender and class*, London: Rivers Oram, 1996, pp. 10–15.
22. M. Tanner to her sisters, 30 December 61, MIL 31/01(2).
23. M. Tanner to My Priestman, 12 May, 7 June 1865, MIL 31/01 (2); H. Bright to W. Clark, 15 June, 22 June, 15 July, 2 December 1865, MIL 55.
24. HCD, 3 April, 16 April, 24 April, 27 April, 4 May, 3 July 65, MIL 69.

25 On parliamentary reform, the language of capacity and of social representation in Britain at this time see A. S. Kahan, *Liberalism in Nineteenth Century Europe. The political culture of limited suffrage*, Basingstoke: Palgrave Macmillan, 2003, esp. pp. 122–49.
26 On divisions among suffragists at this time, see B. Caine, 'John Stuart Mill and the English Women's Movement', *Historical Studies*, 1982, vol. 18, pp. 52–67; 'Feminism, Suffrage and the Nineteenth-Century Women's Movement', *Women's Studies International Forum*, 1982, vol. 5, pp. 537–50; S. S. Holton, *Suffrage Days. Stories from the women's suffrage movement*, London: Routledge, 1996, pp. 27–31.
27 On notions of nation in this period, see C. Hall, K. McClelland, J. Rendall, *Defining the Victorian Nation: class, race, gender, and the Reform Act of 1867*, Cambridge: Cambridge University Press, 2000. On the 'constitutional idiom' in English radicalism, see, J. Epstein, *Radical Expression. Political language, ritual, and symbol in England, 1790–1850*, Oxford: Oxford University Press, 1994. On the adoption of the rhetoric of radical constitutionalism by suffragists, see S. S. Holton, 'British Freewomen. National identity, constitutionalism and languages of race in early suffragist histories, in E. J. Yeo (ed.), *Radical Femininity: women's self-representation in the public sphere*, Manchester: Manchester University Press, 1998. Many within the Priestman–Bright circle retained an undiminished hostility to British imperialism throughout their lives, further dividing them from the mainstream movement. On British women and the imperialist project, see A. Burton, *Burdens of History. British feminists, Indian women and imperial culture, 1865–1915*, Chapel Hill, NC: University of North Carolina Press, 1994; V. Ware, *Beyond the Pale. White women, racism and history*, London: Verso, 1992.
28 On the shifts and cross-currents in suffrage ideology, see S. S. Holton, *Feminism and Democracy. Women's suffrage and reform politics, 1900–1918*, Cambridge: Cambridge University Press, 2002 paperback edn (1986), pp. 9–28.
29 H. Bright to W. Clark, 25 November, 29 December 1864, MIL 55.
30 Ibid., 15, 20, 28 June, 14 November 1865.
31 Ibid., 20 June, 28 July, 25 August 1865.
32 Ibid., 15 October 1865.
33 Ibid., 15, 22, 26 October 1865; M. Tanner to My Priestman, 11 March 1865, and to A. M. Priestman, 4 November 1865, both MIL 31/01(2).
34 H. Bright to W. Clark, 8, 14, 17 November 1865, MIL 55.
35 HCD, 13 December 1865; 3 January 1866, MIL 69.
36 H. Bright to W. Clark, 17, 22 November 1865, MIL 55.
37 Ibid., 29 November 1865, 2, 11, 16 December 1865, 16 February 1866.
38 Ibid., 22 November 1865, 9, 18 January 1866; J. Priestman II to M. Tanner, 16 April, 18 May 1867, MIL 10/05.
39 Ibid., 11, 17, 20 March 1866, 24 April, 4 July 1866.
40 Ibid., 28, 31 March 1866, 8, 13, 16, 18 April 1866.
41 Ibid., 17 May 1866, 18 May 1866.
42 Ibid., 22 June 1866, 4 July, 6 July 1865.
43 Ibid., 22 June 1866, 6 July 1866, 12 July 1866, 13 July 1866, 17 July 1866, 19 July 1866; J. Priestman II to M. Tanner, 17 November 1865, MIL 10/05.

10 Marriage, money and the networked family

1 H. Clark to A. M. Priestman, 1 September 1866, MIL 57/06.
2 This account draws on M. McGarvie, *The Book of Street. A history from the earliest times to 1925*, Buckingham: Barracuda Books, 1987. Helen Clark always thought of Rochdale as a village, and continued so to think of Street throughout her life.
3 W. S. Clark, 'A History of the Business of C & J Clark of Street', Appendix in [L. H. Barber], *Clarks of Street 1825–1950*, [Street]: C. J. Clark, n.d., p. 158.

4 Ibid., pp. 158–9, records that James Clark's capital in the firm was £1,070 in 1833, £1,000 of which was lent him by his father who raised it by mortgaging a field. On the 'networked family' and the middle class in the nineteenth century, see R. J. Morris, *Men, Women and Property in England, 1780–1870. A social and economic history of family strategies among the Leeds middle classes*, Cambridge: Cambridge University Press, 2005, esp. p. 233, and see also 8, 41, 301–2, 324, 329, 330, 334–6, 374.

5 On the processes and the 'backshops' in the homes of outworker shoemakers, see B. Lehane, *C. & J. Clark 1825–1975*, Street: C. & J. Clark, 1975, pp. 7–8. For further accounts of the company's history, see [R. Clark], *One Hundred Years. C & J Clark, Street Somerset, 1825–1925*, [Street]: C & J Clark, n.d., also reproduced as the first chapter in Barber, *Clarks of Street*; G. B. Sutton, *C & J Clark, 1833–1903. A History of Shoemaking in Street*, York: William Sessions, 1979; M. McGarvie, *Bowlingreen Mill. A centenary history*, [Street]: Avalon Leatherboard Co, 1979; K. Hudson, *Towards Precision Shoemaking*, Newton Abbot: David & Charles, 1986.

6 McGarvie, *Book of Street*, p. 129.

7 Trust for Eleanor Stephens, 16 September 1835, NO. ONE, 24, CA.

8 Cyrus Clark's separate wool-stapling business was amalgamated with his partnership with James Clark, the latter's capital in the firm being assessed as £720 in recognition of his contribution to that business. By 1839 James Clark's capital was assessed as £2,500, £800 of which was saved from his share of the profits, W. Clark, 'History', pp. 158–63.

9 Ibid. Losses in the corn-factoring business left C. & J. Clark owing £13,000 to the Sturges and £1,500 to Stuckey's Bank. The bank agreed to regular periodic payments and this debt was cleared by 1850. The brothers mortgaged all their private property to repay £8,000 to the Sturges, a member from each of the Sturge and Clark families mediating an agreement whereby they paid 10s in the pound (a Clark ancestor had earlier similarly helped the Sturge family). C. & J. Clark also lent Joseph Clark II, the other partner in the corn-factoring business, £3,000 to clear his liabilities, a debt eventually written off in 1856. On these grounds William Clark argued both his uncles remained in debt to C. & J. Clark, and Cyrus Clark could be said to have had no capital remaining in the business after the early 1840s. James Clark by his calculations still had capital in the company, the stocktaking accounts for 1850 showing this to be £3,819, while Cyrus Clark still owed the firm money.

10 Ibid., pp. 172–4; cutting of obituary of W. S. Clark, *Central Somerset Gazette*, 27 November 1925, HSHC 52, H. S. H. Clark papers, CA.

11 W. Clark, 'History', p. 172.

12 A. Fox, *History of the National Union of Boot and Shoe Operatives, 1874–1957*, Oxford: Basil Blackwell, 1958, esp. pp. 17, 262, 315,428. On H. J. Bostock, who became part of the management of the company, and his role as President of the Employers' Federation in the 1920s, ibid., pp. 442, 443, 444, 447–8, 449, 604.

13 W. Clark, 'History', p. 167; Barber, *C. & J. Clark*, p. 17. By 1872 the loans had been reduced to £4,925, Sutton, *C. & J. Clark*, pp. 131f.

14 *Central Somerset Gazette*, 8 April, 22 April, 6 May, 10 June 1865 on the controversy surrounding the establishment of a Health Board, and references to the 'family clique' responsible. One of William Clark's younger brothers and one of the firm's foremen had died in a typhoid outbreak in Street a decade or so before.

15 HCD, 19 January, 9 February, 11 February, 27 February 1869, MIL 69.

16 L. Sturge, typescript recollections of Dr Anne E. Clark, 4 March 1924 and see also cuttings of obituaries in *The Times*, n.d., and *The Friend*, 14 March 1924, all MIL 51/01(j).

17 H. Clark to A. E. Clark, 14 May 1873, MIL 58/03. The original group of aspiring women medical students originally met at Newington House, the McLaren family home, cutting of Sophia Jex Blake obituary, *The Tablet*, 26 April 1913, MIL 51/01(j). Duncan McLaren apparently doubted his daughter's intellectual capacity, while

Priscilla Bright McLaren wanted Agnes McLaren by her side in managing Newington House and the younger children.
18 Resistance from some lecturers and students left them unable to continue their medical training in Edinburgh. Annie Clark continued her studies in Berne (teaching herself German), then studied midwifery in Paris and homeopathy in the United States.
19 E. Clark to J. Clark, 19 September 1866, HSHC 53. On the teacher training programme established by Lydia Rous, see H. W. Sturge and T. Clark, *The Mount School, York, 1785–1814, 1831–1931*, London: J. M. Dent, 1931.
20 S. S. Clark, Diaries (henceforth, SSCD), 12 May, 19 June, 10, 15 August, 4 September 1868, 22 March, 13, 25 April, 7, 20 May, 26 November 1870, HSHC 52.
21 Ibid., 27 April, 3, 19, 23 May, 27 August, 1, 14/15 November 1871, 19 January, 4 February, 4–6 March, 20 April 1872; E. Stephens to J. Clark, 13 August, 23 August, 15 September 1876, HSHC 53.
22 H. Clark to W. Clark, 24, 25 October 1866, MIL 55.
23 Ibid., 28 October 1866.
24 H. Clark to My Priestman, fragment dated 27 April 67, MIL 58/01. HCD, 29 November 1866, 17 January, 25 February, 9 March, 6 April, 15, 30 May, 3, 21, 25, 27 July 1867, MIL 69; H. Clark to W. Clark, 6, 7, 8, 10 August 1867, MIL 55; M. Tanner to her sisters, n.d., MIL 31/01(2).
25 H. Clark to her aunts, 16 August 1867, MIL 58/01.
26 Ibid., 23 January 1868; HCD, 15, 17, 21, 26 August, 12, 13 September 1867, 25 December 1868, 6 January 1869, MIL 69; H. Clark to W. Clark, 5 September 1867, MIL 55.
27 H. Clark to her aunts, 14 January 1881, MIL 58/01.
28 H. Clark to W. Clark, n.d., 6 October 1878, MIL 55.
29 Ibid., 13 June 80; 19, 20, 21, 25, 27 August 1880; 7 October 1880; 13, 18 May 1881; H. Clark to her Priestman aunts, 16 Feb 1871, MIL 58/01.
30 H. Clark to W. Clark, 6, 7 December 1870, MIL 55; M. Tanner to her sisters, 1 August 1871, MIL 31/01(2).
31 HCD, 14 December 1866, 26 February, 1 March 1868.
32 W. Clark, op. cit.
33 H. Clark to A. M. Priestman, 11 November 1869, MIL 57/06; H. Clark to her aunts, 16 February 71, MIL 58/01.
34 H. Clark to W. Clark, 26 June 1867, MIL 55; HCD, 19 November 1866, MIL 69.
35 H. Clark to W. Clark, 2 June 1867, MIL 55; HCD, 26 April 1868; 21 April 1870, 3 September, 10 November 1874, MIL 69.
36 'Settlement for the benefit of H. Clark', 9 February 1872, NO. ONE, 24, CA.
37 E.g. J. Bright to H. Clark, 24 December 1872, MIL 34/01. These quarterly cheques were usually for around £70, and represented only a part of her income from her marriage settlement. H. Clark to W. Clark, 14 October 1866, MIL 55.
38 H. Clark to My Priestman, 27 April 1867.
39 H. Priestman on behalf of Priestman & Son, which was an executor of the estate in question, to H. Bright, 24 October 1865, MIL 66, explaining that the legacy could not be used speculatively and would have to be invested in securities.
40 H. Clark to J. Priestman, II, 9 November, 28 December 1877, MIL 58/04.
41 HCD, 9 October 1866, MIL 69; H. Clark to W. Clark, 9 October 1866, MIL 55.
42 H. Clark to My Priestman, n.d. [1867], MIL 57/07.
43 H. Clark to W. Clark, 1 February, 17 April, 20 April, 28 October 1868, MIL 55 In the correspondence of Helen Clark and her aunts, laughter was indicated by one or more upright squiggles.
44 HCD, 14 April, 26 October 1868, 17, 18 November 1868, MIL 69; H. Clark to her Priestman aunts, 21 November 1868 MIL 58/01.
45 HCD, 14, 19 October 1868, 2, 20 November, 7 December 1868, MIL 69.

11 Helen Clark, family life and politics

1. Isabella Pasley is shown among the first class in a photograph of students at the Mount, in H. W. Sturge and T. Clark, *The Mount School, York, 1785–1814, 1831–1931*, London: J. M. Dent, 1931.
2. J. Clark to H. Clark, 9 October 1886, MIL 62.
3. HCD, 9 February 1881, 10 October 1881, MIL 69; H. Clark to her aunts, 14 January 1881, MIL 58/01; H. Clark to J. Bright, 28 December 1884, MIL 57/02.
4. HCD, 1 January 1892, MIL 70.
5. H. Clark to W. Clark, 25 February 1880, 18 March 1883, MIL 55.
6. H. Clark to J. S. Rowntree, 25 May 1889, MIL 58/04; J. S. Rowntree to H. Clark, 19 August 1889, and 23 October 1889, MIL 62. A committee, established to investigate these matters, concluded the hours of study were too long and provision for exercise insufficient, see E. B. Clark to H. Clark, 27 October 1889, MIL 62.
7. H. Clark to W. Clark, 6, 7 August 1879; 25 February 1880, 21 August 1880; 30 November 1883; 2 May 1884; 6, 24 February1885, MIL 55. The death of a consumptive Reynolds niece after being brought to Street to be cared for by Sophia and Edith Clark, could only have increased such anxiety, see H. Clark to her aunts, 1 May 1879, MIL 58/01.
8. H. Clark to A. M. Priestman, 15 February 1885, MIL 58/06.
9. [L. H. Barber), *Clarks of Street 1825–1950*, [Street]: C. & J. Clark [*c.* 1950], pp. 8, 22; M. McGarvie, *Book of Street. A history from the earliest times to 1925*, Buckingham: Barracuda Books, 1987, p. 142.
10. H. Clark to W. Clark, 6 April 1882; 2, 6 May 1884; 24 February 1885, MIL 55.
11. Papers relating to the Ashworth Trust, MIL 51/01(b); J. Bright to H. Clark, 26 April 1872, MIL 93.
12. S. J. Tanner, *How the Women's Suffrage Movement Began in Bristol Fifty Years Ago*, Bristol: Carlyle Press, 1918. On the friendship circles there of which the Priestman sisters were a part, see J. Hannam, 'An Enlarged Sphere of Usefulness: the Bristol Women's Movement, *c.*1860–1914, in M. Dresser and P. Ollerenshaw (eds), *Making of Modern Bristol*, Tiverton: Radcliffe, 1996.
13. S. S. Holton, *Suffrage Days. Stories from the women's suffrage movement*, London: Routledge, 1996, pp. 20–25. On women's growing role in local government, see P. Hollis, *Ladies Elect. Women in English local government, 1865–1914*, Oxford: Clarendon Press, 1985.
14. J. R. Walkowitz, *Prostitution and Victorian Society. Women, class and the state*, Cambridge: Cambridge University Press, 1980; P. McHugh, *Prostitution and Victorian Social Reform*, London: Croom Helm, 1980.
15. See S. S. Holton, 'State Pandering, Medical Policing and Prostitution. The controversy within the medical profession over the Contagious Diseases legislation 1864–86', *Research in Law, Deviance and Social Control*, 1989, vol. 9, pp. 149–70.
16. Holton, *Suffrage Days*, pp. 30–3.
17. H. Clark to W. Clark, 6 December, 9 December 1869, MIL 55.
18. Ibid., 9 December 1869, 6, 10 September 1871.
19. Ibid., 23 April, 26 April, 24 August 1870, 17 March 1872.
20. H. Clark to her aunts, 25 October 1870, MIL 58/01.
21. J. Bright to H. Clark, 26 April 1872, MIL 93.
22. S. S. Clark, draft and final letters to Dear Friend, n. d. [*c.* November 1883], and replies from M. Tanner, 23 November, 18 December 1883, S. A. Pease, 12 December 1883, C. Sturge, 13 December [1883], all MIL 51/01(K).
23. For more detailed accounts of this topic, see S. S. Holton and M. Allen, 'Offices and Services: women's pursuit of sexual equality within the Society of Friends', *Quaker Studies*, 1997, vol. 2, pp. 1–29; T. C. Kennedy, *British Quakerism, 1860–1920. The transformation of a religious community*, Oxford: Oxford University Press, 2001.

256   *Notes*

24 HCD, 15 March, 25 March, 30 March 1869, MIL 69; H. Clark to W. Clark, 26 March, 27 March 1869, together with several undated letters, MIL 55; M. Tanner to My Priestman, 28 July 1869, MIL 31/01(2).
25 H. Clark to W. Clark, 28 July 1871, MIL 55.
26 H. Clark, to A. M. Priestman, 22 April 1878, MIL 57/06. H. Clark to W. Clark, 27 April 1878, MIL 55.
27 H. Clark to W. Clark 27 April, 13 May, 20 May, 27 May 1878, MIL 55.
28 Ibid., 26 May, 27 May 1878, though she doubted her sister would be strong enough to marry.
29 Ibid., 27 September 1879; 8 April 1882.
30 Ibid., 5 February 1888.
31 H. Clark to J. Crosland, 24 October, 7 November 1861, 18 May 1869, MIL 58/02.
32 Ibid., 11 October, 30 November, 3 December 1869; H. Clark to W. Clark, 30 September, 1 October 1879, MIL 55; E. Oldham to H. Clark, 26 [January?] 1870, 9 October 1870, 3 December 1879, MIL 64/01.
33 E. Oldham to H. Clark, 25 November 1889, MIL 64/01.
34 Ibid., pm 25 April 1881; 11 May 1883; 13 May 1889.
35 Ibid., 24 July 1881; 23 July 1884; 8 September 1884; 28 October 1884.
36 Ibid., e.g., 18 July 1882, 1 July 1885.
37 Ibid., 25 March 1888.
38 Ibid., 25 March 1888; 11 July 1882; 23 July 1884; n.d. October n. y., 23 October 1885.
39 Ibid., 11 May 1883; 21 December 1883; n.d. [probably October 1885].
40 Ibid., n.d. October n.y. [1885]; 23 October 1885; 3 November 1885.
41 Ibid., 28 April 1885; 1 July 1885.
42 For a further discussion of these links see E. C. DuBois, 'Woman Suffrage and the Left: an internationalist socialist-feminist perspective', *New Left Review*, 1991, no. 186, pp. 20–45; S. S. Holton, '"Educating Women into Rebellion". Elizabeth Cady Stanton and the creation of a transatlantic network of Radical suffragists', *American Historical Review*, 1994, vol. 99, pp. 1112–36.
43 E. C. Stanton to Miss Priestman, 20 January, p. m. 1883, to 'Dear Widow and Spinsters' [the three Priestman sisters], 30 October [1883], MIL 27/01; E. C. Stanton to A. Clark, 20 October [1890], MIL 90.
44 Holton, *Suffrage Days*, pp. 56–8.
45 HCD, 23 April, 24 May 1880; 22 November 1881; 21 February 1882.
46 P. B. McLaren to H. Clark, 9 October 1883, MIL 43; H. Clark to P. B. McLaren, 10 October 1883, MIL 50.
47 L. Walker, 'Party Political Women: a comparative study of Liberal women and the Primrose League, 1890–1914', in J. Rendall (ed.), *Equal or Different. Women's Politics, 1800–1914*, Oxford: Basil Blackwell, 1987, pp. 165–91. See also C. Hirschfield, 'Fractured Faith: Liberal Party women and the suffrage issue in Britain, 1892–1914', *Gender and History*, 1990, vol. 2, pp. 173–97.
48 D. Rubinstein, *New World for Women. The life of Millicent Garrett Fawcett*, Brighton: Harvester Wheatsheaf, 1991.
49 For a summary of these divisions, see S. S. Holton, 'Women and the Vote', in J. Purvis (ed.), *Women's History, 1850–1945*, London: UCL Press, 1995.

12 The changing order

1 H. Clark to W. Clark, 4, 5, 13 February 1888, MIL 55.
2 Ibid., 16 April 1888.
3 Ibid., 29 May, 30 May, 30 June, 4 July 1888.
4 Ibid., 4, 8, 9 July 1888.

5 Ibid., 28, 29 October 1888.
6 Ibid., 26, 27, 28, 29, 30 November 1888.
7 Ibid., 3, 5, 7, 10 December 1888, 17 March 1889.
8 Ibid., 20, 22 December 1888; 26, 28 February, 9 March 1889.
9 E. Oldham to H. Clark, 13 May, 1 July 1889; 28 November 1889, 16 October 1890; 30 December 1891. H. Oldham to H. Clark, 16, 19, 28 January 1892, all MIL 64/01.
10 HCD, 25 February, 24, 26 October 1891, 20 November 1892, 16 July, 24 September, 16 November 1894; 1 January, 27 March 1895, MIL 70.
11 Ibid., 21 April, 28 June, 10 July, 1895; 16 November 1896.
12 Ibid., 24, 26 October 1897.
13 Ibid., 14 June 1889, 22 November 1896, 18 February 1897; H. Clark to W. Clark, 20 February 1891, MIL 55; A. Clark to H. Clark, 19 May 1898, MIL 57/01. On Radical Liberalism, see F. A. Biagini, *Liberty, Retrenchment and Reform. Popular Liberalism in the age of Gladstone, 1860–80*, Cambridge: Cambridge University Press, 1992; M. Finn, *After Chartism. Class and nation in English radical politics, 1848–1874*, Cambridge: Cambridge University Press, 1993, though neither discusses in any detail the role of Radical Liberals with regard to women's rights.
14 M. Barrow, 'Teetotal Feminists: the temperance leadership and the campaign for women's suffrage', in C. Eustance, J. Ryan, and L. Ugolini (eds), *A Suffrage Reader. Charting directions in British suffrage history*, Leicester: Leicester University Press, 2000.
15 I. Tyrrell, *Woman's World, Woman's Empire: the Women's Christian Temperance Union in international perspective, 1800–1930*, Chapel Hill, NC: University of North Carolina Press, 1996.
16 Compare with A. Burton, *Burdens of History. British feminists, Indian women and imperial culture, 1865–1915*, Chapel Hill, NC: University of North Carolina Press, 1994. I discuss the discourses of race and of constitutionalism and their role in suffrage historiography in 'British Freewomen: national identity, constitutionalism and languages of race in early suffrage history', in E. J. Yeo (ed.), *Radical Femininity. Women's self-representation in the public sphere*, Manchester: Manchester University Press, 1988. On suffragists and the South African Wars see L. E. N. Mayhall, *Militant Suffrage Movement. Citizenship and resistance in Britain, 1860–1930*, Oxford: Oxford University Press, 2003, pp. 25–39.
17 For an account of some of these periodicals, see, H. Brown, *'The Truest Form of Patriotism'. Pacificist feminism in Britain, 1870–1902*, Manchester: Manchester University Press, 2003, pp. 26–43; D. Doughan and D. Sanchez, *Feminist Periodicals 1855–1984. An annotated, critical bibliography of British, Irish, Commonwealth and international titles*, Brighton: Harvester, 1987. The *Women's Suffrage Journal* did not long survive the death of Lydia Becker, its founding editor, in 1890.
18 A. Clark to H. Clark, 12 March 1895, 15, 20 May 1898, MIL 87/1; D. Rubinstein, *Before the Suffragettes. Women's emancipation in the 1890s*, Brighton: Harvester Press, 1986, and esp. pp. 44, 144–5 on the Women's Franchise League; S. S. Holton, *Suffrage Days. Stories from the women's suffrage movement*, London: Routledge, 1996, pp. 76–86, 88–9, 100–02. On the historiography of this period, see also, S. S. Holton, 'Now You See It, Now You Don't: the Women's Franchise League and its place in contending narratives of the women's suffrage movement', in M. Joannou and J. Purvis (eds), *The Women's Suffrage Movement. New feminist perspectives*, Manchester: Manchester University Press, 1998.
19 Holton, 'Now You See It'.
20 On the WEU, see Rubinstein, *Before the Suffragettes*, pp. 82–6, 88–9, 102–5; Holton, *Suffrage Days*, pp. 61, 76, 81–2, 86–9, 104, 106, 109.
21 On some of the continuities between late nineteenth-century Liberal-Radical suffragism and militancy, especially in terms of the Priestman–Bright circle, see S. S. Holton, '"To Educate Women into Rebellion". Elizabeth Cady Stanton and the

258 Notes

creation of a transatlantic network of Radical suffragists,' *American Historical Review*, 1994, vol. 99, pp. 1112–36; S. S. Holton, 'From Anti-Slavery to Suffrage Militancy: The Bright circle, Elizabeth Cady Stanton and the British women's movement' in C. Daley and M. Nolan (eds), *Suffrage and Beyond. International feminist perspectives*, Auckland: Auckland University Press, 1994; Holton, *Suffrage Days*, pp. 106–9.

22 HCD 12, 23 April 1890, 19 January, 8, 10 August 1894, 7 June, 27 July, 8 September 1895, MIL 70.

23 F. Douglass to Helen Clark, 19 July 1894, MIL 67.

24 On Catherine Impey and *Anti-Caste*, see V. Ware, *Beyond the Pale. White women, racism and history*, London: Verso, 1992; on Catherine Impey and the International Order of Good Templars, see D. M. Fahey, *Temperance and Racism: John Bull, Johnny Reb and the Good Templars*, Lexington, KY: Kentucky University Press, 1996; on the Priestman–Bright circle and these questions, see S. S. Holton, 'Segregation, Racism and White Women Reformers: a transnational perspective, *Women's History Review*, 2001, vol. 10, pp. 5–25.

25 Holton, 'Segregation', pp. 11–15 and Tyrrell, *Woman's World*, pp. 192–203, discuss further tensions in the World Women's Christian Temperance Union around the figure of Lady Henry Somerset.

26 'Hannah Wallis' entry in QDB; M. Wallis to H. Clark, 7 January, 9 May 1892, MIL 65, and 6 September 1896, MIL 68.

27 On the impact of TB on the life of Alice Clark, see, S. S. Holton, 'To Live "Through One's Own Powers": British medicine, tuberculosis and "invalidism" in the life of Alice Clark (1874–1934)', *Journal of Women's History*, 1999, vol. 11, pp. 75–96.

28 H. Clark to W. Clark, 10 December 1889, MIL 55; HCD, 31 July 1891, 20 September 94; 6, 25 March 1895, MIL 70.

29 I. Pasley to H. Clark, 20, 24, 27 January 1892, MIL 64.

30 HCD, 1 August 90, 1 May 1891, 15 June 1892, 29 May 1895, 22 June, 5 July, 15–17 May 1897, MIL 70; *Calendar of the Durham College of Science, 1897–98* for E. Clark's qualifications; A. Clark to H. Clark, 2 November 1892, MIL 87/1; A. Clark to W. Clark, 12 December 1892, MIL 87/2.

31 P. Lovell, *Quaker Inheritance, 1871–1961. A portrait of Roger Clark of Street based on his own writings and correspondence*, London: Bannisdale Press, 1970, pp. 36–68; R. Clark, *John Bright Clark of C. & J. Clark Ltd*, Street: privately published, [c. 1934]; HCD, 1 October 1890, MIL 70; cutting of obituary of John Morland, *Central Somerset Gazette*, 10 August 1934, HSHC 53, CA.

32 J. A. Bright to W. Clark, 13 May 1889; W. Clark to J. A. Bright, 16 May 1889, both in 'Details of J. Bright's Estate', MIL 51/01(f). William Clark may also have been an executor. Albert Bright anticipated his future annual income as £2,781 in dividends from the family firm, £175 interest on his legacy from M. E. Bright, and £250 in salary as managing director of the firm, 'so I shall not be rolling in wealth'.

33 Envelope labelled 'HPBC Settlement and Mortgage', which includes A. Molesworth, Solicitor to Mrs Clark, 8 February 1890; Indenture and mortgage agreement between J. A. Bright, as trustee for H. Clark, and W. Clark, 2 June 1890; H. Clark, Deed Poll, 10 July 1905 regarding her marriage settlement of 1872; Transfer of Mortgage on Millfield from J. A. Bright to H. Clark, 21 September 1905, assigning both the principal of £7,000 and any further interest to her, subsequently assigned by H. Clark to W. Clark, 1 December 1919, NO. ONE, 24, CA.

34 [L. H. Barber], *Clarks of Street 1825–1950*, Street: C. & J. Clark [c. 1950], pp. 19–20.

35 HCD, 24 September, 17 October 1894, 28 June 1895, MIL 70; on women as Poor Law Guardians, see P. Hollis, *Ladies Elect. Women in English local government, 1865–1914*, Oxford: Clarendon Press, 1987, esp. pp. 246–99.

36 G. B. Sutton, *C & J Clark, 1833–1903. A history of shoemaking in Street*, York: William Sessions, 1979, p. 159; [R. Clark], *One Hundred Years. C & J Clark, Street Somerset,*

1825–1925, [Street]: C & J Clark, n.d., p. 14; M. McGarvie, *Book of Street. A history from the earliest times to 1925*, Buckingham: Barracuda Books, 1987, p. 144.
37 On the recurrent episodes of ill health among her children, and the medical advice received, see HCD, 9, 30 August, 26 September, 16, 18, 25 October, 7, 8 November 1889; 28 February, 4 September 1890; 30 September, 4 November 1891, 25 August, 7, 15, 16, 20 October 1892, 4, 10 February, 22 March, 16 June, 20 October, 16 December 1893,11, 24 May, 5 July, 9, 24 November 1894, MIL 70.
38 H. Clark to W. Clark, 24 April 1890, 15, 18 March 1891, MIL 55.
39 Ibid., 30 October 1892; HCD, 7, 10, 15, 20 October 1892, MIL 70.
40 HCD, 3, 20, 25, 29 November 1892, 3, January 1894, MIL 70; H. Clark to W. Clark, 30 October 1892, 2, 7, 8, 21, 22, 28 November 1892, MIL 55, and 14, 19, 22 December 1892, 2, 10 January 1894, MIL 56.
41 HCD, 7, 11, 12 February, 7, 20 March, 10 April, 25 August, 8 September, 8 November, 8, 9, 21 December 1894, MIL 70. On the Nordrach system, see Holton, 'Through One's Own Powers'.
42 HCD, 11, 12, 18 August, 3 November, 17 December 1897; Holton, 'Through One's Own Powers'.
43 Holton, op. cit., pp. 85–6, 100–01, 104, 106–7. On the National Union, see L. P. Hume, *National Union of Women's Suffrage Societies, 1897–1914*, New York: Garland Publishing, 1982; S. S. Holton, *Feminism and Democracy. Women's suffrage and reform politics, 1900–1918*, Cambridge: Cambridge University Press, 2002 paperback edn (1986).

13 Suffragism and democracy

1 HCD, 31 December 1897, MIL 70.
2 H. Clark to A. Clark, 24 May 1898, MIL 88/2; A. Clark to H. Clark, 19 May 1897, MIL 87/1.
3 H. Clark to A. Clark, 1 March and 8 March 1898; see also, 31 October 1899, both MIL 88/2. On the Theosophical Society, see, J. Dixon, *Divine Feminine. Theosophy and feminism in England*, Baltimore, MD: The Johns Hopkins Press, 2000.
4 HCD, 23 January 1901, MIL 70.
5 Margaret Bright Lucas, Priscilla Bright McLaren, Margaret Tanner and Anna Maria and Mary Priestman lent their support to various women's peace organisations, H. Brown, *'The Truest Form of Patriotism'. Pacificist feminism in Britain, 1870–1902*, Manchester: Manchester University Press, 2003, esp. pp. 65, 72, 73, 118, 121, 145.
6 A. Clark to H. Clark, 19 and 27 February, 1 March 1898; A. Clark to P. B. McLaren, 6 March 1898, all MIL 87; HCD, 4 March 1894, MIL 70.
7 HCD, 13 August, 15 September, 23 September, 5 October, 8 November, 10 October 1901, MIL 70.
8 Ibid., 11 June 1901, 26 October 1901.
9 Ibid., 4 November, 9 December 1901, 26 February 1902.
10 Ibid., 18 February 1903, 20 April, 13 February, 22 July 1904, 26 January 1905, 26 March 1906.
11 Ibid., 7 May 1898, 14 November 1901, 5 June 1902, 17 February 1903.
12 Ibid 4 August 1904, 21 November 1904, 14 July 1906. On I. O. Ford, see J. Hannam, *Isabella Ford*, Oxford: Basil Blackwell, 1989.
13 HCD, 10, 21 November 1901, 6 January, 10 November 1902, 17 November 1903, 3 June 1904, 6, 23 January, 10 December 1905, 14, 27 January 1906, MIL 70.
14 On the textile workers and women suffrage, see J. Liddington and J. Norris, *One Hand Tied Behind Us. The rise of the women's suffrage movement*, London: Rivers Oram Press, 2000 reprint (1978). On the WSPU, see J. Purvis, *Emmeline Pankhurst. A biography*, London: Routledge, 2002; A. Rosen, *Rise Up Women. The militant campaigns*

260 *Notes*

    of the Women's Social and Political Union, 1904–14, London: Routledge and Kegan Paul, 1974. For a broader exploration of twentieth-century suffragism and its meanings, see L. Tickner, *The Spectacle of Women. Imagery of the suffrage campaign, 1907–14*, London: Chatto & Windus, 1987. On rank-and-file militancy, see L. Stanley with A. Morley, *The Life and Death of Emily Wilding Davison*, London: Women's Press, 1988. On the shifting meanings of militancy, see S. S. Holton, *Feminism and Democracy. Women's suffrage and reform politics in Britain, 1900–1918*, Cambridge: Cambridge University Press, paperback reprint 2004 (1986), esp. pp. 29–52. On radical constitutionalism and suffrage militancy, see S. S. Holton, '"In Sorrowful Wrath". Suffrage militancy and the romantic feminism of Emmeline Pankhurst', in H. L. Smith (ed.) *British Feminism in the Twentieth Century*, Aldershot: Edward Elgar, 1990, and 'British Freewomen: National identity, constitutionalism and languages of race' in E. J. Yeo (ed.), *Radical Femininity: women's self-representation in the public sphere*, Manchester: Manchester University Press, 1998. A similar line of argument has also subsequently been pursued, though strangely only with regard to militancy, in L. E. N. Mayhall, 'Defining Militancy: radical protest, the constitutional idiom, and women's suffrage in Britain, 1908–1909,' *Journal of British Studies*, 2000, vol. 39, pp. 340–71, and *Militant Suffrage Movement. Citizenship and resistance in Britain, 1860–1930*, Oxford: Oxford University Press, 2003, esp. pp. 40–8.

15 S. S. Holton, *Suffrage Days. Stories from the women's suffrage movement*, London: Routledge, 1996, pp. 166–73 on the response to militancy among the Priestman–Bright circle.

16 I discuss such historiographical questions further in S. S. Holton, 'The Making of Suffrage History', in J. Purvis and S. S. Holton (eds), *Votes for Women*, London: Routledge, 2000, and 'Reflecting on Suffrage History', in C. Eustance, J. Ryan and L. Ugolini (eds), *A Suffrage Reader. Charting directions in British suffrage history*, Leicester: Leicester University Press, 2000; S. S. Holton, 'Now You See It, Now You Don't: the Women's Franchise League and its place in contending narratives of the women's suffrage movement', in M. Joannou and J. Purvis (eds), *The Women's Suffrage Movement. New feminist perspectives*, Manchester: Manchester University Press, 1998; Holton, 'Romantic Feminism'. Compare with the discussion in Mayhall cited in n.14.

17 D. Montefiore, *From a Victorian to a Modern*, London: E. Archer, 1927, pp. 40–1.

18 HCD, 26 August, 29 September 1904, MIL 70.

19 Ibid., 27, 29 June, 12 July 1906.

20 Ibid., 16, 21 March 1905, 11, 25 April 1906.

21 Ibid., 31 October, 5, 8, 9 November 1906; 6, 8, 9 December 1906; E. J. Bennett to H. Clark, 18 April 1907, MIL 61, on her new post. This correspondence stretches from 1898–1923 and refers to holidays spent at Millfield.

22 H. Clark to A. Clark, 20 May 1907; 10 April 1908, MIL 87/1.

23 HCD 7 August 1898, 16 November 1898, 20 April 1899, MIL 70. See also A. Clark to P. B. McLaren, 4 December 1899, MIL 87/1. On these new communities of single women, see M. Vicinus, *Independent Women. Work and community for single women 1850–1920*, London: Virago Press, 1985.

24 A. Clark to H. Clark, 1 February 1902; on an earlier occasion she had visited Margaret Clark at Newnham College, when she had been introduced to Ann Jemima Clough, its head, A. Clark to P. B. McLaren, 11 October 1900, both MIL 87/1.

25 HCD, 6, 12 January 1902, 15 August 1902, 1 October 1902, 4 September 1905, MIL 70.

26 H. Clark to W. Clark, June 1901, 18 June, 6 July 1901, MIL 56.

27 HCD, 25–26 December 1906, MIL 70; A. Clark to P. B. McLaren, 22 April 1901, MIL 87/3.

28 H. Clark to A. Clark, 21 April 1901, 6 June 1901, MIL 88/2; A. Clark to P. B. McLaren, 11 July 1901, MIL 87/3.

29 HCD, 24 February 1904, MIL 70
30 Ibid., 31 July, 13 August 1908; H. Clark to A. Clark, 13, 18, 20 August 1908, MIL 88/2.
31 H. Clark to A. Clark, 21 August, 16 November 1908, 13 September 1909, MIL 88/2.
32 Ibid., 6 December 1906, 20 August 1908, 2 April 1909.
33 Ibid., 17 September 1909. On Chenies Street Chambers, see E. Crawford, *Enterprising Women. The Garretts and their circle*, London: Francis Boutle Publishers, 2002.
34 H. Clark to A. Clark, 21, 22 March, 20 June, 13 July, 20, 30 September 1910, MIL 88/2.
35 Ibid., 17, 19, 22 September 1909, 14 January 1910.
36 Ibid., 6, 10, 14, 17 January 1910.
37 Ibid., 5, 8, 15 January 1910.
38 Ibid., 8, 10 January 1910.
39 Ibid., 16, 17, 19, 21, 22 January 1910.
40 Ibid., 22 January, 3 February 1910.
41 S. S. Holton, 'To Live "Through One's Own Powers": British medicine, tuberculosis and "invalidism" in the life of Alice Clark (1874–1934)', *Journal of Women's History*, 1999, vol.11, pp. 75–96.
42 On women's suffrage and party politics, see C. Rover, *Women's Suffrage and Party Politics in Britain, 1866–1914*, London; Routledge & Kegan Paul, 1967; D. Morgan, *Suffragists and Liberals. The politics of woman suffrage in Britain*, Oxford: Basil Blackwell, 1975; Holton, *Feminism and Democracy*.
43 On the Peoples Suffrage Federation and democratic feminism, and on the Conciliation Bills, see Holton, *Feminism and Democracy*, pp. 53–75, 69–75. For an alternative account of the former, see also J. Hannam and K. Hunt, *Socialist Women. Britain, 1880s–1920*, London: Routledge, 2002, esp. pp. 107–8, 123. On the latter see also L. P. Hume, *The National Union of Women's Suffrage Societies 1897–1914*, New York: Garland Publishing, Inc., 1982, pp. 61–97. On the Women's Cooperative Guild, see G. Scott, *Feminism and the Politics of Working Women. The Women's Cooperative Guild, 1880s to the Second World War*, London: UCL Press, 1998, pp. 102–11.
44 H. Clark to A. Clark, 2 December 1908, MIL 88/2; A. Clark to A. M. and My Priestman, 26 June 1908, 18 November 1908, MIL 87/6. See also Holton, *Suffrage Days*, pp. 161–82 on Alice Clark's role at this time.
45 H. Clark to A. Clark, 16 June 1911, MIL 88/2.
46 Ibid., 18 June 1911.
47 'A Note by Alice Clark' in N. Penney, *The Household Account Book of Margaret Fell of Swarthmore Hall*, Cambridge: Cambridge University Press, 1920; A. Clark, *The Working Life of Women in the Seventeenth Century*, London: Routledge, 1992 reprint (1919), p. lviii; file on the Shaw Fellowship, Central Filing Registry, 835, Archive Department, London School of Political and Economic Science.
48 For fuller accounts, see, J. Vellacott, *From Liberal to Labour with Women's Suffrage. The story of Catherine Marshall*, London: McGill-Queen's University Press, 1993, pp. 172–202; Holton, *Feminism and Democracy*, pp. 76–96 and *Suffrage Days*, pp. 175–81.
49 H. Clark to A. Clark, 30 July, 1 August 1914, MIL 88/2; HCD, 5 August 1914, MIL 70.
50 H. Clark to A. Clark, 11, 12 August and 6, 8, 10 September 1914; H. Clark to Ha Clark, 26 August 1914 (among her letters to A. Clark), all MIL 88/2.
51 H. Clark to A. Clark, 14 and 15 October 1914, MIL 88/2; HCD, 4, 6, 8, 25 September and 10, 15 October 1914, MIL 70. See also the obituaries of Anna Maria and Mary Priestman, *The Friend*, 1914, pp. 817, 818, and entries in the QDB.
52 H. Clark to A. Clark, 2, 29 January, 14, 16, 26 October 1915, MIL 88/2.
53 Ibid., 11 August 1914.

54 H. Clark to Ha Clark, 26 August 1914 (located among her letters to Alice Clark); H. Clark to A. Clark, 17, 24 September; 15 October 1914, 8, 12 April 1915, all MIL 88/2.
55 NUWSS, Election Fighting Fund circular, 10 August 1914, enclosed with H. Clark to A. Clark, 11 August 1914, MIL 88/2.
56 HCD, 26 February, 15 March, 14 April 1915, MIL 70; H. Clark to A. Clark, 31 January, 1 February, 23 February, 29 March 1915, MIL 88/2.
57 A. Clark to H. Clark, 5 January 1915, MIL 87/1; H. Clark to A. Clark, 8 February 1915, MIL 88/2. On the divisions among suffragists occasioned by the war, see J. V. Newberry, 'Anti-War Suffragists', *History*, 1997, vol. 62, pp. 411–25; J. Vellacott, 'A Place for Pacifism and Transnationalism in Feminist Theory: the early work of the Women's International League for Peace and Freedom', *Women's History Review*, 1993, vol. 2, pp. 23–56; S. S. Holton, *Feminism and Democracy. Women's suffrage and reform politics, 1900–1918*, Cambridge: Cambridge University Press, 2002 paperback edn (1986), pp. 116–50.
58 A. Clark to H. Clark, 8 March 1915, MIL 87/1; HCD, 12 May, 23 October, 29 November 1915, MIL 70; H. Clark to Alice Clark, 30 November 1915, MIL 88/2.
59 HCD, 9 February 1916, MIL 70; H. Clark to A. Clark, 14 January, 11 February 1916, MIL 88/2. On the divisions within the Society of Friends regarding the war and conscription, including Esther Clothier's role, see T. C. Kennedy, *British Quakerism, 1860–1920. The transformation of a religious community*, Oxford: Oxford University Press: 2001, pp. 357–420, esp. pp. 364–5.
60 H. Clark to A. Clark, 15 September, 14 October, 3, 13, 31 December 1914, 15, 19 February, 29 March 1915, MIL 88/2. For an account of Hilda Clark's work, see H. Clark, *War and its Aftermath: Letters from Hilda Clark, MB, BS, from France, Austria and the Near East, 1914–1924*, E. Pye (ed.), Wells: Clare & Sons, n.d.; S. Spielhofer, *Stemming the Dark Tide. Quakers in Vienna 1919–1942*, York: William Sessions Ltd., 2001, pp. 4–74.
61 W. Clark to A. Clark, 10 September 1914, 6 December 1915, MIL 88/1; H. Clark to A. Clark, 30 December 1914, MIL 88/2; A. Clark to H. Clark, 12 October 1914, 14 February 1915, 27 March, 8 May 1915, MIL 87/1; Alice Clark's fellowship records, Central Filing Registry, 835, Archive Department, London School of Political and Economic Science.
62 H. Clark to A. Clark, 29 March, 30 April 1915, MIL 88/2; A. Clark to H. Clark, 8 May 1915, MIL 87/1.
63 H. Clark to A. Clark, 25 November, 6 December 1915, MIL 88/2.
64 Ibid., 8, 12 April, 1, 27 August 1915; A. Clark to Ha Clark, 29 October 1915, n.d. [*c.* early November 1915], in her Letterbook, October 1915–June 1916, MIL 91; R. Fry, *A Quaker Adventure,* London: Nesbit & Co., 1926, gives minimal recognition to the role of Hilda and Alice Clark in the work of the committee.
65 H. Clark to A. Clark, 6, 19 October, 25 December 1916, MIL 88/2; A. Clark to H. Clark, 14 October, 14, 27 December 1915, MIL 87/1.
66 H. Clark to A. Clark., 7 May 1918, MIL 88/2; A. Clark to H. Clark, 30 March 1918, MIL 87/1.

14 The Priestman–Bright circle and women's history

1 H. Clark to A. Clark, postmark 12 November 1914, MIL 88/2; HCD, 23, 27, 30 October, 6, 8, November 1914, MIL 70.
2 HCD 3 October, 1 November 1915, MIL 70. See also the wills of Anna Maria and Mary Priestman, NO. ONE, Box 42, CA, which after small gifts to one or two more distant kin, divided the rest of estate equally among their surviving nieces and nephews.

3 HCD, 24 July, 10 October 1915; 31 March, 7, 29 April, 2 May, 21 June, 20 December 1916; 3, 12 August 1917, MIL 70; H. Clark to A. Clark, 19, 23 February 1915, MIL 88/2; W. Clark to A. Clark, 12 December 1916, all MIL 88/1.
4 HCD, 23 August, 9/10, 25 September, 5, 6 October 1917, MIL 70; H. Clark to A. Clark, 5 November 1918, MIL 88/2.
5 HCD, n.d. entry headed 'New York Nation Feb 21 1918', MIL 70, presumably referring to a newspaper or periodical report. On the negotiations between suffragists and government members over the content of the act, see S. S. Holton, *Feminism and Democracy. Women's suffrage and reform politics in Britain*, 1900–1918, Cambridge: Cambridge University Press, 2004.
6 Ibid., 18 January, 7 February, 22 April 1918.
7 Ibid., 19 March, 13 April, 3 May, 20 June 1919; A. Clark to H. Clark, 3 October 1921, MIL 87/1.
8 W. Clark to A. Clark, 22 October 1921, MIL 88/1.
9 W. Clark, 'Memorandum to his children for after his death', n.d. [*c.* 1906], MIL 79.
10 For further discussion of this point, see S. S. Holton, 'The Suffragist and "the Average Woman"', *Women's History Review*, 1992, vol. 1, pp. 9–24.

Select bibliography

Manuscript collections

Millfield Papers, Clark Archive.
Sarah Bancroft Clark Papers, Clark Archive, most of which is available on microfilm at the Somerset Record Office, Taunton.
W. Bancroft Clark Papers, Clark Archive.
Helen S. H. Clark, Papers, Clark Archive.
No. One Office Papers, Clark Archive.
Roderick D. F. Clark Papers, Clark Archive.

Friends' House Library collections

Central Education Board Minutes.
Friends' War Victims' Relief Committee Minutes
Quaker Dictionary of Biography.

Local history department Bolton Public Library

1811, 1821, 1831 Census Index and Returns for Bolton
Bolton Poor Law Rate Assessment Book, 1805

Local studies department, Rochdale public library

Poor Law Collecting Book, Wardlesworth Township, 1825–6.

Archive department, British Library of Political and Economic Sciences, London School of Economics

Central Filing Registry, file 835.

Journals and newspapers

British Friend.
Central Somerset Gazette.
The Friend.
Friends Quarterly Examiner.

Works of reference

Baines, E., *History, Directory and Gazetteer of the County Palatine of Lancaster.*
Bolton Directories, 1818, 1821–2, Manchester: T. Rogerson, 1818, 1821.
Commercial Directory of Rochdale, 1814–15, Manchester: Wardle and Bentham, 1814.
Crawford, E. *The Women's Suffrage Movement*, London: UCL Press, 1999.
Crawford, E. *The Women's Suffrage Movement in Britain and Ireland. A regional survey*, London: Routledge, 2006.
Doughan, D. and Sanchez, D., *Feminist Periodicals 1855–1984. An Annotated, Critical Bibliography of British, Irish, Commonwealth and International Titles*, Brighton: Harvester, 1987.
Jolly, M., *Encyclopedia of Life Writing*, London: Fitzroy Dearborn, 2001, 2 vols.
Oxford Dictionary of National Biography, eds H. C. G. Matthew and B. Harrison, Oxford: Oxford University Press, 2004.
Parson, W. and White, W., *History, Directory and Gazetteer . . . of Durham and Northumberland*, Newcastle: White & Co., 1827 (2 vols).
Pigot and Dean's New Directory of Manchester, Salford, Etc., 1821–22, Manchester: R. and W. Dean.
Slater's Directory of Bolton, 1814.

Books

Aylmer, G. A. (ed.), *Public Duty and Private Conscience in Seventeenth Century England*, Oxford: Clarendon Press, 1993.
Banks, O., *Becoming a Feminist. The social origins of first-wave feminism*, Brighton: Wheatsheaf Books, 1981.
[Barber, L. H.], *Clarks of Street 1825–1950* [Street: C. & J. Clark Ltd., *c.* 1950].
Benson, R. S. (comp.), *Photographic Pedigree of the Descendants of Isaac and Rachel Wilson*, Middlesbrough: William Appleyard, 1912.
Biagini, F. A., *Liberty, Retrenchment and Reform. Popular Liberalism in the age of Gladstone, 1860–80*, Cambridge: Cambridge University Press, 1992.
Binding, T., *On Ilkley Moor. The story of an English town*, London: Picador, 2001.
Boyce, A. O., *Records of a Quaker Family. The Richardsons of Cleveland*, London: Samuel Harris, 1889.
Braithwaite, J. B., *Memoir of Anna Braithwaite*, London: Headley Brothers, 1905.
Brown, Heloise, *The Truest Form of Patriotism. Pacificist feminism in Britain, 1870–1902*, Manchester: Manchester University Press, 2003.
Brooke, S. A. (ed.), *Life and Letters of Frederick W. Robertson*, London: Smith, Elder, & Co., 1865, 2 vols.
Burton, Antoinette, *Burdens of History. British feminists, Indian women and imperial culture, 1865–1915*, Chapel Hill, NC: University of North Carolina Press, 1994.
Caine, B., *Victorian Feminists*, Oxford: Oxford University Press, 1992.
—— *Destined to be Wives. The sisters of Beatrice Webb*, Oxford: Oxford University Press, 1986.
Castren, A., Lonkila, M. and Peltonen, M., *Between Sociology and History. Essays on microhistory, collective action and nation-building*, Helsinki: SKS/Finnish Literature Society, 2004.
Clark, Alice, *Working Life of Women in the Seventeenth Century*, London, George Routledge & Sons, 1919, reprinted with an Introduction by Chaytor, M. and Lewis, J., London: Routledge & Kegan Paul, 1982; reprinted with an Introduction by Erickson, A., London: Routledge, 1992.

Clark, Anna, *Struggle for the Breeches: gender and the making of the British working class*, London: Rivers Oram, 1995.

Clark, H., *War and its Aftermath: Letters from Hilda Clark, MB, BS, from France, Austria and the Near East, 1914–1924*, Pye, E. (ed.), Wells: Clare & Sons, c.1956.

Clark, R., *John Bright Clark of C. & J. Clark Ltd*, Street: privately published [c.1934].

[Clark, R.], *One Hundred Years. C & J Clark, Street, Somerset, 1825–1925*, [Street]: C. & J. Clark, c.1925.

Clark, W. S., 'A History of the Business of C & J Clark of Street, Somerset', written 1914, and published as Appendix of [Barber, L.], *Clarks of Street*, [Street]: C. & J. Clark Ltd., c.1950.

Clarkson, T., *A Portraiture of Quakerism . . .*, London: Longman, Hurst, Rees & Orme, 1806, 3 vols.

Colls, R. and Lancaster, B., *Newcastle-upon-Tyne: a modern history*, Chichester: Phillimore & Co., 2000.

Crawford, E., *Enterprising Women. The Garretts and their circle*, London: Francis Boutle Publishers, 2002.

Daley, C. and Nolan, M. (eds), *Suffrage and Beyond. International feminist perspectives*, Auckland: Auckland University Press, 1994.

Davidoff, L., *Worlds Between: Historical perspectives on gender and class*, Cambridge: Polity Press, 1995.

—— and Hall, C., *Family Fortunes: men and women of the English middle class c.1780–1850*, London: Routledge, 1992.

Davidoff, L., McClelland, K. and Varikas, E., *Gender and History: retrospect and prospect*, Oxford: Blackwell, 2000.

Dixon, J., *Divine Feminine. Theosophy and feminism in England*, Baltimore: Johns Hopkins University Press, 2000.

Dresser, M. and Ollerenshaw, P. (eds), *Making of Modern Bristol*, Tiverton: Radcliffe, 1996.

Dyhouse, C., *Girls Growing Up in Late Victorian and Edwardian England*, London: Routledge & Kegan Paul, 1981.

Epstein, J. A., *Radical Expression. Political language, ritual, and symbol in England 1790–1850*, Oxford: Oxford University Press, 1994.

Eustance, C., Ryan, J. and Ugolini, L. (eds), *A Suffrage Reader. Charting directions in British suffrage history*, Leicester: Leicester University Press, 2000.

Fahey, D. M., *Temperance and Racism: John Bull, Johnny Reb and the Good Templars*, Lexington, KY: Kentucky University Press, 1996.

Finn, M. C., *Character of Credit. Personal Debt in English Culture, 1740–1914*, Cambridge: Cambridge University Press, 2003.

Finn, M., *After Chartism. Class and nation in English radical politics, 1848–1874*, Cambridge: Cambridge University Press, 1993.

Fletcher, S., *Women First: the female tradition in English physical education, 1880–1980*, London: Athlone Press, 1984.

Ford, J., *Memoir of William Tanner*, York: William Sessions, 1868.

Fox, A., *A History of the National Union of Boot and Shoe Operatives, 1874–1957*, Oxford: Basil Blackwell, 1958.

Fry, R., *A Quaker Adventure*, London: Nesbit & Co., 1926.

'MCG' [Margaret Clark Gillett], *Alice Clark of C. & J. Clark Ltd*, Street: Somerset, privately published, n.d., [c.1934].

Ginzberg, L. *Work of Benevolence. Politics, morality and class in the nineteenth century United States*, New Haven, CT: Yale University Press, 1990.

Gleadle, K., *Early Feminists: radical Unitarians and the emergence of the women's rights movement 1831–51*, Basingstoke: Macmillan, 1995.
—— and Richardson, S. (eds), *Women in British Politics, 1760–1860. The power of the petticoat*, Basingstoke: Macmillan Press, 2000.
Grubb, G. W., *Grubbs of Tipperary. Studies in heredity and character*, Cork: Mercier Press 1972, p. 94.
Gunn, S., *Public Culture of the Victorian Middle Class*, Manchester: Manchester University Press, 2000.
Hall, C., *White, Male and Middle-Class. Explorations in feminism and history*, Cambridge: Polity Press, 1992.
Hall, C., McClelland, K. and Rendall, J., *Defining the Victorian Nation: class, race, gender, and the Reform Act of 1867*, Cambridge: Cambridge University Press, 2000.
Hamm, T., *The Transformation of American Quakerism. Orthodox Friends, 1800–1907*, Bloomington, IN: Indiana University Press, 1992.
Hannam, J., *Isabella Ford*, Oxford: Basil Blackwell, 1989.
—— and Hunt, K., *Socialist Women. Britain, 1880s-1920s*, London: Routledge, 2002.
Hewitt, N. A., *Women's Activism and Social Change. Rochester, New York, 1822–1872*, Ithaca, NY: Cornell University Press, 1984, esp. pp. 36, 42, 163–6, 169, 254.
Holcombe, L., *Women and Property: reform of the married women's property law in nineteenth-century England*, Toronto: Toronto University Press, 1983.
Hollis, P., *Ladies Elect. Women in English local government, 1865–1914*, Oxford: Clarendon Press, 1985.
Holton, S. S., *Feminism and Democracy. Women's suffrage and reform politics, 1900–1918*, Cambridge: Cambridge University Press, 2002 paperback edn (1986).
—— *Suffrage Days. Stories from the women's suffrage movement*, London: Routledge, 1996.
Howsam, L., *Cheap Bibles: nineteenth-century publishing and the British and Foreign Bible Society*, Cambridge: Cambridge University Press, 1991.
Hudson, K., *Towards Precision Shoemaking*, Newton Abbot: David & Charles, 1986.
Hume, L. P., *The National Union of Women's Suffrage Societies, 1897–1914*, New York: Garland Publishing, 1982.
Ingle, H. L., *Quakers in Conflict. The Hicksite reformation*, Wallingford, PA: Pendle Hill Publications, 2nd edn, 1998 (1986).
Isichei, E., *Victorian Quakers*, London: Oxford University Books, 1970.
Jalland, P., *Women, Marriage and Politics, 1860–1914*, Oxford: Clarendon Press, 1986.
—— *Death in the Victorian Family*, Oxford: Oxford University Press, 1996.
Jensen, J., *Loosening the Bonds. Mid-Atlantic farm women, 1750–1850*, New Haven, CT: Yale University Press, 1986.
Joannou, M. and Purvis, J. (eds), *Women's Suffrage Movement. New Feminist perspectives*, Manchester: Manchester University Press.
Joyce, P., *Democratic Subjects. The self and the social in nineteenth century England*, Cambridge: Cambridge University Press.
Kahan, A. S., *Liberalism in Nineteenth Century Europe. The political culture of limited suffrage*, Basingstoke: Palgrave Macmillan, 2003.
Kennedy, T. C., *British Quakerism, 1860–1920. The transformation of a religious community*, Oxford: Oxford University Press, 2001.
Lehane, B., *C. & J. Clark Ltd, 1825–1975*, Street: C. & J. Clark, n.d.
Levine, P., *Feminist Lives in Victorian England. Private roles and public commitment*, London: Women's Press, 1990.
Liddington, J., *Female Fortune. Land, gender and authority: the Anne Lister diaries and other writing, 1833–36*, London: Rivers Oram, 1998.

―― and Norris, J., *One Hand Tied Behind Us. The rise of the women's suffrage movement*, London: Rivers Oram, 2000 reprint (1978).
Lovell, P., *Quaker Inheritance, 1871–1961. A portrait of Roger Clark of Street based on his own writings and correspondence*, London: Bannisdale Press, 1970.
Mackie, J. B., *The Life and Work of Duncan McLaren*, London: Thomas Nelson & Sons, 1888 (2 vols).
Mayhall, L. E. N., *Militant Suffrage Movement. Citizenship and resistance in Britain, 1860–1930*, Oxford: Oxford University Press, 2003.
McGarvie, M., *The Book of Street. A history from the earliest times to 1925*, Buckingham: Barracuda Books, 1987.
―― *Bowlingreen Mill. A centenary history*, [Street]: Avalon Leatherboard Co., 1979. Mack, P. *Visionary Women: ecstatic prophecy in seventeenth-century England*, Berkeley, CA: University of California Press, 1992.
McHugh, P., *Prostitution and Victorian Social Reform*, London: Croom Helm, 1980.
Midgley, C., *Women against Slavery. The British campaigns 1780–1870*, London: Routledge, 1992.
Milligan, E., *Quaker Marriage*, Kendal: Quaker Tapestry Books, 1994.
Mills, J. T., *John Bright and the Quakers*, London: Methuen, 1935, 2 vols.
Montefiore, D., *From a Victorian to a Modern*, London: E. Archer, 1927, pp. 40–1.
Morgan, D., *Suffragists and Liberals. The politics of woman suffrage in Britain*, Oxford: Basil Blackwell, 1975.
Morris, R. J., *Cholera 1832. The social response to an epidemic*, London: Croom Helm, 1976.
―― Men, *Women and Property in England, 1780–1870. A social and economic history of family strategies among the Leeds middle classes*, Cambridge: Cambridge University Press, 2005.
Muir, E. and Ruggiero, G., *Microhistory and the lost peoples of Europe*, Baltimore, MD: Johns Hopkins Press, 1991.
Penney, N., *The Household Account Book of Margaret Fell of Swarthmore Hall*, Cambridge: Cambridge University Press, 1920.
Peterson, M. J., *Family, Love and Work in the Lives of Victorian Gentlewomen*, Bloomington, IN: Indiana University Press, 1989.
Phillips, M., *A History of Banks, Bankers, Banking in Northumberland, Durham and North Yorkshire*, London: E. Wilson & Co., 1894.
Pickering, P. A. and A. Tyrrell, *People's Bread. A history of the Anti-Corn Law League*, Leicester: Leicester University Press, 2000.
Priestman, S. H., *Priestmans of Thornton-le-Dale and Some of Their Descendants*, Sutton on Hull: privately published, 1955.
Prochaska, F., *Women and Philanthropy in Nineteenth Century England*, Oxford: Clarendon Press, 1980.
Punshon, J., *Portrait in Grey: A short history of the Quakers*, London: Quaker Home Service, 1984.
Purvis, J. (ed.), *Women's History, 1850–1945*, London: UCL Press, 1995.
―― *Emmeline Pankhurst. A biography*, London: Routledge, 2002.
―― and Holton, S. S., *Votes for Women*, London: Routledge, 2000.
Rendall, J. (ed.), *Equal or Different. Women's Politics, 1800–1914*, Oxford: Basil Blackwell, 1987.
Richardson, A. D., *Memoir of Anna Deborah Richardson, with Extracts from her Letters*, J. W. Richardson (ed.), Newcastle: privately published, 1877.

Richardson, J. W., *Memoirs, 1837–1908*, Glasgow: privately published, n.d.
Robbins, K., *John Bright*, London: Routledge and Kegan Paul, 1979.
Roberts, M. J. D., *Making English Morals. Voluntary association and moral reform in England, 1787–1886,* Cambridge: Cambridge University Press, 2004.
Robertson, F. W., *Sermons on Religious Life*, London: J. M. Dent, n.d. [1906].
Robertson, W., *Life and Times of the Right Honourable John Bright*, London: Cassell, 1883, 2 vols.
Rosen, A., *Rise Up Women. The militant campaigns of the Women's Social and Political Union, 1904–14*, London: Routledge & Kegan Paul, 1974.
Routh, M., *Memoir of the Life, Travels and Religious Experience of Martha Routh*, York: W. Alexander, 1822.
Rover, C., *Women's Suffrage and Party Politics in Britain, 1866–1914*, London; Routledge & Kegan Paul, 1967.
Rowntree, J. R., *Quakerism, Past and Present*, London: Smith, Elder & Son, 1859.
Rubinstein, D., *Before the Suffragettes. Women's emancipation in the 1890s*, Brighton: Harvester Press, 1986.
Rubinstein, D., *New World for Women. The life of Millicent Garrett Fawcett*, Brighton: Harvester Wheatsheaf, 1991.
Sansbury, R., *Beyond the Blew Stone. 300 Years of Quakers in Newcastle*, Newcastle: Newcastle Upon Tyne Preparative Meeting, 1999.
Scott, G., *Feminism and the Politics of Working Women. The Women's Cooperative Guild, 1880s to the Second World War,* London: UCL Press, 1998.
Shanley, M. L., *Feminism, Marriage and the Law in Victorian England 1850–95*, London: I. B. Tauris, 1989.
Singh, S., *Marriage Money. The social shaping of money in marriage and banking*, St Leonards, NSW: Allen & Unwin, 1997.
Smith, H. L. (ed.), *British Feminism in the Twentieth Century*, Aldershot: Edward Elgar, 1990.
Somervell, J., *Isaac and Rachel Wilson, Quakers of Kendal, 1714–85*, London: Swarthmore Press, 1924.
Spielhofer, S., *Stemming the Dark Tide. Quakers in Vienna 1919–1942*, York: William Sessions Ltd., 2001.
Stanley, L., with Morley, A., *The Life and Death of Emily Wilding Davison*, London: Women's Press, 1988.
Staves, S., *Married Women's Separate Property in England, 1660–1833*, Cambridge, MA.: Harvard University Press, 1990.
Stebbings, C., *Private Trustee in Victorian England*, Cambridge: Cambridge University Press, 2002.
Steedman, C., *Dust*, Manchester: Manchester University Press, 2001.
Steel, J. W., *A Historical Sketch of the Society of Friends 'In Scorn Called Quakers' in Newcastle and Gateshead, 1653–1898*, London: Headley Bros, 1899.
Stewart, L., *Memoirs of a Quaker Childhood*, E. Roberts (ed.), London: Friends' Home Service Committee, 1970.
Stobart, J. and Owens, A. (eds), *Urban Fortunes. Property and inheritance in the town, 1700–1900*, Aldershot: Ashgate, 2000.
Sturge, H. W. and Clark, T., *The Mount School, York, 1785–1814, 1831–1931*, London: J. M. Dent, 1931.
Summerfield, P., *Reconstructing Wartime Lives. Discourses and subjectivity in the oral history of the Second World War*, Manchester: Manchester University Press, 1988.

270 Select bibliography

Sutton, G. B., *C & J Clark, 1833–1903. A history of shoemaking in Street*, York: William Sessions, 1979.

Szreter, S., *Fertility, Class and Gender in Britain, 1860–1940*, Cambridge: Cambridge University Press, 1996.

Tanner, S. J., *How the Women's Suffrage Movement Began in Bristol Fifty Years Ago*, Bristol: Carlyle Press, 1918.

Thompson, F. M. L. (ed.), *Landowners, Capitalists and Entrepreneurs. Essays for Sir John Habakkuk*, Oxford: Clarendon Press, 1994.

Tickner, L., *The Spectacle of Women. Imagery of the suffrage campaign, 1907–14*, London: Chatto & Windus, 1987.

Tolles, F. B., (ed.), *Slavery and 'The Woman Question'. Lucretia Mott's diary of . . . the World Anti-Slavery Convention, 1840*, Haverford, PA.: Friends' Historical Society, 1952, Supplement no. 23, *Journal of the Friends' Historical Society*.

Tozer, J., and Levitt, S., *Fabric of Society. A century of people and their clothes, 1770–1870*, Carns: Laura Ashley, 1993.

Trevelyan, G. M., *Life of John Bright*, London: Constable, 1913.

Trevett, C., *Women and Quakerism in the Seventeenth Century*, York: Sessions Book Trust, 1991.

Tyrrell, A., *Joseph Sturge and the Moral Reform Radical Party in Early Victorian Britain*, London: Croom Helm, 1987.

Tyrrell, I., *Woman's World, Woman's Empire: the Women's Christian Temperance Union in international perspective, 1800–1930*, Chapel Hill, NC: University of North Carolina Press, 1996.

Vann, R. T., *Social Development of English Quakerism, 1655–1755*, Cambridge, MA: Harvard University Press, 1969.

—— and Eversley, D., *Friends in Life and Death: the British and Irish Quakers in the demographic transition, 1650–1900*, Cambridge: Cambridge University Press, 1992.

Vellacott, J., *From Liberal to Labour with Women's Suffrage. The story of Catherine Marshall*, London: McGill-Queen's University Press, 1993, pp. 172–202.

Vickery, A., *The Gentleman's Daughter: Women's Lives in Georgian England*, New Haven, CT: Yale University Press, 1998.

—— (ed.), *Women, Politics and Power: British Politics, 1750 to the Present*, Stanford, CA: Stanford University Press, 2001.

Vicinus, M., *Independent Women. Work and community for single women 1850–1920*, London: Virago, 1985.

Vincent, J., *The Formation of the British Liberal Party, 1857–1868*, Harmondsworth: Penguin, 1972 (London: Constable, 1966), pp. 196–7.

Walkowitz, J. R., *Prostitution and Victorian Society. Women, class and the state*, Cambridge: Cambridge University Press, 1980.

Walvin, J., *Quakers: Money and morals*, London: John Murray, 1997.

Ware, V., *Beyond the Pale. White women, racism and history*, London: Verso, 1992.

Watts, R., *Gender, Power and the Unitarians in England, 1760–1860*, London: Longman, 1998.

Winter, J., *Sites of Memory, Sites of Mourning. The Great War in European cultural history*, Cambridge: Cambridge University Press, 1986.

Wright, S. *Friends in York. The dynamics of Quaker revival, 1780–1860*, Keele: Keele University Press, 1995.

Yeo, E. J., *Contest for Social Science: relations and representations of gender and Class*, London: Rivers Oram, 1996, pp. 10–15.

Yeo, E. J. (ed.), *Radical Femininity: women's self-representation in the public sphere*, Manchester: Manchester University Press, 1998.
Zelizer, V. A., *Social Meaning of Money*, New York: Basic Books, 1994.

Articles and book chapters

Bacon, M. H., 'The Establishment of London Women's Yearly Meeting: a transatlantic concern', *Journal of the Friends' Historical Society*, 1992, vol. 57, pp. 151–65.

Barrow, M., 'Teetotal Feminists: the temperance leadership and the campaign for women's suffrage', in Eustance, C., Ryan, J. and Ugolini, L. (eds), *A Suffrage Reader. Charting directions in British suffrage history*, Leicester: Leicester University Press, 2000.

Berg, M., 'Women's Property and the Industrial Revolution', *Journal of Interdisciplinary History*, 1993, vol. 24, pp. 233–50.

Bronner, E. B., 'Moderates in London Yearly Meeting, 1857–1873', *Church History*, 1990, vol. 59, pp. 356–71.

Caine, B., 'John Stuart Mill and the English Women's Movement', *Historical Studies*, 1982, vol. 18, pp. 52–67.

—— 'Feminism, Suffrage and the Nineteenth-Century Women's Movement', *Women's Studies International Forum*, 1982, vol. 5, pp. 537–50.

Callcott, M., 'The Governance of the Victorian City' in R. Colls and B. Lancaster, *Newcastle-upon-Tyne: a modern history*, Chichester: Phillimore and Co., 2000.

Chalus, E., 'Women, Electoral Privilege and Practice in the Eighteenth Century', in Gleadle, K. and Richardson, S. (eds), *Women in British Politics, 1760–1860. The power of the petticoat*, Basingstoke: Macmillan Press, 2000.

Clark, A., 'A note by Alice Clark', in N. Penney, *The Household Account Book of Margaret Fell of Swarthmore Hall*, Cambridge: Cambridge University Press, 1920.

Combs, M. B., 'Wives and Household Wealth: the impact of the 1870 British Married Women's Property Act on wealth-holding and share of household resources', *Continuity and Change*, 2004, vol. 19, pp. 141–63.

Cook, K., 'Nineteenth Century Diaries', in M. Jolly (ed.), *Encyclopedia of Life Writing*, London: Fitzroy Dearborn, 2000, 2 vols.

Cragoe, M., '"Jenny Rules the Roost": Women and electoral politics, 1832–68', in Gleadle, K. and Richardson, S. (eds), *Women in British Politics, 1760–1860. The power of the petticoat*, Basingstoke: Macmillan Press, 2000.

Crawford, P., 'Public Duty, Conscience and Women in Early Modern England', in Aylmer, G. A. (ed.), *Public Duty and Private Conscience in Seventeenth Century England*, Oxford: Clarendon Press, 1993.

Crossick, G., 'Meanings of Property and the World of the Petite Bourgeoisie', in Stobart, J. and Owens, A. (eds), *Urban Fortunes. Property and inheritance in the town, 1700–1900*, Aldershot: Ashgate Press, 2000.

Davidoff, L., '"Where the Stranger Begins": the question of siblings in historical analysis', in her *Worlds Between: Historical perspectives on gender and class*, Cambridge: Polity Press, 1995.

Dubois, E., 'Woman Suffrage and the Left: an international socialist-feminist perspective', *New Left Review*, 1991, no. 186, pp. 20–45.

Green, D. R., 'Independent Women, Wealth and Wills in Nineteenth Century London', in Stobart, J. and Owens, A. (eds), *Urban Fortunes. Property and inheritance in the town, 1700–1900*, Aldershot: Ashgate, 2000.

Hamm, T. D., '"A Protest against Protestantism"; Hicksite Friends and the Bible in the Nineteenth Century', *Quaker Studies*, 2002, vol. 6, pp. 175–94.

Hannam, J., '"Suffragettes are Splendid for any Work": the Blathwayt Diaries as a source for suffrage history', in Eustance, C., Ryan, J. and Ugolini, L. (eds), *A Suffrage Reader. Charting directions in British suffrage history*, Leicester: Leicester University Press, 2000.

—— 'An Enlarged Sphere of Usefulness: the Bristol Women's Movement, *c.*1860–1914', in M. Dresser and P. Ollerenshaw (eds), *Making of Modern Bristol*, Tiverton: Radcliffe, 1996.

Hirschfield, C., 'Fractured Faith: Liberal Party women and the suffrage issue in Britain, 1892–1914', *Gender and History*, 1990, vol. 2, pp. 173–97.

Holton, R. J. and Holton, S. J., 'From the particular to the global: some empirical, epistemological and methodological aspects of microhistory with regard to a women's rights network', in R. Lenton and K. Fricker (eds), *Performing Global Networks*, Cambridge Scholars' Publishing, forthcoming, 2007.

Holton, S. S., 'State Pandering, Medical Policing and Prostitution. The controversy within the medical profession over the Contagious Diseases legislation 1864–86', *Research in Law, Deviance and Social Control*, 1989, vol. 9, pp.149–70.

—— '"In Sorrowful Wrath". Suffrage militancy and the romantic feminism of Emmeline Pankhurst', in H. L. Smith (ed.) *British Feminism in the Twentieth Century*, Aldershot: Edward Elgar, 1990.

—— 'The Suffragist and "the Average Woman"', *Women's History Review*, 1992, vol. 1, pp. 9–24.

—— '"Educating Women into Rebellion." Elizabeth Cady Stanton and the creation of a transatlantic network of Radical suffragists', *American Historical Review*, 1994, vol. 99, pp. 1112–36.

—— 'From Anti-Slavery to Suffrage Militancy. The Bright circle, Elizabeth Cady Stanton, and the British women's movement', in Daley, C. and Nolan, M. (eds) *Suffrage and Beyond. International feminist perspectives*, Auckland: Auckland University Press, 1994.

—— 'Women and the Vote', in J. Purvis (ed.), *Women's History, 1850–1945*, London: UCL Press, 1995.

—— 'British Freewomen. National identity, constitutionalism and languages of race in early suffragist histories', in Yeo, E . J. (ed.), *Radical Femininity: women's self-representation in the publics sphere*, Manchester: Manchester University Press, 1998.

—— 'Now You See It, Now You Don't: the Women's Franchise League and its place in contending narratives of the women's suffrage movement', in Joannou, M. and Purvis, J. (eds) *Women's Suffrage Movement. New feminist perspectives*, Manchester: Manchester University Press, 1998.

—— 'To Live "Through One's Own Powers": British medicine, tuberculosis and invalidism in the life of Alice Clark (1874–1934)', *Journal of Women's History*, 1999, vol. 11, pp. 75–96.

—— 'Reflecting on Suffrage History', in Eustance, C., Ryan, J. and Ugolini, L. (eds), *A Suffrage Reader. Charting directions in British suffrage history*, Leicester: Leicester University Press, 2000.

—— 'The Making of Suffrage History', in Purvis, J. and Holton, S. S. (eds) *Votes for Women*, London: Routledge, 2000.

—— 'Segregation, Racism and White Women Reformers: a transnational perspective', *Women's History Review*, 2001, vol. 10, pp. 5–25.

—— 'John Bright, Radical Politics and the Ethos of Quakerism', *Albion*, 2002, vol. 34, pp. 584–605.

—— 'Family Memory, Religion and Radicalism: the Priestman, Bright and Clark kinship circle of women Friends and Quaker history', *Quaker Studies*, 2005, vol. 9, pp. 156–75.

—— 'Religion and the Meanings of Work: four cases among the Bright circle of women Quakers', in Cowman, K. and Jackson, L. (eds), *Women and Work Culture in Britain circa 1850–1950*, Aldershot: Ashgate Press, 2005.

—— 'Kinship and Friendship: Quaker Women's networks and the women's movement', *Women's History Review*, 2005, vol. 14, pp. 365–84.

—— and Allen, M., 'Offices and Services: women's pursuit of sexual equality within the Society of Friends', *Quaker Studies*, 1997, vol. 2, pp. 1–29.

——, Mackinnon, A. and Allen, M., 'Between Rationality and Revelation: women, faith and public roles in the nineteenth and twentieth centuries', *Women's History Review*, 1998, vol. 7, pp. 195–8.

Kerber, L., 'Separate Spheres, Female Worlds, Woman's Place: the rhetoric of women's history', *Journal of American History*, 1988, vol. 75, pp. 9–39.

Kerman, C. E., 'Elias Hicks and Thomas Shillitoe: Two paths diverge?', *Quaker Studies*, 2000, vol. 5, pp. 19–47.

Lane, P., 'Women, Property and Inheritance: wealth creation and income generation in small English towns, 1750–1835', in Stobart, J. and Owens, A. (eds), *Urban Fortunes. Property and Inheritance in the Town, 1700–1900*, Aldershot; Ashgate, 2000.

Lendrum, O., 'An Integrated Elite. Newcastle's economic development, 1840–1914', in R. Colls and B. Lancaster, *Newcastle-upon-Tyne: a modern history*, Chichester: Phillimore & Co., 2000.

Lenton, R. and Fricker (eds), *Performing Global Networks*, Cambridge Scholars' Publishing, forthcoming, 2007.

Malmgreen, G. 'Anne Knight and the Radical Subculture', *Quaker History*, 1982, vol. 71, pp. 100–12.

Mayhall, L. E. N., 'Defining Militancy: radical protest, the constitutional idiom, and women's suffrage in Britain, 1908–1909,' *Journal of British Studies*, 2000, vol. 39, pp. 340–71.

Michaelson, P. H., 'Religious Bases of Eighteenth-Century Feminism: Mary Wollstonecraft and the Quakers', *Women's Studies*, 1993, vol. 22, pp. 281–95.

Morgan, S., 'Domestic Economy and Political Agitation: women and the Anti-Corn Law League', in Gleadle, K. and Richardson, S. (eds), *Women in British Politics 1760–1860. The power of the petticoat*, Basingstoke: Macmillan Press, 2000.

—— '"A Sort of Land Debateable": Female influence, civic virtue and middle class identity, c. 1830–c. 1860', *Women's History Review*, 2004, vol. 13, pp. 183–209.

Morris, R. J., 'Men, Women and Property: the reform of the Married Women's Property Act', in Thompson, F. M. L. (ed.), *Landowners, Capitalists and Entrepreneurs. Essays for Sir John Habakkuk*, Oxford: Clarendon Press, 1994.

—— 'Voluntary Societies and British Elites, 1780–1870: an analysis', *Historical Journal*, 1982, vol. 26, pp. 95–118.

Newberry, J. V., 'Anti-War Suffragists', *History*, 1997, vol. 62, pp. 411–25.

O'Donnell, E. A., '"On Behalf of All Young Women Trying to Be Better Than They Are": feminism and Quakerism in the nineteenth century: the case of Anna Deborah Richardson', *Quaker Studies*, 2001, vol. 6, pp. 37–58.

—— 'Deviations from the Path of Safety: the rise and fall of a nineteenth century Quaker Meeting', *Quaker Studies*, 2003, vol. 8, pp. 68–88.

Onslow, B., 'Britain: Nineteenth-Century Letters' in M. Jolly (ed.), *Encyclopedia of Life Writing*, London: Fitzroy Dearborn, 2000, 2 vols.

Rendall, J., 'Women and the Public Sphere', in Davidoff, L., McClelland, K. and Varikas, E., *Gender and History: retrospect and prospect*, Oxford: Blackwell, 2000.

Richardson, S., '"Well-neighboured Houses": the political networks of elite women', in Gleadle, K. and Richardson, S. (eds), *Women in British Politics, 1760–1860. The power of the petticoat*, Basingstoke: Macmillan Press, 2000.

Shammas, C., 'Re-assessing the Married Women's Property Acts', *Journal of Women's History*, 1994, vol. 6, pp. 9–30.

Stanley, L., 'The Epistolarium: on theorising letters and correspondence', *Auto/biography*, 2005, vol. 13, pp. 201–35.

—— 'Romantic Friendship? Some issues in researching lesbian history and biography', *Women's History Review*, 1992, vol. 1, pp. 193–216.

Vellacott, J., 'A Place for Pacifism and Transnationalism in Feminist Theory: the early work of the Women's International League for Peace and Freedom', *Women's History Review*, 1993, vol. 2, pp. 23–56.

Vickery, A., 'Historiographical Review. Golden age to separate spheres? A review of categories and chronology of English women's history', *Historical Journal*, 1993, vol. 36, pp. 383–414.

Walker, L., 'Party Political Women: a comparative study of Liberal women and the Primrose League, 1890–1914', in Rendall, J. (ed.), *Equal or Different. Women' politics, 1800–1914*, Oxford: Basil Blackwell, 1987.

Unpublished research

Clark, S. B., 'Aunt Wood', BC 249/1, W. Bancroft Clark Papers, CA.

Dingsdale, A., 'Generous and Lofty Sympathies: the Kensington Society, the 1866 women's suffrage petition and the development of mid-Victorian Feminism', PhD thesis, University of Greenwich, 1995.

O'Donnell, E. A., 'Woman's Rights and Woman's Duties. Quaker Women in the Nineteenth Century, with Specific Reference to the North East Monthly Meeting of Women Friends', PhD thesis, University of Sunderland, 2000.

Plant, H., 'Gender and the Aristocracy of Dissent: a comparative study of the beliefs, status and roles of women in Quaker and Unitarian communities, 1770–1830', with particular reference to Yorkshire, DPhil thesis, University of York, 2000.

Index

Ackworth School 13, 21, 64, 124
Anti-Caste 190, 258n24
Anti-Corn Law campaign 36, 81–5
Anti-Corn Law League 71, 74, 80–5, 87, 93, 97, 140; Covent Garden bazaar 93, 95; and gender roles 81–2, 229; and kinship networks 85; Priestman–Bright circle and 82, 83, 84; women's participation in 81–5, 87
anti-imperialism 201–2, 252n27
anti-lynching campaign 190
anti-slavery movement 4, 55, 67, 69–71, 85, 100, 142, 151, 189–90, 205
'Ashley Down', nr Bristol 97, 104
'Ashley Grange', nr Bristol 97, 101, 103, 104, 106
Ashworth (Cross), Anne Frances 128
Ashworth (Hallett), Lilias 178, 179
Ashworth, Sophia *see* Bright
Ashworth, Thomas 76
Ashworth sisters 94, 156, 167, 171; Ashworth Trust 167
associational life 22, 49, 53, 150, 152, 193
aunts and nieces 2, 7, 29, 34, 38, 39, 49, 50, 61, 73, 78, 94, 27, 102–4, 106, 112, 123, 124, 136–7, 152, 154, 155, 156, 157, 159, 161, 227

Backhouse, H. C., Quaker woman minister 63
Baltimore Yearly Meeting 25; *see also* Hicks, Elias; Hicksites
Bancroft, Elizabeth *see* Wood
Bancroft, Esther 18, 31
Bancroft, John, jnr 15
Bancroft, John, snr 14, 15, 26, 31, 38
Bancroft, Joseph 15, 23, 26, 33, 38, 40, 42, 134

Bancroft, Margaret 31, 34
Bancroft (Mellor), Martha 31, 33, 34
Bancroft, Samuel 32
Bancroft (Clark), Sarah 2, 205, 218
Bancroft (Lawton), Sarah 31
Bancroft, Sarah Poole *see* Poole
Bancroft, Thomas 31
Bancroft family, of Manchester, and Providence and Wilmington, Pa 2, 13, 15, 29, 31, 32, 34, 41, 185, 238n44; Bancroft family money 40
Bancroft sisters 23, 32
Barclay, Robert 11
Bath, and Priestman–Bright circle 174; and women's rights movement 140, 165, 168
'Beaconite' schism 62
Becker, Lydia 138, 178, 179, 180, 223
Ben Rhydding, Ilkley 100, 126, 129; *see also* water therapy
Benwell House, nr Newcastle 108, 114, 130, 137
Besant, Annie 200
Bible Society 54
Birmingham University 192
Blackpool 75
black rights campaigns 190; *see also Anti-Caste*; anti-slavery movement; Douglass, Frederick; Impey, Catherine; Jabavu, John D. T.; Wells, Ida B.
Blake, Sophia Jex 18
Blakey, Esther, snr *see* Crosland
Bootham School, York 140, 148, 152, 164
Bragg, Charles 73, 90, 107
Bragg, Hadwen 47
Bragg, John Hadwen 73
Bragg, Margaret, *see* Wilson
Bragg, Mary 50, 59

276 *Index*

Bragg (Priestman), Rachel, snr, Quaker minister 48, 49, 50, 51, 54, 55, 56, 57, 58, 73, 75, 80, 81, 90, 93, 97, 107; and aunts 49, 50, 61; and Bright, John and M. E. 104–5; and family enterprises 50, 54; last illness and death 129–30; life writing of 46, 47, 54, 56–8; personal papers of 130; ministry of 56, 57, 61, 62–3, 80–1, 130; religious values of 54, 55–6; spiritual life of 46, 47, 49–50, 56–8, 78, 80
Bragg family of Whitehaven and Newcastle 47, 49, 50, 53, 54, 55, 78, 137, 170
Braithwaite family, Kendal 61
Bridport 148, 151, 152
Bright, Benjamin 76
Bright, Elizabeth *see* Priestman
Bright (Vaughan), Esther 46, 77, 85, 94, 125
Bright, Gratton 129
Bright (Clark), Helen Priestman 73, 74, 75, 88, 95, 99, 154, 185, 195; and aunts 2, 98, 104, 106, 112–13, 123, 125–6, 127, 155, 159, 163, 166, 172, 179, 184, 185, 190; and Bright, John 74, 75, 127, 128, 133, 155, 161, 168, 170, 171, 173, 178, 181–4, 187; and Bright, M. E. 98–9, 104–5, 126, 128, 132, 135, 168, 170, 173; and C. & J. Clark 158; and children 156, 157, 163–5; and Clark family 152; confinements of 155, 156, 164; and diary keeping 123–4, 133; education of 112, 123–30; and family archive 78–9, 124, 127; and family memory 184–7; on higher education for women 129; and Irish Home Rule 182, 187; and Ladies National Association for Repeal of the Contagious Diseases Acts 168–70; and Leatham family 127; legacies received 159–60, 192–3; and Liberal party 168, 187; and life writing 78, 123–4, 126, 164, 184, 196; and local government 156, 157, 193; and McLaren family 128; and maintenance of kinship relations 160; marriage of 141–3, 144, 146, 154–5; marriage settlement of 158–9, 173, 254n37; and Married Women's Property Committee 168, 172; and Oldham family 69, 126, 177; and 'One Ash' 126, 127, 154; personal wealth of 159, 160, 191–2, 254nn39, 40; and Priestman–Bright circle 76, 112, 128, 160; and Priestman–Bright network 160–2, 178, 190; and Priestman family 2, 79, 101–2, 114, 120, 124; and public affairs 128, 225n7; and public speaking 179; and Quaker 'peculiarities' 125; and radical politics 151, 155, 160, 187; reading 128–9, 155, 185; and reform of Society of Friends 125; religious views of 129, 132, 140–1, 151; and Rochdale 154; and sisters 173–4; social identity of 187; on vowing obedience in marriage 141; and women's money 159–60, 254nn39, 40; and women's rights movement 169, 171, 187; and working-class education 156
Bright, Jacob, jnr 46, 94, 125, 162, 168, 170, 172, 187, 189, 200, 223
Bright, Jacob, snr 15, 17, 18, 22, 23, 26, 27, 29, 33, 34, 35, 36, 39, 40, 66, 74, 76–8, 94, 112–13
Bright, John 15, 79, 85, 87, 95, 112, 160, 172; and Anti-Corn Laws campaign 71, 74, 80–4; and Ashworth Trust 167; and Bright (Clark), Helen 46, 74–6, 98, 127, 155, 171, 179, 181; and Cobden, Richard 80, 82; collected speeches 161; and Contagious Diseases Acts 169–70; courtships of 64–8; diaries of 185; and domesticity 66, 67, 71–2, 73, 74; election as MP, Durham 87; and family firms 27, 74; financial affairs of 173–4, 182–3; first marriage of 63, 68; in government 161, 162; and humanitarian and moral reform movements 67, 70–1; and Jamaica committee 142; last years of 181–4; and Leatham (Bright), Margaret Elizabeth 98, 160, 162, 173; library of 184; and marriage settlement of Bright (Clark), Helen 158–9, 173; masculine identity of 87; parliamentary career 129, 133; and parliamentary reform 35, 88, 132–3, 144, 146, 160; patriarchal attitudes of 87, 171, 175, 179; peace testimony 129; and 'Peterloo' 35, 83; and 'Plug Plot' 82; and politics as vocation 80, 81; and Priestman family 67, 76, 78, 99, 129, 130; and Queen Victoria 70, 162; and

radical politics 35–6, 67, 71, 74, 85; rhetoric of 70–1; Rochdale gift of library 105; Rochdale memorial to 187; second marriage of 97, 99, 105, 113; and sisters 75, 76, 87–8, 94; social identity of 17, 82; and Society of Friends 46, 70, 100; spiritual life 66, 67, 87; and Unionists 179, 181, 182; widowerhoods of 18, 81, 85, 95, 173, 174; on women in public life 69–70, 79, 85, 87, 160, 171, 179; and women's rights 171; and Wood, Margaret, jnr, 35, 64, 68
Bright, John Albert 173, 174, 181, 182–3, 184, 192–3
Bright, Leonard 136, 141
Bright (Roth), 'Lillie' 173, 174
Bright (Lucas), Margaret 64, 76, 77, 88, 112, 132, 135, 161, 169, 187–8
Bright, Martha *see* Wood
Bright (Curry), Mary 173, 174, 182, 208, 218
Bright, Philip 182
Bright (McLaren), Priscilla 2, 9, 46, 66, 68, 71, 75, 76, 77, 80, 81, 86, 87–8, 93–5, 98, 100, 105, 115, 144, 113, 121, 127, 130, 135, 136, 138, 160, 161, 162, 169, 173, 185, 188, 189, 199, 203, 207, 208
Bright, Samuel 27, 34
Bright (Ashworth), Sophia 27, 34, 68, 74, 76, 88, 94, 167
Bright (Cash), Sophia 175
Bright, Thomas 20, 34, 46, 76, 168, 170, 174, 183
Bright, Ursula *see* Mellor
Bright, William 160, 182
Bright family 2, 15, 17, 20, 39, 46, 69, 72, 76, 87, 112–13, 114, 165, 167, 176, 185
Bright family firms 74, 113, 174, 182–3, 206
Bright family money, 40, 192
Brighthelmstone school, Southport 190
Bright sisters 75, 76, 77, 81, 83, 88, 112–13, 135, 259n5
Bristol 165, 206; voluntary associations and institutions 112; Women's Liberal Association 178, 202, 204; women's rights movement 168, 169; women's suffrage society 140
British and Foreign School Society 54, 156; *see also* working-class education

Index 277

British Women's Temperance Association 176, 188, 202
Butler, Josephine 169, 170

C. & J. Clark 147–50, 192, 193, 195, 196, 207, 218, 225–6; in arbitration 1868, 158, 253n9; financial crisis of 1863, 150; kinship basis of 147, 192; and unionisation 195
Cady Stanton, Elizabeth 178, 205
Cash, Sophia *see* Bright
Chartism *see* working-class radicalism; parliamentary reform
cholera epidemics 34, 47, 114, 115
Christian citizenship 81, 86, 118
churches 2, 82, 85; and citizenship 86; and civil society 54; *see also* Quakers and Quakerism; Society of Friends; Unitarians
church rates, resistance to 36, 71
citizenship 2, 54, 139
civil society 2, 5, 7, 53, 54
Clark, Alice 164, 165, 173, 184, 187, 189, 190–1, 192, 195, 196–8, 199, 201, 202, 203, 209, 210, 211, 212, 213, 214, 215, 216, 217, 219, 220, 221, 223, 225–6, 254n18
Clark, Dr Annie 144, 151, 152, 154, 158, 161, 166, 171, 172, 191, 196, 198
Clark, Beavan 158
Clark, Cyrus 147, 148, 150, 158
Clark (Hinde), Edith 152, 154
Clark, Eleanor *see* Stephens
Clark (Clothier), Esther Bright 164, 165, 184, 191–2, 196, 198, 200, 209, 218–20, 222
Clark (Reynolds), Fanny 152, 154
Clark (Impey), Florence 154
Clark, Francis J. 195, 220
Clark, Helen P. B. *see* Bright
Clark, Hilda 164, 192, 198, 201, 207, 208, 209, 211, 217, 220–2
Clark, James 147, 148, 150, 163, 195
Clark, John Bright 155, 164, 165, 184, 195–6, 205, 208, 209
Clark, Joseph, jnr 148, 159
Clark, Joseph, snr 147
Clark (Gillett), Margaret 164, 192, 202, 207, 209
Clark (Morland), Mary 151
Clark, Roger 164, 165, 187, 192, 196, 204, 205, 212

Clark, Sarah Bancroft *see* Bancroft
Clark, Son and Morland 165, 192
Clark, Sophia Sturge 208, 218; and associational life 152, 198; as aunt 152, 198; Bridport kindergarten of 152–4; and diary keeping 7, 152, 198; and family networks 158, 171–2; and family obligations 152; and 'Greenbank' (Street) family 7, 151; and housekeeping 152; and local government 157, 171, 198; nursing 154; and Priestman–Bright circle 168; and reform of Society of Friends 171–2; and sisters 152; and Street School Board 7; teacher-training of 152–3; and temperance 152
Clark, William Bancroft 201
Clark, William Stephens 140, 141–4, 146, 148, 150, 151, 156–8, 160, 162–4, 166, 167, 169–70, 172, 173, 182, 183, 192, 193, 195, 196, 220, 224–5
Clark family firm 195
Clark family of Street 140, 147–9, 151, 152, 156, 158, 163, 166, 191–2, 193, 191
Clarkson, Thomas 4
Clothier, Esther Bright *see* Clark
Clothier, S. Thompson 198–9
Cobbe, Frances Power 143
Cobbett, William 13
Cobden, Jane 179
Cobden (Unwin), Kate 142, 144
Cobden, Richard 80, 82, 84, 133, 139
Consett Iron Co. 109
constitutionalism *see* radical constitutionalism; women's suffrage movement
consumption *see* tuberculosis
Contagious Diseases Acts 168–70, 176, 177, 179
Corder, Susanna 60
Coultate (Bright), Caroline 76
coverture 139, 178, 189, 199, 228; *see also* femes covert
Crawford, P. 246n16
Crewdson family 61
Crosfield (Reynolds), Harriet 128, 142
Crosland (Blakey), Esther, snr, of Bolton and Halifax 174
Crosland (Crossland in some sources), Jane, 27, 29, 34, 38, 39, 126, 134, 135, 154, 170, 174, 176

Crosland (Patching), Martha, 29, 39
Crosland (Crossland in some sources), Robert 18, 26, 27, 29
Crosland family (Crossland in some sources) 2, 27, 34, 39
Crossland *see* Crosland
Curry, Mary *see* Bright
Curry, Richard 174

Davidoff, L. 7, 235n24
Davidoff, L. and Hall, C. *Family Fortunes*, 38, 233n4, 235n18, 240n23, 242n22, 246n16
Davies, Emily 108, 138
Derwent and Consett Iron Co. 109
diaries and diary keeping 2, 7, 123–4, 133, 152, 222, 225, 228
Dilke, Charles 189
Doeg, William 59–60
domestic cultures *see* Quaker domestic cultures; *see also* diaries and diary keeping; domestic ideology; family archives; family chronicles and history; family memory; letters and letter writing; memoirs and memorials; men Friends; personal papers; Priestman–Bright circle; servants; women Friends
domestic ideology 51, 53–6, 155, 235n16
Douglass, Frederick 70, 190
dower rights 6, 37
Dunbar, Dr Elizabeth 208
Durdham Park, Bristol 157, 165
Durham College of Science 191

East London Federation of Suffragettes 215
Edinburgh women's suffrage society 140
Education Act 1870, 157
Elmy, Elizabeth *see* Wolstenholme
English, Elizabeth 49
epilepsy 136–7
Estlin, Mary 169, 228
evangelical religion 5, 25, 46, 55, 56, 58, 61–2, 78, 81, 118, 140, 151

factory system 147–8, 150
family archives 2, 8, 78–9, 123–4, 127, 130, 137, 175, 185, 209, 217, 226; as historical sources 5, 6; and Priestman–Bright circle 8, 137; and women Friends 2, 6

family chronicles and history 2, 5, 24, 38, 229
family firms 6, 15, 50, 56, 74, 77, 119, 121, 147, 148, 150, 158, 165, 193, 196, 228; and family money 167; women's involvement in and absence from 20, 21, 32, 39, 42, 53, 69, 89, 158; women's money and 39, 42, 159; *see also* Bright, Jacob, snr; C. & J. Clark; Clark, Son and Morland; John Bright and Brothers; 'networked' families; Priestman, Jonathan, snr; Tanner Brothers
family memory 2, 5, 6, 24, 78, 137, 183, 184–7; *see also* family archives; family chronicles and history; letters and letter writing; memoirs and memorials; memoranda; 'networked' families
Fawcett, Henry 133
femes covert 17; *see also* coverture; married women; middle-class married women
femes sole 17; *see also* aunts and nieces; governesses and teachers; middle-class single women; middle-class women; nursing
Ferris, Matilda 98–9
Ford, Isabella O. 202
Ford family of Leeds 128
Freedmen's Aid Society 138
Friends, *see* Quakers and Quakerism; Society of Friends
Fry, Ruth 221, 222

Garrett (Anderson), Elizabeth 138, 143, 144, 151
Garrett (Fawcett), Millicent 116, 161, 179, 188, 199, 202, 219
Garrison, William Lloyd 69, 205, 228
gender distinctions and gender relations 4, 5, 6, 7, 22, 51, 53, 76, 77, 79, 85, 86, 87, 226, 229; *see also* Quaker domestic cultures
Gibb (Bright), Selina 125, 155, 223
Gilpin, Charles 147
Gladstone, William Ewart 133, 143, 161, 179, 182, 183, 187
Gould (Pankhurst), Emmeline 189
governesses and teachers, 89, 98, 99, 102–3, 112–13, 132, 148, 152, 154, 163, 166, 191
'Greenbank', Rochdale 15, 26, 27, 66, 75, 76, 77, 83

'Greenbank', Street 143, 147, 151, 166
Grubb, Sarah Lynes, Quaker minister 45
Gurney, Joseph John, Quaker minister 25, 115

Halliwell family 30
Hague peace conference of women 219
Hicks, Elias, Quaker minister 24
Hicksite schism 25, 45, 61, 62, 70; *see also* Baltimore Yearly Meeting
Hunt, 'Orator' Henry 35
Hustler, John 33
hydropathy *see* water therapy

Impey, Catherine 190
Impey, Florence *see* Clark
Impey family, Street 151, 190
Independent Labour Party 202
International Order of Good Templars 190
International Women's Suffrage Association 178
Irish famine 97
Irish Home Rule 179, 182, 189, 223, 225

Jabavu, John D. T. 201
Jabavu family 228
Jackson, Mrs 85, 86
Jamaica rebellion and committee 142, 146
John Bright and Brothers 74, 174, 182–3, 192–3

Kerber, L. 235n16
King (Wood), Margaret, snr 12, 18–19, 26, 39; and family business 20; and women's money, 20
kinship 227, 229; and Anti-Corn Law League 85; and care of dependants 23; and civil society 5; cousinages 7; density of among Quakers 19; and economic opportunity 20; and family memory 2, 24; and gender order 2, 7; interlocking family circles 15; and networks 2, 7, 190, 233n4; and Priestman–Bright network 2, 5, 7–8; and property 37; and public life 5; and transatlantic networks 29; and women's rights movement 7; *see also* aunts and nieces; family archives; family firms; family memory; money; 'networked'

families; Priestman–Bright circle; Priestman–Bright network; Quaker domestic cultures; siblings; sisters

Labour party 191, 215
Ladies National Association for Repeal of the Contagious Diseases Acts 168–71, 176, 218
Lancashire and Cheshire Textile and Other Workers Representation Committee 203
Lawton, Sarah *see* Bancroft
Leatham (Bright), Margaret Elizabeth 97, 99, 107, 113, 128, 141, 146, 160, 162, 172, 173
Leatham family 97, 123, 127, 162
letters and letter writing 2, 21–2, 24, 37, 57, 77, 123, 175, 177, 209, 223, 225, 228, 229, 249n38
Liberal party 151, 161, 176, 179, 182, 187, 188, 189, 202, 203, 204, 209, 225
life writing *see* diaries and diary writing; family archives; family memory; letters and letter writing; memoirs and memorials; memoranda; microhistory
Liverpool and Manchester District Bank 40
Lloyd (Braithwaite), Anna, Quaker minister 61, 62
local government and women 7, 177, 192, 193, 199
London National Society for Women's Suffrage 139–40
Lucas (Thomasson), Kate 159, 160, 189
Lucas, Margaret Bright *see* Bright
Lucas, Samuel, snr 76–7, 78, 133, 139
Lucas family 77
lynching 190, 223, 228

McLaren, Agnes 151
McLaren, Charles 100, 162, 188
McLaren, Duncan, snr 93–5, 98, 100, 113, 130, 136, 151, 162, 179
McLaren, Eva *see* Muller
McLaren (Rabagliati), Helen 113
McLaren, Priscilla *see* Bright
McLaren, Walter S. B. 138, 162, 180, 188, 193, 205
McLaren family, Edinburgh 113–14, 162

Manchester, election 1867, 161; and Priestman–Bright circle 162, 168; reform meeting 1866, 160; women's rights movement 168; women's suffrage movement 139, 140, 168, 199
marriage portions and settlements 6, 50, 109, 112, 141, 148, 158–9, 173, 258n33; *see also* Bright (Clark), H.; Bright, J.; Leatham, M. E.; Priestman, J., snr; Stephens, E.
married women 6, 37, 103, 120–1; *see also* coverture; dower rights; femes covert; marriage portions and settlements; middle-class married women; money; trusts
Married Women's Property Act 1882, 178
Married Women's Property Committee 168–9, 171, 172
Marshall, Catherine 214, 215, 219
Mellor, Martha *see* Bancroft
Mellor, Thomas, of Philadelphia 33
Mellor (Bright), Ursula, of Liverpool 125, 133, 168, 170, 178,189, 200, 203, 218
memoirs and memorials 57, 78, 127, 130, 185
memoranda 60–1, 64, 72–3, 78, 124, 229
men Friends 76–7; attitudes to women 170, 171, 174, 175; patriarchal attitudes among 76
Merrit, James 30
Metcalfe (Bright), Mary 94, 112
microhistory 6, 235n21; *see also* particular persons; personal papers
middle-class married women, dower rights 6, 37; and property 6, 17–18; and shopkeeping 22; and trusts 6, 18, 37; *see also* family firms; marriage portions and settlements; middle-class women; money; Quaker domestic cultures; trusts
middle-class radicalism 2, 22, 35–6, 67, 71, 74, 79, 85, 87, 138, 139, 142, 146; 252n27; *see also* Anti-Corn Law League; Liberal Party; Priestman–Bright circle; Priestman–Bright network; Women's Liberal Federation
middle-class single women 6, 7, 28, 152, 154, 157, 198, 199; choosing

spinsterhood 110; and family life 6, 7, 8, 19, 24, 112; and higher education 129; and household labour 32; and independence 89; new opportunities for 6, 7; personal papers of 7; and property 17; and trusts 167; and 'usefulness' 20, 21, 89; as widows 110; *see also* aunts and nieces; femes sole; governesses and teachers; middle-class women; nursing; Quaker domestic cultures; shopkeepers and shopkeeping; siblings; sisters
middle-class women 6, and associational life 22; and civil society 5, 53; and class interests 4, 81; and domestic ideology 51, 53, 85; economic contributions of 38; and evangelical religion 5; and family businesses 20, 37, 38; and family money 37, 113; and 'female worlds'; and fund-raising 82; and gender relations and roles 5, 81, 89; and higher education 129, 151, 192, 198, 207, 209, 217, 226; and letter writing 21–2; and life writing 123–4; and local government 139; and medical education 151; and money 6; occupations of 20; and philanthropy 22, 69–70; and politics 22, 53; and property 6, 37; and public speaking 69; and 'separate spheres' 84; and shopkeeping 20, 22, 37, 38; and use of trusts 37; and 'woman's mission' 81; and women's money 38; and 'work of kin' 21–2, 24, 28, 85; *see also* Davidoff, L. and Hall, C.; married middle-class women; Morgan, S.; Morris, R. J.; single middle-class women; Vickery, A.; women Friends
middle-classes, and masculinity 87; necessary income for 38; *see also* domestic ideology; evangelical religion; family firms; gender distinctions and gender relations; life writing; middle-class married women; middle-class single women; middle-class women; 'networked' families; Quaker domestic cultures; women Friends
Mill, John Stuart 141, 143, 144, 146, 161
'Millfield', Street 183, 190, 193, 216, 220
Miller, Florence Fenwick 188
'Mizzy', Rochdale 26, 35, 38, 40, 126, 133, 172, 174

money: Bright family money 40, 112–13, 192; and domestic culture 40; as 'family money' 37, 38, 112, 166–7, 258n33; as international 'family money' 12–13, 37; meanings of 37, 38; and middle-class status 38; Priestman family money 159, 166; Tipping family money 41, 42; women's inheritances 37, 41–2, 73, 112–13, 120–1, 137, 159–60, 166–8, 173, 192–3; as 'women's money' 6, 37, 38, 39, 40, 159, 166, 217, 227, 258n33; Wood family money 28, 38, 39, 40
Montefiore, Dora 189, 204
More, Hannah 50, 124
Morgan, S. 53, 84
Morland, John 151, 158, 187, 192, 225
Morland, 'Pollie' 191, 196
Morris, R. J. 227, 233n4, 235n18, 240n24, 253n4
Mott, Lucretia, Hicksite Quaker minister 70
Mount School, York 152, 163, 164, 165
Muller (McLaren), Eva 180, 188
Municipal Corporations Acts 1869 and 1894 168, 199

National Association for the Promotion of Social Science 138, 169
National Society for Women's Suffrage 179; Central Committee of 171, 179; 'Great College Street' society 179; 'Parliament Street' society 179
National Union of Women's Suffrage Societies 199, 202, 203, 204, 215, 218–19
'networked' families 2, 13, 15, 109, 132–3, 148, 161; and Anti-Corn Law League 85; and economic intelligence 30; among Friends 139, 150; and radical politics 131, 138; transatlantic family networks among Friends 24, 28–30; and women's movement 139–40; and women's work of kin 24; Wood–Bright–Bancroft family network 22–4, 28–30, 31; *see also* Morris, R. J.; networks; Priestman–Bright circle; Priestman–Bright network
networks 2, 7, 22–4, 28, 30, 31, 79, 131, 138, 233n4; and family business 147–8, 150; international networks

188, 190; and kinship 7, 147, 185; and politics 161, 162, 190; transatlantic 148; *see also* 'networked family'; Priestman–Bright circle; Priestman–Bright network
Newcastle 47, 49, 54–5, 68, 69, 83, 84, 107, 108–9, 115, 187
nieces *see* aunts and nieces
Nordrach 196, 199
Nordrach-sur-Mendip 210–11
Northumberland and Durham District Bank, failure of 108–9, 137
nurses and midwives 155, 178, 184
nursing 112, 114, 130, 136, 155, 157, 167, 172, 175, 184, 202, 209, 220, 227

'Oakridge', Sidcot 120, 155, 157, 172, 205
O'Donnell, Elizabeth 53, 55
Oldham, Benjamin 69, 126, 174–6
Oldham, Eliza 43, 126, 134, 135, 174–7, 178, 184
Oldham, Hannah 177–8, 184
'One Ash', Rochdale 62, 68–9, 72, 75, 78, 82, 98, 99, 105, 112, 113, 126, 131, 133, 134, 135, 143, 157, 170, 174, 181, 182, 184, 205
oppositionism 9, 229

Pankhurst, Emmeline *see* Goulden
Pankhurst, Richard 189
Pankhurst, Sylvia 215
parliamentary reform 35, 55, 81, 86, 132, 138, 139, 142, 143, 146, 155, 160, 161, 176, 179
Parnell, Charles S. 182
particular persons and history 6, 226, 235n21; *see also* microhistory
Pasley, Isabella 163, 166, 191
Patching, Martha *see* Crosland
Pease (Clark), Caroline 100, 205, 208, 209
Pease (Nichol), Elizabeth 100
Pease, Jane, Quaker minister 106, 110, 115, 118
Pease, Joseph 70
People's Suffrage Federation 212, 261n43
personal papers 57; *see also* diaries and diary keeping; family archives; family chronicles and history; family memory; letters and letter writing; life writing; memoirs and memorials; memoranda

'Peterloo' 35, 83, 176
Philadelphia Yearly Meeting 25, 62; *see also* Baltimore Yearly Meeting; Bancroft family; Hicksite schism
Pickering, P. and Tyrrell, A., *People's Bread* 81–2, 84
Pickering Monthly Meeting 63
Plant, Helen 53
Pochin, Laura 188
Poole (Bancroft), Sarah 32
Poole family
Poor Law Guardians, women 13, 189
Priestman and Son 254n39
Priestman, Anna Maria 51, 76, 128, 217, 222; and Anti-Corn Law League 117; and 'Ashley Grange' 101–2, 106; and Bright, John and M. E. 105; and Bright family 113, 128, 129, 164; and Bristol Women's Liberal Association 178, 202; and Christian citizenship 118; and diary keeping 123; education of 101–2; and education of Bright, Helen 102, 106, 112, 123; and evangelical religion 101–2, 115–17; and family archive 185; friendship with Pease, Jane 106; friendship with Richardson, Anna D. 106–7; and gender differences 118; housekeeping 130; on marriage 110; on ministry of women 118; and Newcastle meeting 108; nursing 130, 136, 267, 202; philanthropy 102; and radical politics 117, 160, 167; reading 102, 105–6, 116, 117; and religious 'heterodoxy' 115; and sisters 96; and Society of Friends 115, 116, 117; and spinsterhood 110; and Wheelers 96; and 'Woman Question' 117, 118; on women public speakers 118; and Women's Emancipation Union 189; and Women's Liberal Federation 189; and women's suffrage movement 178, 179; *see also* Priestman–Bright circle; Priestman–Bright network; Priestman sisters
Priestman, David, jnr, of Malton 60
Priestman, David, snr, of Malton 61
Priestman, David, of Newcastle 51, 57, 59
Priestman (Bright), Elizabeth 1, 2, 46, 51, 60, 61–2, 63, 64–8, 69, 70–5, 78, 99, 126, 127, 175

Priestman, Emily, of Manchester *see* Slagg
Priestman, Emily, of Newcastle 51, 57–8
Priestman (Pumphrey), Frances 27
Priestman, Hadwen 51, 60, 77–8, 115, 126, 166, 167, 254n39
Priestman, Jonathan, jnr, of Newcastle and Shotley 51, 106–7, 108–9, 167, 184
Priestman, Jonathan, snr, of Malton and Newcastle 50, 66, 71, 74, 78, 108–9, 137, 138, 141
Priestman, Joseph, of Malton 60
Priestman (Wheeler, then Tanner), Margaret 2, 51, 68, 69, 78, 81, 82, 83–4, 85, 86, 87–93, 94, 95, 155, 157, 160, 205, 209, 228; and Anti-Corn Law League 81, 82, 83, 84, 85; on Arthur Tanner, jnr 120; benevolence 110, 111; and Bright, John and M. E. 104, 113, 123; and Bright family 68–9, 75–6, 86, 88, 89, 91, 93, 94, 95, 110, 112, 113, 121, 127, 131; childhood 55, 58–9; and church discipline 78; courtship of 90, 91–3, 120, 121; education 58–60, 7; and education of Bright, Helen 102–6, 112, 131; and evangelical religion 61–2; and family archive 137; financial affairs of 103, 106, 120–1; first marriage of 95, 96–7; first widowhood 101, 103, 110, 112; and gender differences and relations 89, 119; housekeeping of 96–8, 160; illness and death of Daniel Wheeler 100–2; and marriage 89–95; memoir and memorial writing 57, 101, 130; and nieces 136–7; opposition to capital punishment 112; reading 96; and reform movements 69; and reform of Society of Friends 117, 118; relationship with Wheeler (Tanner), Sarah 101, 103, 104, 121; relationship with Tanner, Sarah and William 112, 121; religious values and politics 62, 81; second marriage 120, 121, 130, 141; second widowhood 172; servants of 97; and social identity 121; and spinsterhood 89, 90, 92; and Tanner Brothers family firm 121; and women's rights 85, 90, 119; and working-class education 55, 140

Priestman, Mary 51, 76, 101, 107, 112, 114, 130, 136–7, 142, 144, 157, 160, 172
Priestman, Rachel, jnr, of Newcastle 51, 60, 73, 77, 78, 81, 83, 85
Priestman, Rachel, snr *see* Bragg
Priestman, 'Rachie', of Shotley and Bristol 136, 137, 157
Priestman family, of Malton 50, 112
Priestman family, of Newcastle 2, 46, 50, 51, 53, 54, 55, 58, 61, 62, 67, 68, 70, 78, 79, 83, 86, 89, 90, 92, 98, 102, 106, 107–9, 112, 113, 114, 117, 138, 146, 254n39; Priestman family money 137, 159, 166–7
Priestman family, of Yorks 50, 51, 61, 63
Priestman sisters 101–2, 107, 108, 109, 136–7, 202, 205, 209, 216, 217, 218; and Anti-Corn Law League 83, 129; as aunts 2, 102–6, 112–13, 123–6, 133–4, 136; and Bright (Clark), H. 104, 106–8, 155, 157, 166, 167; and Bright, J. 113; and Bright, M. E. 114; and Bright sisters 2, 13; and Christian citizenship 81; and diary keeping 123; and evangelical religion 81; financial position of 137, 157; and gender order in Society of Friends 118; and pacifism 259n5; teachers 89; and WSPU 203
Priestman–Bright circle 2, 5, 6, 7, 19, 22, 53, 64, 71, 76, 77, 78–9, 82–3, 85, 86, 89, 93, 95, 100, 110, 113–14, 125, 126, 130, 133, 135, 138–40, 151, 161–2, 168, 169, 228, 229
Priestman–Bright network 36, 37, 79, 82, 160–1, 190, 203; anti-imperialism of 252n27; formation of 76; and international reform networks 185, 188; and radical politics 138–40, 144, 160–2; reform of Society of Friends 5, 171–2; and women's rights movements 2, 5, 36, 37, 38, 140, 143, 168–72, 180, 187–90, 199; and WSPU 203; *see also* Anti-Corn Law League; Ladies National Association; National Society for Women's Suffrage; National Union of Women's Suffrage Societies; Radical Liberals; Union of Practical Suffragists; Women's Franchise League; Women's Freedom League; Women's Liberal Federation; Women's Social and Political Union

private and public life, links between 61, 79, 80, 81, 85, 95, 97, 160–1, 168, 171–2
Pye, Edith 209, 220

Quaker domestic cultures 2, 5, 6, 7, 17, 40, 46, 49, 51, 53–55, 64, 65–6, 68–9, 73, 74, 77, 78, 93, 151, 155, 156, 159, 162, 167, 174, 175, 182–3, 184–7, 192–3, 202; *see also* family archives; family chronicles and history; family firms; family memory; kinship; life writing; money; Priestman–Bright circle; servants

Quakers and Quakerism 4, 5, 11, 202, 227, 228, 229, 230; and associational life 4; business arbitration practices 158; civil disobedience and passive resistance of 11, 35, 36; and civil society 55; and consensus-building 180; courtship 18–19, 64–8, 91–5, 120, 121, 140–2; cousinages among 49; and education of girls 4, 21, 190–2; emphasis on mutual trust 42, 43; endogamy 12, 19; and evangelical religion 5, 25, 45, 55, 61–2; and family limitation 4, 51; 'gay' Friends 76, 125; and gender differences 11, 40, 53, 69, 70, 77, 79, 90; and 'guarded' upbringing of children 40, 59; history of 4, 10, 28; ideals of marriage 18–19, 50–1, 53, 64, 65–6, 69, 94, 110; inheritance practices 73, 112, 113, 167, 182–3; among local elites 54, 55; and masculinities 156; networks of 2, 30, 31; and 'oppositionism' 9, 11, 13, 55; 'peculiarities' of 11, 37, 45, 46; and philanthropy and personal benevolence 4, 22, 69; 'plain' Friends 37; and politics 12, 22, 35, 62, 79; quietism of 11, 22, 55, 81; refusal of public offices 161; and social mobility 90; and social reform 54; use of informal wills 42; varieties of 4, 12; and working-class education 67, 69, 72, 193; *see also* evangelical religion; men Friends; money; 'networked families'; Quaker domestic cultures; Priestman–Bright circle; Priestman–Bright network; Society of Friends; women Friends

Rabagliati, Helen *see* McLaren
race and racism 257n16, 258n24; *see also Anti-Caste*; anti-lynching campaign; anti-slavery movement; black rights campaigns; segregation
radical constitutionalism 139, 188–9, 203–4, 252n28, 257n16, 259–60n14; *see also* National Union of Women's Suffrage Societies; women's suffrage movement
Radical Liberals 88–9, 139, 178–80, 200–1, 202, 257n13
railways 44
Red Cross School, Bristol 112
Reform Bills 34, 35, 55, 132, 133, 142, 144, 155, 160, 161, 176, 179
religion *see* Evangelical religion; Quakers and Quakerism; Society of Friends; Unitarians; women Friends
religious mentalities and values 1, 2, 4, 5, 7, 6, 8, 9, 11, 12, 17, 22, 26, 37, 43, 45, 46, 47, 49–50, 55–6, 61–3, 78, 80, 101–2, 114–18
Religious Society of Friends *see* Society of Friends; *see also* Beaconites; evangelical religion; Hicksites; Quakers and Quakerism
Remond, Sarah Parker 138
Richardson, Anna Deborah 106–7, 108
Richardson, Isaac 50
Richardson, Jane *see* Wigham
Richardson, John Wigham 108
Richardson, Jonathan, of Shotley 108–9
Richardson (Priestman), Lucy 108–9
Richardson family of Newcastle 50, 107, 108
Richardson family of Shotley 107, 109
Robertson, Frederick 132
Rochdale, Lancashire 1, 9; Anti-Corn Law League 83; Bright (Clark), Helen and 172–3, 175; church rates controversy 71; commemoration of John Bright 187; Cooperative Society 141; Friends' Meeting 12, 75; gift of library to John Bright 105; local government election 177; parliamentary election 74; parliamentary representation 35; 'Plug plot' 82; Reform Bill demonstration 144; women's suffrage petition 144
Rogers, Thorold 161
'romantic friendships' between women 88

Romilly, Sir Samuel 151, 185
Rooke, Jane 83
Roper, Esther 199, 203
Roth, Dr Bernard, jnr 166, 176, 199
Roth, Dr Bernard, snr 126
Rous, Lydia 132, 152, 163
Rowntree, John S., of York 165
Rowntree, Mary, of Scarborough 174, 181

Sayles, Ann 76
Schnell, Emilie 127, 128
Scott, Job, Quaker minister 21
segregation 190
servants 43, 69, 72, 76, 97, 126, 143, 156, 157, 174, 175, 176, 177–8, 184
settlements *see* marriage portions and settlements
shoemakers and shoemaking 147, 148, 195, 205, 253n5; *see also* C. & J. Clark
shopkeepers and shopkeeping 12, 22, 23, 37, 142, 148, 152
siblings 7, 19, 20, 64, 68, 79, 93, 94, 98, 106–8, 119, 152, 154, 159, 160, 182, 227, 228; *see also* aunts and nieces; kinship; sisters
Sidcot school 124–5, 140
Singh, S. xii, 240n25; *see also* money
single women 6, 28, 207; *see also* middle-class single women
sisters 19, 20, 24, 64, 66, 68–9, 71, 73, 74, 75, 76, 77, 78, 79, 88, 96, 101, 103, 106, 110, 119–20; *see also* aunts and nieces; kinship; siblings
Slagg (Priestman), Emily 125, 137, 166, 167
Smith, Joseph 94, 95
Smuts, Jan 201
Society of Friends 4, 8, 11, 220, 221, 222, 241n49; and baptism 72; 'Beaconite' schism 45, 58, 61; belief in 'Inner Light' 62, 72; church calendar 49; church culture 11, 54; church government and organisation 9, 11; discipline regarding bankruptcy 109, 148; discipline regarding church rates 35, 36; discipline regarding marriage 11,19, 76; discipline regarding 'plainness 45; 'disownment' of members 11, 19, 46, 76, 77, 78, 94, 100, 109, 115 125; divisions within 24, 25, 45; Durham Quarterly Meeting 64; elders and overseers of 4, 47, 78, 115; and evangelical religion 1, 5, 24, 45, 61–2, 63, 101, 115, 140; FWVRC 220–2, 228, 229; gender order within 4, 11, 53; Hicksite schism 24–6, 45, 238–9n51; kinship networks of 19; London Yearly Meeting of 44, 45; membership of 11, 62, 77; ministers as 'public' Friends 80; ministry of women 7, 10, 45, 46, 47; Newcastle Meeting 47, 49, 68; peace testimony 129, 138; Philadelphia Yearly Meeting 5, 238–9n51; Pickering Meeting 63; and Quaker 'peculiarities' 116, 117; reform of 2, 37, 171–2; Rochdale Meeting 12, 75, 135; schisms 5; theology 9, 11; *see also* men Friends; Quaker domestic culture; Quakers and Quakerism; women Friends
Somerset, Lady Henry 188, 202
South African Conciliation Committee 201
South African Wars 201–2
spinsters *see* femes sole; middle-class single women; single women
Stacey family 49
Stephens (Clark), Eleanor 144, 148, 151, 152, 154, 155
Stickney, Esther 58, 59, 61, 62, 101
Stowe, Harriet Beecher 138
Street, Somerset 147, 150, 184, 193, 195, 199, 202; *see also* C. &. J. Clark; Clark family; 'Greenbank', Street; 'Millfield', Street
Sturge, Charles 148
Sturge, Eliza 141
Sturge, Joseph 46, 55, 148
'Summerhill', Newcastle 47, 50, 55, 62, 65, 66, 67, 69, 74, 76, 81, 89, 96, 105, 183

Tait, Dr Lawson 198
Tanner, Arthur, jnr 119, 120–3, 141, 172, 210–12
Tanner, Mary Anne 119
Tanner, Sarah *see* Wheeler
Tanner, William, Quaker minister 104, 115–16, 119, 124
Tanner Brothers 119
Tanner family 119
Taylor, Clementia and Peter A. 138, 143, 190
Taylor, Ralph 33

temperance movement, 54–5, 67, 68, 69, 85, 118, 151, 152, 176, 188, 190, 193
Theosophical Society 200
Thomasson (Winkworth), Emma, of Bolton 159
Thomasson, John Pennington, of Bolton 140, 143, 156, 160
Thomasson, Thomas, of Bolton 140, 160
Thompson, Colonel George 82
Thorp, Fielden, Quaker minister 140, 143, 152
Tipping, John, and Wood family 29, 41; as father's executor 41; Tipping family money and -women's money 41, 42
trusts 6,18, 159, 167, 193; *see also* Ashworth Trust; Bright (Clark), Helen
tuberculosis 154, 165, 184, 191, 195–6, 199, 210–12, 217, 220, 221, 222, 227
typhoid 130, 154, 218, 253n14

Uhde, Ferdinand 103
Union of Boot and Shoe Operatives 195
Union for Democratic Control 219
Union of Practical Suffragists 202, 204
Unitarians 5, 12, 70, 140

Vaughan, Esther *see* Bright
vegetarianism 129
Vickery, A. 7, 234n8, 235nn16 and 20, 249n38
Vigilance Association for the Defence of Personal Rights 188
Vigilance Society 188

Wallis, Hannah 190
Wallis, May 190
water therapy 71, 77, 100, 156, 176; *see also* Ben Rhydding, Ilkley
Wells, Ida B. 190
Wells Board of Poor Law Guardians 193, 217
Wheeler, Daniel, jnr 91–3, 95, 97, 100–1, 103
Wheeler, Daniel, snr 91, 93
Wheeler (Tanner), Sarah 93, 101, 103, 104, 106
widows and widowers 18, 19, 23, 27, 39, 40, 41, 50, 81, 85, 93–4, 95, 98, 100, 102, 103, 105, 110, 167, 208
Wigham, Eliza 100
Wigham (Richardson), Jane 106–7

Willard, Frances 190
Wilson (Bragg), Margaret, of Kendal and Newcastle, Quaker minister 47, 49, 50, 53, 55, 59, 60, 66, 72–3
Winkworth, Emma *see* Thomasson
Winkworth, Stephen 159
Wolstenholme (Elmy), Elizabeth 168, 169, 178, 189
women Friends 2, 5, 8, 45–6, 53, 65, 110, 230; and Anti-Corn Law League 80–4; and associational life 4, 22, 49, 53, 54–6, 67, 69, 97, 135; and civil society 53, 69; and consumption 90, 97; courtship, marriage and domestic life 65, 69, 93, 119, 135, 140, 141, 154, 157; and domestic ideology 53; education of Quaker girls 4, 13, 18–19, 21, 49, 54, 58–60, 125; and family archives 2, 4, 57; and family limitation 4, 51; and family memory 2, 6, 57, 78–9, 137; and family money and property 73, 112–13, 166–7; and gender differences 2, 4, 53, 118, 130; and Ladies National Association for Repeal of the Contagious Diseases Acts 169; and life writing 5, 57, 78–9, 123–5; ministry of 6, 9, 10, 45–6, 50, 80; personal benevolence and philanthropy of 4, 22, 54, 81, 84, 85, 96; position in Society of Friends 4, 9; private papers of 57, 78, 79; public character of 4, 61, 79; and public life 4, 5, 69, 70, 82–7, 90–1; and public speaking 85; and sexual division of labour 53, 79, 84, 85; and social mobility 90, 120–1; stereotypes of 4; and women's rights 5, 24–8, 139; and working-class education 54; and work of kin 85; *see also* middle-class married women; middle-class single women; middle-class women; Quaker domestic cultures; Quakers and Quakerism; Society of Friends
women in local government 7, 157, 168; *see also* Bright (Clark), Helen; Clark, Sophia Sturge; Municipal Corporations Acts; Wells Board of Poor Law Guardians
Women's Emancipation Union 189
Women's Franchise League 188–9, 203
women shoemakers 148
Women's International League for Peace and Freedom 219

Women's Liberal Associations and Women's Federation 178, 179, 189, 202, 219
Women's Penny Paper 188
women's rights movement 7, 138, 139–40, 151, 168, 176, 177; Priestman–Bright network and 2, 5, 36, 37, 138, 140, 168–72, 178, 180, 187–90, 199, 203, 204
Women's Signal 188, 189
Women's Social and Political Union 203, 204
Women's Suffrage Journal 177
women's suffrage movement 139, 202, 215, 219; formulation of demand 140, 178, 189, 199; and Gladstonian Liberals 179, 180; historiography of 260n16; and Irish home rule 179; and married women 178; and 'militancy' 204, 215, 223, 229, 259–60n14; and peace movements 262n11; and Radical Liberals 178, 188, 257–8n21; and Reform Bills 1867, 1884 147, 179–80; and Representation of the People Act 1917, 263n23; women Friends and 5, 139, 140; and Women's Liberal Associations 179; working women and 177, 189, 199, 203; *see also* National Society for Women's Suffrage; National Union of Women's Suffrage Societies; radical constitutionalism; Radical Liberals; Union of Practical Suffragists; Women's Emancipation Union; Women's Franchise League; Women's Freedom League; Women's Social and Political Union
women's work of kin 94–5; linking private and public lives 81, 94; in 'networked' families 24; *see also* private and public life, links between; Vickery, A.
Wood (Bancroft), Elizabeth 13, 25, 31, 33, 38, 40, 45
Wood (Crosland), Esther 18, 20, 25, 27
Wood, Henry 31
Wood, John, jnr 12, 13, 22, 23, 31, 33, 38, 39, 41
Wood, John, snr 12, 18–19
Wood, Joseph 31, 34, 41
Wood, Joseph, Quaker minister 12
Wood, Margaret, jnr, of Bolton and Rochdale: as aunt 29, 31, 33, 34, 38, 39; and Bancroft, Joseph 23, 26, 33, 38, 40, 42; and Bancroft family 2, 31, 41, 42; on Bright, John 64, 65, 68, 77; and Bright family 2,19, 20, 26, 27, 34–5, 37, 39, 42, 43, 74, 76, 83, 94, 126, 127, 128, 133–4; and commercial intelligence 28, 32, 33; and Crosland family 27, 29, 34, 38, 39; cultural legacy of 7; economic independence of 22, 37, 38; education of 21; employment and business of 9, 20, 22, 32, 37, 38; employment of servants 38, 43; and evangelical religion 12, 25, 56; executor and estate of 42; and family businesses 28, 38; and family memory 24, 38, 39, 137, 184; family obligations 27, 28, 29, 31, 32, 33, 34, 38, 39, 44; and Hicksite schism 25–6; and humanitarian and moral reform 70; and kinship networks 2; last illness and death 134–5; and letter writing 21–2, 24, 37, 57, 77; on marriage 18; on ministry of women 118, 124; on money, wealth and business ethics 22, 23, 32, 37–8, 42, 43, 44, 68; and nieces 18, 23, 39, 94; as petite bourgeoise 23, 38; property and income of 38, 39, 40, 42, 68; and Quaker 'peculiarities' 37; Quaker values 12; quietism 12; and radical politics 12, 36, 83; reading 21; religious values 17, 22, 23, 25, 26, 32, 45, 47, 54; retirement from business 22, 24, 56; on schism 62; on shopkeeping 22–3; as single daughter 20, 23; as single woman 18, 89; as sister 23, 31, 33; and sisters 19, 24, 33; social identity of 12, 17; and Society of Friends 70; spiritual life and aspirations of 22, 45, 46, 66; transatlantic networks of 29–31, 33; use of informal will 42; visit to USA 24, 28–35; as women of affairs 22, 28; and women's money 39, 40; and Wood, John, jnr 20, 23, 41; and Wood family 31; and Wood family money 28, 39, 40; and work of kin 22, 24, 25–6, 27
Wood, Margaret, snr *see* King
Wood (Bright), Martha 13, 15, 17, 18, 21, 26, 27, 39, 40

Wood family, of Bolton, Rochdale and Schuylkill 12–13, 15, 79, 205, 227; Wood family money 28, 39, 40, 41
Wood sisters 13, 21
working class education 135, 154, 156–7, 193; *see also* Quakers and Quakerism; women Friends
working-class radicalism 35, 82, 83, 84
working-class women and women's suffrage 199
World Women's Christian Temperance Union 190
Wright, Sheila 53

York College, Leeds 192

Feminist History Reader

Edited by
Sue Morgan

The Feminist History Reader gathers together key articles, from some of the very best writers in the field, that have shaped the dynamic historiography of the past thirty years, and introduces students to the major shifts and turning points in this dialogue. The *Reader* is divided into four sections:

- early feminist historians' writings following the move from reclaiming women's past through to the development of gender history
- the interaction of feminist history with 'the linguistic turn' and the challenges made by post-structuralism and the responses it provoked
- the work of lesbian historians and queer theorists in their challenge of the heterosexism of feminist history writing
- the work of black feminists and postcolonial critics/Third World scholars and how they have laid bare the ethnocentric and imperialist tendencies of feminist theory.

Each reading has a comprehensive and clearly structured introduction with a guide to further reading, this wide-ranging guide to developments in feminist history is essential reading for all students of history.

978–0–415–31809–9 (Hardback)
978–0–415–31810–5 (Paperback)

Sceptical History

Feminist and Postmodernist Approaches in Practice

Helen Bowen Raddeker

A highly original work in history and theory, this survey considers major themes including identity, class and sexual difference, weaves them into debates on the nature and point of history, and arrives at new ways of doing history that – very unusually – consider non-Western history and feminist approaches. Using wide range of historical and cultural contexts, the study draws extensively on feminist scholarship, both feminist history and postcolonial feminism.

978–0–415–34115–8 (Hardback)
978–0–415–34114–1 (Paperback)